NEO~
NEUTRALITY

NEO-NEUTRALITY

By GEORG COHN

Translated from the Danish by

ARTHUR S. KELLER

AND

EINAR JENSEN

NEW YORK : MORNINGSIDE HEIGHTS
COLUMBIA UNIVERSITY PRESS
1939

Published 1939

Printed in the United States of America

FOREWORD

THIS FOREWORD is being written in the midst of a European crisis and while hearings on neutrality occupy the center of the stage in Washington. There could scarcely be a more appropriate time for the publication of this book in the United States. For a little more than a decade after the close of the World War, governmental, academic, and popular thought largely ignored the problems of neutrality. For the last five years, neutrality has been a dominant theme in discussions by all of these groups. In both its period of practical obliteration and its present period of vitality, the subject has been complicated and confused by intellectual and emotional reactions for or against the League of Nations and the system of collective security. It is now the turn of the League to be considered nothing but a remnant of the historic past, but in the current discussions of "aggressors," the themes of collective security find new applications.

It is surely a curious thing that for some fifteen years the United States refused to be a party to any policy which involved an alignment against an "aggressor" although we would then have had some forty to fifty allies, while today, when the League's collective front is broken, the demand that the United States play the rôle of a world power is more vociferous than ever before. Nor is this curiosity peculiar to the foreign policy of the United States. There are reasons, to be sure, but not a few of them stem from a lack of foresight. All the more necessary at this critical juncture in world affairs is an American reappraisal of these questions with all the wisdom which can be brought to bear.

In such a reappraisal, it cannot but be helpful to have available the views of an experienced European who surveys trends in thought and in diplomacy from the vantage point of one who is both scholar and statesman. Dr. Cohn's book, which now appears for the first time in English, was published in Danish about a year ago. The author is the Chief of the International Law Section of the Danish Foreign Office and has frequently represented his country at Geneva. It is well for citizens of the United States who pride themselves upon the traditional neutrality of the United States to recall that Denmark has as fair a claim to the title of a "traditional neutral." There is an underlying intellectual kinship, therefore, between Danish and American thought on neutrality despite the many differences due to geographical location and political heritage. Dr. Cohn surveys the history of neutrality from its earliest era down through the World War. He appraises the League system and its relation to neutrality. He is a frank critic of many features of the League of Nations and is by no means a partisan of the view that the world can be saved by some simple formula for defining aggression. He evaluates the recent neutrality acts of the United States and the current developments in Pan Americanism. He has thoughtfully considered the inescapable relationship between peace, neutrality, and war and has propounded his own concept of Neo-neutrality which insists upon non-participation in war while at the same time seeking to make a contribution to war prevention. This, in its essence, is what many persons in the United States are searching for today as an American policy.

In a final section prepared for the American edition, Dr. Cohn states his conclusions, which reject both the traditional neutrality and the system of sanctions developed under Article XVI of the Covenant of the League. Whether or not one agrees with all of the author's conclusions, one cannot help but find stimulation and inspiration in his scholarly realism.

PHILIP C. JESSUP

Columbia University
April, 1939

TRANSLATORS' PREFACE

In the preparation of this book for the English-reading public, the translators have endeavored to reproduce faithfully the original Danish treatise of Dr. Cohn. Where there were available English texts of some of the references originally cited by him from texts in various other languages, the former have been used. This is particularly true of the League of Nations references, where Dr. Cohn consulted and quoted the official French texts and where the present translation has used the English ones.

Where quotations in the Danish edition were originally made from Danish, Norwegian, Swedish, and Dutch authors by Dr. Cohn in their original language, we have in general translated these for the English reader; material in other languages has generally been left in its original form.

Our sincere gratitude is due Dr. Cohn, who checked a preliminary draft of the manuscript of this translation, for his many helpful corrections and suggestions. Responsibility for the final English text must, however, be assumed by the translators.

Arthur S. Keller
Einar Jensen

CONTENTS

NEO-
NEUTRALITY

I

TRADITIONAL NEUTRALITY

Plans for the Abolition of Neutrality Following The World War

1. When the League of Nations came into being it was the general opinion that the old law of neutrality had no further part to play, not only because the new system of the League Covenant failed to mention the status of neutrality,[1] but also because the two systems were regarded as diametrically opposed, the acceptance of one excluding consideration of the other. Special importance had been attached to certain negative aspects of the legal status of neutrality, namely, nonparticipation and impartiality, which were indicated quite clearly by the etymology of the word *neutrality*, the *neutral* being one who took sides with neither party. On the other hand, there was the positive side of the law of neutrality—the admission that the neutral continued in a state of peace which was not always understood. It included, and in general still does, the traditional concept of neutrality as an indivisible whole in the form which its development had reached at the close of the nineteenth century. Impartiality created the basis of the right to keep out of war.

This one-sided and in reality misleading concept of the nature of neutrality appears very clearly in modern theoretical statements of its "meaning" or in definitions of the term. It is characteristic, for example, that Haase, in his work *Wandlung des Neutralitätsbegriffes*,[2] poses and thoroughly discusses (1) war, (2) nonparticipation, and (3) freedom of action, subject always to qualifica-

[1] President Wilson's original draft had suggested the possibility "that the smaller members of the League be excused from making any contribution to the armed forces to be used against the covenant-breaking states," but this was not synonymous with neutrality. The draft is printed in U. S. Senate, 66th Congress, *Hearings before the Committee on Foreign Relations*, Washington, 1919, p. 1168.

[2] Leipzig, 1932, p. 14.

tion, as being the three essential elements of neutrality. These concepts prevent him in advance from even grasping the real meaning of neutrality. In this he but follows the pattern of higher authorities. Oppenheim [3] defines the concept of neutrality simply as an attitude of impartiality. Bonfils-Fauchille [4] attaches importance to the purely negative idea of nonparticipation in war. Nys [5] also asserts that, among the innumerable definitions that have been laid down and which attach more or less weight to impartiality, "la plus simple consiste à montrer dans la neutralité la situation de l'État qui reste étranger à la guerre." From the American point of view, neutrality has been defined as merely a condition of recognition that the causes of both belligerents are just.[6] Instead of examining the situation from the viewpoint of the law of neutrality and assuming a position thereon, these authorities have thus made neutrality, in theory as well as in practice, an adjunct to the law of war.

They define it as something purely negative, or mistake a single historically and politically established legal *consequence* (impartiality) for its actual substance. Instead of regarding neutrality as a normal and positive condition of the law-abiding states, and war as an abnormal disturbance of public order, they reverse matters, regarding war as an extensive and productive legal system of which neutrality is a negligible by-product, a precarious and, correctly speaking, an inferior status, which a state accepts because it cannot or dare not expose itself in the arena of war.

In natural consequence, the League of Nations likewise placed the protection of important interests—among them world peace—in the hands of belligerent Powers; they seemed unable to realize that neutrals might have certain interests of their own to safeguard or to

[3] *International Law*, II (1935), 15: "Neutrality may be defined as the attitude of impartiality adopted by third states towards belligerents, such attitude creating rights and duties between the impartial states and the belligerents."

[4] *Droit international public*, II (1921), 635: "La neutralité est la situation de tout État qui reste étranger à la guerre survenue entre deux ou plusieurs autres États"; for a purely formal definition, see also Matzen, *Den positiv Folkeret*, p. 302.

[5] *Droit international*, III (1912), 551.

[6] Moore, *International Law*, Washington, VII (1907), 860: "the state of neutrality recognizes the cause of both parties to the contest as just."

support. In other words, neutrality was held to be something purely negative: nonintervention, egoism, the desire to feather one's own nest while others were fighting for right and justice. Neutrals were to be forced to accept a morally inferior position, to agree with both sides, however much the injustice of one side might be evident, for when one cannot or dare not fight one must keep entirely silent. This was the view of neutrality generally held just before and during the World War and also during the period of the preparation of the Covenant of the League of Nations.

From this viewpoint the principles of neutrality necessarily ran counter to the League's new maxim of the international solidarity of the states in their efforts for the prevention of war. On this subject there are numerous statements and expressions of opinion. President Wilson for example, declared, in his address of April 2, 1917, that neutrality was neither possible nor desirable when world peace and the liberties of people were at stake.[7] In his Fourteen Points he had laid down the principle of the freedom of the seas as one of the most important principles in the new order of justice; he later waived this point, taking the position that this subject only concerned neutrals during maritime war, "but when we have the League of Nations, there will be no neutrals in time of war." [8] In the famous declaration of February 13, 1920, by which the League Council allowed Switzerland to enter the League without abandoning its historic rights of neutrality, it was again stated that the idea of neutrality was not compatible with the general principle that each and all of the members of the League should act jointly in carrying out their obligations.[9] As late as 1929 we find the British government declaring officially in its *White Book*, regarding its acceptance of the optional provisions of Article 36 of the Statute for the Permanent Court of International Justice,[10] that as "between members of the League there can be no neutral rights because there can be no neutrals," a concept which is natural enough,

[7] Cohn, *Kriegsverhütung und Schuldfrage*, p. 32.

[8] Gilbert, *The Mirrors of Washington*, New York, 1921, p. 40; Cohn, "Neutralitet i Fremtid," *Jur. Tidsskrift*, 1924, p. 41; Politis, *La Neutralité*, p. 102; Whitton, *La Neutralité*, p. 453.

[9] Huber, *Die schweizerische Neutralität und der Völkerbund*, p. 127.

[10] *British White Book*, Miscellaneous No. 12, 1929, Cmd. 3452, p. 10

since the English theory regards complete impartiality as the essence of neutrality.[11]

It was further stated during the discussions in the Assembly of the League in 1929 regarding the incorporation of the Kellogg Pact into the League Covenant that, from the Belgian viewpoint, claims for recognition of a status of permanent neutrality were monstrous.[12] In the Assembly in 1931 (the session of September 11)[13] the Spanish delegate, Madariaga, declared that the combining of the Kellogg Pact with the League Covenant would cause the complete collapse of the law of neutrality: "Il n'y a plus de neutralité." The most active opponent of neutral rights, namely the Greek delegate, Politis,[14] has drawn the practical conclusions of his position. When the Institute of International Law, during its meeting in Cambridge in 1931 (July 31), discussed a draft convention on international rivers, Politis insisted, and gained his point, that any position recognizing a legal status under the laws of neutrality was no longer tenable,[15] giving as his reasons that "dans le cadre de la Société des Nations, l'hypothèse de la neutralité paraît exclue." [16]

At its thirty-seventh conference at Oxford in August, 1932, the International Law Association discussed a draft convention dealing with neutrality in warfare on land and on sea, but it met with fundamental objections upon the part of a group of members, especially from the Englishmen, Professor Brierly and Dr. McNair. The former declared [17] that the concept of neutrality "belongs to an utterly outlawed order of ideas." For him, the demand for im-

[11] Explicitly referred to on page 9 of the *British White Book*.

[12] League of Nations, *Official Journal*, Special Supplement No. 76, Geneva, 1929, p. 32: "Peut-on imaginer la monstruosité que serait dès lors la prétention au droit à la neutralité."

[13] League of Nations, *Official Journal, Special Supplement No. 93*, Geneva, 1931, p. 79.

[14] *La Neutralité et la paix*, Paris, 1935.

[15] *Annuaire de l'Institut de Droit International*, II (1931), 176.

[16] Among other writers with similar views may be mentioned Calogeropoulos-Stratis, *Le Pacte général de renonciation à la guerre*, p. 202: "La neutralité donc n'est plus juridiquement possible à la suite de la transformation des régles du droit des gens. A l'heure actuelle, elle est même dépourvue de base juridique, de fondement et d'utilités"; and p. 204: "La neutralité . . . est déjà passée dans l'histoire."

[17] The International Law Association. *Report of the Thirty-Seventh Conference*, London, 1933, p. 175.

partiality in the concept of neutrality is incompatible with the position of the League Covenant toward the aggressor. A similar irreconciliable conflict existed in the rules of free passage, extension of credits, and others. The Kellogg Pact [18] also abolished the laws of war and neutrality. Dr. McNair agreed wholeheartedly with this position and declared "that the whole conception of neutrality is in the melting pot." [19]

Miss Crichton, in an article in the *British Yearbook of International Law*,[20] "The Pre-War Theory of Neutrality," goes so far as to take a purely historical view of the law of neutrality as that of a thing of the past. She asserts "that the pre-war theory in its entirety has become a matter of history." [21]

In certain respects there is something most remarkable in this resolute and unconditional rejection of the law of neutrality by these writers, who at the same time assume that war and the laws of war are by no means repealed or nullified by the League Covenant. In a system which aims at the abolition of war, they take the position that only such states as are prepared for and willing to wage war may be considered members of it. To a great extent this inconsistency arises from their misunderstanding of neutrality as being something purely negative and permeated throughout with the idea of impartiality.

2. When, despite this repudiation in principle, the fundamental ideas of neutrality still failed to disappear from international law, it was not due to any recognition by the states of a positive content of neutrality, that is, its endeavors to keep nations out of war, which at least were in complete harmony with the new system. It was primarily due to the great technical and political difficulties which were found to be connected with the carrying out of the new system under the Covenant. As early as 1921 the International

[18] *Ibid.*, p. 177.

[19] *Ibid.*, p. 185: "I can tell you where to find what was the law of neutrality in 1914, but I cannot conscientiously tell you what it is to-day."

[20] London, 1928, pp. 101 ff.

[21] See also the *Séances et travaux*, of the Union juridique internationale, which had during its fifth session a proposal by Alvarez for a resolution declaring: "Il n'y a pas de neutralité possible entre membres de la Société des nations"; see *Handbuch des Völkerrecht*, Bd. 2, abteil 2, Strupp, "Neutralisation, Befriedung, Entmilitarisierung," p. 349.

Blockade Committee had pointed out the technical difficulties within the system, indeed the practical impossibility of applying it in its then existing form.[22] The Committee was faced with the fact that certain large exporting countries stayed outside the League and thereby in advance put obstacles in the way of carrying out a system of sanctions. Articles XVI and XVII of the Covenant, it is true, were explicitly designed to carry out the system, despite the fact that such states remained outside the League. But it was just here that the system encountered legal difficulties impossible of solution.[23]

It was necessary to still take into consideration the law of neutrality, which the United States and various other countries outside the League resolutely refused to abandon.[24] It was only by states within the League that, for political and legal reasons, recognition of neutrality was not extended openly. But even here there was an interesting development, at first in a theoretical and later also in a practical form, which in more recent times has led to an entirely revised view of the concept and legal aspects of neutrality within the League system. This new view rests, in the first place, upon the thesis that traditional neutrality does not actually constitute a uniform and static condition of law. In its historical aspects neutrality has assumed various forms[25] which did not always express the disinterestedness and passivity which it had assumed by the end of the nineteenth century. The content of the law of neutrality showed in its historical evolution as well, certain positive features

[22] League of Nations. *Reports and Resolutions on the Subject of Article XVI of the Covenant*, 1927, p. 16. Report of the Committee. "The Committee considered, however, that the application of Article 16, even if the League was universal in its character, might have formidable consequences either for the League in general or for certain of its members."

[23] Cohn, *Neutralité et Société des nations*, p. 184; *Kriegsverhütung und Schuldfrage*, p. 52; Whitton, *La Neutralité*, p. 398; Oppenheim, *International Law*, pp. 508 ff.

[24] Jessup, *The United States and the Stabilization of Peace*, pp. 131 ff., U. S. Senate. *Hearings before the Committee on Foreign Affairs* (Jan. 7-15, 1936), Washington, 1936; Whitton, pp. 541 ff. (Situation des États-Unis); Moore, "An Appeal to Reason," *Foreign Affairs*, New York, XI (1933), 558 ff.; Jessup, "The Birth, Death and Reincarnation of Neutrality," *American Journal of International Law* XXVI (1932), 789 ff.

[25] Bourquin (ed.), *Collective Security*, p. 455: "But the idea of neutrality has by no means always had the same content."

which were not entirely at variance with the idea of the solidarity of nations in their efforts for the prevention of war.[26]

The Negative Character of the Concept of Neutrality

1. When the traditional law of neutrality attached such great importance to its purely negative side—passivity, disinterestedness, and impartiality—this viewpoint had its explanation in different facts. Traditional neutrality rules were developed in close association with the laws of war, and did not constitute a contrast to a condition of war nor did they receive equal rights with it thereunder. War was the sun, about which the law of neutrality was to revolve like a planet. It was not due alone to its "precarious" condition, i.e., that the neutral state could at any time itself abandon its neutrality, or, by a single act of one of the belligerents, become spontaneously involved in the war, whereupon the whole system of neutrality, together with the rights and duties connected with it went into abeyance.[27] This was furthermore due to the prominent part which war played in earlier international law and the overwhelming influence which it exerted on all internationally legal conduct.

It would not be too broad a generalization of the earlier condition of law in this field if we were to say that war was legalized and that the status of war and the status of peace were situations of equal legal right. In such case the impartial neutral state could simply hold that war between two other countries was not its affair. It might then have the right to continue its own peaceful existence undisturbed as before. But on what ground could the bel-

[26] *Ibid.*: "This lesson of the past therefore justifies us, if the need arises, in relaxing the excessive strictness of our pre-war ideas, and without destroying the idea of neutrality, in giving it a meaning consistent, if not with all forms of repression of war, at least with that minimum degree of partiality without which the collective reaction is inconceivable."

[27] Haase, *Wandlung*, p. 25: "freiwilliger, stets aufhebbarer Zustand." Instead of voluntary it should be denoted as "precarious," for the free will of a neutral state is not sufficient to keep it out of the war; Oppenheim, p. 525, considers, however (likewise outside the League), that it is contrary to international law to involve a State which desires to remain neutral in the war. (See also Bonfils-Fauchille, *Droit international public*, II (1921), 640; Kleen, *Krigets Lagar*, p. 655; Fenwick, *International Law*, p. 619.

ligerent claim (except by special treaty agreement)[28] a right to demand impartiality of the neutral, and at the same time to insist upon its neutrality, while subjecting it to serious encroachments upon its commerce, to visit and search of its ships and their seizure? It is clear that this condition of neutrality could not be characterized either legally or actually as mere nonparticipation in war, with the natural consequences resulting therefrom.[29]

No better understanding of the law of neutrality could be obtained than by reference to the theories advanced in earlier international law regarding such concepts as sovereignty, nonintervention,[30] and the like. The badly misused concept of sovereignty[31] nowhere more clearly shows its insufficiency than in the laws of war and of neutrality. A sovereignty which might at any time, in complete harmony with international law, be brought to an end, or be arbitrarily limited by an unrestricted application of the laws of war and conquest, naturally could not be sufficient as a basis for legal benefits which reposed in the law of neutrality. The principle of nonintervention and the unlimited application of the laws of war form such an obvious self-contradiction[32] that their simultan-

[28] Some (e.g., Heilborn) believe that all neutrality rests on an explicit and implicit agreement; opposed to this position is Oppenheim, p. 526. It is therefore impossible to characterize ordinary neutrality as "protection" or "preservation" of a condition (as does Krauel, *Neutralität, Neutralisation und Befriedung im Völkerrecht;* Gareis, *Neutralität;* and Strupp, *Wörterbuch* II, 125 ff.); opposed to this, with regard to permanent neutralization of certain countries or territories, see Liszt, *Das Völkerrecht,* 1925, p. 466.

[29] Opposed is Descamps, *La Neutralité de la Beligique,* p. 353: "La neutralité en général, est l'état particulier d'une nation qui, demeurant étrangère aux conflits armés entre d'autres nations, poursuit avec elles le cours de la vie internationale pacifiques"; Heffter, *Das europäische Völkerrecht,* p. 315: "Fortbestand aller Rechte des Friedens"; Hautefeuille, *Histoire . . . du droit maritime international,* p. 43: "La guerre ne modifie pas la position de l'état neutre"; Kleen, *Lois et usages de la neutralité,* I, 75: "Elle constitue un état juridique nouveau, qui se distingue de l'état de paix ordinaire."

[30] This is the reason most frequently advanced; for example, see Kleen, *Krigets Lagar,* p. 655; Oppenheim, *op. cit.,* p. 519; Bonfils-Fauchille, II, 640; Politis, *La Neutralité et la paix,* pp. 19 ff.

[31] Cohn, *Kriegsverhütung und Schuldfrage,* pp. 57 ff.; Ross, *Folkernes Forbund og Staternes Souveraenitet,* p. 445.

[32] Numerous authors maintain that it is a question in international law whether a neutral State can be implicated in war without its consent, but declare at the same time that the neutral State at any time is entitled to abandon its neutrality

eous recognition in the earlier international law made any arguments for the law of neutrality on this basis quite untenable. The principles of sovereignty, independence, nonintervention, and so forth are thus always stated in the earlier international law with the implied limitation that they collapse upon a declaration of war.

The most adequate interpretation of the traditional law of neutrality, therefore, is undoubtedly the idea that it constitutes a part of the law of war itself.[33] This proves its historical evolution [34] as well as the origin of its different rules. They were not in the first place dictated, from the standpoint of the neutral's existence, for the maintenance or continuous development of its own peaceful existence, independent of and unaffected by the war, although such a hope naturally underlay this system. But what these states had attained through centuries of development was only to be tolerated under certain conditions and with broad privileges of interference, conditions and privileges which were dictated entirely by and in the interests of the belligerents.[35]

2. Historically therefore the law of neutrality has evolved as a supplement to the law of war, and not as an independent form of law. In the following pages we propose to present some outstanding characteristics of the development of the idea of neutrality. Formerly a distinction between belligerents and peaceful states of course was recognized in fact. But the two situations have not

and to declare itself a participant in the war. But why should the neutral State in this respect have greater freedom than the belligerent?

[33] So, to a certain extent, says Waldkirch, *Das Völkerrecht*, 1926, p. 370: "Begleiterscheinung des Krieges"; Liszt, *Völkerrecht*, p. 532: "Der Krieg erzeugt ... ein Rechtsverhältnis" and p. 534: "eine wesentliche Verschiebung des Friedensverhältnisses"; Rivier, *Droit des gens*, II (1896), 370: "La notion de la neutralité est inséparable de la notion de la guerre."

[34] For reference to this historical development itself, see, for example, Ullmann, *Völkerrecht*, p. 515 ("Begriff der Neutralität ist das Ergebnis eines geschichtlichen Prozesses"); Despagnet, *Droit International*, p. 689: "la détermination de l'ensemble de ces droits et devoirs constitue l'object de la théorie de la neutralité"; but such a reference gives no explanation of the nature of neutrality.

[35] Bonfils (especially p. 638), insists that the possibilities of neutrality are founded in "la jalousie des belligerants voulant empêcher un État tiers de devenir l'allié de l'ennemi." From a purely economic approach to war and neutrality, Jessup, Neutrality, IV, "Today and Tomorrow," pp. 20 ff., arrives at a similar conclusion; neutrality is a part of war, it is to some extent "a euphemism for economic war."

kept legal connection with one another.[36] If a non-warring state, for example, permitted the free passage of foreign troops through its territory, or extended aid to them, whether of financial, material, or military nature, there were no legal consequences with respect to the position of the state so acting. On the other hand, the belligerent states permitted themselves to be guided by self-interest alone in their relations with the nonparticipating states.[37]

Historically, through different cycles of civilization, there had evolved highly specialized rules under the law of war governing reciprocal relations between the belligerents themselves, but we find no rules which regulate the relations between a belligerent and a nonparticipant.[38] The Roman Empire, which, at the close of the period of antiquity, came to play a considerable political rôle in Western civilization, rejected, as a matter of principle,[39] any idea of a neutral or impartial status: "*aut socius aut hostis.*"

When the law of neutrality, like international law as a whole, was first accorded independent status in the Middle Ages, it was naturally because new economic and political conditions forced this development. A number of states, having more or less similar military and economic resources, came into existence, and at the same time commercial relations rapidly increased among them,[40] although they might be situated a considerable distance apart. It could hardly be in the interest of a belligerent state to make enemies of such distant countries. Its interest dictated only that the belligerent states aim to prevent the supplying of its opponents by

[36] The law of neutrality is, however, considerably older than is generally stated, especially in English references, where the theory of complete impartiality quite naturally leads to a dislocation of its historical lines. See, for example, Oppenheim, II, 494: "Indeed, the practice of the seventeenth century shows in numerous instances that neutrality was not really an attitude of impartiality," from which that author concludes that real neutrality did not develop until the eighteenth century.

[37] *Ibid.*, p. 492; Hall, *International Law*, pp. 691 ff.

[38] See Cybichowski, *Das antike Völkerrecht*, p. 82, giving however the text of a treaty between Rome and Astypalaea, which strongly resembles modern day agreements with respect to neutrality (prohibition of passage and supplying of arms, money or ships to the enemy); see also Séfériadès, *La Conception de la neutralité dans l'ancienne Grèce*, pp. 641 ff.

[39] Rivier, *Droit des gens*, II, 371.

[40] Jessup-Deák, *Neutrality, Its History, Economics and Law*, I (1935), 10 ff.; Rivier, II, 370 ff.; see also Nys, *Le Droit international*, III, 535 ff.; Boye, *De vaebnede Neutralitetsforbund*, pp. 3 ff.

sea, i.e., the recognition of the right of blockade and of the capture of merchant vessels carrying contraband of war,[41] while, on the contrary, innocent shipping was to be respected. During the thirteenth century certain practices arose which may be described as rules of neutrality during maritime warfare, finding formal expression in the famous *Consolato del mare*.[42] The law of neutrality in maritime warfare is thus much older than that of neutrality in land warfare and is essentially different from it; the latter had an independent origin and developed much later. Even for several centuries after that time, rules of law were recognized in which it was considered entirely legal and normal that a nonparticipating state should permit passage through its territories or might render support to a belligerent in the form of soldiers, provisioning, or loans. This was not considered as incompatible with its status as a neutral. Thus, neutral governments frequently lent or hired out numbers of their troops for payment. On the other hand, belligerent states often paid subsidies to other states to keep them neutral. It was at times a purely business arrangement, in which the highest bidder was successful.[43] A lack of definite provisions for neutrality necessitated the insertion of such provisions in treaty agreements made between various countries. Thus Article 3 of the Danish-English treaty of 1670 [44] provides that the kings of the two countries respectively shall not supply the other's enemies (when these are aggressors)[45] with munitions, soldiers or arms, nor permit their

[41] Jessup-Deák, pp. 50 ff. and 105 ff.

[42] Heffter, p. 316; Boye, pp. 5 ff.; Jessup, I, pp. 4 f.; Hall, p. 543; Nys, III, p. 537.

[43] For example, see Laursen, *Danmark-Norges Traktater 1523-1750*, IX (1933), 114, regarding the negotiations preceding the Danish-French Treaty of Neutrality of March 17, 1691: "The Danish Minister was dissatisfied with the subsidy, 100,000 Rixdalers (annually) which Martangis (the French Ambassador) offered for neutrality, and demanded 200,000 Rixdalers and furthermore payment of subsidies owing under the treaty of 1682.... The situation became even more difficult for Martangis when the British Ambassador (Molesworth) at the end of July was granted authority to negotiate with the Danish government for the delivery of 7,000 to 8,000 men to England. Martangis did all that he could to prevent this...."

[44] Laursen, VI (1923), 319.

[45] "Qui aggressores fuerint." The theory of aggression, with its significance for the law of neutrality is thus quite old. It is interesting, too, to note that England at that date by no means regarded impartiality as an essential of neutrality.

subjects to do so, and provides for the most severe penalties in case of violation.

When a state thus undertook to extend subsidies to another, or, on the other hand, to maintain its neutrality under certain conditions, such treaty agreements envisaged a state of war. That a positive agreement upon peace is the purpose is, in fact, specifically stated at times, as many of these treaties aim at the declaration of an "everlasting state of peace between the contracting parties." [46] But the obligations of neutrality were not understood to be a guarantee for a general condition of peace. They obtained actual and legal significance only when the condition of peace had ended and a state of war had succeeded it.

This is also in harmony with the ideas of the time and with the then existing theories of international law. The term "neutrality" itself was in common use from the beginning of the seventeenth century (Neumayer von Ramsla, 1620),[47] but had been used at times in documents as early as the fifteenth century. It is of great significance that a scientific study of the concept of neutrality shows that it did not originally lay stress upon impartiality and passivity.[48] On the contrary, we find that Hugo Grotius, in his famous work *De jure belli ac pacis*, is influenced by canon law in the expression of an idea which, in its fundamental aspects, is not far removed from that which underlies the system of the League of Nations. According to Grotius, the question of guilt, that is, the moral judgment of the belligerents as to the justice or injustice of the war, is to be a guide for determining the attitude of the non-participating states.[49] States are obligated to act in such manner that a bad cause is not strengthened nor a good one weakened.[50] They should even intervene in the conflict to defend the latter.

[46] See, for example, the above-mentioned treaty of 1670, Art. I.

[47] Nys, III, 538 ff. on the older theories of neutrality, from which it appears likewise that the expression is of a much earlier origin.

[48] Jessup, I, 8 ff.: The notion of "just" and "unjust" war, of Ayala, Vitoria, Suarez and Gentilis.

[49] Grotius' theory of neutrality is set forth in his famous 17th chapter in Part III of his work *De jure belli ac pacis* (here quoted from the Marburg edition of 1734): "De his qui in bello medii sunt."

[50] Page 722: "nihil facere, quo validior fiat is, qui improbam fovet causam, aut quo justum bellum gerentis motus impediantur."

Only when the moral and legal judgment of the issues seems to be in doubt were they obligated to extend equal treatment or impartiality to both belligerents. For example, as to the right of passage or economic aid, such support was in no way regarded as prohibited to neutrals.[51] Impartiality, to Grotius, is therefore neither passivity nor disinterestedness, nor do its origins nor its reasons lie there. The law of neutrality, on the contrary, evolved in the theories of a positive and active attitude toward war, on the part of outside states, for the purpose of assisting a just cause to become a victorious one.

3. This view of the concept of neutrality was, however, soon to be replaced by an entirely different one, answering better the political realities of its time. Since international organizations capable of passing judgment upon the moral or legal character of a particular war did not exist, the states were thrown upon their own judgment, which naturally was not unaffected by their own political interests. This was shown by the manner in which the writers attempted to separate the concept of neutrality from a moral and legal judgment of the war. In Vattel, for instance, we notice this development. He demands from neutrals complete impartiality[52] toward the belligerents, while he insists at the same time that, even if it is possible through equal treatment of both parties, the neutrals must not give actual support to a state in an evidently unjust war.[53]

Vattel bases his reasons upon the distinction between just and unjust wars[54] and lays down the remarkable thesis that a state which wages an unjust war, secures thereby no legal rights: "Une guerre injuste ne donne aucun droit."[55] There is therefore no obligation of neutrality toward such a state. For example, Vattel permits the right of passage over neutral territory only where it is conceded to both belligerents under the same conditions, but it may be refused to a state waging an obviously unjust war.[56] He

[51] "In re vero dubia ad aequos se praebere utrisque in permittendo transitu, in commeatu praebendo legionibus, in obsessis non sublevandis."

[52] *Le Droit des gens,* III, 99: "exacte impartialité."

[53] *Ibid.,* p. 102.

[54] *Ibid.,* pp. 26 ff.

[55] *Ibid.,* p. 204.

[56] *Ibid.,* p. 131.

seems to imply here the legality of a sort of passive support to one of the parties, and it is interesting to note that Vattel does not in any way regard such action as incompatible with the concept of neutrality.

Moreover, Vattel takes the position that assistance given one of the belligerents in accord with a previous treaty engagement is not contrary to neutrality.[57]

Theoretical Development of the Concept of Neutrality During the Eighteenth Century

1. The first to expound the traditional concept of neutrality in complete clarity and consistency was the Italian Galiani.[58] He gave it the actual form which it retained up to the period just prior to the outbreak of the World War in 1914. He separates completely the connection between the law of neutrality and a moral or legal evaluation of the war, or rather, he points out correctly that such evaluation is not the only factor for the non-participating state to consider when it faces a decision as to what position it should take toward the outbreak of war. The neutral state has an equally important obligation to consider with regard to its own citizens. No moral or legal duty can exist to oblige a state to participate in a war in which the weight of its share by intervention would be slight or the possibility of its being able to take a decisive part in the victory of a good cause be very questionable.

He correctly distinguishes between individual morality and international morality, which in many details are so different and therefore must lead to such different consequences. When one speaks of the "duty" of a non-belligerent state to intervene in any war for the purpose of extending assistance to the victim of an aggression, it is due to a confusion of the notions of legal and moral obligations. He cites instances where moral duty requires such intervention, for example,

[57] *Ibid.*, p. 101: "Les exemples en sont frequens en Europe."

[58] *De' doveri de' principi neutrali*, 1782. We here use Cäsar's translation, Leipzig, 1790.

where the state attacked by an aggressor is in no way guilty of provoking such attack and at the same time is connected by the closest of ties of friendship, of gratitude, or of consanguinity, and where finally the pleas for assistance are so strong and the danger so slight that the ruler risks little. A Prince who under these circumstances would refuse to extend such aid would fail in his most humane obligations.[59]

But conditions might be quite different, so that it might be unpardonable foolhardiness, even a crime against one's own subjects, to intervene. Galiani describes graphically the economic and moral decay which follows in the track of war.[60] Should one be obliged to expose the people of one's own country to these ofttimes irreparable catastrophies, merely because two or more foreign governments have worked themselves up to that point where their differences may be resolved only by war? Moreover, the neutral state has probably been poorly informed of the actual causes of the war, and often its assistance will contribute nothing decisive toward its conclusion. Galiani refuses as a matter of principle to place upon a nonparticipating state any obligation to intervene in the war. Even where very great services have been rendered by one state to another, he declares that this cannot put upon the latter an obligation of such far-reaching nature that in gratitude it should enter the war to aid the former.[61] And as a consequence, it is a condition of the maintenance of the legal status of neutrality that the nonparticipant is not *entitled* to intervene in the war.[62] It is possible that law and morality are both on the side of one of the belligerents, when one considers only the mutual relationship of the parties. But this is not a sufficient reason to require the neutral state to enter the war. Had it been in the position of the injured belligerent state, it might for example have averted the war by a compromise. It is impossible to turn over the decision to another state in a case where its own

59 *Ibid.*, I, 36, 42 ff.

60 *Ibid.*, saying that an earthquake, a dangerous epidemic, a fire, or a financial panic, which destroys one or more communities, cannot be compared with war, which may deprive a whole nation of its independence and liberty forever.

61 *Ibid.*, I, 59. Galiani makes an exception only in the case where a State owes its very existence and independence to the other; p. 62.

62 *Ibid.*, I, 85, on Treaties of Neutrality.

political freedom of action with regard to the important question of war or peace is at stake. Upon this point, for the sake of its own people and their interests, it must reserve its freedom of action.

2. These points of view, which are rooted basically in the general political and economic conditions of their day, were further elaborated by Galiani into special rules of law, and with such striking clarity and consistency that his ideas gained general acceptance. Neutrality had now attained a relatively independent position as a legal institution. It was based upon the compelling interests of the neutral states, and was no longer to be derived solely from the question of guilt between the belligerents. This new theory, however, did not quite attain the end which is the real object at which it aimed, namely, the right of outside states to continue their peaceful existence in the same manner as in time of peace. In so far as individual rules of neutrality were concerned, these were to retain their dependence upon a state of war, so that the law of neutrality was still for the non-warring states a sort of supplement to the laws of war. The impelling force in the developmental history of the law of neutrality was neither the independent interests of neutral states in the maintenance of a peaceful existence, in so far as this was not interrupted by war, nor a complete formal impartiality toward the belligerents; but rather a purely psychological (and political) evaluation of that kind of behavior on the part of the neutral state which would be permitted it by the belligerents without exposing it to a declaration of war.

From this developed the maxims of impartiality, passivity, and disinterestedness, among others, while the theoretical principles of state sovereignty, of non-intervention, and others, had very little to do with it. The law of neutrality is a very weak expression of state sovereignty; it has thus quite a precarious nature, not only in the sense in which all international law formerly held it, where access to war was always free, but since it was designed throughout, not in the interest of neutrals, but in the interest of the belligerents.

Efforts to Enforce the New Concept (Armed Neutrality)

1. Coincident with the theoretical development[63] of new principles, an attempt was made to carry them out in practice through the so-called Armed Neutrality Leagues of 1780 and 1800. A sharp controversy arose between the belligerents and the neutrals with regard to limitations upon the freedom of trade of the latter, especially as to the extent to which enemy goods might be seized aboard neutral merchant ships. Diplomatic negotiations led nowhere, and, during the war between England and America, a group of European states united, agreeing to use military force, if necessary, to maintain the neutrality rules for maritime warfare which had developed through customary usage. Besides defining contraband, they particularly required: (1) the recognition of the right of neutral merchant ships to navigate freely in the ports and along the coasts of belligerent countries;[64] (2) that enemy private property, with the exception of war contraband, be free from seizure aboard neutral merchant ships ("free ships, free goods"); (3) that only an actual effective blockade of enemy ports was to be respected (as distinct from the so-called "paper blockade"); and (4) that neutral ships could be captured only for clear and just reasons, and that the prize court must promptly and legally pass judgment.[65] The agreements in these conventions were gradually accepted by a considerable number of nations and constituted in a sense the first codification of neutrality law during maritime warfare. The Danish-Russian Convention of July 9, 1780, in Article X, provided that all other neutral powers were to be entitled to accede to the agreement, with the same rights and duties as the original parties. In Article IV it was stipulated that each of the contracting parties was to arm a suitable number of

[63] See regarding Hübner and his importance, Boye, *De vaebnede Neutralitets-forbund*, pp. 123 ff. Earlier attempts in the same direction are mentioned by Kulsrud, "Armed Neutralities to 1780," *American Journal of International Law*, *XXIX* (1935), 423 ff.

[64] So, Bergbohm, *Die Bewaffnete Neutralität*, p. 34, who states however that these principles were not of great practical interest at the time.

[65] Danish-Russian Convention of July 9, 1780, Martens, *Recueil*, II (1791), p. 106.

war vessels to enforce the principles established by the Convention; Article VIII bound the parties to mutual defense, if, in consequence of their being a party to this agreement, they should be attacked. In the year 1800 a new attempt was made to assert these principles, with the addition of a rule concerning the inviolability of convoys.

In principle, these conventions recognized that the right to use military force to maintain rights was not incompatible with neutrality, and we may therefore see in the Armed Neutrality Leagues an evidence of the thesis that it should be possible to combine the present sanctions system of the League of Nations, with the idea of neutrality. However, one must not overlook the fact that the Armed Neutrality Leagues aimed primarily at the defense of impartiality and of disinterested neutrality. They find their parallel in modern times, rather, in the Fifth Hague Convention of 1907, Article X, under which a neutral state may resist by force violations of its neutrality without such resistance being regarded as a hostile act. In accord with the Thirteenth Hague Convention, Article XXV, a neutral power, in proportion to the resources at its command, is further obligated to use all necessary means to prevent violations of its neutrality. The provisions thus imply the right and duty of a neutral to use armed force to protect its neutrality. The sanctions system of the League Covenant goes, however, beyond the bounds of nonpartisan neutrality in so far as it is specifically intended to intervene in the relations between the belligerents to prevent or to stop the war. Nonetheless, the armed neutralities have a special significance in the development and the correct understanding of the law of neutrality which makes desirable a further examination of their underlying points of view.

2. In any discussion of the possibility of a continuous existence of neutrality law after the establishment of the League of Nations, there is too much importance given to the *negative* side of neutrality, that is, to the refusal of a state to associate itself with one of the belligerent parties; while the *positive* element of this, to which Galiani attached prime importance, is overlooked, that is, the desire to keep one's own country out of war with all

the economic and moral decay which accompanies it. Far too much importance has been attached to absolute passivity and impartiality, which characterized the laws of neutrality at the end of the nineteenth century and at the beginning of the twentieth. When these laws were codified in recent times, it was overlooked that passivity and impartiality were, at best, merely the *means* by which neutrality, under given political conditions might be maintained, and that they were not under all circumstances necessary *elements* of neutrality itself. If we go back a hundred or two hundred years, we find that the nonparticipating states were struggling for recognition of their rights by methods which give us an entirely erroneous impression. First, unconditional impartiality was rarely a required condition of neutrality, particularly where assistance was given to a belligerent under the terms of a preëxisting agreement, and in actual practice even without such prior agreement. And, further, the neutrals were anything but passive toward the belligerents; on the contrary, the Armed Leagues of Neutrality, with their use of substantial mutual assistance even by armed force, required that their rights be respected. Such attempts moreover date back to a much earlier period than the end of the eighteenth century.

As early as March 10, 1691, in the treaty between Denmark and Sweden,[66] there was an agreement for the protection and maintenance of their trade as neutral powers. The two countries promised mutual assistance in matters of trade, shipping, and cargoes during wars between certain foreign powers. If any harm were done to the subject of either party through search, seizure, or capture in any way contrary to the law of neutrality, the parties were to make common cause by jointly requiring that the injury be repaired; or, if such satisfaction were not obtained within four months, they were to undertake retaliatory measures or reprisals against the offending belligerent. If because of this any of the belligerents should resort to hostilities against either of the contracting states, the situation would create a *casus foederis* within the meaning of the provisions of their treaty of defensive alliance

[66] Laursen, IX (1933), 86; Bergbohm, 1884, p. 49; Boye, *De vaebnede Neutralitetsforbund*, pp. 55 ff.; *Haandbok i Folkret*, pp. 165 ff.

dated February 1, 1690.[67] The two states mutually obligated themselves, in addition, to fit out convoys to escort the merchant vessels of either party, and also to furnish a number of warships to patrol the areas considered dangerous to their merchant shipping. Notification of the agreement was to be sent to the belligerent powers.

These measures were further expanded and made more pointed in the treaty[68] of March 17, 1693, for the maintenance of free trade between the states, as it was desired upon the part of the Danes that the convoys should be jointly representative of the fleets of both states, thus giving them greater emphasis. It was furthermore desired—and this is of great interest to us here—that the signatories make a *joint effort at mediation between the belligerent parties.*[69] This mediation was to have an entirely different character from that called for two hundred years later in Articles V and VI of the First Hague Convention of 1907,[70] according to which the mediators' task was apparently ended at the moment such proposal had been made and rejected, and moreover was to have only the character of disinterested advice. The 1693 treaty, however, took a far more positive position by providing for the exercise of real diplomatic and political pressure upon the belligerents, thus being something comparable to that collective and united action against the belligerents which the South American Saavedra Lamas Treaty has in view. In the Danish draft of February 14, 1693, it was stated that the two kings could not show their friendship for the participants in the war in any better manner than by expressing their deep concern and interest in any means by which peace might be reëstablished. It was therefore

"mutually decided to extend mediation from time to time, and to negotiate with each other frankly and fully concerning this and all such other related questions as might arise, and to confer, through their respective ministers at the courts of the belligerents and at each other's courts, frankly and fully upon any measures to be taken. If any of the participants in the war should not state its position regarding

67 Laursen, *op. cit.*, pp. 17 ff.

68 *Ibid.*, pp. 517 ff.

69 *Ibid.*, pp. 502, 507. The Danish agent Juel felt that "it was almost a matter of conscience that the two kings put an end to the bloodshed."

70 Martens, *Nouveau recueil général de traités,* 1910, p. 378.

this proffered mediation, the two kings were jointly to declare that, although they had no intention of forcing mediation upon any of the participants in conflict with its own interests, they agreed not to conduct separate negotiations in this matter, and they likewise solemnly agreed that no mediation would be tendered without prior consultation together. Should one of the participants refuse the proffered mediation or put it off with an equivocal reply, or put the responsibility upon the other, the two kings would coöperate diligently with the other participants for the reëstablishment of peace. Should the King of Sweden consider it necessary, in order that such mediation receive sufficient respect, that he make extraordinary increases in armament on land or sea, the King of Denmark agreed to do the same." [71]

The Treaty of 1693 denounced as "almost indescribable" the devices, violence, and chicanery practiced against neutral ships and their convoys, and the consequences therefrom in the deprivation, restriction, losses, and irreparable injuries done to them and their countries and people, the destruction of ships, the loss of human lives and of property and possessions; they stated that the two contracting parties were therefore agreed to put into effect the terms of the treaty of alliance previously concluded by them. If further applications to the belligerents should fail to lead to a satisfactory result, the parties mutually engaged themselves to halt and to seize as many of the vessels of the belligerent countries as was necessary to afford full satisfaction or indemnification for the existing damages, and not to release any such ships until both the contracting parties had been fully recompensed for their losses.

Economic sanctions were considered in Article IV of this treaty in a manner peculiarly modern, in that the two kings mutually engaged themselves to forbid their subjects to transport their goods upon the ships of the belligerent concerned, and they were likewise temporarily to prohibit their subjects from purchasing or loading such ships. That these sanctions might result in an unequal treatment of the two belligerents was in no way regarded as in conflict with neutrality. Article VII expressly provided that when a belligerent state respected the rights of neutrals, the ships and goods of its subjects were not liable to capture and sale in Danish and Swedish ports; while on the contrary it was permissible to

[71] Laursen, p. 513.

seize the ships and goods of a belligerent who did not discharge its obligations in that respect, thus evidently discriminating between the two belligerent parties. Should a belligerent take counter measures, the provisions of Article IX become effective, under which the contracting parties might resort to such further measures as general seizure, embargo, boycott, or a blockade by land and sea. In Article XII the two monarchs engaged themselves to equip and keep in readiness a certain number of war vessels for the maintenance and execution of this agreement. In a secret codicil to the above, the number of such vessels was set at eight from each party.[72]

3. Almost a hundred years later the first Armed Neutrality League was formed under similar legal and political circumstances, but on a much greater scale. The reason behind it was that American privateers sent out during the war between England and her North American colonies had rendered the North Sea unsafe. In August, 1778, the Russians made a proposal to Denmark to end this nuisance by joint action. A. P. Bernstorff prepared a draft treaty containing the five fundamental rules which later (in 1780) were taken up in the Russian proposal, but which at first were not approved by the Russian government.[73] In 1779, however, an understanding was finally effected between the three northern powers, Denmark, Sweden, and Russia, in which it was resolved to keep privateers away from their coasts and to "neutralize" the waterways of the North Sea, this including an agreement for the building and fitting out of a number of naval vessels to carry out the provision. The initiative in the League of 1780 came from Russia, for the Empress of Russia dispatched a copy of the Declaration of February 28, 1780,[74] to England, France and Spain in which the rules of neutrality which the Russian government would uphold—if necessary, by force of arms—were further elaborated. Shortly thereafter (May, 1780) the Danish government made a

[72] On the League of Neutrality of 1756, see Boye, *Die vaebnede Neutralitets-forbund*, pp. 97 ff.

[73] Bergbohm, p. 4 ff.; Boye, p. 147 ff. A comparison of the literature with the official documents may be found in Scott, *The Armed Neutralities of 1780 and 1800*.

[74] Martens, *Recueil des principaux traités*, II (1791), 74.

declaration [75] concerning the Baltic Sea which clearly established the essentially protective tendencies of the law of neutrality. In order to preserve a free and unimpeded connection between Denmark and Norway, the king declared the Baltic to be a closed sea in which the ships of all nations might sail in peace and enjoy all the advantages of its peaceful status.[76] The king therefore prohibited the entry of armed vessels of a belligerent into the Baltic for the purpose of hostile action against any other party. He referred to the fact that all countries which bordered on the Baltic lived in conditions of sincere peace and "regard it as one of the greatest blessings a Prince can secure for his people." [77] It was thus not merely a question of establishing certain rights for neutrals, but of a common localized limitation of the right to make war, with the idea of the protection of the commerce of all nations including that of the belligerents. The thought behind this declaration is quite different from that in the common opinion of its time (and of later times) regarding passivity toward war, as a necessary element of traditional neutrality. The Danish viewpoint was further expressed at the same time in agreement with Russia and Sweden and was accepted by the belligerents.[78]

The Danish government further issued a declaration [79] under date of July 8, 1780, regarding the rights of neutrals. Notifications along the lines of the Russian one, were sent to the belligerents (England, France, and Spain), and in the same month a convention was concluded between Denmark and Russia [80] which reasserted these rights in treaty form, the contracting parties engaging to equip

[75] *Ibid.*, p. 84. The question of the neutralization of the Baltic had already been taken up in the Peace of Roskild of February 26, 1658, Article III; Laursen, V (1920), 232; Bergbohm, p. 171; Boye, *Die vaebnede Neutralitetsforbund*, p. 41; and later aimed at in the Danish-Swedish Convention of July 12, 1756 (*Danske Traktater*, 1882, p. 83) Article III: "The Baltic Sea, which must remain free from war itself as well as from all its consequences...."

[76] "Ou toutes les nations doivent et peuvent naviguer en paix, et jouir de tous les avantages d'un calme parfait."

[77] See footnote 75 above.

[78] The French reply of May 25, 1780 is in Martens *Rec.* VI, 202. For the separate articles between Russia and Sweden see Bergbohm, p. 171, and Boye, *Die vaebnede Neutralitetsforbund*, p. 191; England and the Netherlands also gave their adhesion.

[79] Martens *Rec.* IV, 360 ff.

[80] *Ibid.*, II, 103 ff.

a number of naval vessels to support their position. They engaged further to give mutual diplomatic support and to undertake common reprisals against the belligerent who failed to comply. Its terms were, in essentials, the same as those in the Danish-Swedish agreement of 1693. The convention was to remain open for the accession of other states. A similar convention [81] was concluded between Sweden and Russia on August first of the same year.

At about the same time a supplementary agreement [82] was concluded (July 9, 1780), in which it was asserted, not only that the Baltic Sea was to be regarded as "outside limits" of war operations, but it further attempted to extend this prohibition to the North Sea areas. In Article II of this agreement the parties declared (in accord with the Danish draft of 1693) that they would coöperate for the reëstablishment of peace and a fair settlement of the dispute, so that further bloodshed might be avoided.

Denmark and Sweden further gave their accession respectively to the convention [83] concluded between Russia and other countries, of which notifications were sent by Russia to the belligerents.[84] The Netherlands [85] gave its adherence on January 3, 1781, and the Emperor of Austria [86] on July 10 of that year. Portugal's acceptance of its terms came through a separate convention made by it with Russia on July 13, 1782.[87] Prussia also associated itself with this system,[88] as did the Kingdom of the Two Sicilies.[89]

There was thus created a rather comprehensive system for limiting the effects of the war upon outside states. This system accepted war as a fact and made no distinctions between the belligerents with respect to the guilt of the parties, or between aggressive and defensive war. This League was, however, neither passive nor impartial. It asserted its claims as of right against the belligerents,

[81] *Ibid.*, 110.
[82] *Ibid.*, IV, 357 ff.
[83] *Ibid.*, 369 and 371.
[84] *Ibid.*, 372.
[85] Documents hereof; *ibid.*, 375 ff.
[86] *Ibid.*, 404 ff.
[87] Martens, *Rec.*, II, 208 ff.
[88] *Ibid.*, 418 ff.
[89] Also see Bergbohm, pp. 188 ff.; Boye, *Die vaebnede Neutralitetsforbund*, pp. 200 ff.

and presupposed the maintenance of its position by force of arms.[90] The weaknesses of the system lay in the lack of any legal organization and the consequent jealousies and mutual suspicions among the participants, which are evident even in the Danish-Swedish agreement which was made toward the end of the seventeenth century. Fixed forms of common action against the belligerents had not been created, and one might therefore suspect that one or another of the neutrals would attempt to gain special advantages for itself by adopting toward one of the belligerents a more favorable attitude than that of the others. The difficulties inherent in this lack of organization may be seen in an interesting exchange of notes between Sweden and Russia in 1780, to be found in Martens' treaty series.[91] The Swedish government asked a question as to the manner in which mutual assistance was to operate: was each participant to be responsible for the peaceful commerce of all the other participants, or was each one to protect only his own commerce? The Russians answered that an explicit convention should be concluded to which all neutral powers should be invited. Any of these powers might take part for the general security of their common commerce. The warships of all should be so stationed geographically as to form a continuous chain designed for mutual support. Each would thus have equal standing.

Sweden then asked what measures were to be employed against a belligerent if the common efforts of the neutrals failed to attain their aims. Should remonstrances be made jointly, or was each member state to act for itself? Finally, if a member neutral power was, as a last resort, compelled to use extreme measures against a belligerent, should it not have the right to demand the support of the other members? How could this be guaranteed? Reprisals, for example, should not be made in the name of the offended state alone, but only after the previous vote of all had been taken. Otherwise a single power might, by its individual action and con-

[90] Bergbohm, p. 96 agrees that the Armed Leagues of Neutrality are in direct conflict with the status of belligerency, but believes—without sufficient reason—in accord with more modern views, that they are therefore in conflict with international law: "die neutralen Staaten sind überhaupt und principiell nicht berechtigt, von sich aus den Operationen der kämpfenden Mächte willkürlich Schranken zu setzen."

[91] Martens, Nouveau Recueil de Traités d'Alliance ... de l'Europe, IV, 354 ff.

trary to the desires and interests of the others, drag all into war, and thus defeat the purpose of the League or render it ineffectual.

To this the Russian reply was that remonstrances should first be made directly by the offended state, but that this should be simultaneously supported in an active manner, through diplomatic representations by the envoys of the other participants. There must, moreover, be a distinction between the various types of complaints. If one of the League states were guilty of a violation of its neutral obligations, and if this were to occasion a controversy with one of the belligerents, the remaining neutrals would not be bound to support it. But if the act of a belligerent was in the nature of a violation of the principles now established, or if it expressed opposition to the League of Neutrality itself, it was to be regarded as a "devoir indispensables des Puissances unies, d'en faire une cause commune." However, this duty of making common cause was to apply only to the sea, without any obligation for the other neutrals to participate in further military operations (on land). And only jointly ("la volunté commune de tous") might such decisions be made. The Russians moreover believed that the belligerent would respect, without further measures, this common action of neutrals, "dont l'idée seule a été reçue avec l'applaudissement de toutes l'Europe impartiale."

Like the Danish-Swedish agreement of 1693, the League of 1780 played an immediately important rôle in limiting encroachments by the belligerents. But England later involved the Dutch in the war, in order to destroy the League.[92] When the latter applied to the other members for help, they were faced with a very difficult situation, of which an account is given in a Swedish memorandum [93] of February 17, 1781; if they sided with Holland, they would be drawn into the war and the real purpose of the League would be defeated. If, on the other hand, one maintained that the Dutch incident fell outside the scope of the League, the latter would be weakened in the eyes of the world, since it was aimed, as all knew, at mutual assistance against encroachments by the belligerents. It was therefore suggested by Sweden that diplo-

[92] Martens, *Rec.* IV, 389 ff.
[93] *Ibid.*, 394.

matic representations on behalf of the Dutch be made to England.

4. A fundamental difficulty had been discovered here (which has likewise arisen in more recent times) with regard to any system of restricting war without provision for a positive obligation upon the members to participate in the war if necessary. The same difficulty came up for instance in the English examination of the problem of security in 1934-35, where it was then pointed out that economic sanctions, not backed by a threat or readiness to participate in war, would be insufficient. In the Swedish-Russian exchange of notes of 1780, emphasis had been laid on the fact that an attack from a belligerent which was aimed at the League itself was to be regarded as calling emphatically for united action. And England's attack in 1781 was to be so regarded, according to the assertions of the Dutch government.[94]

On the other hand, Russia had laid stress upon the idea that mutual support need not imply a declaration of war, and it may therefore be said that the Swedish position—that the League should *not* enter the war on Holland's side—was undoubtedly correct. The decisive consideration, as logical as it was practical, was that by a declaration of war the League would lose its own *raison d'être*. It was not a defensive alliance, with possible engagements of a military nature, but a league for the maintenance of peace and the restriction of war. It is true that Holland's involvement might have weakened the League's authority, but this was an inevitable consequence of the unlimited absolute right to declare war, as recognized by international law at that time, and of the limited means and forms of organization available to the League. It is, in fact, similar to the situation which Neo-neutrality must face in our own time with regard to Article XVI of the League of Nations Covenant. A belligerent may actually commence hostilities against one of the sanctioning powers. This, however, creates the necessity for the other members to participate in the hostilities if they did not participate in the original war which was the occasion of the sanctions. Neo-neutrality asks in such a case, as in all cases of war,

[94] The English declaration of war, however, gave a different reason, and Bergbohm (pp. 185 ff.) thinks that the Dutch statement was merely an excuse to draw the League into the controversy.

that the peaceful sanctions which are available to the League be extended and made sufficiently severe to compel cessation of the war.[95]

5. Following the treaty of peace in 1783, the first Armed League of Neutrality lost its significance, and there was no attempt to incorporate its principles into the treaty after Russia [96] and other European states associated themselves to form a common front against the French Revolution. None the less, the principles which the League had defended in the field of neutrality were embodied more and more frequently in commercial treaties between nations. Denmark and Sweden did not abandon the fight for the cause of peace in a war-mad world. On March 27, 1794,[97] they renewed a mutual agreement for defense and security of commerce and navigation, "following the model of its predecessor." Both states were to equip eight ships of the line and a sufficient number of frigates to carry out the aims of the convention, so that ships and subjects of both countries might have equal protection.[98] The Baltic, in Article X of the agreement, was again declared a closed sea, and armed vessels were prohibited access to it, if from "distantly situated belligerent parties." The two states declared themselves to be firmly agreed upon the preservation of conditions of perfect peace in these waters. In the face of continued aggression from belligerents, Denmark and Sweden engaged to resort to reprisals everywhere, "the Baltic Sea, however, excepted."

There is no doubt but that the first armed League of Neutrality

[95] See the Danish proposals in League of Nations, International Studies Conference. *Collective Security*, Bourquin (editor) Paris, 1934, pp. 48 ff.

[96] Bergbohm, (pp. 236 ff.) gives an interesting explanation of the diplomatic game going on behind the scenes between the English envoy Harris, who through Potemkin drew Catherine II over to the English side, and the Russian Prime Minister Panin, who, under the influence of Frederick the Great, was working in opposition to these plans. Bergbohm thinks that the Armed Neutrality was the result of this "pulling strings" by which Panin had given to the Empress' ideas (which were not at all aimed thus) a direction against England and the maritime war. Thereafter the fame of Catherine as the "northern Semiramis" and "lawgiver of the Sea" was to be considerably deflated. On the other hand it is understandable why there was no attempt made to place the basic principles of the League in the treaty of peace.

[97] Martens, *Rec.* V, 274.

[98] Danish and Swedish territories in Germany were excepted (Article IX).

played a very important rôle and strengthened the interest in peace and neutrality. The threat of entering the League was used by Prussia as an effective weapon against English encroachments.[99] Privateering gradually ceased,[100] says Bergbohm:

> Armed neutrality had shown that even the strongest maritime Power may be forced to adapt its policies to the demands of the neutrals, when these are in mutual agreement, and especially during the period of a long naval war. But it has at the same time been proved that its existence depends upon throwing its real power into the scales whenever there is a question of establishing the new principle of law, especially in the law of war, and of its recognition by independent nations. The relations between neutrals and belligerents making for the creation of new laws of maritime warfare were stated in a surprising manner.[101]

Of lesser significance is the second Armed Neutrality of 1800 which, because of England's determined and heavy-handed opposition, had but a brief existence. Amid a general disregard of neutral rights, England went so far as to announce her intention to seize convoy vessels, which led to bitter controversies with Denmark (C. G. Bernstorff).[102] Russia (Czar Paul) again took the initiative toward an Armed League of Neutrality, which Denmark, Sweden, and Prussia joined.[103] This League reiterated the principles of the 1780 agreement, and added obligations of belligerents to notify neutrals of the establishment of a blockade and to accept, as being sufficient to grant immunity from search,[104] the declaration of the neutral convoy commander that there was no contrabrand aboard the convoyed vessels. England regarded this as a challenge, and demanded explanations from Count Bernstorff, who replied that Denmark had never abandoned the principles of 1780. There-

99 Bergbohm, p. 192.

100 *Ibid.*, p. 212.

101 *Ibid.*, pp. 216 ff. (Translation.)

102 See Cohn, "Danske Neutralitetsforanstaltninger for et Aarhundrede siden" in *Juridisk Forenings Aarbog 1915;* Bergbohm, pp. 256 ff.; Boye, *Die vaebnede Neutralitetsforbund*, pp. 241 ff.; Schmidt-Phiseldek, *Versuch einer Darstellung des Dänischen Neutralitätssistemes.*

103 These negotiations and acts are found in Martens *Rec.*, Supplement II (1802) 344 ff.

104 See the Danish-Russian Treaty of December 4, 1800, Article III; Martens *Rec.*, Supplement II, 402.

after followed the Battle of Rheden, April 2, 1800; Denmark was forced to abandon its position; the death of the Czar (Paul) in Russia and the advent of a new czar, Alexander I, created a new situation; Alexander associated himself with the English policy toward neutrals (English-Russian Treaty, June 5, 1801 [105]) and Denmark and Sweden were forced to accept it.[106]

The Establishment of the Traditional Concept of Neutrality during the Nineteenth Century

1. Armed neutrality thus could not be carried out in practice, and the period of the Napoleonic wars at the beginning of the nineteenth century witnessed a decline in the law of neutrality similar to that during the World War period a hundred years later. But the law of neutrality which had been established in the eighteenth century was later revived and came to be recognized as an important part of international law. In addition to actual neutrality, there came into existence in the nineteenth century a new legal institution, the neutralization by treaty [107] of certain states and territories,[108] which procedure naturally assisted in the evolution of neutral rights and duties. The neutralization [109] of Switzerland took place under the Act of November 20, 1815; and at the same time, in accord with the Final Act of the Congress of Vienna (June 9, 1815), Article XCII, and with the second Treaty of Paris (November 20, 1815), Article III, section 2, certain territories (Chablais, Faucigny, and others) were likewise neutralized.[110] Later provisions of a similar nature were approved with

105 *Ibid.*, 476.

106 Bergbohm, p. 261; Boye, *Die vaebnede Neutralitetsforbund*, pp. 298 ff.

107 Herein are included unilateral declarations of permanent neutrality, which in the case of Iceland is expressed in the Danish-Icelandic Alliance Statute, *Law No. 619 of November 30, 1912* Denmark-Statutes. Lovtidende-A (*1918*), p. *1424* § 19, according to which Denmark is to notify the foreign powers "that Iceland declares itself to be permanently neutral."

108 Neutralization may be of a positive or a negative character; Møller *Folkeretten in Fredstid ag Krigstid*, II, 2, p. 19; Liszt, pp. 107 ff.; see further Richter, *Die Neutralisation von Staaten*, pp. 37 ff.; and Strupp, *Neutralisation, Befriedung, Entmilitarisierung*, pp. 373 ff.

109 Schweizer, *Geschichte der schweizerischen Neutralität.*

110 Cohn, *Folkeretskilder*, p. 17.

regard to Belgium[111] (1839) and Luxemburg (1867). In so far as these states are concerned, their permanent neutrality is recognized as a valuable link in the general preservation of peace. Still more important was the fact that certain countries, among them especially the United States[112] and the Scandinavian countries,[113] in their own interest, followed a purposeful *neutrality policy*, that is, they attempted to adapt their foreign policy in such manner that they would under no circumstances be brought into armed conflict with other states. For the United States it was mainly a question of keeping itself aloof from European politics (the Monroe Doctrine). Such efforts, under the conditions of international law prevailing at the time, were bound to be as precarious as the rules of neutrality themselves. But they have a special significance in that they cleared the way for an entirely new and independent evaluation of the law of neutrality as a defense of peace and not as a mere supplement to the laws of war.

By the Declaration of Paris[114] regarding maritime law (April 16, 1856), certain principles were established; the maxim "free ships, free goods" was again asserted, and at the same time privateering—that is, the right of private merchant vessels of a belligerent authorizing them so to act, to seize hostile merchant vessels—was declared abolished. The demand that a blockade, to be entitled to recognition, must be effective, was recognized. It was also conceded that neutral goods—with the exception of contraband—could not be seized on enemy ships ("enemy ships, free goods"). From that time, all these rules formed constituent elements of the law of neutrality and, as such, became important milestones in the development of the rights of neutrals.

Somewhat similar, with regard to the duties of neutrals, are the so-called Washington rules[115] of May 8, 1871, which hold that a

111 Descamps, *La Neutralité de la Belgique.*

112 Scott, *The Controversy over Neutral Rights between the United States and France (1797-1800).*

113 Schmidt-Phiseldek, *Versuch einer Darstellung des dänischen Neutralitätssistemes*, I-II; for the early materials on the Armed Leagues of Neutrality, Frederik Bajer, *Nordens, saerlig Danmarks Neutralitet under Krimkrigen*, Copenhagen, 1914; Hedin, *La Neutralité des États scandinaves;* Waultrin, *La Neutralité scandinave.*

114 Martens, *Nouveau Recueil Générale*, Ser. 1, XV, p. 791.

115 *Ibid.*, XX, p. 698.

neutral must prevent the fitting-out within his own territory of any vessel for participation in the war or must prevent the departure of such a vessel therefrom; and that a neutral power shall not permit a belligerent to make use of its territory as a base for military operations, nor for increasing the military effectiveness of a vessel or its armament, nor for recruiting.

2. The rules of neutrality evolved along with the laws of war and as a supplement to them in the nineteenth century also. A new notion, however, appeared, which is described in Descamps' attempt to revalue the idea of neutrality.[116] Starting from the position that nonparticipants and belligerents must be deemed to have equal rights during a state of war, he created a new designation for such special condition of peace ("pacigérat").[117] But this idea was of no practical significance. The final form and the codification of traditional neutrality law was bound up with the laws of war and in close dependence upon them. The Brussels Conference of 1874, convened upon the initiative of Russia, had already codified the laws of land warfare. (The Hague Conventions of 1899 and 1907 largely rested upon that preliminary work [118]), but the legal status of neutrals in warfare was made the object of further detailed study. The right of permanently neutralized states (Belgium) to wage defensive war was recognized.[119] There followed a discussion of the rights and duties of neutrals with regard to the entry of belligerent forces into their territory, especially of the sick and wounded and of prisoners of war.[120]

By 1874 when an effort was being made for the codification of the laws of war and neutrality, the object of these efforts, of course, was the limitation of war. In the proposals of the Russian government there was expressed the hope that the growth of education

[116] "Nécessité d'une revision de la donnée de la neutralité." (see footnote 117).

[117] See especially his article in the *Revue Générale de Droit International Public*, VII (1900) pp. 629 ff.: "Le pacigérat ou régime juridique de la paix en temps de guerre"; and pp. 705 ff.: "Les grands étapes du progrès dans le droit des neutres et la vocation de notre temps à la constitution du pacigérat"; see also his book: *La Neutralité de la Belgique*, p. 353, where he distinguishes between simple, integral and disarmed pacigérat.

[118] Martens, *Rec.*, Ser. 2, IV (1879-80), pp. 21, 162, 197 and 225.

[119] *Ibid.*, 21

[120] *Ibid.*, p. 163.

and civilization would make war more and more rare. It was emphatically stated that the condition of war was not a normal, but rather an abnormal and exceptional one, but they nonetheless continued to regard neutrality as merely a restriction upon military operations, and its rules as merely a component part of the laws of war. The fundamental outlawry of war and the treatment of neutrality from the standpoint of the interests of the neutrals themselves was still far beyond the horizon for the Powers.

3. When the codification of the laws of war and neutrality finally took place at the Hague in 1899 and 1907, this too was due largely to the desire to decrease the frequency of war.[121] But the law of neutrality was regarded as having no value for that purpose. It was by no means within the scope of neutrality to lessen the probability of war, nor to brand aggressive war as illegal. Neutrality was designed only to assure a juridical status between the belligerents and the non-belligerent states. The device intended to control war was to be a judicial or arbitral settlement of international controversies. When disagreements should occur which were capable of settlement by arbitration, there was indeed no reason for the states to resort to war. War prevention itself, that is to say, the legal procedure which might be used to delay or prevent the outbreak of the war, was not carried far in the Hague Conventions. First, these Conventions imposed upon the disputants no binding obligation to submit questions to arbitration. With respect to mediation between nations, the Conventions explicitly declared that they were not designed to prevent the outbreak nor the continuation of war. Thus[122] Article VII in the First Hague Convention states that mediation does not have the effect that "mobilization or other war preparations are to be prevented, halted or hindered." This mediation, commencing after the outbreak of hostilities, will not cause interruption of existing military operations (except by express agreement between the parties). And in Article XXXV of the same Convention,[123] the International Commission of Inquiry's report permits the parties

[121] Art. I, First Hague Convention (1907); for further reference see Cohn, *Kriegsverhütung und Schuldfrage*, pp. 2 ff.

[122] Martens', *Nouveau Recueil Générale*, Ser. 3, III, 379.

[123] *Ibid.*, p. 387.

to retain full freedom of action with regard to whatever interpretation they wish to give it.

The inherent idea behind the war and neutrality rules of the Hague Conventions continued to be the same, namely, a complete and unfettered privilege to make war, the law of neutrality, which preserves throughout them a precarious existence, being still only an adjunct to that of war, or as one might say, the application of the laws of war to non-belligerent states. There is a further distinction between the laws of neutrality in land warfare (Fifth Convention)[124] and laws in maritime warfare (Thirteenth Convention).[125] Both are to be governed by the principles of impartiality and equal treatment,[126] but the principle of non-intervention is asserted in a more diversified form[127] than previously, while the idea of neutrality is set forth with much greater clarity in the case of land warfare than in that of maritime warfare.

Apart from this, the Hague Conference's system of neutrality distinguishes between a neutral state and the private citizens[128] of such state. Of this instances are given of situations in which the neutral state is to be held responsible for the actions of its private citizens,[129] and of others where no such responsibility exists, the consequences of certain unneutral acts devolving directly upon the private persons themselves.[130] For example, it is a violation of neutrality for a neutral state to aid one of the belligerents by furnishing arms, ammunition, and the like; but none the less Article VII of the Fifth Convention explicitly provides that there is no

[124] *Ibid.*, p. 504.

[125] *Ibid.*, p. 713.

[126] See particularly the Fifth Hague Convention, Article IX ("in identical manner") and the introduction to the Thirteenth Convention ("without partiality") and also Article IX ("equally").

[127] See particularly the absolute prohibition against entry or passage in the Fifth Convention, Articles I and II in contrast with the broad permission under the 13th Convention, Articles X, XI, XII, XIV, XV, XVII, XIX, XX, XXI and XXIII granted the belligerents for the use of neutral territory in their own interest. Under the subject of navigation the London Naval Conference Declaration likewise granted far-reaching privileges to the belligerents against neutrals.

[128] Article V of the 5th Convention, in contrast with Articles VII and VIII.

[129] Article IX, Sec. 2.

[130] Article XVII and the Rules of Capture and Prize under the London Naval Conference rules of 1909 (Cohn, *Folkeretskilder*, pp. 265 ff.).

obligation upon a state to prevent its citizens from selling or carrying such materials to one or the other of the belligerent governments. The state is thus not held responsible for the acts of its citizens. The same is true with regard to the carrying of contraband during maritime war. Indeed, even if a private citizen of a neutral country commits a hostile act against one of the belligerents, it is not (according to Article XVII of the Fifth Convention) the affair of his government, since the only consequences would be that such neutral private person "would no longer be regarded as neutral." [131] Under Article IX of the same Convention, however, a neutral state is responsible for seeing that export prohibitions, or restrictions upon the use of telephone, telegraph, and so forth, are applied equally to both belligerents, and *in this respect* it is to be held responsible for the acts of private citizens or corporations within its territory.

Positive obligations are also placed upon the neutral state when it receives armed forces of a belligerent into its territory. These are to be interned.[132] On the other hand, prisoners of war, brought by such belligerent forces, are to be freed within the neutral's territory; the same rule applies to escaped prisoners of war [133] who enter such territory.

4. These rules indicate that the neutral states, even during conditions of land warfare, are not in all cases obliged to refrain from any form of interference in the war or in its consequences. In still greater degree is this the case during maritime warfare, because the open sea provides a broad common field for the activities of neutrals as well as belligerents. There are thus frequent conflicts of interest, resulting from inevitable misunderstandings of reciprocal rights and duties. Because neutrality rules for maritime warfare have a much longer history than those for land warfare, they rest upon different fundamental points of view.

[131] This seems to be a clear statement that private persons can have an independent legal status under the rights and obligations of international law. For this question in general see Politis, *Les Nouvelles Tendances du droit international*, pp. 55 ff.

[132] 5th Convention, Article XI; 13th Convention, Article XXIV.

[133] 5th Convention, Article XIII.

The need for impartiality is, however, fully recognized in the preamble of the Thirteenth Hague Convention, and all war operations upon neutral territory are prohibited.[134] But upon the open sea very broad rights against neutral shipping have been granted the belligerents. Normal passage through neutral territorial waters is permitted.[135] In connection with this permission there is a long list of privileges for belligerent war vessels, permitting calls at neutral ports for the purpose of provisioning and taking on fuel, to repair damages, indeed even to bring in with them and carry away again their prizes (Article XXI). To realize the principles of non-intervention and its desire to remain at peace, undisturbed by the war, is therefore not possible to the neutral under conditions of maritime warfare. The answers to particular questions given by the Thirteenth Hague Convention could not be understood as the logical or legal consequence of a principle of this kind.[136] They arise in the main, from the conflict of interests between the belligerents themselves, and are only in slight degree related to the desire of the neutrals to keep out of the war. This conflict of interests [137] between various countries (England among others) having great and widely dispersed points of support, on the one side, and other countries (Germany) with relatively smaller forces of this nature on the other,[138] is clearly revealed in the discussions which took place during the negotiations prior to the Hague Conference of 1907. The decisions reached there were largely the expression of the hierarchy of interests of that time, rather than the expression of any universal principles of neutral-

[134] 13th Convention, Article II.

[135] *Ibid.*, Article X.

[136] See also Jessup, *Neutrality* IV, "Today and Tomorrow," p. 16: "nothing could be more fallacious than the attempt to test the application of any one of these rules of neutrality by the principles of logic. Since they are products of compromise and of experience, logic has found practically no place in their development and cannot properly be used in their application."

[137] Regarding the conflicting interests of this kind at the Hague Conference of 1899, see Meurer, *Die Haager Friedenskonferenz*, II, pp. 625 ff.

[138] Liszt, p. 541, note 3: "es ist einleuchtend, dass die Beschränkungen die Kriegführung um so mehr erschweren, je weniger Flottenstützpunkte der Kriegführende in den verschiedenen Teilen der Erde besitzt. Daraus erklärt sich die verschiedene Haltung Grossbritanniens und des Deutschen Reichs."

ity,[139] and it may be taken for granted, therefore, that discussions of these questions today the latter would result in entirely different rules of neutrality.

5. The Declaration of the London Naval Conference[140] of 1909 is also an expression of the same tendency to satisfy the interests of the belligerent at the expense of the neutrals. In not recognizing the inviolability of private property in contradistinction to the rules for Land Warfare of 1907 [Article XLVI]),[141] maritime law bears in general a more primitive and uncivilized character than the laws of land warfare. The Declaration of London was never generally ratified, it is true, but in a preliminary provision ("disposition préliminaire") it was expressly stated that the Declaration essentially corresponds to the recognized principles of the maritime law of its time.[142] Article LXIII, moreover, declares that the rules therein form an indivisible whole, and it was therefore not permitted to any signatory state to make reservations with regard to any of its provisions.

The Declaration of the London Naval Conference can thus be regarded as a supplement not only to the Fourth Hague Convention of 1907 regarding the laws of war, but also to the Thirteenth Hague Convention on the laws of neutrality. It repeats the demands of the Declaration of Paris of 1856 for the need of effectiveness as a test for the legality of a blockade, and it gives detailed rules for the enforcement of such blockade with regard to the rights of neutrals. Of special importance is its classification of the kinds of contraband[143] (unconditional and conditional contraband, and especially the free list in Article XXVII on the subject of what can in no case be declared contraband) and of its rules for

[139] Cohn, "Haevdelsen af Danmark's Neutralitet under Verdenskrigen," in *Juridisk Tidsskrift, XIV* (1928) p. 41. "The concept of neutrality suffered from an internal inconsistency even before the outbreak of the World War"; Einicke, *Rechte und Pflichten der neutralen Mächte im Seekrieg*, p. 374 ("*Kompromisscharakter*").

[140] Cohn, *Folkeretskilder*, p. 265.

[141] Martens' *Nouveau Recueil Générale* Ser. 3, III, 500.

[142] See further the reference under Note 139 above, p. 39, "it is in reality a series of compromises, and this can be demonstrated for each individual article."

[143] Liszt, pp. 548 ff.; Møller, II, 2, pp. 78 ff.; Oppenheim, II, pp. 655 ff.; Hall, pp. 765 ff.; Bonfils, II, 896 ff.

the treatment of neutral prizes.[144] Neutral ships accompanied by war vessels of their own nationality (convoys) are to be free from search.[145]

Such, in the main, was the condition of the law of neutrality which was to face its test during the World War of 1914-18. It was an expression of the commonly accepted principles of international law, as understood during the nineteenth century. Rights and obligations had an undefined character, as a consequence of the fact that they could be brought to an end upon the wish of the neutral state by its voluntary entry into the war, or if it were forced by one of the belligerents to enter. There was some talk of the obligations of neutrality; for instance, that if the rules of neutrality were not enforced by the neutrals there might be created a legal claim for damages against the neutral for his negligence in this case.[146]

The fundamental ideas referred to were non-intervention and impartiality; these, in turn, were related to the prevailing notions of sovereignty, but in reality not based upon them. None of these general points of view can be regarded as a satisfactory explanation for their concrete elaboration. The deciding factor here, in so far as the laws of land warfare were concerned, was the resolving of the conflict of interests between neutrals and belligerents; while with regard to naval warfare, it was essentially a resolving of the conflicting interests of some assumed future belligerents.[147]

Efforts to Maintain the Principles of Traditional Neutrality during the World War

1. Conditions during the World War became quite different from those contemplated in the codifications of 1907-9. There was lacking, particularly, the relative freedom of movement on the high seas which had formed the background for the Declara-

[144] Article XLVIII.

[145] Articles LXI-LXII.

[146] Møller, II, 2, pp. 60 ff.

[147] Cohn, "Haevdelsen af Danmark's Neutralitet under Verdenskrigen," *Juridisk Tidsskrift, VI* (1920), 41. "The 13th Hague Convention here holds solutions which have as little as possible to do with the real nature of neutrality, but aim only to bring about a compromise of the interests of the belligerents."

tion of London.[148] The blockade of the Central Powers by the Allied and Associated governments was so strict as to constitute an absolute domination of the world's waterways. No regard was paid in any way to the interests of the other belligerent, which found itself impelled to resort to counter measures, such as unrestricted submarine warfare, and which of course merely made conditions worse for the neutral. The distinction between the various types of contraband of war and the free list could no longer be of any importance when one party was cut off completely from all supplies.[149] The rules of visit, search and seizure could have slight meaning when any neutral ship might be taken for examination into the ports of a belligerent, even before it had attempted to pass the blockade. The freedom of entry and departure assumed under the Fifth Hague Convention on Neutrality during Land Warfare had to be dropped when the neutral state itself was thrown upon the benevolence of one of the belligerents for the most necessary supplies for its own people. It was forced to submit to conditions laid down regarding reëxport, and to the whole system of control and restrictions thus created.[150]

When now it is inferred from this, as was often asserted, that the law of neutrality became bankrupt during the World War, and that this example proves that neutrality is unworkable during conditions of modern warfare, that would be a false conclusion.[151] If the heart of the law of neutrality were not the maintenance of neutral trade, impartial treatment of the belligerents, nor in any manner the carrying out of any of the other theories or ideas of the older system of neutrality, but was merely an effort to keep the neutral state away from the horrors of war with its consequent wholesale slaughter of the nation's youth and the moral decay of one or two succeeding generations, still it may be claimed that those countries which remained neutral during the World War have demonstrated that neutrality is both feasible and useful, even during conditions as they exist today. Complaints that economic

[148] *Ibid.*, 42, 55 ff.

[149] *Ibid.*, 58 f.

[150] Cohn, "Haevdelsen . . ." p. 59.

[151] *Ibid.*, pp. 65 ff.; see also van Eysinga, *Die Niederlande und das Neutralitätsrecht während des Weltkrieges*, pp. 604 ff.

collapse during modern wars may be as fatal in neutral countries as in those of the belligerents, that they are more and more being drawn into the blockade system and so into the general destructive effects of the war,[152] are facts which can only lead to the conclusion that neutrals, no less than belligerents, are vitally interested in preventing or stopping war. Such facts must never lead them to abandon their last line of defense [the law of neutrality] and to throw themselves into the conflict. A partial involuntary involvement resulting in economic distress and destruction resulting from the war has ever been the lot of the neutrals, and this was true even in the best times of traditional neutrality.

2. A detailed study of conditions in the individual neutral states during the World War period shows that they made considerable use, in numerous ways, of the rules of neutrality established in 1907 and 1909.[153] There were some instances in which direct application of the rules for internment in neutral territory was made, and here a new problem arose under these rules, namely, the question of "hospitalization" of prisoners of war and of belligerent sick and wounded on neutral territory,[154] also the question of belligerent naval vessels and their prizes entering under the right of repair and provisioning in neutral harbors and in neutral territorial waters was of practical importance.[155] There were also many instances involving the practice of neutrals with respect to similar questions, also not known or contemplated in 1907 and 1909; for example, the treatment of armed and unarmed belligerent sub-

152 This is what Politis (*La Neutralité et la paix*, pp. 69 ff.) regards as "le déclin de la neutralité" and he, therefore thinks that "la guerre de 1914 a porté à la neutralité un coup mortel"; see also p. 95: "la faillite du compromis historique entre belligérants et neutres... aucune conciliation, aucun accomodement ne sont plus possible." This is clearly an error, which can only be explained by the fact that the author sees the main object of neutrality as an attempt to make profits at the expense of the belligerents.

153 When Vandenbosch, *The Neutrality of the Netherlands during the World War*, p. 315, states that "the history of neutrality during the World War would indicate that neutrality is a makeshift, based upon expediency, made possible only by the unstable condition of international society," one can only reply that a substitute may still be an extremely valuable thing so long as one is unable to obtain the genuine article.

154 Cohn, "Haevdelsen af Danmarks Neutralitet," p. 54; Vandenbosch, p. 160 f.

155 On the internment of the crew of the "Igotz Mendi" see Cohn, *Kriegsverhütung und Schuldfrage*, pp. 46 ff.; Møller, *Folkeretten in Fredstid og Krigstid*, II, 2, p. 71 f.

marines,[156] armed merchant vessels,[157] aircraft [158] flying over neutral territory, and others. It would be more correct, therefore, to say that it was only with respect to the problems of purely economic war that the rules of 1907 and 1909 were ineffectual. In a way, one might further assert that the conditions which prevailed in the World War have been a great object lesson in the carrying out of traditional neutrality in all other respects, in spite of the fact that it failed in the purely economic field. Article XVI of the League Covenant has to a certain extent established the legal basis for an international system of blockade for use in future wars, without definitely taking a stand upon the question as to whether the situation created might be characterized as *war*, or could be regarded as affecting the neutral status of the participants. In any case, it is evident that its authors had in mind the circumstances and conditions of the World War, and copied from them,[159] and in the fact that real neutrality could be carried out under the conditions of the World War, there can therefore be found confirmation of the thesis that Article XVI is not inconsistent with a position of neutrality.

Conflicts Concerning Neutrality within the Framework of the League

1. When the World War was entering its final phase and the war-weary nations were longing for a system of international order and law which would make a repetition of such war impossible, it was quite natural that a system of neutrality would not be uppermost in their minds. The war of the victorious powers had been waged, and one country after another had been drawn into it, under the slogan of "a war to end war," or the "last war" which would be fought ("never again,") through propaganda and agi-

[156] Vandenbosch, *The Neutrality of the Netherlands during the World War*, pp. 88 ff.; Møller, pp. 98; Perrinjaquet, *La guerre européenne et le commerce des belligerants et des neutres*, pp. 225 ff.; Savage, *Policy of the United States toward Maritime Commerce in War*, II, 50 ff.

[157] Vandenbosch, pp. 124 ff.; Møller, p. 96 f.

[158] Vandenbosch, pp. 77 ff.; Møller, p. 74; Cohn, pp. 62 ff.

[159] Cohn, *Neutralité et Société des nations*, p. 153.

tation unparalleled in former wars. This "moral" war had aroused public opinion to a passionate condemnation of the opponent, had created the questions of war guilt and of punishment for that responsibility, and had naturally considered also the creation of a new international order, in the light of these points of view. Apparently no consideration was given to the paradox which that view contained, namely, that they were to fight war with war.[160] Such a viewpoint was at the same time in the interest and the unexpressed desires of most of the belligerent governments, who wished to maintain or augment their military strength, thus continuing their former security and supporting their world policies.

Moreover, as a consequence of this feeling, toward the end of the war, a certain sentiment had been created against the neutrals.[161] Amid such violently aroused passions, those states which had refused to recognize that all criminal responsibility belonged to the other side, or at least would not give public expression to that idea, were naturally the objects of strong disapproval among the belligerents. The belligerents claimed, however unfairly, that the neutrals aimed only at profiting financially at the expense of the sacrifices of blood and wealth of others, and ascribed to them only the basest motives for their abstention from the war. When the cry became "a war against war," any efforts to maintain neutrality for the future were construed as deliberate attempts to oppose the creation of a new international order and to sabotage the abolition of war as desired by the opinion of the world. If there were to be no more war, of what importance could neutrality be in the future?

2. In opposing such reasoning, the neutral countries found themselves in a difficult position. No one, of course, wished more strongly than they to promote international order and to work for

[160] Cohn, *Kriegsverhütung und Schuldfrage*, p. 179.

[161] See, for example, Politis, *La Neutralité et la paix*, p. 96, in which he works himself up to uttering the following statement: "Le spectacle offert par les neutres, qui ne se sont pas révoltés contre la cynique violation des traités les plus sacrés, qui ont profité de leur situation pour continuer et parfois developper leur commerce avec tous les belligérants, sans se demander si l'un d'eux n'était pas coupable d'une injuste agression . . . a paru à tous les esprits éclairés être en flagrante contradiction avec les données actuelles de la vie internationale et mériter, en conséquence, d'être taxé de profonde immoralité."

the establishment of a permanent peace. If it were really possible to obtain a legal system of international organization, where war in the future would be abolished, it was their duty to work for this, regardless of their own special interests and experience. This "conscience conflict" appears in the proposals of almost all such countries prior to their entering the League, and in the preparatory work for the establishing of this new world order.[162]

This preparatory work and the proclamations that were submitted regarding war aims (for example the celebrated Fourteen Points of President Wilson) presupposed a reorganization of an essentially different character from that which was realized in the Covenant of the League. Public opinion[163] called for a general and effective disarmament, prohibition of the private manufacture and sale of munitions, compulsory arbitration in all cases, parliamentary control of foreign policy, the abolition of customs barriers, and equal freedom of trade for all nations with colonial possessions. Many believed in the possibilities of still more far-reaching reforms of a social and political nature, of the equality of races East and West, of an international agreement for the reapportionment and distribution of raw materials; and, first and foremost it was universally agreed that the chief objective was to be the definitive and final abolition of war itself from the lives of the peoples. It was not easy to forsee just how many or how few of these ideals would be realized. In this imagined league of nations, the neutral would also find security for its existence. If war, and especially what at that time were regarded as *the causes of war*, could be abolished, the logical consequence was that along with it the law of neutrality would be abolished.

This ideal league of nations and the real League as it was later constituted at the Peace Conference and for the first time made

162 See for example the Danish memorandum of January, 1920, regarding Denmark's entry into the League of Nations; for the memoranda of other neutrals see Cohn, *Kriegsverhütung und Schuldfrage*, pp. 31 ff.

163 In this connection, see the Dutch "Organisation Central pour une paix durable," setting up a "minimum program" and the *Recueil de rapports I-IV*, The Hague, 1916-18, also the American "League to Enforce Peace." For the preparatory work on the Covenant, see Miller, *The Drafting of the Covenant*, I, 3 ff.; a survey of almost all published proposals, both official and private, can be found in Schücking, Die Satzung des Völkerbundes, pp. 6 ff.

public in the draft[164] of January 14, 1919, certainly differed greatly. This draft was bound to and did evoke bitter disappointment. Membership in the League was to be restricted, and later admission was to be made dependent upon majority consent and the acceptance of rigid conditions.[165] The universality which had been regarded as the essence of the League and necessary for the fulfillment of its most important objects, was thus at once made impossible, and this was further evidenced in Articles XVI and XVII regarding the attitude to be taken with respect to outside states. The right of withdrawal was reserved in Article I, section 3.

It was a one-sided League of Nations, the effectiveness of which had further been weakened by incorporation of the antiquated and vague concept of absolute state sovereignty with its corollary principle of non-intervention (Article XV, section 8) and the still more far-reaching Monroe Doctrine (Article XXI).[166] Article V required unanimity for the decisions of both the Assembly and the Council, and a similar requirement was made applicable to the war prevention activities of the League. According to Article XVI, it was, in the final analysis, to be left to the sovereign opinion of each separate and individual state as to whether League intervention would or would not go into effect.

Instead of real disarmament, Article VIII was a greatly restricted proposal for the reduction of armaments; instead of abolition of the private manufacture and trade in arms, there was merely, in section 5 of that article, an argument for the necessity of continuing it. About compulsory arbitration of all international controversies, there was not a word. The application of Article XIII was made dependent upon the will of the parties concerned ("a leur avis"). War was not abolished at all; on the contrary, it was recognized as a legal means, if only the formal procedure and the delay specified in Articles XII and XV were observed beforehand. Articles XVI and XVII, instead of abolishing war, placed

[164] Published as an annex to the Danish memorandum of 1920; for further reference see Miller, D. H., *The Peace Pact of Paris*, pp. 118 ff.

[165] Article VII in its final formulation.

[166] Whitton, "La Doctrine de Monroe et la Société des nations," in *Revue de Droit International*, VIII (1927) 561 ff.; and *La Neutralité et la Société des nations*, pp. 542 ff.; see also Baty, "Note sur la Doctrine de Monroe," in *Revue de Droit International, IX* (1928) 157 ff.

a series of obligations upon the members, practically involving them in intervention in the war. In lieu of parliamentary control of foreign policy, Article XVIII laid down a rule that the publication of a treaty is a requirement for its validity, while secret engagements were in no wise prevented. Instead of carrying out broad socio-political reforms, there were in Article XXIII some vague efforts made to list a number of points desirable for such a program; instead of the freedom and equality of trade in the colonies, of equality of the colored and white races and of raw-material distribution, Article XXII provided merely for a division of the conquered colonies among the victorious great powers.

So great was the disappointment, the "tragedy's second act," that the neutrals were convinced that their hesitation was justified and even reinforced. They, too, tried to get some degree of acceptance of their various points of view, but without much luck.[167] This was due to many different causes. First, the changes were so sudden and so revolutionary that many circles hardly grasped their significance in the short time given for accession, which, under Article I, had to be done without reservation. Next, many of the particular decisions, and particularly the most important, following the English practice with regard to the editing and rewording of legal texts, left them so vague and ambiguous that it was difficult to point out in just what particulars they differed from the demands made by public opinion. This was openly acknowledged by the English themselves, who regarded such vagueness as an advantage, or even as an essential, for securing the acceptance of such a novel and far-reaching arrangement.[168]

[167] On the negotiations between the neutrals and the International Commission in the Hotel *Crillon* in Paris on the 20th and 21st of March, 1919, see Munch, "Les États neutres et le Pacte," in *Les Origines*, I, 163 ff.; the Danish memorandum and annex of January, 1920, appendix 3; D. H. Miller, *The Drafting of the Covenant*, I, 303 ff.; Schücking, p. 17.

[168] The official English commentary on the League Covenant which was submitted to Parliament (printed as an enclosure to the report of the Danish memorandum of January 1920) reads as follows: "Acknowledging the fact that one generation cannot expect to bind the next through mere written words, the Committee has throughout proceeded from the point of view that the League must ultimately depend upon the future favor of the member states for its continued existence.... A series of amendments aiming at the establishment of rules of procedure, after which the League should work... intended to make for greater exactness in general, *has been purposely rejected* [present author's italics] not

With regard to the most important question, that is, the coöperation of the states in the prevention of international war, a special difficulty resulted from the formulation of the text itself. The original form of Article XVI had presupposed a general condition of war, and the particular and separate provisions as to the measures to be used especially against those belligerent states which were not members of the League were based upon this presupposition. But even before the final draft had been prepared, President Wilson, prompted by his advisers, had abandoned this condition as impracticable both from the standpoint of constitutional and of international law,[169] while the particular provisions of the Article were left unchanged. The result was an Article XVI which comprehends a series of unsolved and partly insoluble problems concerning the contemporary application of laws of peace and war [170] and of the possibility of combining the system of sanctions with the system of neutrality, although the latter is not even mentioned in the Covenant. From the text of Article XVI, it was impossible to determine whether the legal status of neutrality was to be abandoned or to be kept and strengthened.

because the Committee has no sympathy for the proposals, but because they felt it was better to permit the statesmen of the future to be as free as possible, and let the League itself exist as a living organization, determining the lines of its own development."

[169] See further Cohn, *Neutralité et Société des nations*, pp. 156 ff.; *Kriegsverhütung*, pp. 54 ff.; United States Senate, Hearings before the Committee on Foreign Relations, 1919, pp. 1194 ff. This change which had already been made in the original, and which was of fundamental importance for the interpretation and evaluation of the whole legal situation presupposed therein, had previously been overlooked; see Schücking and Wehberg (1924) p. 621: "Die Worte 'ipso facto' lassen die *Vermutung* aufkommen, es solle gleichsam automatisch durch den Beginn des Ueberfallkrieges der Kriegszustand zwischen dem überfallenen (überfallenden) Staate und den andern Mitgliedern des Bundes eintreten. *Vielleicht* war dies auch . . . ursprünglich der Sinn, den die Urheber dem Art. XVI beimessen wollten" [present author's italics]. *Contra*, Oppenheim, II, 510; Michäilidès, *La Neutralité et la Société des nations*, pp. 97 ff.

[170] For further reference, see Cohn, *Kriegsverhütung*, pp. 56 ff.; Møller, *Folkeretten*, II, 1, pp. 101 ff., who thinks that a state of war does not exist but that Article XVI, nevertheless is incompatible with the member's neutrality; Schücking (1924), p. 632, in which is laid down inaccurately a distinction between participation in war (instead of *military* sanctions) and participation in economic sanctions; and holds that in the latter case there will not be a question of rights and obligations as a neutral but of a law *sui generis;* other authors (Gonsiorowski, Ray, Politis, Rolin, and others) deny the possibility of combining neutrality with the obligations under Article XVI. See below.

This confusion was augmented by the fact that one of the neutral countries, namely Switzerland, gained full recognition of her neutrality and at the same time was granted unreserved admission to the League.[171] It was in the interest of the Swiss government that this legal status should be announced as something quite exceptional, and this also was the purpose of the declaration made by the League Council on February 13, 1920, in which Switzerland's exceptional position was stressed, and in which it was further stated that neutrality in other cases was not compatible with the system created under the League Covenant. This very exception thus came to be a corroboration of the idea that neutrality had been abolished, and that the Swiss case was the exception which was intended to prove the rule.

In other quarters [172] the opposite idea was maintained, namely, that Switzerland's reservationless admission to the League, despite her elsewhere authorized neutrality (Article 435, Treaty of Versailles), was proof in itself that these two situations were not mutually exclusive. See also Article XX of the Covenant, according to which neutrality would have been void if it had really been in conflict with the provisions of the Covenant of the League of Nations. This view received definite support from the circumstances under which Luxemburg was later admitted to the League.[173]

[171] Møller, *Folkeretten*, I, 80; II, 1, 101 ("special status"), which is also the commonly accepted view. Declaration of the League Council of February 13, 1920 ("situation unique"); Oppenheim, II, 515 ("special status"); Ray, *Commentaire du pact de la Société des nations*, p. 104; Schücking, *Die Satzung*, pp. 299 ff. (1924 edition, pp. 633 ff.); Huber, "Die schweizerische Neutralität und der Völkerbund" (in *Les Origines*, II) 68 ff.; Whitton, p. 537 ("de caractère exceptionnel"); Gonsiorowski, *Société des nations*, II, 419 ("situation exceptionelle").

[172] Cohn, *Neutralité et Société des nations*, pp. 194 ff. (on Luxemburg p. 195, Note 1); *Kriegsverhütung*, pp. 71 ff.; Bonfils, II, 653, also appears to regard the Swiss entry as evidence that Article XVI is consistent with neutrality. On the other hand, the following have considered Switzerland's legal status as inconsistent with the principles of the League Covenant: Michaïlidès, p. 192 and the article of A. François quoted therein.

[173] Wehrer, "Le statut international du Luxembourg et la Société des nations," in *Revue Générale de Droit International*, XXXI (1924) 169 ff.; also "La Politique de securité . . . de Luxembourg," in *Revue de Droit International*, XIII (1932) 326 ff.; Michäilidès, p. 215 ff., is reluctant to admit the consequences, but on p. 227 had to admit that "le Luxembourg entend maintenir après la guerre et dans le cadre de la Société des nations, une politique de neutralité." The whole question is examined in some detail in the following pages.

3. But there are other and deeper reasons, of a political and international nature, which prevented the question of neutrality itself from being mentioned at all within the system of the Covenant. In interpreting the scope of each particular provision in the light of the fundamental aspect of the legal and political character of the new system, there were from the very beginning strongly divergent, even diametrically opposite, opinions upon the very points involved in this question. Even the fundamental view that the League had been created a new instrument for the maintenance of peace was ambiguously and variously interpreted in different quarters. Some—and especially those former neutrals just entering the League—understood by the word "peace" a *general* condition of peace, and that this was to be maintained by the abolition of war itself or at least by counter measures to oppose it. Others—and especially France and the pro-French nations—understood it as something of an entirely different nature; "peace" meant that condition which had been gained through the World War, that is to say, the particular condition of peace which had been established in law and incorporated in the Versailles Treaty.[174] This was the "peace" of which the League was to be the guarantor.

This profound difference had already been expressed in the first Assembly of the League, when from various sides, and especially from the three Scandinavian countries, proposals were made calling for certain changes in the Covenant. Opposed to these proposals was the opinion that amendments of a political and legal nature in the Versailles Treaty, of which the Covenant was an integral and component part,[175] were of doubtful legality. This view, how-

[174] See further Cohn, "Forbundspagtens Udvikling," in the volume *Folkeforbundets Forste Tiaar* (1930), pp. 21 ff.

[175] Said Mr. Balfour, during the session of December 2, 1920: "If you change the Covenant you change the Treaty of Versailles. The Covenant is embodied in the Treaty; it is an integral part of the Treaty . . ." League of Nations. *Records of the First Assembly. Plenary meetings*, p. 247. M. Bourgeois: "The insertion of the Covenant in the same diplomatic document as the Treaty is not merely a device of the drafters; it is the expression of a carefully considered determination. It is important that these two diplomatic documents, bound together by the same signatures, should retain in respect of each other the mutual relationship conferred upon them by their common signatories and that the obligations which result therefrom should be carried out loyally and in their entirety." *Ibid.*, p. 258.

ever, was immediately attacked by the neutrals (Switzerland), who would not grant in any way that, because the Covenant had been inserted as the first twenty-six articles of the Treaty of Versailles, this had any legal significance or created a relationship between the League members and the treaty of peace.[176]

The same differences occurred with regard to almost all other important questions, such as the demand for the reduction of armaments, security, treaty revision, treaty interpretation (Article XIX), and others. Such ideas gained quite different significance and importance when examined from these differing fundamental points of view. For the common preservation of peace, for example, a far-reaching general disarmament is, by all states, greatly to be desired. On the other hand, the need of maintaining the political alignments created by the Versailles Treaty, the fear of a war of revenge, and similar ideas made it necessary that considerable military forces be maintained to preserve the status quo. That the position of the neutrals must be entirely different when we change from one fundamental position to the other, is obvious, but it was not possible in this respect to determine which of the two positions was the right one. Both tendencies were still trying to control the development of the League but the final result was a restraint and an inhibition of real progress and inevitably contradictory interpretations of the meaning of the text of any particular provision or ruling.

4. Even within the circle of those countries which preferred to regard the League Covenant as a guarantee of security for the preservation of the situation created by the Versailles Treaty, opposing counsels existed with regard to the extent of this guarantee, as to how far the signatories had bound themselves in the matter of war and peace, and also whether they could preserve their position as neutrals should an emergency arise. Here the French and their friends interpreted the provisions as broadly as possible.

176 Mr. Motta: "...there is one argument which we cannot admit so far as the modification of the Covenant is concerned, and that is the argument based on the fact that the Covenant is bound up with the Treaty of Versailles.... The Treaty of Versailles, as regards its main contents is a treaty which concerns only the parties signatory thereto." *Ibid.*, p. 256.

France had, as we know, placed the question of its security foremost,[177] and had at first desired a direct alliance or a definite understanding with England and America, which should promise them military assistance in case of attack. Since this, from the beginning, met with difficulties, it was not unnatural for France to seek to read into the provisions of the Covenant a similar obligation. Others, however, did not desire to pledge themselves in advance to obligations or understandings of so broad a nature. Their position here was consistent in general with the policy of Great Britain, as well as with certain particular English principles of interpretation and formulation. Even among this group, however, there was no strong desire to assert a restricted or narrow interpretation of its obligations. Just because such members did not wish to go beyond the obligations[178] undertaken in the Covenant, they were the more anxious to insist that the obligations actually assumed should be sufficient to fulfill the guarantees demanded by the other side.

Through the Locarno Treaty[179] of 1925, a certain clarification of these contradictory positions was obtained, as it was expressly provided therein that the signatory states obligated themselves to extend military aid whenever a particular state was convinced ("aura pu se rendre compte") that an unprovoked attack has been committed. By this device a formula was created which made possible Germany's entry into the League in 1926.

There was at the same time, however, in Supplement F[180] a declaration (not formally binding) under which the fulfillment of obligations under Article XVI, requiring aid in resistance to an aggression[181] is made dependent[182] upon the "situation militaire" and "position géographique" of the particular member of the League. This broad limitation, which, so far as military sanctions are concerned, might to a certain extent be held to be implicit in the construction of Article XVI, section 2, aims at, and

177 Cohn, "Kollektiv Sikkerhed," *Tilskueren*, April, 1936.

178 This viewpoint was again and again officially asserted by the English.

179 Martens, *Nouveau Recueil Générale* (1927), p. 7.

180 Martens, *op. cit.*, p. 32.

181 This is not correct, as the obligation only existed after a formal violation of Articles XII, XIII and XV of the Covenant, and in such case even where actual aggression was not present.

182 "Dans une mesure qui soit compatible."

opens up the possibility of, a consideration of neutrality, even if it be expressed merely in an implied form.[183] While strengthening the special obligations of the Locarno powers against a German attack, they thus weakened the general obligations of all, under Article XVI with regard to the law of neutrality.

The Locarno Treaty, however, concerned only the boundaries on the west, and was, moreover, made dependent in such a way upon the coöperation of the League Council that France in the last analysis, did not regard its claims for security as sufficiently satisfied. They therefore were unable to make any broad gesture for a reduction of armaments. When Germany, in 1933, announced its intention of withdrawing from the League; then, in 1935, when it unilaterally freed itself from its disarmament obligations; and finally when, in March, 1936, again by unilateral action, it abolished the provisions for demilitarization of the Rhine region, the French demand for security was naturally still further from fulfillment. It was therefore to be expected that France would be particularly anxious to emphasize the collective obligations contained in Article XVI, while Britain was now more interested in minimizing them.

Developments, however, led both the French and the British to directly opposite views during the Italo-Ethiopian conflict in 1935-36. Here it was Great Britain which, at the beginning, took the lead in asserting that Article XVI obligated all League members to intervene, while France held back and took the position that the application of military sanctions at least must be excluded. This remarkable development shows how extremely difficult it is to couch political interests in advance in terms of universal legal obligations, and is in a way a victory for the British argument for a vague formulation of treaty engagements.

5. Opposed to these conflicting and changing tendencies in the interpretation of Article XVI of the Covenant of the League stood the independent endeavors of the neutral states. These en-

[183] It was particularly the engagements to afford passage under Article XVI, sec. 3, to which Germany took exception; see Wehberg, "Der Pakt von Locarno," in Strupp, *Wörterbuch,* III, 986; Gonsiorowski, II, 500 (vague); Politis, "Les Accords de Locarno," in *Revue de Droit International,* VI (1925) 713 ff.; Strupp, *Das Werk von Locarno,* p. 87.

deavors were directed, as far as possible, toward strengthening the League in its efforts to move in the direction of maintaining peace, while at the same time giving these efforts such form as would serve at all times, and not merely under the threat of a particular war situation, to preserve the general peace. The neutral states, at the same time, had to be on guard lest the war prevention activities of the League assume such form that individual members would find themselves under direct obligation to intervene or participate in military operations. These efforts sometimes coincided, and sometimes were at cross purposes, with the tendencies mentioned above, in the neutrals' interpretation of Article XVI. Least of all was an interpretation of any value which was dependent upon the immediate political situation for the application of sanctions, or otherwise, as the neutral states did not have the same possibilities as the Great Powers had for the control of this situation. It seems however to be the condition under which they must exist to retain their status as League members, and this fact makes their legal position under the system of sanctions and the question of a combination between neutrality and sanctions a very real one.

The neutrals had succeeded besides, as early as the beginning of the League, in obtaining recognition to a certain extent of their special interests.

In the very first Assembly of the League in 1920, the three Scandinavian countries proposed an amendment [184] to Article XVI, section 1, according to which there should be added to the general obligations to participate in economic pressure, the following rule: "At the request of a member for which the application of the above provisions might entail serious danger, the Council may authorize this member to maintain intercourse, in such measure as the Council may decide, with the Covenant-breaking state." This proposal, it is true, was not accepted at the time, but it served to cause the appointment of the so-called Blockade Committee, which was to make a general study of the question of the application of

[184] Denmark. Rigsdagstidende. *Report to the Rigsdag,* 1921; see discussion on this proposal in League of Nations. *Records of the First Assembly. Plenary meetings,* p. 248 ff., also League of Nations. *Document A.14.1927.V.* cited in the following footnote.

Article XVI. The result was a surprisingly severe criticism [185] of the entire system of Article XVI and an acknowledgment that it was completely impracticable in its existing form. It was held, albeit incorrectly—as the text of Articles XVI and XVII indicates—that the system presupposes universality and that it could not be carried out so long as large export countries remained outside. Several amendments to these articles were therefore proposed, and the Assembly in 1921 passed unanimously a series of so-called "Resolutions" [186] which were to be their guide for applying the system until the proposed amendments had been carried. These rules were later approved by the Council and modified the sanctions system to a considerable extent from its original form; they likewise opened up certain possibilities for the consideration of the special interests of the neutral states. They retain the admission that Article XVI as a whole must be regarded as a compulsory means of exercising economic pressure, but that this does not presuppose a real state of war,[187] and that the Council of the League, even where the decision has been left to the individual members, still has left to it important tasks in the planning and carrying out of the whole sanctions program.[188] The fundamental idea of the proposed amendment of the northern Powers was also recognized,[189] especially the desirability of the successive application of increasingly [190] severe economic measures as a means of compulsion. If more far-reaching measures, such as the effective blockade of the coasts of the violator of the Covenant, were required, the duty of carrying the

185 Cohn, *Kriegsverhütung und Schuldfrage*, p. 79 f. This memorandum is published in League of Nations. *Reports and Resolutions on the subject of Article 16 of the Covenant, Document A.14.1927.V.* and Schücking (1924 ed.), pp. 608 ff.

186 League of Nations. Assembly. *Reports and Resolutions Adopted by the Assembly* (1921) p. 24.

187 Article I, section 2 of the Resolutions "Unilateral action on the part of the defaulting State can not create a state of war . . . it is in accord with the spirit of the Covenant that the League of Nations . . . should attempt to avoid war and to restore peace by economic pressure."

188 Article II, section 8: "The Council shall recommend the date when the enforcement of the economic pressure in Article XVI is to begin."

189 II, 9, b, of the Resolutions of 1921.

190 II, 14. "Measures of increasing stringency may be taken. The cutting-off of the food supplies of the civil population of the defaulting state shall be regarded as an extremely drastic measure which shall only be applied if the other measures available are clearly inadequate."

decision into effect should be placed upon particular League members.[191] In this way the other League members would avoid being drawn into the war.

6. These Resolutions of 1921 were opposed by the so-called Geneva Protocol of 1924, and especially by the Belgian delegate Brouckère's, Report of 1926. The former [192] attempted to give new life to the system of Article XVI by laying down various presumptions concerning the question of aggression and by organizing a common front against aggressors. Here again sounded the fanfare of trumpets:

> The prohibition applies to aggressive war only. It naturally does not extend to defensive war.... Without waiting for the assistance which it [the victim of aggression] is to receive from international society it may and should defend itself with its own resources.[193]

The League members are likewise authorized to conduct wars of sanctions, concerning which the General Report [194] says:

> For this reason we have not hesitated to speak about special authorization to make war. It has been requested that the word "force" be used, to avoid any mention of "war" to save the people from any disappointment they might feel when they discover [!] that war, in spite of its solemn condemnation, is still permitted in special circumstances. We preferred however, to frankly acknowledge [and so forth.]

Brouckère's Report [195] of 1926 is generally mentioned in the literature of international law [196] as an effort to show the great possibilities for the prevention of war in Article XI of the Covenant. Actually, it aims to weaken the "Resolutions" of 1921 and to prove that they cannot be of consequence because of the text of Article XVI, with which Brouckère claims they are in conflict.[197]

[191] IV, 18, a.

[192] The protocols, together with the general report prepared by Beneš and Politis is printed as Annexes B and C in Miller, *The Geneva Protocol*, pp. 132, 156.

[193] General Report, p. 56 f. (in Miller, *op. cit.*, p. 56).

[194] *Ibid.*, p. 57.

[195] Published in League of Nations. *Document A.14.1927.V.*, *Reports and Resolutions*, p. 60 ff.

[196] See for example Kunz, *Die intrasystematische Stellung des Art. XI des Völkerbundpaktes*, p. 77.

[197] See further, Cohn, *Kriegsverhütung und Schuldfrage*, p. 83 f.

The viewpoint expressed in this report is restated in a report by the Dutch delegate, Rutgers to the Committee on Arbitration and Security in 1928,[198] a rather abstruse document which does not bring any of the questions discussed nearer a solution.

That the Geneva Protocol of 1924 and Brouckère's Report contained no recognition or clarification of the legal status of neutrals within the sanctions system, goes without saying. Actually neither the Blockade Committee nor the Resolutions of 1921 brought up for examination the problem of the relation between neutrality and the system of sanctions. They do not even mention the neutrality question, still less make any contribution toward its solution; nor did the report prepared by the Secretary-General of the League[199] on May 17, 1927, indicate a desire to disentangle the legal status of the members of the League with respect to war and neutrality during the application of military sanctions. Of course, to a certain degree, this was due to political "wire-pulling," such as that described above with respect to the interpretation of Article XVI. But it is also owing to the unfathomable technical difficulties which beset such explanations, and which are in no small measure due to the ambiguous wording of the Article and to the vagueness which from the beginning confused its real aims. When, however, the Covenant itself, as well as all of the documents mentioned here, assumed that war, in the international law sense of the word, continued to exist, and when all were forced at the same time to admit more or less definitely that not all states would be required to participate in war, at least not from its beginning, the questions of the law of neutrality and of its status within the League system thrust itself forward for that solution which sooner or later must be made. Efforts to close one's eyes to the existence of the problem and to the realities of the situation can not in the long run be successful.

[198] Printed in League of Nations. *Official Journal, 1928*, p. 670 ff.

[199] League of Nations, *Reports and Resolutions, Document A.14.1927.V*, pp. 83 ff.; Cohn, *Kriegsverhütung*, pp. 84 ff.

II

THE TECHNICAL PROBLEM

Conflicting Ideas not Resolved

1. THE POSITION of the law of neutrality within the system of the League of Nations system is necessarily and primarily a *technical problem.* Can the two systems be envisioned at all as combined? The fathers of the Covenant had rather taken the position that it was impossible, and this opinion was clearly expressed in the Declaration of the Council of February 13, 1920, on the occasion of Switzerland's entry into the League.[1] This was really practically a matter of course, so long as one takes for granted that the situation envisioned under Article XVI was that of a general state of war between all of the members of the League on one side and the Covenant-breaker on the other. But the situation had already been changed through President Wilson's final formulation of the article,[2] while the report of the Blockade Committee and the Resolutions of 1921 had completely rejected it. But what rules were then to be applied to those states which stood outside the League, whether by League members or not, if not the rules of neutrality? International law recognized in a situation of war only two legal systems—the law of war and the law of neutrality. The Covenant of the League had not prepared a third system to cover the quite special situations created under Article XVI, which put the impracticable demand upon the League members to act in conflict with the laws of neutrality, without pointing out to them a way to avoid being brought into the war, although such a position was not only assumed to be tenable but was indeed the legal basis for the whole system created by the

[1] "While affirming that the concept of neutrality of the members of the League is incompatible with the principle that all members," etc. See League of Nations, *Council Minutes (1920)*, p. 23.

[2] Cohn, *Neutralité et Société des nations*, pp. 156 ff.; *Kriegsverhütung*, pp. 54 ff.; Michäilidès, p. 98; Oppenheim, II, 510.

Article. It was of no use to refer to Article XVI as constituting a new element in international law, standing outside the whole question of neutrality and war.[3] In the first place, this simply was not what the Covenant said; for not only in Article XVI, but also in Articles XI, XII, XIII, and XV, it was presupposed that war would continue to exist (as would also neutrality) in the form which had been handed down historically as legal procedures for the settlement of international disputes, if only the formal methods and delays of the Covenant had been observed beforehand. Further, would such a concept not require a still more complicated and extensive system of legal rules of international law than the present laws of war and neutrality, to be capable of resolving the interminable conflicts of interest and of legal situations which, under such a system, would arise between the states?

There is not a hint, however, of all this to be found, nor any attempt in such direction, in the Covenant or elsewhere. Thus, apart from the fact that it is not easy to discover the legal basis upon which this new system could be erected, we are left without resource, in this vast and complex situation of conflicts, unless we fall back upon the laws of war and neutrality.[4]

[3] See however Møller, *Folkeretten*, II, 1 (1931), p. 101, who says "that for the remainder of the League members there will be no question of neutrality, either economic or military, when an illegal war (under the terms of Article XVI) exists," and (on p. 102), "The Hague Conventions regarding the obligations and duties of neutrals are inapplicable in such a situation." . . . "Moreover, for that matter the other member States could only obtain a position as a neutral in the situations dealt with under Article XVI by denying that the basis for the application of Article XVI exists in the present situation." On the other hand, "it cannot be assumed that the League members in such case [under Article XVI] are to be considered as belligerents with respect to the law-breaking State." See further Gonsiorowski, II, 422 f.; Politis, *La Neutralité et la paix*, p. 113: "ni belligérants ni neutres"; Michäilidès, p. 108 ff. (indefinite); Ray, p. 528: "On ne peut plus user des conceptions traditionelles relatives à la guerre et à la neutralité."

[4] Of necessity ("no other course seemed to be possible") we slip back to the positive laws of neutrality even for states which, in any given situation, claim that the application of sanctions under Article XVI of the Covenant is incompatible with fundamental neutrality; this arose in a very interesting fashion in the debates in the English parliament on October 23, 1935, concerning the Italo-Ethiopian conflict. There had been applied to Italian naval vessels in the ports of the British colonies and protectorates the rules of the 13th Hague Convention of 1907 concerning the question of neutrality at sea. In his speech, the English Foreign Secretary *Eden* remarked (*The Times*, London, October 24):

"The Leader of the Opposition had referred yesterday to instructions given by

2. It was also quite certain, and easily demonstrable, that the Great Powers had not contemplated such a sweeping reform of the whole legal system in this field, but rather had regarded Article XVI as but one forward step in the evolution of existing international law. Even as early as 1922 an official conference had been held at the Hague, in accordance with a decision of the Washington Conference, at which the United States was represented, together with England, France, Italy, Japan, and Holland. This was planned to supplement the rules of neutrality of 1907 by taking into consideration the technical developments in military science which had taken place since that time. The draft conventions [5] prepared by this Conference,[6] particularly regarding control of radio-telegraphy during time of war and of aerial warfare through all its sixty-two articles do not refer by so much as a word to the system of sanctions under Article XVI nor give any special consideration to the problem from the standpoint of belligerent or neutral states.[7]

authorities in British Colonies and Protectorates to apply towards Italian warships and auxiliaries a rule of the Hague Convention No. 13. Owing to the fact that this Convention was one which defined the duties of a neutral, the right honorable gentleman seemed to infer that the Government had made something equivalent to a declaration of neutrality. This was a complete misunderstanding of the position. If the Government had regarded themselves as neutrals they would have taken the regular step of issuing a proclamation of neutrality. No such step had been taken, and he quite agreed that such action would be inconsistent with their duty under Article 16 of the Covenant.

"They did not consider that any Covenant-breaking State had any legal right to require observance by other members of the League of any of the laws of neutrality. On the other hand, any departure from the rules to the detriment of the Covenant-breaking State was action in the nature of a sanction, and therefore, in accordance with their oft-declared policy, could only be taken in common with all the other nations at Geneva.

"In the present case there had been as yet no collective decision, and members of the League had therefore the right to apply the rules of the Hague Convention on a purely *de facto* basis. The Government found that immediate instructions had to be given to our authorities to guide their actions, and for the reason he had given, no other course seemed to be possible except to instruct them to apply the Hague Convention rule on a *de facto* basis."

[5] In the preparation of this certain world-famous jurists participated, such as John Bassett Moore, Cecil Hurst, de la Pradelle, Basdevant, Matsui, Struycken and van Eysinga.

[6] *Algemeen Verslag der Commissie van Rechtsgeleerden*, belast met de studie van- en het uitbrengen van bericht over de herziening van het oorlogsrecht, The Hague, 1923; Sandiford, *La Neutralité aérienne*, pp. 754 ff.

[7] The President of the Conference, J. B. Moore, states in the American periodical *Foreign Affairs*, July, 1933, pp. 560 f.: "The parties to this conference over which I had the honor to preside were the United States, France, Great

In the first-named Convention above, Article IV, section 2, it is expressly provided that all previous limitations upon the use of radio stations within the territory of a neutral power are to be applied uniformly to all belligerents. Article VII extends the rights of the belligerent authorities against neutral merchant vessels and aircraft, since they can assign to them a specific route or prohibit entirely the use of their radio equipment, and violators of these regulations are subject to attack by shell-fire or to capture.

The conventions on aerial warfare lay down a number of new rules, relating both to the laws of war and to the laws of neutrality; to the marking of belligerent airplanes; to the conversion of civil into military airplanes; their nationality; the right to claim the privileges of belligerents; the right to participate in war operations; and others. Persons escaping in parachutes must not be attacked while falling (Article XX). Precise rules give the conditions under which bombardment from the air is permissible or prohibited (Articles XXII-XXVI); and, on the contrary, conditions under which airplanes expose themselves to fire (Articles XXX-XXXV). It is forbidden for belligerent airplanes to invade the territory of neutral states [8] (Article XL). Airplanes on board war vessels are regarded as part thereof [9] (Article XLII). Many additional points regarding war vessels, to establish the rules for military aircraft (Article XLVI of the Washington Rules)[10] are carried over by analogy from the rules regarding war vessels of the Hague Conventions of 1907 and the Declaration of London of 1909. Somewhat

Britain, Italy, Japan, and the Netherlands. The delegates acted under the instructions of their respective governments. An examination of our unanimous report will show that it was largely devoted to the definition of the rights and duties of belligerents and of neutrals in time of war, and that it treated as still existing the Land War Neutrality Convention, the Convention for the Adaptation of the Geneva Convention to Maritime Warfare, and the Convention concerning Neutral Rights and Duties in Maritime Warfare, all made at the Hague in 1907. *The idea that the law of neutrality had become obsolete never was broached.*" (Our italics.)

[8] The rule here given undoubtedly includes the air above the territorial waters (see the *International Air Convention* of October 13, 1919, Article I, sec. 2, "with territorial waters appertaining thereto") and is therefore of interest in the question regarding the right of passage of airplanes over international straits.

[9] In this manner belligerent aircraft may profit by the right of passage over neutral territorial waters and international straits.

[10] Martens, *Nouv. Rec. Gén.*, Ser. I, xx, 698.

similar were the rules applying to the capture of prizes, to prize courts and the destruction of neutral aircraft (Articles LIII-LIX). Article LXII contains a fundamental and interesting interpretation of the question as to whether the laws of war and of neutrality for *land* warfare, or those for *maritime* warfare—which of course are quite different—should apply to aircraft and their crews.

These conventions have not been ratified, but will, like the London Declaration [11] of 1909, have a certain degree of authority and importance during emergencies, because of the eminent character of the jurists responsible for their preparation and of the Powers which took part in the Conference.

From the date of the coming into effect of the Covenant to the present time a number of international conventions have also been concluded which specifically mention the neutrality situation and give some positive rules concerning it. Agreements of this nature include both multilateral international instruments and bilateral treaties between various states, and in both cases also include League members.

The International Air Navigation Convention of 1919 prescribes (Article XXXVI) that in case of war its provisions are not to interfere with the freedom of action of the contracting Powers as belligerents or as neutrals, without any reference to the special arrangement covering this situation under Article XVI of the League Covenant. The statute on freedom of transit of 1921 (Article VIII) likewise retains the traditional freedom of action for belligerents and neutrals.

Similar reservations [12] are to be found in the International Waterways Convention of 1921 (Article XV);[13] and in the Barcelona Conference appear proposals regarding international ports (Article XIII). This Conference explicitly expressed a desire for the preparation of a new convention concerning the rights and duties of belligerents and neutrals with regard to transit in time of war. In the Convention of October 20, 1921, regarding the neutralization

[11] See also Hall, *op. cit.*, pp. 765 f.; Oppenheim, II, 505 f.; Bonfils, *Treatise on International Law*, II, 469; Liszt, pp. 498 f.

[12] Cohn, *Neutralité et Société des nations*, p. 195.

[13] Denmark, Statutes, Proclamation No. 198 of April 19, 1923 (*Lovtidende* [1923], p. 1285).

of the Aaland Islands, it was stated in Article VI, section 2, "in time of war" [regardless of who is the aggressor and with reference to Article XVI of the Covenant] they shall be regarded as neutral and shall neither directly nor indirectly be used for military operations.

In the treaty [14] of February 6, 1922, between the United States, Belgium, the British Empire, China, France, Italy, Japan, the Netherlands, and Portugal regarding their policies in China, Article VI provides that the various Powers bind themselves, in wars in which China is not a participant, to respect scrupulously that country's rights as a neutral Power; on the other hand, China engages that she, while neutral, will observe the rules of neutrality.

The Treaty of Lausanne [15] of July 24, 1923, regulates the status of the Turkish Straits during war and peace, in no way affected by any change in the traditional system applying to such situations. The exact circumstances under which Turkey would be regarded as a neutral were specified in section 1b of these regulations, and under paragraph (c) those determining her to be a belligerent. In the latter case provisions are made for the right of free passage for neutral shipping.

A similar arrangement was made in section 2, dealing with war vessels, transports, military aircraft, and the like, for purposes of war, as well as during Turkey's neutrality.[16] With respect to supplies and repairs, reference was made to the Thirteenth Hague Convention of 1907 concerning neutrality during maritime warfare, stating that its provisions were to be applied analogously to aircraft.[17] When Turkey was a belligerent, neutral aircraft were

[14] Washington, D. C., *Conference on the Limitation of Armament* (1921-22), pp. 1621 ff.

[15] League of Nations, *Treaty Series*, XXVIII (1924), No. 702, pp. 116 ff.

[16] Flying over this area was permitted (sec. 2b): "Les droits et devoirs de la Turquie comme Puissance neutre ne sauraient l'autorsier à prendre aucune mesure susceptible d'entraver la navigation dans les Détroits, dont les eaux et l'atmosphère doivent rester entièrement libres, en temps de guerre, la Turque étant neutre, aussi bien qu'en temps de paix." These regulations are now amended by Article XXIII of the Montreux Convention of July 20, 1936.

[17] "En attendant la conclusion d'une Convention internationale établissant les règles de neutralité pour les aéronefs, les aeronefs militaires jouiront dans les Détroits d'un traitement analogue à celui accordé aux bâtiments de guerre par la Convention XIII de la Haye 1907"; since omitted in the Montreux Convention of July 20, 1936.

to have the right of passage through the Straits, but at their own risk; and in cases where such aircraft were forced to land, the Turkish authorities might require proof of their neutral character (which has since been amended by Article XXIII of the Montreux Convention).

Article IX of the Treaty presupposed—without any direct reference[18] to, or modification of, by the Article XVI of the Covenant—that Turkey and Greece might become belligerents and exercise their "rights as belligerent Powers."

The Treaty of Lausanne has since been superseded by the Montreux Convention[19] of July 20, 1936, which permits the remilitarization of the Straits, but which recognizes war and neutrality, in effect, as in the Lausanne Treaty.

There is here reason only to lay stress upon some of the neutrality provisions originating at the time of, and shortly after, the publication of Article XVI, and in the following period, in which a long series of treaties was concluded, which expressly assumed the continued and unaltered existence of the traditional law of neutrality.[20]

3. The Permanent Court of International Justice at the Hague devoted itself to the question of neutrality as early as 1923, without so much as hinting that any change had taken place in this system because of Article XVI of the Covenant. This was in the case of the British steamship "Wimbledon" and its passage through the Kiel Canal in 1921, with a cargo of munitions destined for

18 See on the other hand Article XVIII, sec. 4 (now Article XXV of the Montreux Convention) in which another question, that of the duties of guarantees by the Powers) under which rights and duties in accord with the League Covenant are discussed.

19 Including correspondence published in the *English White Book: Turkey No. I* (1936).

20 Cohn, *Kriegsverhütung und Schuldfrage*, p. 73, note 19; for similar instances see the neutrality treaty between Hungary and Turkey, in Martens, *Nouv. Rec. Gén.*, ser. 3, XXIX (1934), 372, and the joint neutrality declarations of the Scandinavian countries and the neutrality rules of each (the so-called "Oslo States") in the Danish, Norwegian, Swedish and Finnish law collections for 1938. The Danish declaration was applicable to Iceland. French texts of these neutrality rules for each country may be found in *Finland Statutes*. Finlands Författningssamling, *Fördragsserie Overenskommelser med Främmande Makter* (1938) No. 17, pp. 93-94. See also *Amer. Jour. Int. Law*, XXXII, No. 4 (1938), 141-63, for English text of these rules.

Poland, which passage was opposed by Germany because of its position of neutrality toward the war between Poland and Russia. The Court decided,[21] on August 7, 1923, that the obligations of neutrality on the part of the German government, were not contrary to the clear obligation of the right of passage provided in Article 380 of the Versailles Treaty. Both the majority opinion and the dissenting minority [22] of the Court agreed, however, that the law of neutrality was in full force, just as it had been hitherto.[23] One of the members of the court, J. B. Moore, said: [24] "All the judges of the World Court, in the Kiel Canal case unhesitatingly concurred in the view that the law of neutrality remained unmodified; no one thought of doubting its continuing force." Thus there can be hardly any doubt [25] that the acceptance of Article XVI of the Covenant was not regarded as bringing to an end the entire former system of the law of war and neutrality. Article XVI in no sense created a new system of international law upon this point. In its original form it assumed a general condition of war. This assumption was later revised without, however, changing the remaining text of the article. The result has been, *not a new formation, but self-contradiction.*[26]

Efforts to Solve the Problem of Coördination by Technical Methods

1. The report of the Blockade Committee, and the Resolutions of 1921, had examined the purely *practical* question as to

[21] League of Nations, Hague, Publications of the Permanent Court of International Justice, *Series A, Collection of Judgments I,* No. 1, p. 33, The S.S. "Wimbledon," Williams and Lauterpacht (eds.), *Annual Digest of Public International Law Cases* (1923-24), pp. 99 ff.

[22] Publications of the Permanent Court, *op. cit.*, pp. 35 ff.

[23] See also Cohn, "Kielerkanalens folkeretlige Stilling," in *Juridisk Tidsskrift* IX (1923), 225 ff.

[24] In *Foreign Affairs* (New York, 1933), p. 561.

[25] See also the report of the Secretariat General dated May 17, 1927. League of Nations, *Reports and Resolutions on the Subject of Article 16 of the Covenant (A.14.1927.V)*, p. 84: "The fact, however, that a war has been illegally commenced does not in the present state of international law affect the rights of the belligerent as such." Even this is recognition that the law of neutrality has been continuously in effect.

[26] Cohn, *Neutralité et Société des nations*, p. 157; *Kriegsverhütung*, p. 56.

what might happen if the system of sanctions were put into effect, but had not taken up the study of the neutrality question itself and that of its relation to sanctions. There were *technical* questions, too, of the creation under international law of rules applicable to such a situation. A first attempt toward a solution of this problem was made by the present writer, in an article: "Neutralité et Société des nations," in the Danish publication *Les Origines et l'oeuvre de la Société des nations.*[27]

In that article the system of the League and the system of neutrality are for the first time set forth as two contrasting principles, *which were nevertheless to be combined*[28] *into a single rule of law* as a consequence of the formulation itself of Article XVI. As we have previously noted, a number of agreements *outside* the League had expressly maintained the concepts of war and neutrality. This very fact assumed the need of the joint application of the two systems when, in a given war situation, they should both be applied. It is furthermore an undeniable fact that war and neutrality *within* the League has been maintained in a number of cases (legal wars). In this connection we may refer to Article XII, section 1,[29] in the instance where a controversy has been submitted for arbitration or for consideration by the Council, and three months have elapsed after the arbitral award or the report of the Council. War may also be legal under Article XII, section 2, if the arbitral award is not made within a reasonable time or the Council's report is not rendered within six months.[30] Another instance is to be found in Article XIII, section 4, which presupposes that war is permissible against a League member who refuses to accept the award of the arbitrators (execution war). It is, however, questionable whether this authorization applies to the adversary

[27] Copenhagen, 1923-24, II, 153 ff.

[28] *Ibid.*, pp. 199 ff.

[29] "The Members of the League agree ... in no case to resort to war until three months after the award by the arbitrators or the report by the Council."

[30] There is also the possibility of regarding Article XII, section 2, as imposing upon the arbitrators or the Council members only a ("limited") obligation (without means to enforce it) but in such manner that permission to make war is not granted in any case. See Cohn, *Neutralité et Société des nations*, p. 167; Haase, *Wandlung des Neutralitätsbegriffes*, p. 64; Schücking (2d ed.), p. 515.

in the arbitration alone or applies to all League members.[31] It is furthermore a weakness in the system that the authorization to resort to war in such cases was not specifically limited to securing the attainment of the terms of the arbitral award.

In the same way, Article XV, section 6, permits war against a League member who fails to comply with a unanimous request of the Council. Where the Council's report is not unanimous, the right to wage war is extended to both parties, under section 7. Section 8 of the same article relates to questions coming within the competence of one of the parties alone, and is generally understood to mean that authorization to make war is, in such case also, left open.[32]

One might also imagine that the Council, for one reason or another, avoided [33] dealing with controversial questions, sometimes because these should be treated or are being considered by some other international organization; or because both the Council and the Court each believes that the other international instrument is competent to deal with this controversy, and therefore refuses to interfere. In all such cases it is a consequence of the League system that permission to resort to war is open to disputants.

Finally there is provided in Article XVII, section 4, an instance where a state of war may exist outside the sanctions system, namely,[34] where two states, at least one of which is not a member of the League, refuse to accept the use of the procedure provided under the Covenant. The question of permission to resort to legal

[31] According to the text of the Articles, the latter is rather the case ("The members of the League,") but it would be strange indeed if a completely disinterested third State should be entitled to use an arbitration award between two other States as a cause for war against one of the parties without following the procedure under Article XII of the Covenant.

[32] Cohn, *Neutralité et Société des nations*, p. 168; Haase, *Wandlung des Neutralitätsbegriffes*, p. 59; contra, Schücking-Wehberg (1924 ed.), *op. cit.*, p. 589; "jede Kriegserklärung ausgeschlossen" in which the author concludes that if the Council is not entitled to intervene, individual members are still less entitled to do so.

[33] See on this question particularly Michaïlidès, pp. 57 ff.

[34] One might also restrict the provision to those instances where both States are outside the League, for it says "the two parties invited." *League members* need no special invitation to comply with the provisions of the Covenant.

war is here also left open, since Article XVI is not applicable.[35]

2. Apart from these legalized wars within and without the framework of the Covenant, the text of Article XVI itself points out other wars which may not be affected by this provision and so may only be handled by proceeding under the traditional laws of war and neutrality. First and foremost, Articles XVI and XVII contain a legally and factually impractical attempt to enforce the system of sanctions against states which are not members of the League and which therefore are not bound by its provisions.[36] When Article XVI, section 1, finally obligates all sanctioning nations to break off all relations between citizens of the Covenant-violating state and "citizens of any other State, whether a League member or not," it is making a rule which can be regarded as practicable neither under the assumption that the sanctioning countries are neutrals nor that they are belligerents, since as belligerents they too are bound to recognize the rights of outside states, under the law of neutrality, to continuous peaceful trade with the belligerents (except in contraband). An attempt to deduce this rule from an entirely new legal situation created by the Covenant of the League would have no better chance. For the Covenant as a *res inter alios gesta* cannot bind states which have not voluntarily agreed to become so bound. This is even more obvious because the Covenant, in Article XVI, retains to its full extent (in the case of League members) the traditional conception of the notion of sovereignty. According to Article XVI, it is left to the free judgment of the League member to decide whether a violation of the Covenant has occurred and whether it will therefore participate in sanctions or not. The League member who answers this question in the affirmative has no right whatsoever, merely because of this, to force his decision upon another League member who may have answered it in the negative. It would then not only be unjustifiable but self-contradictory that this member should be entitled to act in such a manner against a state outside the League

[35] Concerning legal wars under the Covenant, see in general Oppenheim, p. 510; Cohn, *Neutralité et Société des nations*, pp. 164 ff.; Schücking (1924), pp. 596 ff.; Haase, pp. 47 ff.; Whitton, pp. 474 ff.

[36] Cohn, *Neutralité et Société des nations*, pp. 184; Haase, p. 145; Whitton, pp. 500 ff.

which did not wish to join the sanctions system. At this point the Covenant of the League must once more yield to the mandates of common sense and logic and apply the customary law by recognizing the neutrality of non-member states.

A condition for the application of sanctions, according to Article XVI, is that a violation of the Covenant has been committed by an individual member of the League. If the Covenant has been violated by both belligerents, sanctions might, of course, be applicable against both, but it is doubtful whether the Covenant intends to cover such a situation, since it has, in the analogous situation in Article XVII, section 4, failed to apply sanctions against non-members under such circumstances. As the questions of guilt and the illegal injury of an adversary play a prominent part in the Versailles Treaty in general, and in Article XVI of the Covenant in particular, it is fair to assume that violation of the Covenant by both parties does not obligate the members to take action under the far-reaching provisions of that article. This especially holds true of the so-called "duel war" situation, where both parties assert that the dispute can be resolved only by war and that compromise, arbitration, or similar legal settlement is of no interest to them. If we assume that a "duel war" lies outside the province of Article XVI, it must of course be judged and treated according to the traditional laws of war and neutrality.

Just as guilt may rest upon both parties, it is possible, conversely, to believe that war might break out with neither party being guilty of a violation of the Covenant, or in a way which does not permit the establishing of guilt. Such cases likewise naturally lie outside the province of Article XVI. It is here again a question of the typical "classical" neutrality, which even Grotius and Vattel recognize as being a situation where outside states are really unable to find a definite basis for their acts in the guilt of one or of the other belligerent. Such cases will be frequent in practice, not only because both parties as a rule will assert that the other is the aggressor and thus throw the blame upon their adversaries, but also because war frequently really does break out owing to some deep and unassignable causes or from reasons which can be understood as not involving guilt of either party. Civil war may occur, as in

Spain, between fascist and communist groups, and this war may gradually result in the involvement of other states adhering to one or the other ideal. Determining the question of guilt here is equivalent to determining the correctness of one of such ideologies of states in time of peace. There is, moreover, the purely factual question as to whether there really has been a "resort to war," the answer to which may be doubtful or indeterminable.

According to the Resolutions of 1921, it lies with the Council to determine whether a state has been guilty of a breach of the Covenant, and the more quickly and energetically the Council acts, the easier it will be for League members to form a reasoned opinion on the question of guilt. If, on the other hand, there is a difference of opinion within the Council's own circle, the opinion expressed will not, of course, be so valuable a guide for League members, and as a result there will rarely be an application of Article XVI. The Council can hardly charge the ordinary members of the League, who will often have but meager information about the legal and political nature of the controversy, with an unconditional obligation to throw themselves into a dangerous system of sanctions, when the members of the Council themselves cannot agree as to whether or not the requirements for the application of the system exist.

3. As we have hinted before, Article XVI presupposes, at least with respect to the duty of the League members to participate in sanctions,[37] the pure classical concept of sovereignty which has come down through tradition. In Article XXI the Covenant goes even further and actually incorporates into the principles of the Covenant[38] the Monroe Doctrine, with its insistence upon the claim of unconditional non-intervention. It appears to be a device to eliminate in advance the concept of neutrality, which historically

[37] See also the Resolutions of 1921 (II, 3): "It is the right of each member of the League to determine whether a breach of the Covenant exists."

[38] As we know, the extent of the jurisdiction of the Monroe Doctrine is a greatly disputed question; see further Alvarez, *Le Droit international americain*, pp. 133 ff.; Møller, *Folkeretten in Fredstid og Krigsted*, pp. 138 ff.; Liszt, p. 121 f.; Strupp, *Wörterbuch*, II, 63 ff., where this is stated, and in "interminable" literature on the subject. A further element of vagueness is thus injected into the Covenant.

and constructively has been so closely associated with the principles of non-intervention.

This much, however, is certain, that all obligation to take part in sanctions under Article XVI is dependent upon the sovereign judgment of each individual League member, which it is expected will, of course, be exercised loyally. No compulsion can be put upon a state, to require its participation in the sanctions. Not even a formal criterion is set up, to make possible a decision as to whether a state has fulfilled its obligations or not. If a League member believes that the conditions required for the application of sanctions do not exist, no other state may change such decision and the state in question therefore has reserved the right to remain neutral. The possibility of such differences in judgment almost always exists, and cannot be resolved in any other way than by the simultaneous application of sanctions and the consequent combination of the two systems.

The problem of the legal relationships between the League members who regard the situation as that called for under Article XVI and the League members who do not, is of course difficult to solve, either practically or theoretically. It is, however, legally analogous in fact [39] to the question of the legal relationships between League members who participate in sanctions and states outside the League which do not.

The real problem arises, however, when we consider the question of the combination of the legal conditions, under the combination of neutrality rules and the sanction system, between the violator of the Covenant and reciprocally between the League members. The Treatise of 1924 emphasized this as the *central problem* [40] and attempted to make an initial contribution toward its solution through an analysis and combination of the basic ele-

[39] The difference is especially in that the legal situation under the Covenant between the League members is not *res inter alios gesta*, so that this particular difficulty at least need not be considered. Any further clarification is not created, however, as there is among the League members no common principle or standard by which one may determine which member is to be entitled to force through its own ideas of the situation.

[40] Cohn, *Neutralité et Société des nations*, pp. 175 ff.

ments of the two systems and their application to various situations and disputes which might arise.

That these two main points of view, on the one side, traditional neutrality, sovereignty, and non-intervention, and on the other, solidarity, war prevention, and the application of sanctions, are direct opposites, each leading in quite contrary directions, was naturally evident in advance. The question was, however, as to what extent these views might be in accord, or in conflict, with those of Article XVI.

We know that none of the opposing viewpoints was either fully accepted or completely rejected in Article XVI, which contains a number of different ideas, the relationships of which are not explained.[41] Article XVI itself, therefore, begs the question as to how far these various points of view may be resolved or combined.

4. This insistence, at the same time, upon two incompatible and contradictory ideas—sovereignty and intervention for prevention of war—has already been touched upon above. It is likewise not clear whether Article XVI is constructed upon the legal supposition that it creates a state of war; or if, on the other hand, it is really a method of opposing a war through unwarlike means, so that the Article may be consistent with the application of the neutrality rules of 1907 and 1909; justification for both positions can be found:

In favor of the assumption that a state of war is created is the explicit assertion in Article XVI, section 1, that the aggressor has committed an "act of war" against all other League members; next, there is the assumption existing in the formal designation itself that this characterization of a state of war is necessary for the creation of a legal basis to justify the exercise of the rights and duties of League members which Article XVI has authorized. If these rights and duties could be deduced from the mere assumption that a state of war does not exist, it would be unnecessary and superfluous to characterize the aggressor's attitude toward the attacked state as an act of war against all other League members, which actually it is not.

The complete discontinuance of commercial relations with an-

[41] See also Cohn, *Kriegsverhütung und Schuldfrage*, p. 69.

other state is, according to many [42] authorities, incompatible with the existence of a condition of law between the states in time of peace (*jus commercii*), and is therefore automatically an expression of a state of war.

The duty of discontinuing relations between the aggressor and all other states, including even those which *are not members* of the League of Nations, and moreover also with those League members who have decided that the conditions necessary for application of sanctions according to Article XVI in their opinion do not exist, can to some extent be founded [43] on international law under the assumption that the nation which participates in sanctions is entering into a state of war and therewith exercises those rights acquired by a belligerent. Likewise, participation in military sanctions under Article XVI, section 2, may, *prima facie*, be presumed to be an expression of actual war. Lastly, the granting of the right of free passage [44] under Article XVI, section 3, seems to be quite consistent with the assumption that the country which grants the right of passage is in a state of war, for as a neutral it would not be entitled to do so.

Against the assumption of the existence of a state of war, we note, on the other hand, the preparatory work and the preliminary discussions of Article XVI, which show that the original intent of its provisions was that the aggressor would be considered as being automatically at war with all League members. This wording was revised [45] to avoid this very consequence. The remaining states are permitted, but not bound, to declare war upon the aggressor. Article XVI in this way does not automatically create a state of war between them.

Article XVI, section 2, further assumes that the League mem-

[42] See for instance Liszt, p. 126: "Ein Staat, der einem anderen Staate das allen andern gewährte *commercium* versagt, begründet damit für diesen einen *casus belli.*"

[43] As already stated above, this conclusion is not quite well founded.

[44] Whitton, p. 510, regards the question as "extrêmement complexe" and has evidently found no satisfactory solution. When he asserts that "Chaque cas doit être considéré à part," he forgets that already the mere availability of passage will in practice compromise its neutrality. Oppenheim, II, 513, himself subscribes to the theory of the Covenant-violator's prior consent.

[45] Cohn, *Neutralité et Société des nations*, p. 157; Michaïlidès, pp. 96 ff.

bers do not, as in ordinary war, participate at once with their entire armed forces or military power; nor is it assumed that all of them need take part in military sanctions. Just on this point there is a very clear difference between the participation in economic and in military sanctions. According to Article XVI, the Council makes its proposals only to "the several governments concerned." There is required only a contribution of forces sufficient to maintain the obligations of the League, and not that of general participation of all members of the League, with their complete military force, to make war upon the aggressor.[46] Finally, in the same sense may be mentioned the possibility of interpreting the system of sanctions as entirely an economic weapon (as did the International Blockade Committee in 1920)—according to which interpretation it would not be incompatible with the non-belligerency of the League members—and in this way of retaining essentially the status of neutrality. Military sanctions and the right of passage might then be regarded as only a device for the enforcement of economic sanctions, and not as an independent system of sanctions of a warlike nature.[47]

Considering the form which Article XVI finally assumed, the most natural assumption is that it does not presuppose an automatic state of war between League members and the aggressor. With this idea as a starting point, the treatise of 1924 is intended to show how the individual obligations[48] assumed under Article XVI are consistent with the neutral status of the members of the League. Regarding economic measures, it is to be noted that the Hague Conventions of 1907 did not require the maintenance of commercial relations with a belligerent. Where equal treatment of the belligerents is discussed in the Fifth Hague Convention of

[46] A very important distinction exists here also in the use of force for only a definite legal purpose, while the concept of war in international law may have unlimited objectives. See, for example, Oppenheim, p. 172: "War is the contention between two or more states through their armed forces, for the purpose of overpowering each other, or imposing such conditions of peace as the victor pleases."

[47] Cohn, *Neutralité et Société des nations*, pp. 188 ff.; Michaïlidés, pp. 127 ff.; Wehrer, *Sécurité et Arbitrage au Luxembourg*, pp. 342 ff.

[48] Cohn, *op. cit.*, pp. 182 ff.

1909, only the export of arms and the use of telephone and telegraph on the neutral's territory are really referred to. On the contrary, there is nothing new in Article XVI of the Covenant which prevents a state which is participating in sanctions from carrying out these limited measures against both parties. An open conflict between the system of sanctions and that of neutrality can thus be avoided.[49] The obligation of "prevention of all financial, commercial or personal intercourse" might conceivably (depending upon its wording) go further than what might be consistent with strict neutrality; it would then have to be interpreted in such a way as to be made consistent with it [50] (territorial limitation, and so forth).

Regarding the provision for participation in military sanctions, in accord with section 2 of the article, it is noteworthy that its terms are somewhat less rigid, since the Council can only make proposals concerning the contribution which each of the interested states may be called upon to make. The Swiss [51] and the Scandinavian neutrals have attached much importance to the distinction between the compulsory character of the obligations under section 1 and those under section 2, for they see in this fact a possibility of combining the application of sanctions with that of neutrality. They take for granted that neutrality is of particular importance in the purely military domain, and believe therefore, since there is here no real obligation to participate, that they might take part in economic sanctions while still retaining the status of neutrals with regard to the military situation.

All this reasoning seems however somewhat questionable. In the first place, it is hardly true that the rules of neutrality relate primarily to purely military questions. On the contrary, the Hague Conventions of 1907, as well as the Declaration of London of 1909, show that the major portion of neutrality law relates to

[49] In practice Switzerland and Luxemburg followed this theory, as in the Italo-Ethiopian conflict of 1935-36.

[50] Cohn, *Neutralité et Société des nations*, p. 183.

[51] This theory is especially maintained in the "*Message du Conseil Fédéral à l'Assemblée Fédérale*" of August 4, 1919, pp. 41 ff.: "la notion de neutralité ... une notion d'ordre essentiellement militaire."

economic matters which the states cannot disregard without compromising their status as neutrals.

Furthermore, Article XVI must be regarded as a unit, so that we have come to consider it impossible to become a member of the League with any tacit reservations, as to the obligations assumed under section 2 of that article. Such tacit reservations would be as unacceptable as those openly expressed, which are precluded by Article I, section 1, of the Covenant. Section 2 of Article XVI, it is true, appears to permit certain limitations of the obligations of participating states ("governments concerned"). But this limitation must be assumed to refer to concrete circumstances, in which military sanctions are to be applied, and not to the ordinary distinctions between League members (the Great Powers versus the smaller states, and so forth).

The treatise of 1924 therefore sought a quite different solution.[52] Article XVI, section 2, can be understood in two different ways; first we may consider military sanctions as an independent measure of compulsion of a warlike nature; in such case participation is inconsistent with the status of neutrality. But we may also consider Article XVI as a whole; *i.e.*, as a single compulsory measure of an exclusively moral and economic character, and the military sanctions under section 2 of significance merely as a means of enforcing an economic boycott as provided in section 1, but not to be used independently for war aims or military objectives (bombardment of cities and fortresses, participation in the war on the side of the aggressor state). The Resolutions of 1921 support this interpretation, since they assume that Article XVI as a whole can and should be applied without actual resort to war, and could be used in the form of economic pressure. At the same time they state that only under very special circumstances would it be desirable to impose upon some of the League members the requirement of establishing an effective blockade of the coasts of the violator of the Covenant—"to reinforce the economic measures," and thus not as an independent military means of coercion. One might also, perhaps, consider the expression used in the beginning of section 2 ("in such case"), which refers to the continuity with the economic

[52] Cohn, *op. cit.*, p. 185.

sanctions in section 1, as pointing toward this interpretation.[53]

If this conclusion is correct, then participation in military sanctions under section 2 cannot be definitely regarded as inconsistent with the rules of neutrality, since military sanctions merely support a system of law of a purely economic nature and not in conflict with the laws of neutrality, a system which is directed toward stopping the war without direct intervention. Even the ordinary system of neutrality, in agreement with traditional international law, might strengthen itself by military means without these being considered as unneutral acts. Thus Article X in the Fifth Hague Convention of 1907 provides that when a neutral resists by force violations of its neutrality, this will not be regarded as a hostile act. A similar rule appears in the Thirteenth Hague Convention, Articles XXV and XXVI. Likewise the Armed Leagues of Neutrality, at the end of the eighteenth century, although they were examples of military force being used to maintain a legal system for the limitation of war (in the interest of the members themselves, it is true), must be regarded, nevertheless, as quite consistent with the law of neutrality.

The same presumption must therefore be made as well for the basis of the right of passage, dealt with in section 3 of this Article.

If, on the other hand, one of the sanctioning countries declares war against the state violating the Covenant—which it is fully[54] entitled to do, because of the principle enunciated in section 1 of the Article, where a breach of the Covenant is characterized *ipso facto* as an act of war against all the other members of the League —a situation is created which is entirely outside the scope of Article XVI.[55] The other sanctioning countries need not participate in such a "sanctions-war," nor does the right of passage apply in such cases.

[53] Section 3 of the Article appears also to assume a continuity of the economic measures with the right of passage of military forces taking part in the joint action.

[54] Without prior obligation to observe the procedures prescribed in Article XII, ff. of the League Covenant.

[55] This position is likewise taken by the International Blockade Committee in 1920 (League of Nations, *Reports and Resolutions*), p. 17: "l'article XVI est essentiellement d'ordre économique, ce qui montre dans quel sens les prescriptions en doivent être interprétées"; and in fact also by the Resolutions of 1921, which are based upon the report of the Blockade Committee.

Criticism of the Coördination Theory

1. This theory asserts as we have seen that Article XVI in its entirety,[56] and when applied as such, is compatible with the rules of neutrality of 1907 and 1909. It caused an extensive discussion of the entire question and a long debate in numerous articles in the literature of international law. It met with strong criticism, but also found support. The criticism was of both a theoretical and a practical nature. The theoretical criticism was naturally based upon the fundamental distinctions existing between the two legal systems, one of which seemed quite incompatible with the other. The system of neutrality belonged to a period in the history of international law now antiquated by the provisions of the Covenant of the League, a period which had been influenced by the principles of non-intervention and political egoism, while the sanctions system is an expression of the modern principles of state solidarity and the right of intervening for the prevention of war. For an example of this, see Gonsiorowski's work, *Société des nations et problème de la paix*,[57] which emphasizes the idea that sanctions under Article XVI are not to be solely of an economic character. When the Council, under section 2 of that Article, makes proposals regarding the military force to be used, nothing is prescribed as to whether first consideration must be given to the sufficiency of the economic sanctions already in effect. But even if one regards the sanctions system as being mainly of an economic character, there is nothing in this, Gonsiorowski says, which makes it clear whether it is or is not consistent with neutrality. In that respect the right of passage is expressly called for as are the obligations of guarantee, in Article X of the Covenant.[58]

This latter argument is frequently advanced in this connection by other authors,[59] but is quite untenable, since Article X does

[56] Cohn, *Neutralité et Société des nations*, p. 191: "L'ensemble de l'art. XVI est compatible avec la neutralité de chacun des Membres de la Société."

[57] II, 421 ff.

[58] *Ibid.*, 422: "La notion de neutralité a donc évolué . . . à l'heure actuelle, elle apparaît comme inconciliable avec l'idée de la solidarité des peuples."

[59] See Whitton, pp. 524 ff., who incorrectly asserts that members of the League are obligated to declare war on an aggressor. Politis, *La Neutralité*, p. 108; Michaïlidès, p. 146, who, in referring to the interpretation of Article X suggested

not prescribe any obligation to go to war, nor does it create a state of war, and the question of neutrality is therefore in no way affected by it.

Michaïlidès, in his book *La Neutralité et la Société des nations*, subscribes, on the whole to the proposals in the Danish treatise of 1924, it is true, but considers, none the less, that military sanctions and the obligation of passage in accord with Article XVI are inconsistent with neutrality.[60]

Among the many other writers[61] who oppose the idea of a possible combination between neutrality and the League system, we must mention particularly Politis, *La Neutralité et la paix*, who has devoted his entire book to this refutation.[62] For him, the ideas of neutrality and of international coöperation for the prevention of war are incompatible; neutrality is a product of international anarchy and has no right to exist in a society of states regulated by law. It is the erroneous theory of unrestricted sovereignty which he holds responsible for rejecting the natural distinction between just and unjust wars. During the World War this distinction, however, proved its legitimacy and necessity, and that in the Covenant of the League this new thought, inconsistent as it is with the idea of neutrality, received its legal expression.

Even during the period of the supremacy of traditional international law, neutrality had always had a confused and uncertain character.[63] Its main tenets were nonparticipation and impartiality, this being a purely passive attitude which gave to war a complete preponderance. Its culmination came at the beginning of the twentieth century, when the law of neutrality was codified at The Hague and at London (1907-9); since that time, however, there has

by the "Institut de Droit International" in 1923 also asserts that League members are obligated to resort to arms in emergencies; Ray, Commentaire, p. 371, note 2; Schücking, p. 464, who carries over these obligations from Article XVI to Article X by analogy.

[60] Page 129: "De nombreuses considérations militent en faveur de la nature belliqueuse de l'action armée et, par suite, de l'incompatibilité de la neutralité et du devoir de livrer passage."

[61] See comment on Ray in Cohn, *Kriegsverhütung*, p. 75 f.

[62] That author, who is the Greek minister in Paris, has on many occasions supported the French views.

[63] Page 37: "il n'est pas dans le droit des gens de matière plus confuse, plus complexe, plus fuyante."

occurred what the author describes as the decline of neutrality. The World War gave it an irreparable blow, as the rights of neutrals were systematically disregarded; and a new moral concept gradually arose, which was no longer compatible with the recognition of the position of neutral states as innocent bystanders—which moreover, under the conditions of modern war, would in any case be practically impossible, he believes:

> The war of 1914 has not only proved that the historical compromise between the belligerents and the neutrals is no longer possible; it has proved the fact that in a war under existing conditions, on one side, especially when it includes the Great Powers, and upon the other side the fundamental rights of outside States to peace and its benefits, no compromise or adjustment is possible. It has also demonstrated that the conscience of the civilized world will no longer regard as justifiable the position of isolation, disinterestedness, and egoism which has hitherto characterized the domain of neutrality.[64]

This "moral theory" thus assumes that responsible statesmen of the neutral states should guide their people into the war for the satisfaction of moral principles and accept their own emotional bias toward one or the other belligerent as justification. At the same time, however, Politis asserts that participation in sanctions should be optional for only the Great Powers, as the smaller countries would have to follow their lead.[65] But when political realities in the world are of such nature, why then set forth such stilted moralizings[66] to the neutrals?

With regard to the technical problem, Politis believes that participants in sanctions are neither belligerents nor neutrals. He refuses to recognize that most economic sanctions should at least be made compatible with neutrality,[67] since unequal treatment of the

[64] Politis, pp. 95 f.

[65] *Ibid.*, p. 111: "A vrai dire, la liberté d'appréciation n'est réelle que pour les grandes Puissances. Elle ne l'est guère pour les petits États. En fait, elle n'existera pas quant à eux, si les grandes Puissances sont d'accord sur l'application des sanctions. Car elles auront, dans ce cas, sur les autres États, de moyens de pression pour les amener à se conformer à leur politique."

[66] *Ibid.*, pp. 121 f.

[67] *Ibid.*, p. 114: "Mais quelle que soit la nature des sanctions exercées, il suffit qu'elles impliquent un traitement différentiel entre les parties en conflit pour qu'il n'y ait pas à proprement parler de neutralité, parce qu'on s'écarte du devoir d'impartialité qui la caractérise."

two belligerents was itself already a violation of neutrality. Here, however, he has overlooked the facts that sanctions may to a certain degree be conducted with *nominally* equal application to both belligerent parties; that the Hague Conventions do not require identical treatment of the belligerents in the economic domain; and that neutrality neither historically nor in principle requires the unconditionally equal treatment which he supposed.

He finally forecasts the future of neutrality, which he avers will divide itself into four stages: the first is to be the abandonment of neutrality based on distinctions between just and unjust wars, and the laying down of a definition of aggression;[68] the second phase would consist in rendering aid to the party attacked; next would follow the treatment of war as an international crime, with penalties and legal consequences; finally there would be the organization of a permanent international military force, as was originally suggested by France. The author then reviews various recent suggestions for a combination between neutrality and the system of sanctions, such as the Saavedra Lamas Treaty, the Danish proposals,[69] relating to the conferences on security in 1934 and 1935. Politis finds insuperable difficulties in the theoretical distinctions inherent in the systems. If we are to have a condition of solidarity and permanent peace which is not utopian in character, he thinks, we must not shun the sacrifices necessary to obtain it.

With regard first to Politis' theoretic objections to a combination of neutrality and sanctions, these are really not well-founded, as the author frequently overlooks the fact that these new principles of solidarity and the right of intervention are not exactly carried out in their purity in the League Covenant, which is rather the expression of a compromise between various contradictory principles, a compromise which itself refers to coördination as the most natural solution. Article XVI, in its final form, does not actually say that a state of war exists between the Covenant breaker and the sanction states, or that the latter should be obliged to make war upon such violator of the Covenant. Further, these

[68] On this question see references below.
[69] Politis, pp. 173 ff.

objections do not, in turn, take into account the facts that the combination theory, to which they are opposed, recognizes the principle of the solidarity of states and the right of intervention, with its corresponding duty to oppose war; and that it is only the *means* of attaining this purpose which causes the difference of opinion.

It was certain in advance that the combination theory would meet political resistance in those countries which—as noted above—were interested in putting into the sanctions system as broad an obligation of guarantee and assistance as possible, or those countries which feared to weaken it because they did not wish to undertake obligations of a still broader nature. These objections were expressed on many occasions, and particularly in 1929, during the discussions in the League Assembly regarding the incorporation of the Kellogg Pact into the League Covenant.

2. The practical objections to this theory are apparently of greater weight than the theoretical ones. They are mainly to the effect that it would be impossible to delay the application of sanctions on a particular point and to weaken their force by combining them with a system which leads in an opposite direction, toward isolation, non-intervention, and a passivity toward the belligerents. If the League's authority once has been engaged, it would be necessary to enforce it to the finish. This point of view has been put forward particularly by the English; it says, in effect, that the application of economic sanctions is in reality war.[70] It must not be forgotten that the question of war or peace does not depend upon the desires of the sanctioning countries alone. The Covenant-breaker has the power to create a state of war with respect to the sanctioning countries, by either making a formal declaration against them or by actually forcing them into the field of military operations,[71] and the theoretical interpretation of

[70] Thus, in an article "Neutrality and Sanctions" in the periodical *The Round Table* for September, 1935, p. 701: "Sanctions mean war" which also discusses the economic boycott under Article XVI, section 1, asserting that it "is meaningless unless there is behind it a readiness to go to war if need be"; see also p. 708: "For the least exercise of sanctions, even though they are purely economic, is an attempt to coerce a sovereign State against its will, and may therefore lead to war."

[71] Concerning the position of the first Armed League of Neutrality, and involvement of the neutral, Holland, in the war, see Politis, pp. 65 ff.

Article XVI in one direction or another will then be of no use. The strength of, and the basis of, the older status of neutrality was that very psychological element which assumed that the belligerents would let the neutrals remain at peace because they did *not at all* interfere in the dispute, did not expose their hand, and no belligerent had any interest in making enemies of them. But when they to some extent did take sides, and even agreed to a far-reaching economic strangulation of one of the belligerents, it would be, in general, of no interest at all to that belligerent to treat them as neutral, but rather, following its own interests, to force them into the war.

As we have already stated, these practical objections have a certain weight, but cannot be recognized as decisive. So long as we continue to regard war as a normal and necessary element in the proceeding of a state, for the safeguarding of its own interests and for the assertion of its sovereign will, this must of course in the last analysis hold true for the sanctioning countries, in any war against a violator of the Covenant, as well as for the violator's counter measures. It would be quite different, on the other hand, if we mean that measures of an economic kind, enforced consistently and universally, and, if necessary, in extreme cases, with certain military support, are really a thoroughly appropriate means to oppose war, and at the same time deny in principle that war is ever a justifiable means for the maintenance of international law and order. In such case the question of war in its former sense does not arise, and there is no more reason for assuming that the violator of the Covenant would care to pull the sanctioning countries into the war than it would have under the old system of neutrality. When the violator of the Covenant knows that the sanctioning countries, or the neutrals among them, will under no circumstances participate in actual military operations against it, so long as it does not itself force them into war; and when at the same time, as was foreseen in the Resolutions of 1921,[72] certain concessions are made to specially exposed members of the League when they participate in the enforcement of sanctions, there seems

[72] See League of Nations, *Reports and Resolutions on the Subject of Article XVI of the Covenant*, pp. 29 ff.

to be no reason for assuming that their situation, actually as well as psychologically, would be any worse with respect to the violator of the Covenant than it would have been toward a belligerent under the former system of neutrality.

Attempts at Solution by Abolition of the Concept of Neutrality

1. While the legal problem of the relationship between neutrality and the sanctions system have been gradually coming to the fore in the literature of international law, efforts have been made for the reasons previously stated, to suppress the discussions thereon within League circles. This especially holds true for the Geneva Protocol of 1924 and for the so-called Brouckère's Report of 1926.

The Geneva Protocol[73] of 1924, which received the unanimous support of the Assembly but which was not ratified by a single member of the League, attempted to carry out the system of Article XVI of the Covenant of the League through an "automatic" determination of the "aggressor" and by laying down a number of "presumptions" in that connection.[74] But all of the technical questions regarding the legal status of the relationship between the members of the League and the Covenant-breaker, or between the former among themselves, have not been explained clearly, since the Protocol merely says that they shall coöperate "loyalement et effectivement" to oppose aggression, to that extent which their geographical position and the particular condition of their armament makes possible. With regard to military sanctions, a state might, under Article XIII of the Protocol, inform the League in advance what, in an emergency, it would be able to place at the disposal of the command. The originators of the proposal (Beneš *and* Politis) explained in their report concerning it, that thereby "la grande lacune du Pacte a été comblée," which was however a somewhat rash hope. Moreover, for that matter, does not the entire report relate to the legal situation between the parties, and thus touch not at all the question of the relation between the sanctions system and the rules of international law?

[73] See especially D. H. Miller, *The Geneva Protocol;* also Wehberg in Strupp, *Wörterbuch*, III, pp. 845 ff. together with bibliographical references, pp. 853 ff.
[74] Cohn, *Kriegsverhütung*, pp. 126 ff.

The purpose of Brouckère's Report[75] of 1926 was to refute the Resolutions of 1921. These Resolutions are in his opinion only the expression of amendments to Article XVI, which were formulated at that time but could not be realized, although they were asserted to be directly opposed to the original and still valid wording of this article.[76] Brouckère's Report may, in one sense, be said to aim at the explanation of the legal situation, since it takes rather the position that Article XVI is an expression of an actual state of war. On the other hand, the complete peaceful and gradual application of moral, legal, and economic measures of compulsion, referred to in these Resolutions of 1921, according to Brouckère's Report may be classified as a means which the Council might propose, under the conditions of Article XI of the Covenant. These measures gain, in such way, a far more prominent position under the system of the Covenant than had previously been assigned them.[77] The Resolutions of 1921 consider purely temporary measures, which are in a way wholly consistent with the notion of the neutrality of the participants. The Report does not mention the problem of neutrality. A different situation arises after Article XVI has been applied. Members of the League, under that Article, certainly need not in all cases regard themselves as being at war with the Covenant-breaking state. But they cannot refuse any of the definite and far-reaching obligations of an economic and military nature laid down in Article XVI by merely declaring that a state of peace and not of war exists. There is for him no idea of a compromise with the law of neutrality. Article XVI must immediately be put into full force and effect, whether it involves war or not.

The reasoning behind Brouckère's Report, which if not sound or tenable in theory,[78] was, in practice at least, rejected by the application of Article XVI to the Italo-Ethiopian conflict in 1935, which followed the Resolutions of 1921 and not Brouckère's

[75] Published in League of Nations, *Reports and Resolutions* (1927), *Doc.A.14. 1927.V.*, p. 60 ff.

[76] See Cohn, *Kriegsverhütung*, pp. 83 f.; Møller, *Folkeretten*, II, 1, p. 97, note 1: Wehberg, *Die Aechtung des Krieges*, pp. 69 ff.; *Die intrasystematische Stellung des Art. XI des Völkerbundpaktes*, pp. 77 ff.

[77] For further reference see Kunz, *ibid.*, pp. 77 ff.

[78] Cohn, *Kriegsverhütung*, p. 83, note 11.

Report. It proved to be quite impossible on this occasion—despite the aggressive nature of the situation, recognized by all parties, including the aggressor itself—to put into immediate effect the system of Article XVI in its original form, while all agreed that the Resolutions of 1921 provided the proper basis for procedure. That the sanctions, for purely political ("irrelevant") reasons, could not be enforced, is beside the point.

2. Meanwhile the question regarding the legal status of a member during the application of sanctions, especially under the earlier law of neutrality, had arisen within the League of Nations, and the Council on December 8, 1926, agreed, among other things, to invite the Secretary of the League to "examine the legal situation which is created by the application in time of peace of economic measures of compulsion under Article XVI, especially through a naval blockade."

The Report of the Secretary-General [79] of May 17, 1927, formulates the problem thus:

How far is it possible for members of the League, other than the state attacked by the Covenant-breaking state, to apply, without resort to war, the economic sanctions contemplated by Article XVI, more particularly by way of a maritime blockade, without violating rights belonging, under international law, to: (1) The Covenant-breaking state itself; (2) other members of the League; (3) third states.

This was a very clear and precise formulation of the problem, but the solution was not so easy:

(1) The right of applying Article XVI for the probable maintenance of a state of peace (neutrality) and particularly against a Covenant-breaking state, is evidently a matter of course when the Covenant-breaker is a League member and has himself agreed to this provision. But how proceed against a non-member under the terms of Article XVII? The Report here concerns itself with the older rules of a defensive alliance, drawing an *a fortiori* conclusion. The Report concludes that if the members are obligated to go to war against an aggressor, they are so much the more obligated to participate in the non-military sanctions provided in

[79] Published in League of Nations, *Reports and Resolutions*, pp. 83 ff.

Article XVI, at the same time maintaining their peaceful and neutral legal status.

This reasoning is, however, invalid.[80] The legal rights of an ally, under the older system of international law, arise exclusively from his declaration of war (or his participation in the war). There is here no question of "more or less," and consequently no possibility of an *a fortiori* conclusion. One is therefore, quite contrary to the conclusions of the Report, forced to conclude that the application of sanctions against non-members involves a state of war, and is therefore inconsistent with the participant's neutrality. Moreover, the Report implies that the application of sanctions against a Covenant-breaker which is at the same time a League member, can and will be regarded as an act of war, if the latter believes that its interests lie in that direction.

(2) The mutual legal relationships among the members of the League under Article XVI are difficult to determine, whether we consider the situation under this Article as one of war or as one of peace (neutrality) [81] or as being something entirely new (*sui generis*). Actually, no legal relationship exists among League members in this respect, since it is left to the free and sovereign judgment of each as to whether or not it will regard a breach of the Covenant as existing. But *if* it answers that question in the affirmative, Article XVI makes it the duty of such state to ensure "prevention of all financial, commercial and personal intercourse between the nationals of the Covenant-breaking state and the nationals of any other state, whether a member of the League or not." [82] If now League member A answers the question in the affirmative, and League member B, on the other hand, in the negative, the question arises whether or not A is entitled and

[80] See also Cohn, *Kriegsverhütung*, p. 85.

[81] The Report of 1927, League of Nations, *Reports and Resolutions*, p. 85, concludes however, "that strict application of the economic sanctions of the Article without resort to war is possible without violating legal rights of the members applying the sanctions or (probably) of members which do not consider the Covenant to have been broken."

[82] One cannot make a restricted interpretation by assuming that compulsion may only be applied through legal means. No legal means exist by which one can force a nonparticipant state to abandon its rights as a neutral; see further, p. 85 of the Report: "notwithstanding that they injure its interests and violate rights for which ordinarily it would be entitled to claim respect."

obligated to enforce the sanctions in the relations between B and the Covenant-breaking state. One cannot say here that B, through its signing of the Covenant, has agreed to permit sanctions to have free rein, for B may deny that the condition exists for their application, and this it is entirely free to do, according to the system of the Covenant. By this argument A would be prevented from enforcing the sanctions. On the other hand, it would be a very strange situation if the Covenant should give to League member B a status superior to that which it gives to a non-member state, C, which according to Article XVI has no option, but must unconditionally participate.[83] From this it would appear that A should not be deterred by B's objections.

The Report of 1927 arrives at the latter conclusion, from the argument that members of the League have, it is true, reserved to themselves the sovereign right to decide whether a breach of the Covenant exists, but from the wording of Article XVI, section 1 they have agreed to permit other members of the League to exercise the same free judgment regarding the right to enforce sanctions according to the rules.

Despite this subtle reasoning, the practical result is that free exercise of judgment exists only so long as none of the League members has taken the initiative in the application of sanctions. The moment this occurs, freedom of action is ended, since—according to this interpretation and in spite of their having taken the opposite view—the other members are obligated on their part to permit the breaking-off of relations. In the Italo-Ethiopian conflict this theory was to some extent asserted by Russia,[84] which proposed the application of the sanctions likewise against such states as might refuse their consent to the suggested proposal regarding Italy.[85] This suggestion was not carried out, however. It seems, moreover, difficult to recognize a system under which a

[83] And even if it has no right as a League member to demand support, pursuant to Article XVI, sec. 3 of the Covenant.

[84] League of Nations, *Official Journal, Special Supplement No. 145* (1935), 40: "The application of certain economic restrictions to member nations which refuse to apply sanctions."

[85] These members recognized however that the situation, viewed from the standpoint of law, was covered by Article XVI. Only where a League member refuses does this question definitely arise.

minority can thus oppose a majority, so that even a single League member, in the face of opposing opinions of all other members, would be able to impose upon the others is probably incorrect conclusion that a breach of the Covenant had occurred and that sanctions should be applied. But in the same sense it could not be admitted that the majority might impose such demands upon a minority, or even upon a single member of the League.

(3) The Report of 1927 admits[86] that the use of sanctions against non-member states raises "les questions juridiques les plus delicats." It assumes also in such situations that the League Covenant *did not create a new legal system* under international law, binding upon all states, but that the positive rules of Article XVI must be coördinated later with the general and common rules of the already existent and valid principles of international law. Non-member states were not bound by the Covenant, under the maxim *pacta tertiis neque nocent neque prosunt.* Article XVI, section 1, must be interpreted in the light of such a stand. The rights of non-member states must be respected unless they themselves agree, in one form or another, to coöperate with the system of sanctions. The Report believes that this will probably be the case, because the Covenant-breaking state has committed a violation of law, and because he also agreed beforehand to the system created under Article XVI. But the legal status of neutral third parties has not been altered by this.[87] The Report of 1927, with this as a basis, sets forth a general summary of the measures which the sanctioning countries may take without infringing upon the rights of outside neutral states. These recommendations do not, however, accord with what is expressly required in Article XVI, section 1. The Report particularly emphasizes the difficulties which might arise if sanctioning countries should charge their subjects then residing in non-member countries with certain obligations

[86] League of Nations, *Reports and Resolutions*, p. 86.

[87] *Ibid.*, p. 87: "These facts do not, however, modify the legal position of the third state, since a belligerent's rights toward neutrals do not depend upon the legality or illegality of its conduct in resorting to war," *Contra* is Politis, who attempts to prove that the legal relationship toward nonparticipating states is likewise altered mainly because wars under Article XVI are thereby different in character and have become an international crime. This attempt must however be described as unsuccessful. Politis, pp. 121 ff.

under sanctions, when such obligations would violate the domestic legislation of that non-member state; also if the sanctioning states should attempt to enforce such obligations against the vessels of non-member states engaged in lawful and innocent transit through the territorial waters of the sanctioning country.

Upon the high seas the difficulties of such a situation might be avoided,[88] according to the Report, if the sanctioning countries declared war upon the Covenant-breaking state. This is not true, however, since nonparticipating neutrals have freedom of trade with the Covenant-breaking state, except with respect to contraband. If war is not declared, use might be made, according to the Report, of the expedient of a "pacific blockade," [89] in the hope that nonmembers would voluntarily respect it, or agree through fear that the sanctioning countries might otherwise be compelled to declare a state of war, in order to institute an effective blockade.

On the whole, it can be said of the Report of 1927, that it attempts to hide the legal difficulties of the system by showing the political possibilities which may nevertheless exist for the enforcement of its rules. It recognizes that Article XVI may build upon—or may be combined with—the existing rules of neutrality and war of international law and that in this way it involves no new situation in international law. Experience has proved that hopes for a political solution of this legally defective system have not been realized.

The Position of the Concept of Neutrality in the Attempts to Harmonize the Covenant of the League of Nations And the Kellogg Pact

1. Despite the legally correct premise upon which the Report of the Secretary-General of 1927 was based, it received slight attention and on the whole remained disregarded. The differences were still those between the Resolutions of 1921, which pointed to a peace-and-neutrality-law interpretation of Article XVI, and

[88] *Ibid.*, p. 87.

[89] *Ibid.*, Appendix II (p. 89), (Report of M. Giraud), however, reaches the conclusion that the enforceability of a pacific blockade on third parties is an open question.

Brouckère's Report of 1926, which assumed a situation under the law of war. Conflict between these two contrasting viewpoints arose in 1929, during discussions concerning incorporation of the Kellogg Pact into the Covenant of the League.

The Kellogg Pact [90] of August 27, 1928, was—in its original form—conceived by the French, as an attempt to bring the United States into the security system. When the United States persistently refused to enter the League and to participate in the system created under Article XVI, the French Foreign Minister Briand tried to make use of an American movement, "The Outlawry of War," as a device for effecting a somewhat analogous system of security. The American movement was an expression of the opposition, which was widespread in certain circles in the United States, against too complete non-coöperation with the war prevention program [91] of the League and which had threatened to wreck the League because of American isolation. There was therefore considerable moral pressure put upon the American government not to deny entirely some measure of sympathetic support to the French proposals.

The American government, of course, which did not desire to enter the League, wished far less to bind itself to the equivalent of a treaty of alliance with France alone, and tried to parry the French suggestions by proposing that the arrangements should include all states. The effect of this was to dilute the plan to an extreme and to cause its alliance-like character to disappear. The French opposed this in vain; the result was the world-famous Kellogg Pact, which was at first looked upon with great hopes, but the realization of its content and real scope caused these to crumble.[92]

[90] D. H. Miller, *The Peace Pact of Paris;* Shotwell, *War as an Instrument of National Policy;* Wehberg, *Die Aechtung des Krieges; Møller, Folkeretten,* II, 1, 130 ff.; Cohn, "Kellogg-Pagtens retlige Betydning," in *Juridisk Tidsskrift* (1928), pp. 1 ff.; same in *Zeitschrift für Völkerrecht* (1929), pp. 169 ff.; Oppenheim, pp. 152 ff.; Strupp, *Elements,* pp. 494 ff.; see especially the comprehensive list of references in Wehberg, p. 22, note 1.

[91] Morrison, *The Outlawry of War,* pp. 231 ff.; Jessup, *The United States and the Stabilization of Peace,* pp. 37 ff.

[92] Jessup, *The United States and the Stabilization of Peace,* p. 39: "As far as public opinion in general was concerned, the legal aspects of the notion of outlawing war were widely misunderstood or wholly ignored."

In Article I of the Kellogg Pact the nations "condemn resort to war for the solution of international controversies and renounce war as an instrument of national policy in their relations with one another." Many governments, as well as writers on international law, believed in the beginning that this implied a general abolition [93] of war as a politically and legally recognized institution, which had also been the original aim of the American movement for the outlawry of war.[94] If so, not only the traditional laws of war, but the entire law of neutrality would have been voided.[95] On the other hand,[96] it was soon proved that nothing of the kind could be read into the Kellogg Pact, and the debates regarding its approval in the American Senate [97] soon removed all doubts about that.

Even within the text itself, the Kellogg Pact included so many limitations ("for the solution of international controversies";—"as an instrument of national policy"; in their relations with one another) that it could not be characterized as a general abolition of war. Further restrictions and reservations are apparent from the address of Kellogg [98] before the American Society of International Law on April 28, 1928, concerning the interpretation of the Pact (defensive war reservations) and from the negotiations with individual states (the American Monroe Doctrine, and so forth). In the preamble of the Pact it is indicated that states which in the future attempt to further their national interests by going to war shall lose the advantages of the Treaty, which is tantamount to saying

[93] Mendelssohn-Bartholdy, Raestad and others; see, for details, Cohn, "Kellogg-Pagtens retlige Betydning," in *Juridisk Tidsskrift*, XV (1929), 31 ff.

[94] Cohn, *op. cit.*, *supra*, pp. 24 ff.; Morrison, *The Outlawry of War*, pp. 42 ff.

[95] G. Rambert, *Le Droit de la guerre et le Pacte Briand-Kellogg*, p. 47: "L'acte juridique le plus remarquable de notre epoque, l'acte par lequel le jus belli dans son ensemble est révoqué."

[96] Cohn's treatises (*supra*); Shotwell, in *L'Esprit international*, II (1928), 483: "Renonciation à la guerre, et non; Mise hors la loi de la guerre"; D. H. Miller, *The Pact of Paris*, p. 127; Shotwell, *War as an Instrument*, pp. 189 ff.; somewhat opposed are Wehberg, *Die Aechtung des Krieges*, p. 109; Rutgers, *La Mise en harmonie du Pacte de la Société des nations avec le Pacte de Paris*, pp. 78 ff.; Hassmann, *Der Kellogg-Pakt und seine Vorbehalte*, pp. 62 ff.

[97] U. S. Congress, *Congressional Record, 70th Congress, 2nd Session*, p. 1267 (Borah's Speech) and p. 1271 (Borah): "When this treaty is ratified it will be for the Government of the United States to determine, upon any particular state of facts or any set of conditions, as to what constitutes a defense of its rights."

[98] Cohn, "Kellogg-Pagtens retlige Betydning," pp. 38 ff.

that the Treaty shall have no significance when it becomes of immediate importance—in other words, when war impends. No other sanction is involved in its violation.

This "epoch-making" document thus could not really be of any legal significance for the future validity of the law of neutrality; there were not even any technical difficulties arising from it in this connection. The law of war, and consequently the law of neutrality, were completely unaffected by the Kellogg Pact, as to their legal validity, and remained in force as before.

2. The social democratic government in England made a motion in 1929 which could at one blow have changed this whole legal system. In the League Assembly on September 3, the British Prime Minister, MacDonald, proposed harmonizing the two pacts (*i.e.*, the League Covenant and the Kellogg Pact) in order to render them more effective, and his initiative received at the beginning the support of a large number of states.[99] In the first session of the Council, the English delegate, Cecil Hurst, explained further[100] that the obligation in the Kellogg Pact to abolish war went "un peu plus loin" than the Covenant of the League,[101] as the gaps in the latter did not exist in the Pact. He considered the changes thus created as "peu importante."[102]

In connection with this motion, the Peruvian delegate raised the question of neutrality.[103] He asserted that prior to the Kellogg Pact states had had the right to declare themselves neutral, whereas they were now forbidden to do so, since "war as an instrument of national policy" had now been forbidden, and thus no state had a right to remain neutral. All states were obligated to defend the principles for which they signed the Kellogg Pact. They should

[99] League of Nations, *Records of the Tenth Ordinary Session of the Assembly. Minutes of the First Committee*, Geneva, 1929, pp. 24 ff.

[100] *Ibid.*, pp. 8 f.

[101] Shortly thereafter he says, however, "les stipulations beaucoup plus étendues du Pacte de Paris."

[102] *Ibid.*, p. 10 says, in the same way: "On constatera que les modifications qu' à son avis il serait nécessaire d'apporter au Pacte de la Société des nations, à la suite de l'acceptation du Pacte de Paris, ne sont que d'une portée très modeste. Elles n'entraînent pas de revision radicale de la charte qui lie tous les Etats Membres de la Société. Ce ne sont que de petites rectifications qu'il semble raisonnable d'effectuer."

[103] *Ibid.*, p. 11.

therefore draw up an amendment to the Covenant of the League explicitly providing that no state should have the right to remain neutral.

These proposals could not but create serious doubt in the minds of the former neutral countries,[104] especially the three Scandinavian countries and Holland. One must of course be satisfied, now that the gaps in the system[105] of the Covenant had been plugged, and a complete legal prohibition of war enacted, but these neutrals could in no wise agree that this was only a question of arranging a few unimportant details of a rather formal nature. They were impelled to regard the proposed change as being of far-reaching and fundamental significance and to ask themselves what was its real purpose. In various quarters it was held that this broadening and generalizing were in reality a diluting and devaluation of the sanctions system of the Covenant, intended to prepare the ground for Germany's admission into the League, which might take place without hesitation on the part of certain Powers, now that the obligations under Article XVI were thus weakened. It was equally dangerous for the smaller countries that neutrality should be abolished, just when the sanctions system was expanded to become legally applicable to *all* wars. It was necessary, in any case, that they gain time for serious consideration of the far-reaching consequences of the proposal, and they would not agree, however much it was desired by the English, to give it their immediate approval.

The northern countries therefore decided, after mutual discussions, to dissociate themselves from these proposals, although their action, in the way that the whole motion was presented by the English, was given a rather dramatic interpretation, and created quite a sensation. The Danish delegate asserted that the Kellogg Pact contained no real abolition of war. If a war did break out, the rules of neutrality of the Hague Conventions, combined with the system of League sanctions, would continue in effect. The Kellogg Pact implied so great an advance, as compared with the Covenant of the League, that Denmark would be much interested

[104] See also Wehberg, *Die Aechtung des Krieges,* pp. 118 ff.

[105] League of Nations, *Doc. C. 499. M. 163. 1929. V.* See footnote 99, *supra.*

to see these two plans worked out together. This meant, however, a radical alteration of the entire system.[106] And although they were ready to agree to this considerable extension of the application of sanctions of an economic and moral type, they would not do so with regard to military sanctions, about which they entertained grave fundamental doubts. Another difficulty in the extension of Article XVI to include all wars without exception, was that this Article had made the question of guilt the very foundation of the sanctions system, this being an unjustifiable extension of the ideas of a national penal code into international law, for which they were unfitted.[107]

The Dutch, Norwegian, and Swedish delegates followed, and stated their objections to the suggested proposals. It had now become evident that the question here involved was not one of merely minor revisions of a formal nature, but rather of some of the most fundamental principles of the system.

From the opposite camp this attitude was bitterly attacked by the Belgian Rolin.[108] The Geneva Protocol of 1924, which, in dealing with this subject, had attempted to make a general prohibition of war, he said, had met with the sympathy of the whole world. This proved that public opinion everywhere felt impelled to common action and loyalty. It was impossible to distinguish between certain prohibitions against war, which were covered by sanctions, and other prohibitions which were not. When, therefore, a general prohibition of all war was agreed upon, it must likewise be put under the protection of sanctions.

He asserted that all talk of neutrality in its traditional sense was

[106] Calogeropoulos-Stratis, *Le Pacte général de renonciation à la guerre*, pp. 215 ff.; Gallus, *Des amendements au Pacte de la Société des nations*. Reprint from *Revue Gén. de Droit Intern. Public*, 1930, pp. 25 ff.; Wehberg, *Die Aechtung des Krieges*, pp. 118 ff.

[107] League of Nations, *Doc. C. 499. M. 163. 1929. V.*, p. 12: "il est nécessaire d'interdire la guerre comme telle, et . . . il est inutile et vain de faire une distinction entre les guerres légales et illégales, entre les guerres d'agression et les guerres defensives, de retenir les idées de crime, de culpabilité ou de responsabilité en cette matière. Ce sont là des conceptions de droit penal national qui ne s'adaptent guère aux relations entre les États." This opinion was for that matter in full accord with the American "outlawry" doctrine. See Morrison, *The "Myth of Aggressive War,"* pp. 215 ff.

[108] League of Nations, *Doc. C. 499. M. 163. 1929. V.* pp. 15 ff.

based on a complete misinterpretation of the new collective obligations to oppose aggression. After the ratification of the Kellogg Pact, no aggression could then occur which did not involve a legal violation of obligations of all the other signatory powers and League members. Under such circumstances, neutrality was not only inconceivable to him, it was monstrous.[109]

Despite this strong support from Belgium and further efforts of like nature from the English side, the proposal proved unacceptable in 1929. This was a natural consequence of the fact that its acceptance would have led to a result going much further than that of harmonizing the two pacts. The Kellogg Pact contained a general prohibition against war, but was without sanctions. The Covenant of the League contained sanctions, but no general prohibition of war. The union of these two systems would therefore have meant such a radical change in both systems that it was impossible to accomplish it through mere editorial changes in the text of the Covenant during an Assembly of the League. On the other hand, it would have been possible, had they but incorporated the general prohibition of war into the Covenant without incorporating it at the same time into the system of sanctions.

3. A committee of eleven was now appointed to give further consideration to this question, and all members of the League were requested to send in proposals for the solution of a difficulty which had arisen, which, in a sense, was only of a formal nature. It was the question of eliminating the presumption that war under certain conditions was permissible, through a construction of the League Covenant, and yet at the same time of not expanding the obligations under sanctions. This task was in itself not insoluble. The Danish delegate had,[110] as early as 1929, pointed out a way in which the difficulty might be avoided: they might let the sanction provisions of the Covenant remain technically unchanged, and then after Article XVII add a new Article, reproducing the unrestricted prohibition of war of the Kellogg Pact.

[109] *Ibid.*, p. 16: "Peut-on imaginer la monstruosité que serait dès lors la prétention au droit à la neutralité en pareille circonstance? Cette monstruosité serait telle que...."

[110] Wehberg, *Aechtung*, p. 119.

The Swedish delegate in 1930 made a similar proposal to incorporate a general prohibition of war in the premable of the League Covenant.

It might be objected, against these proposals, that they still permitted the existence of that situation in Article XII, section 1, which presumes the right to resort to war after the expiration of a three months' delay.

The Danes, therefore, made a new proposal [111] in February, 1931, suggesting that a comparatively simple amendment in that provision would solve all difficulties. Instead of a negative form, that the states were *not* to resort to war until three months had expired, to insert a *positive* ruling to the effect that the states, within three months from the date of the judgment of the Court or the Council, must offer to settle the controversy in accord with the terms of the subsequent Article in the Covenant. In this way it would be *tacitly* assumed that they had accepted the general prohibition against war which was based on the Kellogg Pact (outside the Covenant of the League). Article XVI would not be affected, as the obligation of sanctions would have only the same scope as it had hitherto possessed under the terms of this Article.

From various other quarters, different proposals [112] were made, somewhat resembling the original one of the English, and all aiming at the inclusion of a general prohibition of war under the sanctions system.

It has proved impossible, so far, to secure acceptance of any of these plans. Year after year the Assembly has had on its agenda the problem of harmonizing the Kellogg Pact with the League Covenant, but each year discussion of the question has been postponed until the following year. The question also of the pact of the South American, Saavedra Lamas, which will be discussed below, has been referred to the same committee which was to discuss the "harmonizing" question. This is also quite natural, since the problem which underlies both proposals is the same, namely a combination of the neutrality system with the system

[111] Not published.

[112] See the British White Book: *Papers Regarding the Proposed Amendment of the Covenant of the League of Nations* (Miscellaneous No. 18), London, 1930.

of sanctions. This question got no further within the League structure, until it again arose during the Italo-Ethiopian conflict. For the time being each party retained its own position. The English used the *White Book*, which was submitted to Parliament, regarding England's approval of the optional clauses in Article XXXVI in the statute of the Permanent Court,[113] in order to reassert the English viewpoint, according to which neutrality is inconsistent with the Covenant of the League,[114] a viewpoint which was also pressed by the French and the Belgians, as well as by a number of other states.[115] But the contrary opinion still exists and has received unqualified expression in numerous treaties[116] which have been contracted between various countries, and likewise in the practice of particular countries (Switzerland, Luxemburg) in the Italo-Ethiopian conflict, a discussion of which is given below.

American Attempts at Coördination

1. While the question of the continuing existence of the system of neutrality within the setting of the League must be described as uncertain, the law of neutrality has attained new development outside the League, particularly in the United States and, in a somewhat different way, in South America also. The United States had not entered the League, although President Wilson had done the most for its establishment and creation. The reasons of the United States were varied,[117] but even a complete examination of all of them gives inadequate explanation to the European: conflict with American tradition, the internal political situation at the

[113] British White Book, *Memorandum on the Signature by His Majesty's Government . . . of the Optional Clause of the Statute of the Permanent Court* (Miscellaneous No. 12), London, 1929.

[114] *Ibid.*, p. 10: "In other words, as between Members of the League, there can be no neutral rights, because there can be no neutrals."

[115] In a speech by the Belgian king in 1936; that country is now converted to the neutrality viewpoint even though the term neutrality occurs nowhere in it. See Sforza, *La Belgique et sa politique étrangère*, in *L'Esprit international*, Jan., 1937, p. 32.

[116] Cohn, *Kriegsverhütung*, p. 73; also *supra*, pp. 63 ff.

[117] Schou, *The United States Refusal to Join the League of Nations;* in Munch, *Les Origines et l'oeuvre de la Société des nations*, I, 297 ff.; Morrison *Outlawry*, pp. 231 ff.; Whitton, *La Neutralité*, pp. 541 ff.; Jessup, *The United States and the Stabilization of Peace*, pp. 3 ff.

moment, opposition of individual persons, and narrower motives of national egotism. Unfortunately the development of the League did not show a rising curve, which might have overcome this resistance and have drawn the United States in.

The question of pro-League or anti-League was raised in the Presidential election of 1920, in which the Democratic party, to which Wilson belonged, was defeated, the Republicans winning. Although this was in no way the most important question and much less the only question between the parties, it nevertheless created the impression that the people had voted against the League. During the electioneering, the heads of the voters had been filled with false assertions [118] about the nature of the League, it being pictured as a superstate which would divest the United States of its sovereignty and independence. It was claimed that American tariff provisions were to be abolished for the benefit of the foreigner; that the United States would be forced to submit to an unrestricted immigration from oriental countries; that the Monroe Doctrine would be abrogated; and that the youth of the United States would be used as soldiers in the interest of the foreign policies of alien countries all over the world.

In the Senate the opposition was led by President Wilson's bitterest personal enemy, Lodge, who heaped up arguments against joining. These arguments concerned particularly Article X, which was so interpreted that it was made to appear that the United States would be forced to guarantee with its armed forces the territorial integrity of every individual member of the League. In this way the United States would be obliged to help England to crush the Irish revolt, an argument appealing directly to the Irish population in the United States. The provisions about the rights of states to withdraw from the League and those relating to sanctions in Article XVI gave Senator Lodge an excuse for inserting broad reservations. Added to this were erroneous beliefs of the man on the street about Washington's Farewell Address, in which he advised his countrymen not to meddle in the policies of foreign states, and the popular concept of the Monroe Doctrine, about which most ideas were really of the vaguest sort.

118 Jessup, *op. cit.*, p. 5.

2. The United States, therefore, did not enter the League, but it tried from the very beginning to maintain a certain coöperation with it. Beginning in 1923, it had followed the discussions through an "observer" and had even sent frequent official delegations to the non-political conferences. But after 1928 a change had taken place in this, as the Republican party then took a definite stand that the United States would not enter the League nor undertake any obligation under the League Covenant. The party platform had stated that the United States should maintain its rights as a neutral, but within those limits should support the League's efforts for the prevention of war through parallel action, according to the circumstances of each individual case. Although the fact is not clearly established, it appears in reality to be simply an assertion of the ideas of the Danish treatise of 1924 regarding the possibility of a combination between the law of neutrality and the system of sanctions, or a system paralleling it. Thus the United States coöperated with the League,[119] despite its neutrality, in the Leticia boundary dispute,[120] which had almost resulted in war between Colombia and Peru in 1932; in the Chaco conflict between Paraguay and Bolivia, which resulted in open warfare between the two countries in 1932 and was only rendered capable of settlement in 1936 through the coöperation[121] of the adjacent South American states and the League; and also in the Manchurian controversy between China and Japan, through its non-recognition of any situation brought about by armed force, in accordance with the so-called Stimson Doctrine.[122]

The Disarmament Conference[123] likewise found the United

[119] On American coöperation in the boundary dispute between Panama and Costa Rica (1921), see Conwell-Evans, *The League Council in Action*, p. 15.

[120] Oppenheim, II, 157.

[121] See the exchange of notes in League of Nations, *Official Journal*, XVII, 3 (1936), 279 ff.

[122] This doctrine is actually built upon an originally Danish proposal made officially as early as 1922; see further, Cohn, *Kriegsverhütung*, p. 185, and foot of p. 167.

[123] Regarding the entry of the United States into the International Labour office in August, 1934, and its general attitude toward the Permanent Court of International Justice at the Hague, see Jessup, *The United States and the Stabilization of Peace*, pp. 22 ff.; also Hudson, *The Permanent Court of International Justice*.

States, while fully maintaining its neutrality, holding out a prospect of definite coöperation with the sanctions system of the League of Nations (see below regarding the consultation system).

3. Upon two occasions it appeared as if an understanding, in an indirect fashion, might have been reached between the United States and the League, first through the Geneva Protocol of 1924, and later by the Kellogg Pact in 1928. When the United States was prepared to support the system of sanctions by parallel action, even if upon a neutral and independent basis, it was to the mutual interest of the parties that they be able to lay down definite and uniform rules for the determination of the aggressor. This was exactly the purpose of the Geneva Protocol of 1924, which was designed to solve the question by preparing "automatic" criteria and assumptions. Similar plans for the determination of the aggressor—although on a somewhat different basis—were independently under consideration in the United States, and a proposal directed toward that end was worked out by two noted authorities on international law, James T. Shotwell and David Hunter Miller.[124] But the Geneva Protocol, when it came to the point, was as unacceptable to the United States as it was to the members of the League. In particular, the Americans were sure to see a difficulty in the Protocol's attempt to close the "gap" in Article XV, section 8, of the Covenant, regarding questions which were reserved for the domestic jurisdiction of the parties. It was chiefly with regard to such questions as immigration laws (Japanese) that the United States would in no way surrender its freedom of action. The Geneva Protocol also gave the Council of the League broad powers regarding the time of starting and withdrawing sanctions, which were as unacceptable to the United States as the original provisions of the League Covenant, if not more so.[125]

A second attempt to entice the United States into the great web of the war-prevention system was the proposal of Briand in 1927 for a joint Franco-American agreement for the outlawry of war.

[124] D. H. Miller, *The Geneva Protocol*, pp. 10-12 and 263 (the American plan); Strupp, *Der Kellogg-Pakt*, p. 16.

[125] The proposal prepared by a mixed committee in 1923 concerning a treaty on mutual aid was forwarded by the Secretary-General of the League to the United States for an expression of opinion, but was definitely rejected.

The American government rejected these proposals of alliance in an ingeniously diplomatic manner by insisting that the agreement be a universal one. But the American public nevertheless came to regard the Kellogg Pact, especially in the beginning, as a real instrument for the prevention of war, and it was put into effect by the American government in the following year, forming a starting point for the United States to coöperate with the League without abandoning its traditional neutrality, or, as one might say, a form under which the two systems might be combined.

When the threat of war between China and Soviet Russia arose in 1929, the American Secretary of State, Stimson, after discussion with the representatives of the other Powers in Washington, assumed the initiative in an invitation to the two disputing Powers to remind them of their obligations under the Kellogg Pact. Hostilities broke out in November of that year, and the American government, together with those of England, France, and Italy, renewed this appeal to the parties concerned, and at the same time called upon all other signatories to the Kellogg Pact to do likewise, a request with which many complied.

Likewise, on the outbreak of hostilities between China and Japan over Manchuria in 1931, Secretary Stimson based his original request to the parties upon the Kellogg Pact, and coöperated with the League upon this basis. In January, 1932, he dispatched to the two governments concerned a note stating that the American government would not recognize the validity of "any situation, treaty or agreement" which was in violation of the rules of the Kellogg Pact, of which both China and Japan were signatories. In this way the so-called Stimson Doctrine of non-recognition of such situations, was brought into association with the Kellogg Pact as the system upon which the United States would base its coöperation with the system of the League.[126]

If we examine the three main points of the American war-prevention program, that is, neutrality, non-recognition, and political pressure, it will be seen that it is in reality only slightly different

[126] Concerning the two forms in which the United States is willing to coöperate with the general war-prevention program, see Jessup, *The United States and the Stabilization of Peace*, pp. 131 ff.

from the South American system, based upon just these three elements, which found expression in the Saavedra Lamas Treaty. The League of Nations likewise subscribed to the Stimson Doctrine during the Chinese-Japanese conflict, when the members, following the resolution of the Assembly of February 24, 1933, declared that they would refuse recognition of the new situation in Manchukuo, either *de jure* or *de facto*.[127]

4. Another American form of combination of the two systems exists in the plans for international "consultations" for the fight against war. The origin of this may be found in the Kellogg Pact, since to give that instrument practical importance one had to assume that there would be consultations between the states. President Hoover, as well as his Secretary of State, Stimson, in 1932 emphasized this same logical consequence.[128] In this manner another form of coöperation was found by which neutrality might be combined with a participation in the work of war prevention.

This idea received further impetus from the fact that the Americans associated it with disarmament efforts—making this the form under which the United States would be willing to coöperate for the prevention of war—and thus indirectly with the sanctions system of the Covenant. The American delegate, Norman Davis, declared at the Disarmament Conference in 1933 that his government would be willing to consult with other states, in case of a threat to peace, in order to avert the conflict. If during the conference the members decided that one state had acted contrary to its international obligations, and took measures against the guilty state, the United States, if it agreed upon the fact and upon the nature of the responsibility of the *guilty party, would refrain from any action, which would tend to weaken the general effort for the reëstablish-*

[127] On this non-recognition policy, see the report of the advisory committee of June 7, 1933, League of Nations *Official Journal, Special Supplement No. 113*, pp. 11 ff.; Cavare, *La Reconnaissance de l'État et le Mandchoukouo*, pp. 92 ff.; McNair, *The Stimson Doctrine of Non-Recognition*, pp. 65 ff.; and for the application of its principles to Italy's conquest of Ethiopia, see Garner, "Non-Recognition of Illegal Territorial Annexations and Claims to Sovereignty," *American Journal of International Law* XXX (1936) 682 ff.

[128] Jessup, *The United States and the Stabilization of Peace*, p. 45; Fenwick, "The Implication of 'Consultation' in the Pact of Paris," *American Journal of International Law*, XXVI (1932), 787.

ment of peace—a standpoint which justly could be considered as a combined neutrality and sanctions policy.

In accord with this offer, the English prepared a draft convention [129] on the general obligations of consultation, to the effect that the Council, the Assembly, or one of the contracting Powers not a member of the League (the United States) might, upon a breach of the Kellogg Pact, request "immediate consultation" with the other members, which should consist of (1) an exchange of ideas for the preservation of peace; (2) application of political pressure ("good offices") for the reëstablishment of peace; and (3) determination of the aggressor. Mr. Norman Davis neither accepted nor rejected this proposal, but explained that what his government aimed at was a combined policy of "*consultation and neutral rights by unilateral declaration.*" At the same time he made it a condition of such an American policy that a satisfactory agreement upon disarmament should be reached.

These discussions led to no result, mainly because of Germany's withdrawal from the League and its rejection of its disarmament obligations under the Versailles Treaty, after which the question of disarmament, from the American viewpoint, became a European affair in which the United States did not care to mix.

When the General Commission of the Conference again met in May, 1934, Mr. Davis again explained that, since the United States was most anxious to keep out of war itself, it would in any other way possible assist in a fight against war. This position was very close to that suggested within the League by the Danes and other neutrals, and may well be described as "war prevention without war."

The consultation idea itself was naturally not a new formulation in international law, but was as old as the history of diplomatic intercourse. It had already been applied especially for the prevention of war in agreements entered into on April 23, 1908, concerning the maintenance of the *status quo* in the regions of the North Sea and the Baltic Sea respectively, by which the Powers in emergencies were to meet for purposes of consultation and agreement upon

[129] See League of Nations, *Records of the Conference for the Reduction and Limitation of Armaments.* Series B, Minutes of the General Commission, II, 494 ff.

appropriate measures.[130] The same in general is true of the disarmament agreements signed at Washington in 1922. In the treaty [131] dealing with the island possessions of the Powers in the Pacific Ocean, Article I contains an engagement for a consultation, should any situation arise which might threaten the peace of that area. If the threatened danger came from an outside state, the Powers, under Article II, were to communicate with one another ("entrer en communication") in order to arrive at an understanding as to the most efficient measures to be taken.

In like manner Article VII of the treaty [132] prescribes the policy to be followed in China by the Powers: "whenever a situation arises . . . which involves the application of the stipulations of the . . . Treaty, there shall be full and frank communication between the Contracting Powers concerned."

The system so created, examined from a juridical viewpoint, creates no obligation of common military action, but really creates a solidary front against the state which threatens war, and has both legal and moral significance. Accordingly a general agreement of this type might be useful as a model under which the United States, without abandoning the legal status of neutrality, could cooperate with the members of the League in their struggle against war and threats of war.

5. The United States, however, has not so far signed any such general consultative pact, either under the Kellogg Pact or the League Covenant. There has been some opposition among the American people and in the Senate,[133] by those who feel, not without some justification, that a mere obligation to consult, when expressed in the form of a clear treaty engagement, will mean necessarily something much more than just a promise to talk things over. It would perhaps, just because of its vagueness, be readily

[130] Martens, *Nouv. Rec. Gén.*, ser. III, I, 17; Liszt, p. 44 f.; Møller, *Folkeretten*, I, 243.

[131] Washington, D. C., *Conference on the Limitation of Armament* (1921-22), pp. 1612 ff.

[132] *Ibid.*, p. 1627.

[133] Especially Senators Borah, Shipstead, and Robinson, who on several occasions attacked it. Jessup, *The United States and the Stabilization of Peace*, p. 70 f.; also John Bassett Moore has in his article "An Appeal to Reason," *Foreign Affairs* (New York), 1933, spoken quite definitely against a consultative pact.

understood as a disguised security pact or even as a defensive alliance.[134] The United States did not care to bind itself thus in advance by treaty arrangements with the European Powers, but preferred rather to follow the combination policy, with a unilateral declaration to apply to each particular instance, as Mr. Davis stated in 1934.

On the other hand, in 1934 the United States had no such objections against ratifying the Saavedra Lamas Treaty of October 10, 1933, which obligates its signatories, in Article II, to support every effort to maintain peace which is not inconsistent with their status as neutrals; and as neutrals to maintain solidarity and to apply political, juridical, and economic measures under international law, but without diplomatic or armed intervention. The wording of this pact appears to go further in its assertions than a mere consultative obligation, which, for that matter, must be assumed as a necessary preliminary to the agreed upon mutual support and solidarity. It appears, therefore, the best device for France and England to use in order to bring the United States into a general war-prevention program. Furthermore, the ratification by the United States of this treaty shows that the real policy of that country is in this respect in accord—as we shall point out later—with the proposals of the Danish treatise of 1924. That France and England have thus far not availed themselves of this opportunity [135] is of course due to the explicit assertion in the treaty of a neutrality and sanctions policy in combination, which these countries, for the political reasons already stated, categorically refuse to accept. But it proves that numerous states inside and outside the League, the United States among them, regard this combination system as not only feasible but likewise as appropriate and expedient in a struggle against the danger of war.

In the mutual relations of the countries of both Americas, the United States again took up the consultative idea at the Pan-American Conference in Buenos Aires in December, 1936, and moreover

[134] Senator Borah: "A consultative pact is a security pact in disguise." Senator Shipstead, "To agree to consult is to agree to decide. To agree to decide is to agree to act. To agree to act is to agree that we are going into the next war."

[135] The Saavedra Lamas Treaty may be ratified by any State, and so far has been signed by more than thirty nations.

ascribed to it very important functions in preventing war. There was further created a Permanent Inter-American Consultative Committee, which will be discussed later.[136]

6. The United States, as well as many of the Central and South American states, of which most are League members, thus constantly regarded the law of neutrality as an important element of international law and policy; during the subsequent period it naturally came to play an increasingly important part in the development of American international law. The Pan American Union in 1924-25 took up the question of a general codification of Pan-American international law for further investigation and study, and prepared a number of drafts [137] which are of considerable interest for our purpose. Among the prominent [Pan-] American scholars of international law who aided in the preparation of this code was Alejandro Alvarez,[138] who, like several others,[139] correctly attached importance to the distinction existing between American and European ideas upon many fundamental questions in international law. And these differences have found an expression in the American drafts which differ in details from the system adopted some years earlier when the Covenant of the League was elaborated.

The main distinction between the system of the League Covenant and that of the earlier traditional international law consists, as we know, in the abandonment of the principle of non-intervention for the purpose of preventing war. But we must remember that this principle has a far more distinctive character in America than in earlier European international law. The independence of the individual American nations is not only the concern of every one of them, but is regarded as an important mutual and distinctly American affair. In other words, the principle of non-intervention has crystallized in the Americas into the Monroe Doctrine.

[136] *Infra*, p. 142 ff.

[137] *Codification of American International Law*, Pan American Union, Washington, 1925.

[138] See specially his well-known book: *Le Droit international americain*, pp. 261 ff.

[139] See Cohn, "Kan Staterne samles om en faelles Lovbog i Folkeret?" in *Tilskueren*, 1930, pp. 327 ff.; Strupp *Éléments*, I, 5.

The Pan-American codification draft of 1925 is therefore an extremely interesting effort toward the combination of this principle (and thereby that of neutrality) with a system of war prevention. The codification contains no rules (or practically none) [140] relating to the laws of war.[141] Sanctions, on the other hand, are referred to in Project Number 4, Articles XX-XXII, together with the integrity of the American Republics under sanctions of public opinion; right of protest against violations of international law, even if those do not directly affect the protesting state; permission to injured states to address the Pan American Union direct; and publication of official correspondence with a request for arbitration and the severance of diplomatic relations. To this, Project Number 29 [142] adds two types of permissible action of a non-military character: first, *pacific* means; second, *coercitive* means. The former consists of a pacific *embargo*, and severance of diplomatic and of commercial relations (*non-intercourse*); the latter consists of reprisals, retorsion, hostile embargo, and a pacific blockade which affects only vessels of the blockaded state (Article X). On the other hand, it is forbidden (this being directly inconsistent with the express provisions of the League Covenant) to maintain a commercial blockade, in any manner whatsoever, of the ports or territorial waters of a belligerent state.[143]

The Monroe Doctrine itself is incorporated into the system, as a guarantee of the independence and territorial integrity of the states, corresponding to Article X of the Covenant. Project Number 8, Article I, prescribes, as inherent rights of American Republics, liberty, complete independence, and sovereignty. No American state may—even with its consent—restrict these for the benefit of any other nation. In the same way it may not cede any part of its territory to a non-American nation, nor may any nation occupy, even temporarily, any portion of the territory of an American Re-

[140] The Convention on Neutrality, in Chapter 4, naturally discusses questions of "Rights and Duties of Belligerents."

[141] In his introductory remarks Charles E. Hughes says on p. 3: "Their members were a unit in believing that the law of war should find no place in the relations of the American Republics. We have dedicated ourselves to the cause of peace."

[142] *Codification of American International Law* (1925), p. 115.

[143] *Ibid.*, p. 99, Voeu No. 2.

public, even with the latter's consent. Finally no nation has the right to interfere in the affairs of an American Republic against the latter's will. If these provisions are violated, or if there is threat of using force to do so, all the American states agree to meet to consider the common interests[144] of the continental solidarity uniting its members.

Project Number 26 deals with maritime neutrality.[145] Consideration of this question is stated as being necessary for the maintenance of peace. In fact, Article I does expressly provide that the American states, in case of war between two or more countries, *consider it a duty to remain neutral* and to contribute to ending the dispute by a tender of good offices, or mediation. The thought is in reality basically different from that of traditional neutrality, which was a voluntary matter for each state; it corresponds rather to the general prohibition against war in the League system. The Project reproduces, moreover, in its separate provisions, the rules of the Hague Conventions and the London Declaration regarding maritime neutrality, with a few important innovations, as, for example, the regulations for submarines (Article III, section 2) and for belligerent aircraft (Article XII). According to Article XIV it is especially forbidden to all American states to accept loans or to open credits to any one of the belligerent states.

Finally, Project Number 30 proposes, in agreement with the Danish draft of 1922, rules for non-recognition[146] of territorial

[144] "With the object of bringing about an exchange of views..." *ibid.* p. 37.

[145] *Ibid.*, p. 92.

[146] *Ibid.*, p. 118. In the letter of transmission to Mr. Charles E. Hughes, *ibid.*, pp. 13-14, the origin of this suggestion is stated to be a proposal made at the first Pan-American Conference in 1889 regarding abolition of the right of conquest. It is not likely that this old proposal, not found mentioned further, was referred to, but that, on the other hand, it is the Danish draft of 1922 which underlies this American proposal of 1925. The Danish draft of 1922 was communicated to all foreign governments. Mr. Hughes was at that time Secretary of State for the United States. If we compare this new American proposal with that of the Danish, we see a close correspondence both in form and content. The text of the Danish proposal is (translated):

"In the future, territorial acquisitions in Europe shall not be lawful if resulting from war, conquest or the conclusion of a peace treaty.

"Any agreement or arrangement made contrary to this principle shall be null and void and will not be recognized by the High Contracting Parties."

The text of the Pan-American Project No. 30 was:

"In the future territorial acquisitions obtained by means of war or under

changes brought about by war. This is the proposal which later, under the designation, the Stimson Doctrine,[147] was carried out in American policy and by the League of Nations during the Manchurian conflict, and was reproduced in Article II of the Saavedra Lamas Treaty.

The draft concerning maritime neutrality was made effective, although in a somewhat altered form, through the Convention[148] on Maritime Neutrality at the Sixth Pan-American Conference at Havana, signed by twenty-one American nations, the United States ratifying it in February, 1932. The connection with the great Pan-American work of codification has been discontinued, and the Convention has, upon the whole, a more "purely" neutral character than that of the draft. It coincides essentially with the classical rules of neutrality of the Hague Conventions and the Declaration of London, and the question of a *duty* to remain neutral is not mentioned. The rules of the draft with regard to submarines, aircraft, and loans to the belligerents are preserved in the Con-

the menace of war or in presence of an armed force, to the detriment of any American Republic, shall not be lawful; and that

"Consequently territorial acquisitions effected in the future by these means cannot be invoked as conferring title; and that

"Those obtained in the future by such means shall be considered null in fact and in law."

The determining element of both texts, which agree closely, is that non-recognition is laid down as an *independent principle of international law* which is a legal consequence of the new principle of the outlawry of war, as in both texts decisive importance is attached to the fact that the new principle applies only to future wars and not to conquests in previous wars. Non-recognition is in both cases an *independent sanction in the service of war prevention.*

If we examine the old American proposal of 1889 we shall see that it is both in form and substance quite different from this. It is concerned with *a part of an arbitration agreement* to be understood so that the *purpose of the arbitration* shall not be defeated by one of the parties taking the law into his own hands. Therefore any cession of territory conquered by force of arms must be adjudged by *arbitration. Renunciation of the right to arbitration* of such cases is declared "null and void." There is not even a suggestion of a prohibition of war or of compulsory measures to prevent war. See J. B. Scott (editor), *The International Conferences of American States (1889-1928)*, p. 44 f.: "Any nation from which such cessions shall be exacted may demand that the validity of the cessions so made shall be submitted to arbitration.... Any renunciation of the right to arbitration, made under the conditions named in the second section [threat of war] shall be null and void."

147 Oppenheim, p. 145 f.; Jessup, *The United States and the Stabilization of Peace*, p. 44.

148 U. S. *Treaty Series, No. 845*, Washington, 1932.

vention. The United States put in reservations to a new provision (Article XII, paragraph 3) regarding armed merchant vessels.[149] The Convention as a whole indicates *that the whole American continent* (Canada and the European possessions of course excepted) *maintains the law of neutrality of the traditional type to its fullest extent.*

7. If we next examine the more recent developments of international law in the United States, we find that they reflect in broad outline the policies of that country in this field. An early attempt to explain the technical problems in the relations between neutrality and the League of Nations is John B. Whitton's study, "La Neutralité et la Société des nations." [150] This article is in many respects founded upon the Danish treatise of 1924, even bearing the same title. The author, in accord with the general opinion, assumes that an impassable gulf exists between the two systems, in accord with the ideas expressed in President Wilson's statement that neutrality is neither possible nor desirable when the peace of the world or the freedom of peoples is at stake. An examination of the individual provisions of the Covenant proves, however, that it nowhere forbids all types of war. In cases where war continues to be permitted, the other members of the League are not only allowed but they are required,[151] to remain neutral, simply because they have not the right to make war outside the particular situations reserved in the Covenant. Detailed study of these cases gives us an interesting comparison of various theories,[152] and leads to the conclusion that the Covenant "laisse une large place à la guerre." [153] "La neutralité aussi garde une place importante." [154]

But even under conditions of illegal war the Covenant recognizes the neutrality of League members; [155] economic sanctions are to be

[149] Article XXVIII provides that the Convention does not alter obligations previously assumed in international agreements. The American States which at the same time are League members thus protect themselves against conflicting obligations.

[150] In The Hague, Academy of International Law, *Recueil des Cours de l'Académie de Droit International*, II, 453 ff.

[151] *Ibid.*, p. 478; cf. Cohn's Danish treatise of 1924, in Munch (ed.), *op. cit.*, p. 173.

[152] See *ibid.*, p. 487, for those questions which are reserved for the competence of the individual States.

[153] *Ibid.*, p. 492.

[154] *Ibid.*, p. 493.

[155] *Ibid.*, p. 494 f.

automatically applied, but there exists no legal obligation to participate in military ones. Economic sanctions, moreover, may to a certain degree be consistent with rules of neutrality, and thus their enforcement may not deprive the non-member states of their rights as neutrals,[156] especially because the effect of the sanctions is not equivalent to a general condition of war. The legal situation then becomes very complicated, particularly because the obligation to discontinue ("faire cesser") relations between the Covenant-breaker and the non-member states cannot easily be enforced without a declaration of war.[157]

As to military sanctions, Whitton took over the ideas of the Danish treatise of 1924,[158] so far as these may be regarded merely as a means of enforcing economic measures. The consequence is, of course, that an actual state of war quite exceeds the terms of Article XVI.[159] This appears to be misunderstood to some extent by Mr. Whitton, who (on page 508) seems to consider two classes of military sanctions, accessory and independent. That the latter presuppose an actual state of war is a matter of course. But the final text of Article XVI, as well as the 1920 Report of the Blockade Committee and that of the Resolutions of 1921, all definitely presuppose that Article XVI can be enforced to its last detail without involving the members of the League in a state of war. With regard to the right of transit under Article XVI, section 3, Whitton[160] subscribes also to the conclusions in the Danish proposals of 1924. It would therefore appear that the application of the sanctions system to illegal wars is not inconsistent with neutrality.[161]

On the contrary, Mr. Whitton regards Article X of the Covenant, which guarantees the independence and territorial integrity of the member states, as being basically inconsistent with neutral-

[156] *Ibid.*, pp. 499 ff.

[157] *Ibid.*, p. 505. The author agrees with the general American opinion that a pacific blockade is not valid against the commerce of third parties. His presumption of the necessity of a declaration of war is based on Gonsiorowski, II, 412 ff., also Oppenheim, II, 127; contra is Cohn, Neutralité et Société des nations, p. 183.

[158] Cohn, *op. cit.*, p. 185.

[159] Cohn, p. 186. This is explicitly stated in the Blockade Committee's Report of 1920 and assumed in the Resolutions of 1921.

[160] Whitton, p. 510.

[161] *Ibid.*, p. 520.

ity. He sees in this Article an internationalization of the Monroe Doctrine. To be consistent with the essence of neutrality, one would have to consider Article X as being of an exclusively moral nature. The argument for Whitton's stand (set forth on pages 522 ff.) is not, however, convincing. Article X contains a legally binding obligation. But nothing has been stated as to whether this obligation of guarantee must be carried out by a declaration of war, or through adopting a warlike attitude, or merely through economic sanctions. It might be fulfilled in a great many ways. Its insuperable disagreement with a position of neutrality should not, therefore, be too readily assumed.

The closing pages (541 ff.) of this article contain interesting reflections upon the special position of the United States. Mr. Whitton opposes American isolation and stresses the moral responsibility which it creates. A declaration that the United States will not support an aggressor nation would not, in his opinion, be inconsistent with the Monroe Doctrine.[162]

This book with its sympathetic and friendly attitude toward the League of Nations, is an exception to those of more recent American opinion, which reflect rather an attitude of uncompromising neutrality.

In a brilliant article, "The Birth, Death and Reincarnation of Neutrality" [163] Philip C. Jessup denies that the Kellogg Pact has abolished neutrality. Will not the aggressor apply the existing valid rules of international law regarding visit, search, and capture of vessels of states participating in the boycott? These states have only the choice of taking the position that they are neutrals, or of refusing to the aggressor the right to exercise such authority, subject to being regarded as belligerents.[164] The line of reasoning, the

[162] *Ibid.*, p. 549.

[163] "The Birth, Death, and Reincarnation of Neutrality," *American Journal of International Law, 1932*, pp. 789 ff.; see also his work *Neutrality IV:* "Today and Tomorrow," pp. 86 ff.

[164] *Jessup, The Birth, Death*, p. 792: "But what of the aggressor? Would he not insist that the traditional rights of visit, search and capture still exist since not expressly revoked, and would he not therefore proceed to interrupt the flow of arms, munitions and other contraband to the defender? If he did, the non-participants could either become participants and fight it out, or resort to the practice of the armed neutralities and, by provoking conflicts with their convoying vessels, get themselves into the war by a less direct channel."

manner of oral phrasing and of expressing by written words may have altered greatly since the establishment of the League of Nations, but international law upon this point is unchanged, he believes. The rules of the Hague Conventions regarding the laws of war and neutrality are still in force, even during wars of sanctions. This also appears in the maritime neutrality convention,[165] signed at Havana in 1928 by every American nation.

A view antagonistic to the principles of the League Covenant and adhering uncompromisingly to the system of traditional neutrality, found expression in John Bassett Moore's article, "An Appeal to Reason."[166] The author sharply attacks the belief that by the Covenant of the League or the Kellogg Pact there came into the world a new spirit favorable to peace ("the new psychology"; "the international mind"). Both pacts permit defensive war, both are dependent upon the voluntary acts of the signatory state. But it is obvious, he asserts, that states will not, and do not in practice, doubt the present validity of the laws of war and neutrality. The Hague Conference of 1922-23[167] presupposed the continuing validity of the law of neutrality, and the Permanent Court of International Justice at the Hague did the same in the Wimbledon case.[168] Great Britain and a number of other states remained neutral in the war between Greece and Turkey in 1922 and in that between China and Japan in 1933. When the war between Paraguay and Bolivia broke out in 1933, Argentina, Chile, and Peru issued express declarations of neutrality. To Moore, neutrality contains a moral element, in that, while it takes no stand against injustice, it yet has the highly moral and important purpose of keeping the neutral state out of war. The assertion that neutrality must be obsolete because a will to peace and international solidarity has developed from the rapid growth of communications in modern times, with its consequent mutual exchange of knowledge and comprehension of the culture and economic needs of other states, is patently erroneous. The worst menace of war, Moore asserts, is, and has been for a long time, the state of the relationship between France and Germany, although these countries are adjacent and

[165] *Ibid.*, p. 793.
[166] In *Foreign Affairs*, July, 1933, pp. 547 ff.
[167] *Supra*, pp. 60 ff.
[168] *Supra*, pp. 64 ff.

have extensive economic and cultural relations, with a true understanding of each other's affairs.

Neither would it be correct to say that the neutral state should be compelled to stand by as an idle spectator. It may have its sympathies and it may give them expression. But it must follow certain definitely approved rules; it cannot both participate and remain outside the war. The assertion that neutrality is the expression of an antiquated legal order is, in his opinion, "so visionary, so confused, so somnambulistic" as to be absurd.

Nor is Mr. Moore friendly to consultative pacts, and he warns us strongly against them. So closely was the consultative pact associated by the Americans with the disarmament proposals as a device for securing approval of the latter, that it is obvious that it was regarded as a conclusion, and not merely an obligation to discuss. Europe was divided into hostile camps; why should the United States increase the danger of war by ratifying such a pact, thereby stimulating the appetite of one of the parties? It was just this sort of ambiguous obligations which had in so many cases resulted in war,[169] and which had in particular (in the case of French-English entente) led to the World War in 1914. The article concludes with a strong appeal—which is never in vain in American ears—to remember Washington, Jefferson, Alexander Hamilton, John Adams, and others, and urgently warns the American people against participation in "entangling alliances."

One reads Mr. Moore's article with displeasure because, despite its many apt remarks, it breathes a narrow-mindedness and egoism which can never be the last word in the important problem of the struggle for the prevention of war. Other American writers have attempted to show the extent to which a neutral viewpoint could be made consistent with the sanctions system of the League Covenant. Of these writers, Philip C. Jessup prepared a summary, for the Conference on Security in London in 1935, of the steps which

[169] "Appeal to Reason," J. B. Moore, *Foreign Affairs*, p. 572: "Of all conceivable devices the 'consultative pact' is the most pernicious. It operates both as an incentive and as a lure. While it encourages the co-partner to do what he might otherwise refrain from doing, it fails, by reason of its indefiniteness, to deter the co-partner's antagonist from doing what he might not otherwise attempt. Numerous examples might be adduced to show this."

the United States, despite its neutrality, would be able to take in this direction.[170] He mentions in this connection the obligation of non-aggression as expressed in the Kellogg Pact and in the Saavedra Lamas Treaty, which were both ratified by the United States. Tending toward the same view are the Four Power and Nine Power Treaties of the Washington Conference, wherein the parties agree to recognize their respective possessions in the Pacific Ocean and to consult together if such rights should be threatened by any other power. Jessup also believes that the United States would be willing to enter into an agreement for the determination of the aggressor, only, however, if the designation were finally left to the decision of the individual parties (the United States) and if it involved no obligation to participate in sanctions.

Furthermore, the United States would agree to a disarmament convention and, in connection therewith, an international supervisory control board. The same applies to armament manufacture and sale.[171] The United States would further agree to the internationalization of the Philippines.

The United States would hardly agree to any consultative pact, for the reasons previously stated, except perhaps, as Norman Davis intimated, a unilateral declaration regarding consultation with respect to disarmament. This would have to be on the assumption that it would in no case obligate the signatory States to participate in sanctions. Concerning the purely technical questions relating to the preparation of such consultations a convention might be agreed upon without difficulty. Jessup further implies that it is not impossible that the United States might agree to permit the League Council to consider internationally controversial questions in which the United States was interested, just as is already permitted in the case of numerous international commissions of conciliation and inquiry.

With reference to sanctions, Jessup believes that the United States will not obligate herself to apply them, whether of a military, economic, or financial nature. There are, however, two other

[170] *The United States and the Stabilization of Peace*, pp. 117 ff. ("What might the United States promise to do?")

[171] The international convention of 1925 was ratified by the United States in 1934.

types of sanctions to which the United States, according to its most recent policies, might be willing to agree, namely (1) *non-recognition* of the benefits gained through illegal wars (the Stimson Doctrine, and Article II of the Saavedra Lamas Treaty),[172] and (2) "*modified*" *neutrality*. The latter term, applying to the combination of neutrality and sanctions, is based upon the idea that neutrality involves both rights and duties. The *duties*, of course, cannot be altered without compromising neutrality, but *rights* may be freely relinquished. And, since it is particularly the right of free commercial intercourse with the belligerents which forms the principal obstacle in the enforcement of sanctions under Article XVI, there seems to be a sound basis here upon which neutral countries and sanction countries might coöperate in the service of war prevention.

Mr. Jessup finally refers to the traditional readiness of the United States to permit controversial questions of an international nature to be settled by arbitration and agreement.

So we may say that from the unfertile soil of the law of neutrality there may still spring up shoots which may yet make possible a certain degree of coöperation in the struggle to prevent war. Especially interesting is the theory of relinquishing neutral rights while maintaining neutral obligations toward the aggressor, for this theory recommends to the states outside the League the same procedure as that outlined in the Danish treatise of 1924 regarding non-belligerent League members. The United States has, without actual legal obligation, pursued this course in several instances, in which it did prohibit the export of certain items to both belligerent parties, regardless of the aggressor, while under no obligation to do so, as for example to Paraguay and Bolivia in 1934. In the next year this policy was expressed in legislative form.

8. In August, 1935, a Government bank (the Export-Import Bank) decided to grant no further export credits for goods having the character of war supplies (for example, cotton for use in munition manufacture). Endeavors to put through new legislation on neutrality had been pressed because of the desirability of making revisions in such law during peace time, so that it should not have

[172] Which the United States has also ratified.

the character of legislation directed toward a specific situation or against certain individual states. The new system was to operate upon the principle that, while the *obligations* of neutrality would be rigidly observed, the *rights* of neutrality would be to a certain degree surrendered, to permit coöperation with the League system of sanctions or at least not to oppose it. This trend was further strengthened by some prevailing currents in American legislative circles.

One of these was the notion that the United States, in a new program for neutrality, should abandon those rights which the experiences of the World War period had shown to be untenable during modern warfare. Proposals [173] along this line had been prepared by the jurist, Charles Warren (who had, during the war, dealt with the neutrality problems of the United States), with the intention of surrendering to a limited extent, the principle of freedom of the seas (freedom of neutral trade), provided, in turn, the belligerents would agree *not to confiscate* (*except* to *requisition* for compensation) contraband cargoes and shipping. If the belligerents would not agree to this, the United States should simply prohibit, as a sort of sanctions, exportation of all goods which were specified in the list of contraband, to both belligerents (or permit export limited to the normal peace-time quota).

There were, moreover, in Congress a number of "progressive" Senators (both Republican and Democratic) who, under the leadership of Senator Nye of Michigan, desired new neutrality legislation designed "to take the profits out of war." The idea here was the very natural one that neutral states might render significant but independent coöperation in the fight against war by prohibiting their own people from profiting by it. If all neutral states would carry out such a plan, there would be created thereby a "national" sanction which, without breach of neutrality, might render very effective assistance to international sanctions.

8. The threatened outbreak of hostilities between Italy and Ethiopia was the cause of speeding up these endeavors. A neutrality resolution was prepared with the aid of Mr. Norman Davis and was introduced into Congress on August 17. It gave the President

[173] Jessup, *Neutrality, IV*, "Today and Tomorrow," pp. 142 ff.

certain authority *within his discretion* ("permissive") to prohibit the export of arms to *one or more* belligerent countries. This proposal naturally met with strong opposition from the partisans of "pure" neutrality. The chairman of the Committee on Foreign Relations, Senator Pittman, submitted on the twentieth of the same month a new bill which was prepared with the coöperation of Senator Nye and which limited the President's discretion ("mandatory") and prescribed that the export prohibition was to be applied equally against both belligerent parties. Under strong pressure this bill was passed by vote of both houses on the twenty-fourth of August, and was signed by the President on the thirty-first of that month.[174] It contains further provisions concerning:

(1) Prohibition against shipment of arms, ammunitions, and implements of war to belligerent countries;

(2) Prohibition against the shipment of arms, etc., in American vessels for the use of belligerent countries;

(3) Registration of persons who manufacture, export, or import arms, and so forth, and requirement of a special license therefor.

(4) Prohibition against travel by American citizens on vessels of any of the belligerents.

The President "shall" proclaim the fact of the existence of a state of war between two or more foreign states, whereupon the above prohibitions come immediately into force ("it shall thereafter be unlawful to export," and so forth).

In Section 5, the President is granted the additional right to prohibit the admission of foreign submarines into the ports and territorial waters of the United States.

As will be seen, there is only a very restricted list of war requirements included in the export prohibition. It does not include contraband in general, much less the complete severance of commercial relations equivalent to the economic sanctions of Article XVI of the League Covenant. There is given to the President, it is true, the authority to make public from time to time a list of articles involved in the prohibition. But during the debates on the

[174] U. S. Congress (74th Congress), *Public Resolution No. 67.*

bill in the Senate, a question was put to Senator Pittman as to whether the expression "war materials" might be interpreted to include supplies such as cotton or wheat; he declared that this was not the case,[175] and referred to the use of the term at the Conference on the International Trade in Arms of 1925, a declaration by which the government probably considered itself bound.

This legislation quickly assumed practical importance when the President proclaimed, on October 5, the existence of a state of war between Italy and Ethiopia, so that the provisions went into effect at once.

American efforts to combine a firm and impartial neutrality with a degree of participation in the sanctions program have been severely criticised on various sides.[176] In the first place, the adherents of a policy of neutrality, as well as the adherents of cooperation with a sanctions policy, both felt it was equivalent to attempting to ride two horses at the same time. This one must often do, however, in politics as well as elsewhere. It must be admitted, however, that the bill gave the impression of being a rush job and that a still more pliant adaptation of the two systems would have been possible. It will not always be easy for the President to decide as to whether or not a state of war exists between foreign Powers (as for example in the present conflict between China and Japan). Emphasis has also been placed on the fact that the unconditional character of the provision for equal treatment of the two belligerents abandons the Monroe Doctrine (if, for example, a European Power should unjustly attack an American one). The most important objection naturally can be directed against the narrow limitations of the list of export prohibitions. It was doubted, upon the one hand, if the law would be sufficient to keep the United States out of future wars, since it contains no renunciation of the traditional demand for the freedom of the seas for neutrals, which will probably receive little enough respect from future belligerents in any case. On the other hand, it contributes little to the common efforts for preventing war or to the system of League sanctions, as

[175] "The measure does not include what might prove to be contraband of war." "In this joint resolution we are not dealing with contraband."

[176] Fairman, La Loì américaine de neutralité du 31 aôut 1935 appliquée, au conflit italo-éthiopien, in *Revue général de droit publique* (1935), pp. 682 ff.

compared with what can rightly be expected from such a great and outstanding nation as the United States.[177]

9. Particularly in the latter respect, the American government soon felt the need of supplementing the positive provisions of the bill with a broader voluntary self-restriction upon the part of American trade and shipping, an endeavor which quite naturally met with certain opposition. On October 2 President Roosevelt made a speech at the International Exposition in California, in which he declared that American citizens who voluntarily participated in trade relations ("transactions of any character") with any belligerent did so at their own risk and could not expect the assistance of the American government in case of capture, or being fired upon, or the like. From its text, this important declaration was to be applicable only to the then existing conflict between Italy and Ethiopia,[178] but it not only applied to the belligerents—*it was also applicable to measures which the League of Nations might take in carrying out the sanctions system.* It not only applied to buying and selling, but also to loans and credits, and included American citizens resident or traveling in Italian or Ethiopian territory.[179] It was a significant and extensive addition to the law of August 31 and *a surrender of the demand for freedom of the seas, as well as of American rights under the law of neutrality,* made to carry out combined policies of neutrality and sanctions. There was therefore no reason to ask the United States to comply with the suggestions of the Co-ordination Committee of the League for a successive strengthening of economic sanctions. The United States had indeed taken further steps than had the League members, since it renders such coöperation, whenever the emergency calls, with a complete economic boycott, while the

[177] In our own judgment there is a much too severe criticism of the law of 1935 in Jessup, *Neutrality, IV*, "*Today and Tomorrow,*" p. 125, on the theory that the neutral lessens the danger of being implicated by lessening his commercial contacts with the belligerents. He says: "This theory seems to underlie the United States Neutrality Act of August 31, 1935. It is, however, probably unduly complimentary to that statute to credit it with any one rational underlying thesis. The act is a hodgepodge of ideas scrambled together in the legislative frying-pan in the closing days of a hot summer session in Washington."

[178] Not stated as applying to all cases of future wars.

[179] According to official statements of American authorities.

League itself began with temporary and quite limited sanctions.[180] It follows, however, from this declaration that the United States will under no circumstances go further, as for example to participate in military sanctions, even where this might not be inconsistent with a neutral viewpoint.

This enormous extension of the combination system naturally met the immediate and strong opposition of American exporters. A few days after the President's declaration, the Export Managers Club in New York held a meeting at which they declared that they would maintain trade relations, despite the President's declaration, which had been issued too early and was of too sweeping a character. In consequence Secretary Hull made a further statement, in which he explained the legal situation. From his point of view there was no legal prohibition against exports beyond those in the law of August 31, 1935. But, on the other hand, it could not be the intention of the government to encourage trade relations with belligerents. The government wished at all events to keep this country out of war. In so far as it is consistent with this definite purpose, the government desires, however, to coöperate in an actual boycott of the belligerents.[181] In reality, the United States aligned itself with the League of Nations and its leading countries, England and France. Each party aimed at the same objective, but pursued it with great caution and respect for its difficulties.

These points of view Secretary Hull explained more fully in a very interesting radio address from Washington on October 15: Peace is not and cannot be purely a condition which is won and enjoyed through indifference and selfish indolence. The terms and the policies by which it may be obtained are neither easy nor simple, but require great efforts by the people. The objective of American policy is declared to be an intention to avoid under all circumstances any involvement in war; but apart from this it

[180] The reply of the American Government, October 26, 1935 to the Co-ordination Committee of the League is published in "*American Neutrality Policy,*" United States. Congress. *Hearings before the Committee on Foreign Affairs* (1935) pp. 302 ff.

[181] Under the conditions existing, this naturally affected Italy in particular, since there were no trade relations of consequence with Ethiopia. Scott, *Neutrality of the United States*, pp. 651 ff.

would use all its influence for the prevention of war, which can be possible only through purposeful efforts of many countries.

Under date of October 30, there was again issued a statement, by President Roosevelt as well as by Secretary Hull, which still more earnestly warned American business against using the conditions of the market resulting from the war to promote their trade with the belligerents. This in turn was related to an appeal [182] which had been sent out by the Co-ordination Committee of the League of Nations on the twenty-first of that month to the United States and other non-members of the League, and which was answered by the Americans with a further statement of their policy of co-operation. The United States would assist in the struggle for the prevention of war "in every practicable way within the limitations of our foreign policy." [183] Since this reply met with some criticism in the United States as not being sufficiently favorable to the League's efforts, and because it did not even make a moral distinction between the aggressor (Italy) and its victim, Secretary Hull once more explained in considerable detail the American neutrality position, in a radio talk [184] on November 6, 1936. The bitter experiences of the World War could not be forgotten by this generation, he said. The great majority of Americans were in favor of a policy of neutrality. He further reviewed the historical development of the law of neutrality, recent American neutrality legislation, and the purpose of the President's warning to business against trade with the belligerents. But the American government was not content with a neutrality policy alone. It could not shut its mind to other constructive means for preventing wars between nations. Mr. Hull went on to say:

> Our foreign policy would indeed be a weak one if it began or ended with the announcement of a neutral position on the outbreak of a

[182] League of Nations. *Official Journal (1935). Special Supplement No. 145.* "*Co-ordination Committee*," p. 27.

[183] League of Nations, *Official Journal, Spec. Suppl. (1936).* "Letter of Secretary Hull to the Co-ordination Committee," p. 316. Also see the radio address of former Secretary of State Stimson on the 23d of the same month in the following footnote.

[184] *An Examination of the Neutrality Policy of the United States.* Cordell Hull, "Our foreign policy with respect to Neutrality" (Columbia Broadcasting Company.) New York, 1936.

foreign war. I conceive it to be our duty and in the interest of our country and of humanity not only to remain aloof from disputes and conflicts with which we have no direct concern, but also to use our influence in any appropriate way to procure a peaceful settlement of international differences.

Our own interest and our duty as a great power forbid us to sit idly by and watch the development of hostilities with a feeling of self-sufficiency and complacency, when by use of our influence short of becoming involved in the dispute itself, we might prevent or lessen the scourge of war.

In short, our policy as a member of the community of nations should be twofold—first, to avoid being brought into a war, and, second, to promote as far as possible the interests of international peace and good-will.

A virile policy, tempered with prudent caution, is necessary if we are to retain the respect of other nations and at the same time hold our position of influence for peace and international stability in the family of nations.

We have here dwelt in rather detailed fashion, upon the more recent policies of the United States in this field, because they support the views which underlie the Danish treatise of 1924 and the necessity for coördinating a neutrality and a sanctions policy in an extremely interesting and practical way. Mr. Hull presents in a really striking manner, the opposing view, which in this case, as in most legal situations, and in international law as well, must be taken into consideration and resolved through a mutual adjustment. The assertion that a coördination of the ideas of neutrality and sanctions is impossible because these two viewpoints are diametrically opposed, or impracticable at the same time, or legally and morally "incommensurable," and so on, is not only incorrect, but could in no case prevail against the fact that here at least is a World Power which, after detailed and repeated consideration of all the factors, has arrived at the conclusion that such coördination *is* possible, and has carried out its conclusion in practice. The above opinions of American statesmen point plainly the path which such a coördination policy should follow.

10. This clear path did not, however, so clearly make the policy actually pursued thereafter by the United States. It cannot be denied that it was, on the contrary, encumbered with much un-

certainty. Would the United States abandon neutral rights (freedom of the seas) or not? Would it stop *all* commercial relations with the belligerents with respect to war materials, or prevent only the extraordinary trade created by war conditions? Would it grant equal treatment to both belligerents ("neutrality tendency"), or aim at an arrangement which was unfavorable to the aggressor but favorable to his victim ("sanctions tendency")? These points are not easily answered by examining the speeches of American statesmen, which evidently swing from one side to the other on this subject. A very serious weakness exists also in that it would not formulate its policies into rules of law, but attempted to enforce them by persuasion and pressure upon the export business concerned.

In January, 1936, a new bill appeared, which occasioned lengthy discussions in the Committee on Foreign Affairs.[185] The proposal might be described as an attempt at coördination, but with a very marked neutrality tendency. It declares that the President, when circumstances require it, "shall" issue the necessary proclamation, but the export prohibitions it contains shall apply only to the belligerents expressly named in the proclamation.[186] Thus it would not apply in every case to all belligerent parties. Of special interest in section 4(a) which gives the President broad authority to restrict the exportation of commodities of use in war (with the exception of food and medical supplies) to their normal volume,[187] not only where such action will serve to promote the security of the United States or to preserve its neutrality, but also where the omission of such restrictions *might tend to prolong or widen the extent of the war,* so that this is to be regarded as a means of war prevention.

The possibility of a combination between the systems was further opened in section 6, of this bill, by the provisions of which

[185] U. S. Congress, House of Representatives, *Committee on Foreign Affairs.* Hearings, *74th Congress, "American Neutrality Policy"* (Feb. 5, 1936). Washington, 1936.

[186] At the same time Senators Nye and Clark had made somewhat different recommendations. *Ibid.,* Sect. 3 (a) ... "to any belligerent country, named in the proclamation."

[187] That is, "the average of shipments during a previous period of years to be determined by the President."

the embargo and the restrictions must be applied in identical fashion to all belligerents, unless Congress with the President's approval should direct otherwise. In section 16(b) we read: "Except to the extent that the law and rules of neutrality may be temporarily or provisionally modified by or under authority of this act, the United States reserves and reaffirms its rights under international law as it existed prior to August 1, 1914." [188]

As a consequence of the vague and equivocal position which the League of Nations assumed in the Italo-Ethiopian dispute, opposition to the collective system had naturally grown quite strong in the United States, and this was expressed very sharply in the debates over the bill. It was the war-prevention trend in section 4 with which all were particularly dissatisfied. For the administration, Assistant Secretary Moore attempted to invoke "the moral and political duty" [189] and to argue that it was, from the standpoint of neutrality, entirely lawful [190] to work to prevent the prolongation or extension of the war, since neutral states are more likely to become involved the longer the war lasts. But this idea met no sympathy at all in the Committee. The provision was characterized as being directly inconsistent with the law of neutrality.[191]

American statesmen also discussed in this connection the "cash-and-carry" [192] proposal made by Baruch and Kloeb, which provides that belligerents should transport their purchases from the United States in their own vessels, and pay for them in cash. No doubt this would avoid some of the difficulties arising from neutrality, but, on the other hand, such a program would be destructive to American shipping during war. This plan could not, moreover, be designated as an aiming toward coördination since it contained no war-prevention tendency.

A particularly severe criticism of the whole bill came from Professor Borchard, of Yale University, who had already, in a

[188] U. S. Congress. House. *Hearings*, p. 6. [189] *Ibid.*, p. 16. [190] *Ibid.*, p. 27.

[191] Mr. Tinkham (*Ibid.*, p. 17): "This provision is a declaration of an unneutral policy. It denotes an intention to take one side or the other whenever trouble may arise in the world. . . . That is not neutrality."

[192] *Ibid.*, p. 34 f. See also Dulles and Armstrong, *Can We Be Neutral?* p. 112 f., Jessup, *Neutrality IV*, pp. 139 ff.

number of articles,[193] spoken in favor of a "pure" neutrality system along the lines favored by John Bassett Moore. Borchard had previously prepared a memorandum [194] on this bill, in which he strongly opposed it (in particular, section 4) calling it the "antithesis of neutrality" and "more likely to get us into war than to keep us out." He correctly points out that the question is not that of stopping war at any price, but of the means to be used to stop it.[195] The assertion in the bill that the enforcement of neutrality rules with respect to maritime commerce leads to conflicts with the belligerents and therefore makes for war, he refutes as being false, just as it was false to assert that the United States had become involved in the World War for that reason. The real reason, he believes, was that the American government had not been truly neutral, that it wished to become involved in the war, and that it was not skillful enough in any case to keep from being drawn in.[196]

Well-founded is his criticism of section 9, in which trade relations with belligerents are to be at the risk of the individuals participating, but which, he believes, is in reality a direct invitation to such relations ("a direct temptation to unneutrality"). He is likewise opposed to the explicit reservations of the formal legal status in section 6, since it might be assumed from their text, however incorrectly, that the legal position of the United States had meanwhile been altered.

Mr. Borchard went into further details of this criticism during his appearance before the Committee on Foreign Relations.[197] He

193 See for example "Sanctions vs. Neutrality" in *American Journal of International Law*, XXX (1936), 91-94, "The 'enforcement' of peace by 'sanctions.'"

194 *Ibid.*, (1933) XXVII, 518; The arms embargo and neutrality, *ibid.*, XXVII, (1933), 293 ff. *U. S. Congress. House. Hearings*, pp. 70 ff.

195 *Ibid.*, p. 72: "The defeat of Italy was apparently regarded as the best means of 'shortening' the Ethiopian War. Hence those commodities were selected for prohibition of exports which would handicap Italy and force her the sooner to sue for peace. But this is the very antithesis of neutrality. To promote unneutrality under the guise of neutrality is dangerous and conducive to war."

196 *Ibid.*, p. 73: "It cannot be emphasized too often that we did not enter the last war because of our trade, even in munitions or even in loans. We entered the war because the Executive did not at critical times wish to remain neutral, and in the brief periods when he did, did not know how to maintain American neutrality. Against incompetence in public office there is no protection...."

197 *Ibid.*, p. 74.

asserted that law gives to the President full freedom to act in as unneutral a manner as he sees fit. Section 4 is "one of the most dangerous and needless proposals ever advanced in the United States." [198] It is not a question of creating a better world, or of shortening the war, which cannot be done without taking sides (?). Neither is it correct to say that any modern war must become a world war, as did the last. Experience proves the opposite. Equally false is the notion that the maintenance of neutral rights during maritime warfare must draw one into war. The Scandinavian countries, Holland, and others were able to keep themselves outside the World War because they had the necessary "common sense" and that accurate knowledge of rules of international law [199] which the American government lacked.

On the other hand, Professor Hyde, of Columbia University, spoke strongly in favor of the bill.[200] Among the many other persons and organizations questioned by the Committee may be especially noted various organizations, consisting mainly of persons of Italian descent,[201] who, of course, strongly opposed waiving the traditional policy of neutrality.

Partly because of internal politics, particularly the impending Presidential election, the proposals could not be enacted, and on February 29, 1936, the President approved a new law [202] by which the law of August 31, 1935, was extended to May 1, 1937, with the addition of one new provision against the purchase or sale in the United States of bonds of the belligerent governments, with the significant concession to the Monroe Doctrine that the law would not apply to governments of American republics at war with a non-American state, when such American state was not allied or coöperating with another non-American state in the war. The President at the same time renewed his (legally ineffective) advice to the American people to conduct their trade with belligerent countries as in time of peace. No clear explanation of these instructions was made, but the discussion of this question in the United States brought out a great number of new viewpoints for

[198] *Ibid.*, p. 52. [199] See *Ibid.*, pp. 60 ff. [200] *Ibid.*, pp. 75 ff.

[201] See *Ibid.*, pp. 192 ff., on the "League for American Neutrality."

[202] The text of the law of August 31, 1935, can be found in Dulles and Armstrong, Appendix 5.

the solution of the theoretical and technical problems which inhere in the term "neutrality" and its possible combination with a program of war-prevention. These viewpoints extend all the way from complete isolation, with its surrender of the right of freedom of the seas and the "cash and carry" plan of avoiding all possible conflict by leaving commerce to the belligerents themselves,[203] to traditional neutrality, with its firm insistence upon the freedom of the seas, and the limitation of trade to the normal peace-time volume and to coördination between neutrality and war-prevention ideas in widely different forms.

One reaches quite naturally the conclusion that "the popular ... conception that neutrality is a clearly defined status is erroneous." [204] Neutrality is only a form of international policy which may assume an almost infinite number of permutations and combinations. The expressions "strict neutrality" and "impartial neutrality" are also quite meaningless. Neutrality is "*that policy which a country at peace adopts toward countries at war*." [205] In this way we depart from the principles in the 1907 and 1909 codifications of neutrality law, through which it was of special importance, in advance, "to establish common rules in case of the outbreak of war," and that "these rules shall not be altered by a neutral power during the war" (preamble to the Thirteenth Hague Convention).

"Whatever neutrality legislation we have already adopted or may adopt cannot possibly be more than a framework, raised in the air, to support the specific policy which, in contingencies yet unrevealed, best promises at a moment of crisis to keep us out of war. . . ." [206] If war is being waged, for example, between states which have small navies, the United States would find it possible to maintain its neutrality without serious interruption to normal American trade. It would be quite different if, however, England were involved in a European war or Japan in a war in eastern Asia. There would then "be great difficulty in avoiding dangerous disputes, even if we pressed our renunciation of trade to

203 In a sense this does not result in equal treatment of the belligerents, since one of them will probably control the sea; see also Bernard M. Baruch in his article in *Today* for Nov., 1935.

204 Dulles and Armstrong, *Can We Be Neutral?* (pp. 7 ff.).

205 *Ibid.*, p. 9.

206 *Ibid.*, p. 77.

the limit that the American people would tolerate. Consistency, in other words, is not essential or even possible. And the idea that at the present moment we can be wise and farsighted enough to embody in rigid law the policy which we could consistently follow in varying and even opposite circumstances is positively dangerous."[207]

Dulles and Armstrong here support a policy of the abandonment of a unified concept of neutrality, and would distinguish between "basic" and "supplementary" neutrality. The former is regarded as relating to the measures which a government should apply whenever war breaks out anywhere in the world; the latter concerns those special precautionary measures which should be taken in those particular cases which affect the security of the neutral state itself. These authors admit,[208] however, the moral responsibility of the United States as a great nation which should at all times and under all circumstances be opposed to war and should work for its prevention, in which it has, moreover, a direct and material interest.

From the viewpoint of the smaller states, however, the idea of a divided and varying method of applying the principles of neutrality would be subject to grave doubts, as they might fairly be suspected of changing the rules in the interest of one of the belligerent parties.

South American Attempts at Coördination

1. While the United States has remained outside the League, it has none the less adopted a policy of coördinating neutrality with participation in sanctions. The Central and South American states, most of which are League members, have in other ways reached much the same goal. The South American states have always played a prominent and much appreciated part in the League of Nations, and have contributed a number of useful reforms and have made themselves advocates of modern viewpoints of international law.[209] As early as the first Assembly,

[207] *Ibid.*, pp. 77-78. [208] *Ibid.*, p. 118.

[209] R. Fernandez, "L'Amérique du Sud et la Société des nations" in Munch (ed.), *Les Origines*, pp. 137 ff.; Schücking-Wehberg, *Die Satzung des Völkerbundes* (1931), p. 244.

Argentina had submitted a proposal, which would, if passed, have been of the greatest value for the future universalization and vigorous development of the League, namely, that all states recognized to be sovereign should be regarded as members of the League, so that if any remained outside it would only be through a positive and voluntary act on their part.[210]

In their statement of the reasons and ideas behind this proposal, they correctly asserted that the strength of any such League must be in its comprehensive (universal) character; the greater the number of its members, the brighter the prospect that its efforts to prevent war might succeed; while on the other hand the very fact that a number of states had been kept out would create antagonisms between certain states and the League and be the occasion of constant trouble and threats to world peace. This well-planned and far-sighted proposal was not accepted, as it met immediate opposition from political interests within the League. Argentina took this rebuff so seriously that it for a time discontinued its coöperation, without, however, formally withdrawing from the League.[211] Brazil, on the other hand, did retire from the League in 1928. The reason for this action must be sought in the fact that Brazil, although one of the largest countries in the world and destined some day to become one of the Great Powers, was unsuccessful in obtaining a permanent seat on the League Council. Brazil, which had participated in the World War on the side of the Allies, not without some justification considered that this was a slight, coming as it did at a time when the Council was moving heaven and earth to obtain such a seat for Brazil's former adversary.

The position of the South American states inside the League is a somewhat special one, for various reasons. One of these is that they, together with the United States, consider themselves to be closely associated in a Pan-American regional combination,

210 "The Argentine Republic regards it as essential that all the sovereign states generally recognized as such should be admitted to the League of Nations, unless their non-incorporation is the result of a voluntary decision on their part." League of Nations, *Records of the First Assembly (1920)*, p. 90.

211 The explanation for this step is contained in a letter of M. Pueyrredon dated Dec. 4, 1920, in *Ibid.*, p. 276 f.

that they all follow the typically American policy of avoiding meddling in the affairs of Europe, and, in turn, of not permitting its interference in their own (the original Monroe Doctrine—"America for the Americans"). This policy, however, ran counter to another relating to the unwillingness of the South and Central American states, to recognize that interpretation of the Monroe Doctrine [212] by the United States which assumed that the latter country held a privileged position with regard to interference in the affairs of Pan-America, an extension of the original Monroe Doctrine, with the new slogan "America for the United States," a policy which, by the way, has been more recently abandoned by President Roosevelt.[213] However, all these countries attach great importance to their absolute independence and equal rights; we may see in this fact, one of the reasons for their original entry into the League and the wide extent of their coöperation with it. In contrast with the United States, a further connection with the League of Nations may also be found in the fact that a number of these states feel themselves to be especially attached to Spain or Portugal, from which they have inherited their language and culture and with which they are often pleased to coöperate within the League.

The Monroe Doctrine is explicitly referred to in Article XXI of the Covenant of the League. It is there none too accurately [214] described as a "regional understanding . . . for securing the maintenance of peace," and which as such is therefore not inconsistent with the provisions of the Covenant. Nothing is said as to what the Monroe Doctrine really aims at, or which one of the many and varied interpretations of its text the framers of the Article had in mind.[215] The original purpose, that of making easier the

[212] See further Alvarez, *Le Droit international americain*, pp. 154 ff.

[213] From whose government there have been issued repeatedly statements that the United States is opposed to armed intervention. If such action in a particular case appears to be necessary, it is only to be undertaken after consultation and common action by the Pan-American States. See also recent press reports of discussions at the Lima Conference.

[214] The text of this Article has been properly subjected to adverse criticism from a linguistic point of view; see Ray, *Commentaire*, pp. 575 ff.; also Matos, *L'Amérique et la Société des nations*, pp. 62 ff.

[215] See Ray, p. 576, on the objections of various South American states to the idea underlying Article XXI of the Covenant.

entry of the United States into the League was, however, not attained.

We have noted above that Argentina was one of the original members of the League of Nations. Its all-powerful President Irigoyen decreed Argentina's support of the League on July 18, 1919, without reservations, and "ratified" this decision on January 16, 1930, but he had not secured the necessary constitutional approval of the Argentine Congress. The delegation was, however, withdrawn from the very first Assembly of the League because its above-mentioned proposal was rejected, and Mr. Irigoyen then permitted the whole matter to remain in abeyance. His successor, Alvear (1922-28), saw that the yearly membership dues were regularly paid to the League, but no question of Argentina's membership was submitted by him to the Congress. When Irigoyen again became president in 1922, he vetoed the appropriations to the League for this purpose. In 1932-33 the Congress agreed unanimously, however, to the ratification of the Covenant.

In a manner similar to that of other South American states, Argentina took this occasion to declare "that it is the opinion of the Argentine Republic that the Monroe Doctrine as mentioned in Article XXI of the Covenant is a unilateral declaration which at one time rendered American independence a necessary service, but forms no 'regional understanding' within the meaning of the text of the Article mentioned."[216] None the less Argentina failed to appear at the League Assembly in 1933. It was generally believed that the reason for this was the fear that the country might become involved in the Chaco conflict between Bolivia and Paraguay, through operation of the sanctions system, while Argentina wished to act as a possible mediator in common action with other neighboring countries, particularly Brazil, who, as already noted, was no longer a member of the League.

2. The Argentine Anti-War Pact of October 10, 1933, then, must be examined against this background. In many respects it presents a counterpart to the Kellogg Pact of 1927, not only in

[216] The Argentine representative, Cantilo, had previously made a similar declaration in 1928 in the Committee on Security and Arbitration of the League.

its wording but also in its purpose to act as a link between the sanctions system of the League and the non-member states (in this case, Brazil) which did not wish to enter the League. Just as Briand's original hope that the Kellogg Pact would constitute a special Franco-American agreement was blocked by the insistence of the United States upon universality, so did Foreign Minister Saavedra Lamas of the Argentine first plan his pact as a special agreement between Argentina and Brazil, while the latter country desired that it be extended to include all the American nations, and in reality thus opened it to all countries. Later the Argentine was itself anxious for the acceptance of the pact throughout America and elsewhere abroad, and obtained great success for its efforts in that direction.

What gives this South American agreement for the prevention of war [217] its main interest is the idea already put forward in the Danish treatise of 1924 regarding the *possibility of a coördination of a system of neutrality with the sanctions system;* it is here explicitly provided in the form of an international treaty between a great number of states. Another originally Danish idea was adopted and incorporated in the treaty, namely the Danish proposals of 1922 respecting the non-recognition of territorial changes resulting from war. These two main provisions constitute [218] Articles II and III of the treaty, which read:

> Article II. [The high contracting parties] declare that territorial questions must not be settled by resort to violence, and that they shall recognize no territorial arrangement not obtained through pacific means, nor the validity of an occupation or acquisition of territory brought about by armed force.
>
> Article III. The contracting states undertake to make every effort in their power for the maintenance of peace. To that end they will adopt *in their character as neutrals* a common and solidary attitude; they shall exercise the political, judicial or economic means authorized by international law; they shall bring the influence of public opinion

[217] Published in "Académie Diplomatique Internationale," *Séances et Travaux, VII, 3* (1933), pp. 132 ff. The treaty has also been published together with a number of letters and opinions by the Argentine Foreign Ministry in the Argentine Green Book: *Pacte de Non-Agression et de Conciliation Argentin,* Buenos Aires, 1936.

[218] Article I contains a prohibition against wars of aggression.

to bear; but in no case shall they resort to intervention, either diplomatic or armed, subject to the attitude that may be incumbent on them by virtue of other collective treaties to which such states are signatories. [Our italics.]

This South American treaty is also similar to the Kellogg Pact in so far as it condemns wars of aggression (Article I) and thus by inference permits defensive war. It contains, moreover, a number of provisions relating to the peaceful settlement of international controversies through arbitration. According to its Article XVI, all states are entitled to ratify the Treaty, which membership, under Article XVII, may be terminated upon one year's notice.

It has been brought to public notice on several occasions that the treaty was the work of the Argentine Foreign Minister, Mr. Saavedra Lamas himself. Apart from this, little is known of its preparation.[219] For the sources to be consulted regarding this, we must refer to a discussion which occurred in the Académie diplomatique internationale on October 20, 1933, to the "Exposé des motifs" of Mr. Saavedra Lamas, which he submitted to the Academy, and to the circulars which the Argentine government sent to the various governments together with its proposals relating to approval of the treaty. There can hardly be any doubt hereafter that it was the Danish treatise of 1924 which first pointed out the possibility of coördinating the two systems: the implicit consolidation[220] of the law of neutrality through the war-prevention system of the League and the new and active form of neutrality[221] which formed the basis of the South American treaty. The Argentine circulars of June, 1934, to the various governments, refer to the Danish treatise, and no other sources upon this question are referred to.[222] The fact that the treaty is the expression of an entirely new and modern construction of the concept of neutrality as a "pacigérat international" is strongly emphasized. Traditional neutrality was founded upon passivity and

219 Not given in the Argentine Green Book, 1936.

220 Cohn, *Neutralité et Société des nations*, 172 f.

221 *Ibid.*, p. 203.

222 "L'idée que la neutralité est compatible avec les préceptes du Pacte de la Société des nations a d'ailleurs été brillamment soutenue par"... (the Treatise of 1924) "qui pense que cet instrument, loin d'avoir supprimé ou rendu superflu le droit à la neutralité lui a donné plus d'importance en le pourvoyant d'une véritable base juridique."

impartiality. This form of neutrality was discontinued by Articles X and XVI of the League Covenant. Some believed that the Kellogg Pact should have abolished the notion of neutrality. Contrary to this, the Saavedra Lamas Treaty introduces an active and enlightened neutrality [223] which comes to the aid of an attacked state through reciprocal and joint action by the neutrals.[224]

At the time of signing of the treaty in Rio de Janeiro on October 10, 1933, the Brazilian Minister of Foreign Affairs made an address, in which he stressed the statement that the treaty, unlike the League Covenant, *does not recognize the application of a general state of war as a means of compulsion* against the treaty violator, but follows the principle "*paz pela paz*" ("peace through peace"). This thought was further developed [225] in a number of theses, among which the following may be mentioned: a neutral state must not render aid to an aggressor nation nor recognize the acquisition of territory obtained through violence. It must not act passively toward war between other countries, but shall, on the contrary, coöperate for cessation of the war, since its only purpose is peace and *not the punishment* [226] of a state which was perhaps only denominated the aggressor by a politically influenced decision. Besides Argentina and Brazil, the signatories of the treaty on that occasion were Mexico, Chile, Uruguay, and Paraguay.

The Argentine government has since displayed great energy in its efforts to obtain for the treaty the support of all the remaining American nations, as well as those of Europe, above all Spain, Italy, and the northern European countries.

At the Pan-American Conference in Montevideo in December, 1933, Argentina and Brazil, which had not hitherto signed the Kellogg Pact of 1927, agreed to give these new proposals their

[223] "Neutralité agissante et éclairée."

[224] "C'est cette conception toute nouvelle que M. Saavedra Lamas semble bien avoir inscrite dans l'article 3 de son projet. L'article constate que si la neutralité classique, celle des bras croisés, est perimée, il faut instituer par une attitude commune et solidaire de tous les signataires une neutralité concertée, dirigeant contre l'agresseur les moyens politiques et économiques permis par le droit international."

[225] Thus contrary to the paradox in the League Covenant of "war prevention through war."

[226] Such theses agreed with the conclusions in Cohn, "*Kriegsverhütung und Schuldfrage*," 1931; see especially the conclusions given on pp. 192 ff. of that work.

support, and in turn secured the signatures of the United States and of fourteen South American countries to the Saavedra Lamas Treaty. It was further signed by Italy, Spain, and others.[227]

3. The Argentine government did not address France and England because of the realization that its proposals would hardly meet with a friendly reception in those countries which so positively assert that neutrality is fundamentally inconsistent with the system of the League Covenant. On the other hand, Argentina did submit this treaty to the League Council, with a request that it be referred for further study to the committee dealing with the question of coördinating the League Covenant with the Kellogg Pact. This request was discussed at the meeting of the League Council[228] in January, 1934. States which had already ratified the treaty endorsed the Argentine proposals. The Spanish delegate, Madariaga, also approved it from the view that, just as the Kellogg Pact attempted to bridge the gap between Geneva and the United States, so it was the task of the Saavedra Lamas Treaty to connect South American opinion with the efforts of the League. Warm support was also given by the representatives of Mexico, Portugal, and others; and Sir John Simon (England) and M. Paul-Boncour (France) entirely agreed. The idea that the signatory nations could participate in the fight against war in the capacity of neutrals was not refuted at Geneva by a single word, and the Argentine delegate, Cantilo, took this opportunity to emphasize the general South American desire for pacific solidarity. The Council thereupon accepted the Argentine proposal to refer the treaty to the Co-ordination Committee.

It is strange that Mr. Saavedra Lamas, in his detailed report during the discussion in the Académie Diplomatique, Paris (October, 1933), failed to emphasize the coördination elements but gave first importance to other features of the Treaty. His "motives"[229] for Article III make no mention whatever of neutrality, although the

[227] Norway also signed the Treaty, but Denmark and Sweden have not done so to date.

[228] League of Nations, *Official Journal*. Minutes of the 78th session of the Council (1934), pp. 133-36; 208-12 (treaty text).

[229] Académie Diplomatique Internationale, *Séances et Travaux, VII année, No. 3*, p. 138.

government circulars attached particular importance to it. The explanation is probably to be found in the realization that such an idea would not be very popular in this French *milieu.* His reasons [230] for Article II include a long historical presentation of the principles of non-recognition—which go back to the old principle of *uti possidetis* and which had already been stated by Bolivar in the Panama Congress of 1826—together with the more recent American arbitration programs. As we have shown,[231] all this is quite distinct from the modern doctrine of non-recognition as an independent principle of law resulting from the legal outlawry of war. The "motives" then cite the Pan-American Codification draft November 30, of 1925, as their actual source, but this is again an almost literal reproduction of the Danish proposals of 1922 and is based upon the same ideas.

Of interest is the statement in the "Motives" [232] that the treaty Article III excludes not only armed but diplomatic intervention as well. This is a suggestion of the Calvo and Drago doctrines [233] regarding restrictions upon intervention arising from non-payment of governmental debts, and to similar American doctrines. The latter, however, deal with quite special situations and appear to be in no way applicable to a general program of non-intervention, like that expressed in the treaty, and which must be regarded as particularly objectionable in the light of the need of coöperation for effective war-prevention. It would therefore hardly be incorrect to assume that they are aimed against the North American interpretations of the Monroe Doctrine which give the United States special right to interfere in the affairs of other American states. The expression "diplomatic intervention" (in this case associated with armed intervention) must therefore be understood in a somewhat different way from its normal usage as arbitrary diplomatic intervention in the internal policies of another state. On the other hand, the treaty could hardly exclude those actions based on ordinary international law, and as such fully justifiable proposals

230 *Ibid.*, p. 136.
231 *Supra*, pp. 167 f.
232 Académie Diplomatique Internationale, *op. cit.*, p. 137.
233 See Alvarez, Le Droit international américain, p. 227, Liszt, p. 443; Frisch, in Strupp, (ed.). *Wörterbuch* I, 177 and 252.

to belligerent nations, consisting of representations dealing with the termination of the war or advice regarding the far-reaching compulsory measures of a political, legal, and economic nature of which Article III of the treaty speaks.[234]

Saavedra Lamas tried upon this occasion to avoid a discussion of the problem of neutrality, but since this is so obviously the decisive point in his proposals, it naturally could not be kept out of the debates. In a very detailed statement of the treaty's contents, the Esthonian member of the Academy, Mr. Pusta, went into this question,[235] which he very misleadingly characterized as "benevolent neutrality" ("neutralité bienveillante"). He thereupon[236] quoted verbatim from the Argentine circular, the Argentine statement regarding this new form of neutrality, without his contributing anything new to it. Mr. Guerrero, member of the Permanent Court at the Hague, was more critical in his attitude toward the treaty. He pointed out the textual and material contradictions which Article III appeared to contain. How could one apply the sanctions provided in that article, if even diplomatic intervention is prohibited? In Mr. Guerrero's opinion, a lawbreaker cannot plead the principle of non-intervention. The whole treaty, he said, contributes nothing essentially new toward the solution of the extremely important problem of war-prevention which is not much aided by the assertions of general principles having no legally binding effect.

[234] In his thoroughly detailed study of the particular provisions of the Treaty, the Esthonian Minister Pusta (Académie Diplomatique Internationale, *Séances et Travaux*, p. 149) interprets the term "diplomatic intervention" as referring to an ultimatum and says: "Sans doute nous comprenons l'aversion du projet argentin pour toute intervention diplomatique se manifestant sous l'aspect d'un ultimatum. Mais l'intervention diplomatique, surtout concertée, au nom du droit, de la justice, et de la paix, doit être reconnue. La pratique même des neutres dans le différend bolivo-paraguayen y conduit." By "ultimatum" however is understood in common usage a conditional declaration of war (Møller, *Folkeretten in Fredstid og Krigstid* II, p. 9; Liszt, p. 458) therefore it would have no place in an anti-war pact. Against this idea also are the "Motives" of M. Saavedra Lamas which refer to the American Drago, Calvo, and similar doctrines of non-intervention, constitutional limitations upon state sovereignty (Barbosa) and upon protection of foreigners (Tejedor, Irigoyen) etc.; see also Braun, *Démarche, Ultimatum, Sommation*, pp. 49 ff.

[235] Académie Diplomatique Internationale, *Séances et Travaux*, p. 148.

[236] *Ibid.*, p. 149.

The Spanish delegate, Madariaga, declared that there were already too many pacts. "We are creating an inflation of pacts." [237] In giving a practicable definition of a prohibition of war of aggression, he believed that the Saavedra Lamas Treaty had likewise failed. Madariaga had little sympathy for the new form of neutrality: [238]

> Je crois que la neutralité est équidistante ou elle est inexistante. C'est un peu comme si l'on parlait d'un absolu que seráit relatif ou d'une vertu douteuse ou légère: contradiction bien vivante. Toutefois nous sommes ici encore en présence d'un contraste entre la logique la pratique, entra la théoríe et la pratique, et comme transition entre l'état de fait que nous avons et l'état de droit que nous voulons, il est possible qu'il soit nécessaire d'admettre une neutralité qui ne soit ni chair ni poisson, puisque nous avons pas encore bâti suffisament cette cité internationale qu'il faut absolument bâter en toute logique et en toute efficacité....
>
> Je crois que nous sommes à la veille de l'abolition complète de la neutralité.[239] Tant que nous n'auront pas aboli la neutralité nous n'aurons pas de paix dans le monde. Mais comme pour abolir neutralité, il faudra patienter encore quelques moments, j'applaudis et je trouve que c'est là aussi un des éléments essentiels du Pacte de M. Saavedra Lamas, qui nous sont une guarantie de succès, une des idées les plus originales et les plus intérresantes de ce Pacte: la création de cette neutralité active et pour ainsi dire polarisée qui doit servir en tout cas à l'abolition de la guerre, qui en est le but essentiel.

It is interesting to note that a French member of the Academy, Professor de la Pradelle, as well as other members, highly praised the new ideas in the treaty. La Pradelle, however, did not go particularly into the question of neutrality. However, in a later statement by the Polish writer, M. Rundstein, it is stated more conservatively that Article III appears to recognize the principle of "neutrality," which seems inconsistent with the sanction provision in Article XVI of the Covenant. Consideration is given to this question in the final sentence of Article III of the Saavedra Lamas Treaty, which reads: "with reservation of any obligations

[237] *Ibid.*, p. 156. [238] *Ibid.*, p. 159.

[239] Political developments in the subsequent period have refuted this forecast.

which may be required of them under other collective treaties which such states may have signed." [240]

The Saavedra Lamas Treaty, despite the high praise it received in Paris and despite its acceptance and full recognition at Geneva, has nevertheless not met with the approval of certain countries which seemingly should have been greatly attracted to most of its chief provisions. This is, in the main, due to the fear that it might be used to weaken, both morally and legally, the League sanctions system. The strong emphasis placed upon the principle of non-intervention is a typically American one,[241] since the same importance is not accorded this principle in Europe, where it is held to be rather a backward step, as compared with the League system. A tendency exists among the American nations not to apply evidently compulsory measures, but instead to refer to the value of public opinion, the importance of which in other countries is not estimated so highly. Those European countries which might otherwise wish to recognize the theory of neutrality, desire in no way to weaken the efficiency of the legal, moral, and economic sanctions of the League. On the contrary, they wish rather to strengthen them, in the service of war-prevention, with the single reservation that sanctions must not in themselves go so far as a declaration of war or of a state of war. Through the emphasis which is laid upon the idea of wars of aggression (without further definition of it) and the consequent implicit reservation of the legality of defensive war, the Saavedra Lamas Treaty aligns itself with the Covenant of the League and the Kellogg Pact and therefore assumes a position unfavorable to the newer aspects of neutrality, which in essence presuppose the abandonment of the questions of war guilt and aggressors. We might perhaps say that the Saavedra Lamas Treaty in the last analysis is not in principle so far apart from the other pacts as its author appears to believe. Its elasticity with

[240] These concluding words of Article III constitute a certain weakening of the entire system of the Treaty, since they may be used to make its new provisions invalid for such States as are simultaneously League members. They also indirectly suggest that the two pacts are not held to be altogether consistent with each other.

[241] Alvarez, *Le Droit international americain*, pp. 126 ff.

its regard for other systems is really a liability, rather than an asset.

4. For the consideration of the Pan-American Conference[242] in December, 1936, the Argentine Minister of Foreign Affairs, Saavedra Lamas, had prepared and made public the draft of another "general treaty" to strengthen measures for the preservation of peace,[243] which, while it adhered to the neutrality principle, attached much greater importance to the application of general sanctions than did the treaty of 1933.

This new treaty in a sense aimed at harmonizing the main features[244] of the Kellogg Pact, the Saavedra Lamas Treaty, and the Covenant of the League; but further mentioned a number of other international treaties and special American doctrines ("las doctrinas jurídicas de América") relating to the prohibitions of the use of armed force in the collection of public or private international debts, of extreme exercise of diplomatic protection of citizens abroad, and so on. It was, moreover, aimed at securing the effectiveness of sanctions for strengthening peace and maintaining the principle of non-recognition of acquisitions or occupation of territories brought about through armed force. This pact is not restricted to America, but would secure the blessings of peace to all nations throughout the world by condemning wars of aggression and by abolishing the existing practice of intervention.

In Article III the parties expressly approve the acts of former Pan-American Conferences condemning wars of conquest, and likewise accept the obligations they have assumed under the Kellogg Pact and the Argentine (Saavedra Lamas) Treaty to renounce war as a means for the settlement of international conflicts,[245] to condemn wars of aggression, and not to recognize the

[242] The results of the Conference are published in Inter-American Conference for the Maintenance of Peace, *Final Act*, Buenos Aires, 1936.

[243] Inter-American Conference for the Maintenance of Peace, *Tratado General para reforzar los medios de conservar la paz*, Buenos Aires, 1936.

[244] Argentine also strongly stressed the necessity of harmonizing these pacts in proposals for amendments in 1936; see "Application of the Principles of the Covenant of the League of Nations." (League of Nations *Document A. 31. 1936 VII*, p. 9).

[245] "Como medio de resolver los conflictos internacionales." This is not an exact interpretation of the text or ideas of either the Kellogg Pact or the Saavedra Lamas Treaty.

occupation or acquisition of territory through armed force. Article IV aims at coöperation with the League of Nations for greater efficiency. Article V is an interesting effort to give to special American arbitration boards rights similar to those in the international convention of September 26, 1931, regarding measures for strengthening the means of war-prevention given to the Council of the League of Nations. These American arbitration boards are to be empowered to apply measures of prevention of both military and non-military nature. Among the former, reference is made to the evacuation of armed forces which have invaded the territories or territorial waters of foreign countries, or are in zones demilitarized in accord with international agreements, or which fly over such territories or zones, and to the establishment of boundary lines which such forces may not cross.

Article VI expressly lists a number of sanctions which, regardless of the neutral status, may be applied in the service of war-prevention, namely:

(1) Non-recognition of territorial arrangements ("arreglos territoriales") [246] which may be obtained by non-pacific means,[247] and of occupation or acquisitions obtained by armed force, such action to be taken at the request of the party regarding himself as the injured one. Non-recognition is thus not automatic as it was in the original Danish proposals of 1922 and in Article II of the Saavedra Lamas Treaty, and as actually carried out with regard to the Chinese-Japanese conflict over Manchuria. In certain instances this revision may seem a natural one, but in other cases it will result in weakening the moral and real importance of this policy, particularly where the illegal acquisitions comprise the entire territory of the injured state, as in Ethiopia, so that the presentation of its complaint may meet with difficulties of a formal nature.

The non-recognition under this draft treaty is to be made in the form of a declaration, which is to be published in those instances where pacific means for the solution of the controversy have failed,

[246] The term implies considerably more than mere acquisition or occupation.

[247] This too means much more than the use of armed force, and comprises as well unilateral illegal settlements by private individuals, overthrow of civil authority and the like.

or upon refusal of one or both of the parties to consent to an arbitral adjudication or to comply with an arbitral award, so that it is evidently its intention to occupy the disputed territory with force and to hold it indefinitely.

Such declaration may be made individually or collectively, by the contracting states, and shall be brought to the attention of all the other signatories. It shall contain a proclamation of the moral injustice of the use of violence and declare publicly that they will not recognize any situation or treaty in favor of the pact-breaking state which asserts a claim to the territory thus acquired or thus occupied.

(2) Mutual and common action in the capacity of the signatories as neutrals is considered in Article III of the Saavedra Lamas Pact. Compulsory measures of a political, legal, moral, and economic nature are to be applied. The rights of neutrals with respect to belligerents, as provided in the Hague Conventions of 1907 and the Havana Convention of 1928 regarding maritime neutrality, are to be maintained. The duties incumbent upon them as members of the League are to be reserved. Under these circumstances common action as neutrals ("la actitud commún y solidaria de la neutralidad") in each case is to be agreed upon at the request of any one of the contracting Parties which is not involved directly in the controversy. It is not necessary that such action be delayed until the outbreak of war. Common application of sanctions is made through diplomatic channels or by conferences between the neutrals, who may jointly or individually tender their good offices or mediation to the disputants.

If efforts by the neutral states toward reconciliation are unsuccessful, the contracting parties bind themselves to declare an immediate embargo on all kinds of arms, as well as on petroleum, coal, and similar materials which are of direct use for war; during the period preceding the war this embargo shall be applicable to both parties to the dispute, and after the beginning of hostilities, to the belligerent which, under the circumstances,[248] must be regarded as the aggressor.

[248] Although the draft adhered in principle to the theory of aggression, it made certain reservations in the method of employing sanctions in a broader form

(3) Prohibiting the extension of loans or credits for purposes of war to one or both parties according to circumstances.

(4) Countries bordering on the disputant states may close their ports to one or both belligerents when it is evident these ports are being used for furnishing supplies to the armed forces of such belligerents.

(5) Moral sanctions: pressure of world opinion against the pact-breaker shall be expressed in the form of "censure," that is, in an official and public declaration of disapproval, which is to be endorsed by a majority or by all the contracting powers not party to the dispute. Should such measures fail to obtain the desired effect, they may be succeeded by a temporary severance of diplomatic relations with the pact-breaking state. Such measures may in no case be considered as hostile acts by the state whose action occasioned them.

This draft is remarkable not only for its emphasis upon sanctions while adhering to the law of neutrality, but also because it correctly and expressly distinguishes between the belligerents, and treats them according to their connection with the outbreak of the war, a situation in no way opposed to the natural interpretation of the rules of neutrality or to the moral and legal right which a neutral must be considered to possess, of tendering its coöperation in the service of war-prevention, a coöperation in which it may have a legal and evident self-interest. The new draft follows the earlier proposals in the treatise of 1924 and the Saavedra Lamas Treaty of 1933 toward making possible a coördination of neutrality and war-prevention, and shows how attempts at combination—whatever purely theoretical argument may be offered against them—have continued vigorous and developing.

The Pan-American Conference[249] met in Buenos Aires on December 1, 1936, and its discussion especially concerned itself with a proposal from the United States aimed at closer coöperation

according to the circumstances, as well as their application against both parties in a uniform fashion. In this way it approaches the view of *Neo-neutrality*, which does not prohibit the gradual limiting of sanctions to the party responsible for continuation of the war.

[249] A *Handbook for the Use of Delegates* was published by the Union under the heading: Inter-American Conference for the Maintenance of Peace, Washington, 1936.

and expansion of the existing treaty relations [250] among the American nations. This proposal is inferior to the 1936 draft of M. Saavedra Lamas with respect to the means to be placed at the disposal of the war-prevention machinery and must rather be regarded as an attempt to tie up a few points of the draft with contemporary neutrality legislation in the United States. Its most important and peculiar characteristic is that it places the consultation idea strongly in the foreground with regard to mutual relations of the countries of Pan-America, and creates a solid foundation for the carrying out of such a program.

In Article I the Convention acknowledges the existing inter-American treaties relating to the settlement of controversies (the Gondra Treaty of 1923, the Kellogg Pact, and the Saavedra Lamas Treaty, and emphasizes the duties of non-recognition by its signatories of territorial conquests and of war-prevention in their capacity as neutrals. For this purpose "consultations and coöperation" are considered to be necessary. Under Article II these are to take place through the establishment of a Permanent Inter-American Consultative Committee, whose duty it shall be to prevent controversies from arising and to avoid the use of force while bringing existing controversies to an end. The Committee consists of the foreign ministers of all the American states as obvious members, who however, in special circumstances, may delegate their rights to others. Members of the Committee are to be in close touch with one another (by telegraph and telephone) and to hold meetings whenever it is decided to do so.

Of particular significance is Article IV, which gives to the Committee the right to take the initiative in reminding the states of their obligations under the treaty, to act as mediator between them, and to make proposals to them with regard to the settlement of controversies. In this manner the Committee has been given the functions which the Saavedra Lamas draft intended for the Inter-American Arbitration Board, and which in a sense put it in a position similar to that of the League Council. The people of the Americas have rightly attached great importance and interest to

[250] Convention coördinating the existing Treaties between the American States and extending them in certain respects.

the proposal and have seen in it a reflection of the new Rooseveltian interpretation of the Monroe Doctrine, by which this unilateral North American declaration is to be re-stated in the form of a general all-American agreement.

If war should, nonetheless, break out between two American countries, the reciprocal and uniform stand of the other states, in their capacity as neutrals under Article VI, is to be put into effect through the Permanent Inter-American Consultative Committee. This committee is to examine and report as soon as possible, if a state of war exists, and if it does, the neutrality provisions of the Convention come into effect automatically. In such case each individual American nation *may* put into force prohibitions or restrictions upon its trade with respect to both belligerents equally, unless obligated under a previous agreement to act otherwise (recognition of the principle of qualified neutrality under treaty obligations). On the other hand, it *shall* prohibit the export of weapons, ammunition, and "implements of war," to the belligerents (Article VIII). There are corresponding provisions (Article IX) relating to the extension of credits and loans.

The value of this Convention, which, with regard to the mutual relations between the countries of America rests upon a neo-neutral foundation since the provisions have an undoubted war-prevention tendency, lies in the fact that it has created set forms under which this tendency may be realized. With regard to the means placed at its disposal for this purpose, the Convention is, as we have already noted, inferior to the Saavedra Lamas draft, but it holds the door open for further development in that direction. The important thing is that the correct fundamental viewpoint is recognized to its full extent, that is, collective responsibility for effective prevention of war, in connection with the thought that this war-prevention must not take the form of war itself, but in the participants' capacity as neutrals, with the possibility of a combination of the rules of traditional neutrality with the new system of war-prevention.

Some further remarks on neutrality legislation in the United States may be found in the concluding chapter below.

European Attempts at Coördination

1. While efforts to solve the technical problems of a coördination between neutrality and war-prevention played so important a rôle in both South America and North America—(in Europe, especially because of the French and English attitude, such coordination has been hitherto impossible) the rest of the world was inclined to follow their lead on that question. That international solidarity should require the surrender of neutrality appeared to be a logical necessity, to which no alternative seemed possible. The power of circumstance is, however, much greater than all logical—and apparently compelling—reasons, and consequently doubts arose in some European countries as to the correctness of these conclusions.

An early attempt to combine neutrality with membership in the League of Nations was the position of Switzerland. That country alone, of all the neutrals of the World War, had succeeded in winning an acknowledgment of her exceptional situation in this respect from the Great Powers.[251] Political reasons of both an internal and external nature were urged and recognized in this case as having a quite special nature and a peculiar significance. On the side of its internal politics the circumstance was emphasized that Switzerland was composed of three different population elements, French, German, and Italian, which, while now welded into national unity, could not safely be exposed to the severe test which a war with one of its neighbors of any of these nationalities might create. The century-old [252] tradition of the neutrality of the Swiss people had been so ingrained within their consciousness that it was impossible for them to abandon it. The preservation of the traditional law of neutrality was for them a *conditio sine qua non* for

[251] Huber, "Die schweizerische Neutralität und der Völkerbund," (in *Les Origines et l'oeuvre de la Société des nations, II,* 68 ff.), who, like almost all other writers, emphasizes (p. 136) "die Sonderstellung, welche die neutrale Schweiz im Völkerbunde einnimmt"; Rappard, "L'entrée de la Suisse dans la Société des nations" (*ibid.,I,*361 ff.); Ray, *Commentaire,* p. 105; Whitton, *La Neutralité,* p. 537: "de caractère exceptionnel."

[252] For further reference, see Schweizer, *Geschichte der schweizerischen Neutralität.*

the entrance of that country into the League.[253] The question, under Swiss constitutional law, had to be decided by a referendum vote. But it was a foregone conclusion that an overwhelming majority would vote against the entry of Switzerland into the League in the event that it should involve the forfeiture of their rights under neutrality.

With respect to external policy, it was asserted that the permanent neutrality of Switzerland for over a hundred years had always been recognized as a factor in European politics for preserving peace. In the Treaty of Paris of November 20, 1815,[254] the European Powers had granted "une reconnaissance formelle et authentique de la neutralité perpétuelle de la Suisse" and had guaranteed its territorial integrity and inviolability.

During the discussions concerning the admission of the neutral countries into the League of Nations, Switzerland at first cooperated with the other neutrals, but continued her efforts for special treatment after the others had thrown up the sponge. Whether this alone would have gained her objective is, however, very doubtful, just as it would have been doubtful whether Switzerland would or could have remained outside the League if her demands for special status had been rejected. The fact is that there are others of the smaller neutral countries for whom similar and even stronger arguments might have been advanced—even if of a somewhat different nature—to permit them to continue a neutrality policy of many years' standing, and which had been maintained during the World War. Peculiar, but in no way special, considerations spoke in favor of the recognition of Swiss neutrality within the League.

We therefore must not fail to recognize the fact that Switzerland, in exchange for a re-recognition of its neutrality, made certain concessions[255] of a political nature which were not entirely disproportionate to the object attained.

The initiative in these discussions was taken by France, who

[253] Huber, *op. cit.*, p. 68: "Für de Schweiz konnte es sich nur um Völkerbund mit Neutralität oder um Fernbleiben vom Völkerbund handeln."

[254] Martens, *Nouv. Rec. IV*, 186.

[255] Huber, *op. cit.*, p. 87 f.; Rougier, *Le Traité de Versailles et la neutralité de la Savoie*, pp. 80 ff.

wished to abolish certain inconvenient supplementary provisions of a military and economic nature which had been laid down for Savoy in connection with Swiss neutralization, and which could not be abrogated without the consent of Switzerland. Article 435 of the Versailles Treaty was an expression of a compromise which on the one hand recognized the continued neutralization of Switzerland and on the other hand called attention to the agreement between France and Switzerland regarding the abolition of former restrictions in the neutralized zone of Savoy.

If we examine this question from the position of Swiss foreign policy, there is no doubt that through its perseverance and offer of counter concessions it was able to obtain a result with which the Swiss government has reason to be well satisfied, since it was incorporated as an explicit treaty provision into Article 435 of the Versailles Treaty by the principal Allied Powers, and thus obtained a secure foundation in international law.[256]

2. From the more general standpoint of international law, it is, however, of minor interest what Switzerland or France secured on this occasion. The principle itself is, however, of vital interest. If we assume, as the Council's declaration of February 13, 1920, does, that neutrality is fundamentally inconsistent with the new system of the League Covenant, may we not reasonably inquire: How is it possible within a system which denies, as a matter of principle, the possibility of a member's neutrality; which uses this denial as the very foundation of its war-prevention measures, while recognizing the right to neutrality of one of its members, nonetheless to take the position that this fact promotes the interest of peace? To these questions of principle we might add one of a formal and technical nature: How is it possible to grant one member the special status which Article I, section 1, and Article XX of the Covenant expressly denies, without exception, to all League members? Finally, what rules of international law are to apply to Switzerland during future wars, within a system which no longer recognizes the principle or the laws of neutrality? In

[256] See also Ray, *op. cit.*, p. 105: "Nous sommes persuadé que jamais le Conseil ne sera tenté de méconnaître l'engagement qu'il a pris en 1920; mais nous ne pensons pas qu'on puisse considérer l'accession de la Suisse comme s'étant réalisée sous condition."

efforts to answer these questions various arguments have been put forward.

(1) The Council of the League, which, with its usual superficiality, approved this official act in its declaration of February 13, 1920, passed lightly over these difficulties; it *is* impossible, but yet it is done! Neutrality and the League of Nations are fundamentally inconsistent; but Switzerland has an exceptional position, which is recognized by Article 435 of the Treaty of Versailles. The League Council expects that Switzerland will not withhold support when it is a question of complying with common obligations, especially of an economic and financial nature. But Switzerland is not obligated to participate in military measures nor to permit passage through her territory. Consequently Switzerland's permanent neutrality is dictated by a general desire for peace, and thus, is consistent with the League Covenant.

Whether or not we feel that our fundamental doubts have been removed by these arguments is perhaps a question of personal choice. With regard to the formal and technical aspects, we must understand the Council's statement—if it has any logical basis—as saying that Switzerland's exceptional position is based either upon this declaration of the Council itself or upon Article 435 of the Versailles Treaty. Both positions are, however, untenable. The Council is nowhere given the right to make such exceptions to Article I, section 1, and Article XX of the Covenant. Furthermore, Article 435 of the Versailles Treaty is not obligatory either on the League of Nations or on its individual members merely because its signatories may be the same, and especially since there is no reference in the Covenant to Article 435 of the Treaty or vice versa. The notion that members of the League were to be bound by, or had recognized, the provisions of the Versailles Treaty was clearly and definitely rejected from the beginning, and especially by the Swiss government itself.[257]

(2) Another theory,[258] which at first blush might appear somewhat more acceptable, holds that the other members of the League

257 *Supra*, p. 49.

258 Whitton, p. 537: "le Conseil a approuvé ces réserves expressément, et l'Assemblée tacitment"; also Huber, p. 133, alleging a tacit recognition.

have *tacitly* agreed to permit Switzerland to become a member, despite its permanent neutrality. The question from a purely practical standpoint, was probably regarded in that way by many of the League members. But no adequate interpretation of the legal situation is thus given. In the first place, there can be no question of *tacit* approval of anything so clearly in violation of the explicit and plain provisions of the Covenant. Article I, section 1, demands that entry into the League be made "without reservations." Article XX states plainly and definitely that the Covenant abrogates not only all "obligations,"[259] but also "understandings" between the members which are inconsistent with its terms, and that they bind themselves to make no future engagements of like nature.

It must furthermore be remarked that the entry of Switzerland, like that of the other signatories in the annex to the Covenant, occurred through a unilateral declaration which, since it fulfilled the formal conditions, could not be rejected or criticized by the other members of the League. There would thus be no opportunity nor any reason for such members to raise objections. The legal status had to be determined from the text of the Covenant itself; the mere fact that the other members knew that the new member claimed such an exceptional position, would not be sufficient under ordinary rules of procedure to permit that such position being voted upon or expressed by a special agreement or recognition (which was not the situation in this case) and especially when this claim was, at the same time so clearly at variance with the explicit conditions prescribed in the Covenant.

(3) Switzerland's own statement of the reasons for her exceptional position is based upon Article XXI of the Covenant, under which regional understandings for securing the maintenance of peace, such as the Monroe Doctrine, are not to be regarded as inconsistent with the rules of the League Covenant. The Swiss claim[260] that there is a close spiritual relationship between the

[259] It might be assumed that Article 435 imposes no special obligations on Switzerland but gives it special rights. Such interpretation would likewise be incorrect, as we must assume that the provisions of Article XX, if holding true for obligations must so much the more hold true for rights.

[260] Huber, p. 86, which however only offers as proof the unimportant mere surface resemblance that in both cases it is a question of traditional policies

Monroe Doctrine and Swiss neutrality. The message from the Swiss Council of August 4, 1919, refers expressly to Article 435, which recognizes that Swiss neutrality is granted in the interest of peace and asserts that in consequence of Article XXI of the Covenant it is consistent with its rules.[261]

There is still, moreover, the distinction that the Monroe Doctrine is expressly mentioned in Article XXI and Swiss neutrality is not. The logic in the message of August 4, 1919, is hardly convincing. The assumption in Article XXI is that the Monroe Doctrine—as well as the arbitration treaties referred to—is basically *not* inconsistent with the system of the League Covenant, while the Swiss position assumes definitely that neutrality and the Covenant *are* in principle inconsistent. The mere fact that a special agreement might serve peace better is insufficient justification. If two or more League members should agree that they, in the interest of peace, would abstain from all participation in sanctions under Article XVI, this would be invalid, according to the terms of Article XXI. In all cases of conflict between Articles XX and XXI, the former would govern.

Finally, the Swiss position is inconsistent with that asserted by Switzerland itself, that Switzerland holds a special status based on a positive recognition, which cannot in a corresponding manner be attained by other states.[262] A neutrality agreement between any other group of League members hereafter thus could not be valid

which, in the interest of peace, result in placing restrictions on the political action of a state; see further Borel "La Neutralité de la Suisse dans la Société des nations," in *Revue Générale de Droit International public XVII (1920)*, pp. 159, ff.

[261] "Message du Conseil Fédéral," in Huber, p. 93: "la Suisse ne fera pas une réserve en declarant que sa neutralité subsiste en vertu de l'article XXI, comme engagement international assurant le maintein de la paix et, comme tel, compatible avec toutes les dispositions du Pacte. Car sur ce point, la réserve est faite par le *Covenant* lui-même, comme pour la doctrine de Monroe. Il n'y a pas ici une déclaration faite unilateralement par l'État intéressé. L'Article 435 du traité de paix reconnaît, en effet, que la neutralité de la suisse doit être considérée comme un engagement international pour le maintein de la paix. Le Pacte de la Société des nations, ayant été inséré dans le traité de paix et ayant été signe par les même États, l'article 435 interprète authentiquement l'article XXI."

[262] The Swiss supplementary message of February 17, 1919, says: "Switzerland's legal status within the League of Nations is incontestible and may not be alleged as precedent for other members." See Huber, pp. 93 ff.

through reference to Article XXI. Under such circumstances one might assert that such an entirely special legal status, which is in direct conflict with Article XX, is, without specific agreement, likewise inconsistent with Article XXI, could only obtain legal validity by express provision in the Covenant just as in the case of the Monroe Doctrine.

(4) In the Danish treatise of 1924[263] the opinion was expressed that the question of a neutralized Switzerland's admission to the League of Nations without reservation could only be explained upon the basis of the theory that neutrality and the League of Nations were, in finality, inconsistent. It was therefore neither a question of an interpretation of Article 435 of the Versailles Treaty, nor of tacit recognition, nor of the application of Article XXI of the Covenant. The declaration of the Council that neutrality and the League of Nations are in principle inconsistent is an unproved and unprovable assertion,[264] and the same holds true for Switzerland's stand regarding her absolute and exceptional position. The two facts which stand out are that Switzerland's permanent neutrality is expressly recognized in Article 435 of the Treaty of Versailles and that Switzerland has none the less been admitted to full membership rights in the League without reservation. These two facts, according to the treatise of 1924, permit no other logical or legal conclusion as to the compatibility of the two systems. Since then Luxemburg also has been admitted into the League without surrendering her permanent neutrality established in 1867.[265]

3. Switzerland, however, tried from the very beginning to assert its claim as to an exceptional position, which, from a political standpoint, is easy to understand, since the value of the privilege would naturally disintegrate and disappear to the same degree that it became evident that other states might make similar demands.

[263] Cohn, *Neutralité et Société des nations*, II, 193 ff.; see now also Wehrer in *Revue de Droit International*, XIII (1932), 339: "ce régime accordé à la Suisse n'est pas, lui non plus, un régime dérogatoire au Pacte et n'est pas un régime d'exception."

[264] This is now also recognized by Lauterpacht, "The Notion of Neutrality." In *Some British Views on Collective Security*, II, 3, 9, 12.

[265] Cohn, *Neutralité et Société des nations*, p. 195. (Note 1) insofar as it relates to neutralized states; this is now also acknowledged by Strupp, in *Neutralisation, Befriedung, Entmilitarisierung*, p. 351.

Switzerland, therefore, asserted from the start that, aside from its special case, the League of Nations and neutrality were inconsistent in principle.[266] It then attempted to treat the question as if no combination of the two systems existed, merely the exception which proved the rule; a purely incidental collision between the two legal systems, which required no internal adjustments for adaptation to each other. Switzerland had received the exceptional privilege of living according to the traditional laws of neutrality. For all other states, the law of neutrality was a locked door.

It soon proved, however, that this view was impracticable. It might in any case have followed from the fact that neutrality, like any legal system of international law, may be realized only through the interrelations of several states, and not by a single state. Neutrality is the sum of those rights and duties which can be expressed only in mutual legal relationships with other states, whether participants or nonparticipants in war. Its adaptation to, or combination with, a legal system under which other states are living is therefore in itself an absolute necessity, and the belief that Switzerland alone of all countries could maintain a system so fundamentally opposed to a system valid for all other states, is untenable.

As early as in its first discussions with the Powers, the Swiss government conceded that the neutrality of a League member must in no case lead it to support a Covenant-breaking state.[267] But just what does this mean in fact? It does not merely imply that impartiality and entire equality of treatment of both belligerents—the two corner stones of traditional neutrality—have been abandoned. It also means that the neutral states come to live under a legal system entirely distinct from that of traditional neutrality, under which all rights to freedom of trade have been abandoned, and their duties can be determined only by carefully considering what a combination of the two systems permits or prohibits. In short, the mere recognition that a neutral member of the League

[266] Huber, "Message du Conseil Fédéral of August 4, 1919," p. 27: "Il est indéniable qu'au point de vue de la logique et de la pure raison, neutralité et Société des nations sont deux notions qui s'excluent l'une l'autre."

[267] Huber, p. 85 (n. 1), Swiss note of March 10, 1919: "It is assumed herewith that neutrality will not be capable of such interpretation that support of any kind must be given to a State in conflict with the League of Nations."

of Nations must not aid the Covenant-breaker already leads very far in the direction of a coördinated system which the Danish treatise of 1924 asserted as possible and, in some circumstances, necessary for all members of the League.

The declaration of the League Council of February 13, 1920, went a step further, as it gave full support to the theory [268] which the Swiss government also had asserted in numerous official documents, namely, that the technical problem may be solved in such manner that the neutral state might take part in economic and not in military sanctions.[269] A logical justification for this theory [270] would be difficult to prepare. It has no positive justification and finds no support in the traditional law of neutrality, which developed very detailed rules concerning the rights and duties of neutrals in this very field of economic and commercial relations (the London Maritime Law Declaration of 1909), while on the contrary a certain degree of enforcement of neutral rights by military force (Fifth Hague Convention, Article X, and the Thirteenth Convention, Articles VIII and XXV; compare also the Armed Neutrality Leagues) was not regarded as inconsistent with neutrality. It is, moreover, the far-reaching economic boycott, especially that relating to non-members in Article XVI, section 1, of the Covenant, which is difficult to enforce except by an actual declaration of war by the sanction countries, while the application of those military measures of compulsion mentioned in section 2

[268] *Ibid.*, "la Suisse reconnaît et proclame les devoirs de solidarité qui résultent pour elle du fait qu'elle sera membre de la Société des nations, y compris le devoir de participer aux mesures commerciales et financières demandées par la Société des nations contre un État en rupture du Pacte, . . . mais qu'elle ne sera pas tenue de participer à une action militaire ou d'admettre le passage de troupes étrangères ou la préparation d'entreprises militaires sur son territoire"; for the last request no authority is contained in Article XVI.

[269] The Swiss Government followed this debatable thesis in 1920 to the absurd extent of objecting to the passage of a small contingent of international troops intended for participation in neither war nor in sanctions, but purely for the quite peaceful purpose of supervision of a plebescite in the Vilna area. See League of Nations *Official Journal* (1921), p. 170; *Schücking-Wehberg* (2d ed.), p. 135 ff. who justly remarks: "Die ganze Frage hatte übrigens mit der Neutralität nichts zu tun, da es sich ja nicht um einen Durchzug von Truppen zu kriegerischen Unternehmungen handelte."

[270] Also the Scandinavian countries', and especially Denmark's, policy within the League of Nations relies largely upon this theory; see also Waldkirch, *Das Völkerrecht*, p. 375; Munch, *Die Völkerbundspolitik der drei nordischen Staaten*, p. 12.

of that article has been prescribed in such a noncommittal and qualified fashion that it rather offers an opportunity for coördinating the two systems.[271]

In pertinent official Swiss documents emphasis has been placed upon the fact that the permanent neutralization of Switzerland, Luxemburg, Belgium, and other states, was based primarily upon strategic and not upon economic considerations.[272] Neutrality, it is claimed, is an essentially military idea.[273] But this is hardly a correct statement. Even if strategic considerations do hold a decisive position in the establishment of certain[274] neutral areas, this does not prove that neutrality, once it is created, expresses itself especially in a military form. Even during the régime of traditional neutrality, its rules during maritime warfare were aimed to fully as great an extent against economic as against military warfare, and the greater importance of economic warfare was proved during the World War, just as we must expect it to be in the future. A solution of the technical problem by saying:[275] "full participation in economic sanctions under Article XVI, section 1; no participation in military sanctions under Article XVI, section 2," is therefore hardly possible. Through Swiss participation in economic sanctions during the Italo-Ethiopian conflict, it was, moreover, proved that Switzerland did not follow this theory, but, on the other hand, followed that laid down in the treatise of 1924, under which the combination is made possible by the equal application of sanctions to both belligerents.

271 Cohn, *Neutralité et Société des nations*, pp. 184 ff. (the "Danish treatise of 1924").

272 Huber, p. 101.

273 Switzerland, Conseil Fédéral, *Message du Conseil Fédéral*, p. 41; "une notion d'ordre essentiellement militaire."

274 In no sense all. Huber, *op. cit.*, p. 101, is of the opinion, that neutralization of the Suez Canal, the Congo River, etc. is essentially a matter of commercial policy.

275 See also *Message du Conseil Fédéral, op. cit.*, p. 67: "Au point de vue militaire, nous ne pouvons qu'observer une neutralité absolue." More obscure are the ideas of the memorandum (p. 68 ff.), on economic neutrality; see also p. 46, where it says: "En ce qui concerne la politique de neutralité qui sera suivie en cas d'action collective de la Société des nations, il n'est guère possible d'entrer dans le detail"; but "Dans le domaine économique, nous devrons nous solidariser avec la Société des nations." Also see p. 82 f., and Waldkirch-Vanselow, *Neutralitätsrecht*, pp. 73 ff., opposing the concept of "economic neutrality."

The Swiss finally attempted to contribute to the solution of the technical problem by referring to the distinction between neutrality *law* and neutrality *policy*.[276] What Switzerland reserved to herself at the time of her entry into the League were the rights and duties which flow from neutrality. Participation in the work of the League of Nations requires, on the contrary, an entirely new orientation of Swiss neutrality *policy*. Even before the message of August 4, 1919, there was a reference in this connection to the Belgian writer, Descamps, and his idea that neutrals should depart from the passive and egoistic position they had hitherto held, and assume a positive and active one for the preservation or reëstablishment of peace *(pacigérat)*.

The difference between the traditional and the new neutrality could not, however, be identified with a distinction between law and policy, since it is a question of a new system of law *as well as* a new policy. This new system of law must, as pointed out in the treatise of 1924, be attained by the analysis and synthesis of elements from both systems, to create a vital and living new system, with its future development in view. To separate the legal element from policy in this field is certainly in the long run impossible. A new neutrality policy cannot thrive upon the basis of traditional neutrality law, or vice versa. Switzerland could not, however, admit this, since her political endeavors were directed toward the preservation of this traditional neutrality for her own purposes alone.

4. The untenability of the various Swiss efforts at coördination appeared as soon as they were converted into practice in 1935-36, during the Italo-Ethiopian conflict, in which the question involved economic and not military sanctions. According to the Swiss theory itself, the question of a special status for Switzerland during such a situation should not have arisen. None the less, that country now took the stand that because of its neutrality it could not coöperate with the other members of the League, but could simply follow out the program of the treatise of 1924[277] by applying sanctions in a quite uniform fashion toward both belligerents,

[276] Huber, pp. 99, 105; Switzerland, Conseil Fédéral, Message, p. 39.
[277] Cohn, *Neutralité et Société des nations*, p. 182 f.

that is against attacked Ethiopia as well as against the aggressor, Italy. It is noteworthy that Switzerland, in its note of October 28, 1935, refers to the ordinary rules of neutrality [278] of the Hague Conventions of 1907 before it even mentions its special status as a neutral, and that the latter is in no way asserted as a special status, but merely as "our position as a neutral." This theory of an exceptional position proved altogether to be a less useful argument because other countries declared themselves as being in a similar situation to that of Switzerland, especially Argentina (with her one million of Italian immigrants),[279] Austria,[280] and Hungary.[281] When the Swiss government in its note of October 28, 1935, pleaded [282] "une situation vraiment tout à fait exceptionelle," the Russian delegate, Litvinoff,[283] in the Co-ordination Committee justly asserted the incorrectness of such views. There can be no instances of war, even of obvious aggression, where such situations will not exist for one or more of the members of the League. Application of economic sanctions, he declared, requires unity among all the members, which as we remember, had been Switzerland's own opinion as well.

Moreover, Switzerland's theory of its special neutrality situation also received severe criticism upon this occasion. In the first place Switzerland attempted, as did Argentina,[284] to have it established that the Resolutions of 1921 should be made the basis for League action in this controversy,[285] and not Brouckère's Report, which called for the automatic application of sanctions. From the antineutral countries (the Little Entente, France, and England)

[278] "Vu l'article 9 de la Convention de la Haye du 18. octobre 1907, concernant les droits et les devoirs des puissances et des personnes neutres en cas de guerre sur terre, et notre statut de neutralité, il ne nous a pas été possible de renoncer à l'embargo sur les armes, munitions et matériels de guerre à destination de l'Ethiopie."

[279] League of Nations, *Official Journal, Special Supplement No. 145 (Co-ordination Committee)* (1936), p. 52.

[280] *Ibid.*, p. 22: "situation économique extrêment difficile."

[281] *Ibid.*, p. 23: "situation spéciale."

[282] *Oct. 12, 1935* League of Nations, *Official Journal*, p. 41, in which M. Motta asserts that "couper complètement les relations avec l'Italie" is "une chose absolument impossible, spécialement au point de vue politique."

[283] *Ibid.*, p. 27 f.

[284] *Ibid.*, p. 30.

[285] *Ibid.*, Motta: "il n'est pas douteux qu'elles seules peuvent former la ligne directrice de l'action que doit envisager le Comité."

there was some effort made to object to this, but nothing could be done in face of the fact that the sanctions system of the Resolutions was practical, while the automatic system was not. M. Titulesco (Rumania), as well as Mr. Eden, then expressed the somewhat curious view that there was no practical use in discussing the question.[286] It was thereupon decided "de laisser cette question de côté," which, however, did not alter the fact that in practice they had followed exclusively the program of the Resolutions. At the meeting of the Co-ordination Committee on November 2, 1935,[287] Switzerland's attitude on neutrality was made the subject of a further detailed discussion.

The sub-committee (Politis, chairman) declared that it had taken no action upon the question of the consistency of Switzerland's reply regarding its obligations under the Covenant of the League, which question was therefore open for discussion. Upon an English inquiry, Switzerland declared that the continuance of its commercial relations with Italy would take such form as to gain no special advantage for itself from its exceptional position.[288] As to the details for carrying this out in practice, Mr. Motta could not explain, since "it was a technical question which it would be difficult to discuss to advantage in the committee." Faced with the common displeasure which the Swiss attitude occasioned and the far-reaching consequences which it might have for other countries, Mr. Motta found himself forced to fall back upon the theory of Switzerland's special position, and characterized Swiss neutrality thus:[289]

"the status of Switzerland, declared 'unique' in the Declaration of London was the status of neutrality. It was stated specifically in the Declaration of London that Switzerland's neutrality was compatible with the provisions of the Covenant. Switzerland was neutral in the military sphere, and in those subjects closely akin thereto. In regard to *commercial* and *economic* measures, Swiss solidarity with the League, was complete because she accepted the *financial* sanctions as

[286] *Ibid.*, p. 31.

[287] League of Nations, *Official Journal, Special Supplement No. 146* (1936), pp. 33 ff.

[288] *Ibid.*, p. 35: "il ne veut tirer aucun profit de la situation spéciale dans laquelle se trouve la Suisse."

[289] *Ibid.*, p. 36.

they stood. She accepted the proposals concerning the export of key products as they stood. She has placed an embargo on *arms* consigned to Italy and Ethiopia."

With regard to the latter country, Mr. Motta was prepared, if necessary, to explain the reasons for which Switzerland had maintained the embargo. With respect to *importation* of Italian goods, Switzerland advised that it would apply a system, which, although avoiding losses inconsistent with her situation, would nevertheless accomplish the same result as the import prohibitions proposed by the League of Nations. By this latter phrasing Switzerland intended to say that no complete prohibition of Italian imports was implied, but rather a restriction of them to their normal peace-time volume; otherwise the losses caused to Switzerland by her complete coöperation would be so great and irreparable that the mutual support and indemnification foreseen under Article XVI, section 3, of the Covenant would be of no value to Switzerland.

It could hardly be concealed that this Swiss viewpoint was radically different from the former theory concerning a solidary front in participation in economic sanctions, while at the same time maintaining traditional neutrality in the military domain. As we have already shown, there was no question at all in this case of military sanctions, and under the original Swiss thesis there was no need for that country to take advantage of any special position. To carry out an embargo against both belligerent parties is an expression of a coördination of the two systems, and not of an "acte complet de solidarité"; her demand for freedom of importation from Italy had nothing to do with the neutrality question, but simply said that Switzerland, for economic and political reasons, declined to comply with the provisions of Article XVI of the Covenant, even in a case where this did not conflict with neutrality.

Within the Co-ordination Committee it was at once stated by the French[290] that it would be impossible to accept the Swiss ar-

[290] See also *ibid.*, p. 39, where the French member M. Coulondre declared: "that the government of the French Republic could not admit the validity of the Federal government's argument based on the Hague Convention of 1907 and [to]

gument. South Africa asserted that this was an obstruction set up by Switzerland against enforcement of sanctions. Poland agreed with the French interpretation, and correctly referred to the Swiss action in the Chaco war of canceling the arms embargo against one of the parties (Bolivia). The Greek delegate, Politis, also asserted that Switzerland's attitude was not in accord with the idea underlying the London Declaration of February 13, 1920. The Little Entente, Russia, and England joined in this opposition, the latter adding, however, that it was not expedient at the time to investigate the subject in detail—a helping hand which Mr. Motta promptly grasped in a detailed reply[291] in which he again recounted the Swiss theories. He asserted that neutrality in principle is inconsistent with the principles of the League of Nations, but that Switzerland occupied a unique position under that agreement, which none the less makes a combination of the two systems possible and necessary.

In addition to Mr. Motta's explanations showing at least a strong trend in the direction of a (general) coördination of the two systems, he made reference to the idea that the Swiss embargo on arms, under existing conditions, would not be injurious to Ethiopia and would thus in fact hit Italy alone, and that in this way Switzerland believed that it had brought "her loyalties toward the League into harmony with her fundamental and traditional conception of neutrality."[292] He finally admitted, however, that, in case of the crossing of Swiss territory of arms and munitions for the belligerents, it might nevertheless be possible that Switzerland would make a distinction between an aggressor and an attacked state.

Against these uncertain views the Greek delegate Politis had an easy task as he pointed out that, according to both the London Declaration and to Switzerland's own theories, her traditional neutrality after her admission into the League had a quite different character with respect to economic and financial sanctions. He

its status as a neutral. The French Government considered that the legal arguments put forward by the Swiss Government ran counter to Article XVI of the Covenant and the London agreement between the League Council and Switzerland with regard to the Confederation's entry into the League."

[291] *Ibid.*, p. 40. [292] *Ibid.*, p. 41.

followed this up—and in this M. Politis was eminently correct—by showing that circumstances in a sense make impossible an unaltered maintenance—even in a limited respect—of traditional neutrality, since the members have abandoned the fundamental obligations to make no distinction between the belligerents, not to evaluate the conduct of the belligerents, and to take a perfectly impartial attitude toward both of them. These principles were abandoned by the members of the League, as well as by Switzerland herself, when she agreed, together with the other League members, to accept a decision as to which of the parties to the controversy was the aggressor, as was done in the existing case by expressly recognizing Italy as the aggressor. This decision was itself, according to M. Politis at direct variance with the principles of neutrality. It is true that this same criticism strikes at the position of the London Declaration and the expedient which was there regarded as practicable.

The Swiss plan regarding the possibility of a normal import quota from Italy as not being injurious to the League action, likewise met sharp criticism, which came especially from the English. It appeared as if Switzerland had attempted to avoid further discussions by submitting a written reply,[293] but the meeting was not satisfied with this.[294] The Swiss delegate was recalled for further interrogation, which did not, however, lead to any satisfactory conclusion.[295]

5. An attempt at coördination differing from that of the Swiss theory exists in the case of Luxemburg, and it holds in certain respects even greater interest for the present study, because it is in no way connected with a demand for a special status for Luxemburg, which from the beginning assumed the possibility and permissibility of this combination on the basis of a reasonable interpretation of the Covenant.

It must be remembered in this connection that Luxemburg—even if it is of small extent and population[296]—is a completely in-

[293] League of Nations. *Official Journal, Special supplement no. 147 (1936)*, p. 26.

[294] Paul-Boncour: "la question n'est pas réglée par la lettre de M. Stucki."

[295] See, regarding participation of the principality of Liechtenstein in the Swiss system, League of Nations, *op. cit.*, p. 43.

[296] Its area is about 260,000 hectares and population about 300,000.

dependent state with equal rights; as such, it has participated in a number of international conferences[297] and likewise in this capacity[298] has been admitted as a member of the League of Nations.[299] Luxemburg, even during the Middle Ages, had formed an independent duchy, and was reëstablished as such by the Congress of Vienna in 1815; it was again recognized, with a somewhat restricted territory, in the Treaty of London (1839), which at the same time established the independence[300] of Belgium. By the Treaty of London of May 11, 1867,[301] its permanent neutrality was recognized and placed under the collective guarantee of the contracting powers.[302] Between the neutralization of Switzerland and that of Luxemburg there is this essential difference,[303] however, that while the Swiss are independent as to armament and regard a considerable degree of military preparedness as a necessary condition for the maintenance and enforcement of their neutrality *(neutralité armée)*, Luxemburg is restricted in its military defenses[304] by treaty, and takes the stand that she cannot and should not resist foreign military invasion *(neutralité désarmée)*.

In the Treaty of Versailles the abolition of Luxemburg's neutrality was contemplated, but this idea was later dropped.[305] In

[297] Particularly the Hague Conferences of 1899 and 1907, when the law of neutrality was codified.

[298] League of Nations. *Records of the First Assembly. Report of December 10, 1920, of the Fifth Committee of the Assembly:* "Luxembourg est un État independant qui se gouverne librement sous un régime représentatif, selon ses institutions particulières. Il est reconnu par la généralité des États civilisés."

[299] During the World War Luxemburg was occupied by Germany, but was able nevertheless to maintain its neutrality to some extent. For this story, see a very interesting collection of documents published by the Luxemburg Government: "*Neutralité du Grand-Duché pendant la guerre de 1914-1918. Attitude des Pouvoirs Publics.*" Luxemburg, 1919.

[300] Martens, *Nouv. Rec. XVI*, p. 770.

[301] Martens, *Nouv. Rec. Gén.* ser. 1, XVIII, 445; Dupuis, *Le Droit des gens et les rapports des Grandes Puissances avec les autres États*, pp. 216 ff.

[302] Except Belgium, which was itself a neutralized State.

[303] Wehrer, "Le Statut du Luxembourg et la Société des nations," in *Revue Générale, XXXI (1924)*, 181.

[304] Martens, *Nouveau Recueil Générale XVIII*, p. 448-9. The Treaty of 1867, Articles III and V: "que les fortifications de la ville de Luxembourg ne seront pas rétablies à l'avenir, et qu'il n'y sera maintenu ni créé aucun établissement militaire."

[305] Luxemburg itself was not bound by this provision in the Versailles Treaty; see Wehrer, p. 176.

Article XL, section 2, it is provided that Germany gives its consent that the neutralization of the Grand Duchy may be terminated, and that it accepts in advance any international arrangement which the Allied and Associated Powers may make with regard to the Grand Duchy. Luxemburg was not mentioned in the Appendix to the League Covenant as among those states which were to be invited to join the League, but there naturally existed in this small, exposed state a strong desire for that further strengthening of its position which would result from such membership. In a communication[306] dated February 3, 1920, to the Chairman of the Council of the League, the Luxemburg Minister of Foreign Affairs, Reuter, expressed Luxemburg's desire both to enter the League and to retain her position as a permanent neutral. The Council requested Luxemburg to make her application direct to the Assembly, which under Article I, section 2, of the Covenant was empowered to make such a decision. Action was then taken through a report submitted by the Secretary General, which was approved by the Council on May 15, 1920, and which announced itself as favorable to Luxemburg's desires, special emphasis being laid on the fact that Luxemburg's guaranteed neutrality was to continue during a war between members of the League (for example, those under Article XV, section 7, of the Covenant) so long as such neutrality had not been previously abolished by a decision of the Powers.

It is undeniably strange that the Council, which in the Declaration of London of February, 1920, had categorically denied the possibility of combining membership in the League of Nations with neutrality, would so shortly thereafter (in May of the same year, during the meeting in Rome) approve a report which found no difficulty in combining the two systems.

In the Assembly, toward the close of 1920, verbal discussions took place between the Luxemburg delegation and the subcom-

[306] League of Nations, Report of the Secretary-General to the Council in Rome dated May 15, 1920; Enclosure 42, League of Nations, *Publications (Political)*, p. 5: "The guaranteed neutrality of Luxemburg in its existing form under the Treaty of 1867 will, of course, *stand in case of a war*, contemplated in the seventh paragraph of Article XV of the Covenant, between separate members of the League of Nations, as long as no formal decision to the contrary is taken by the Powers."

mittee[307] concerned with its request. These discussions in no way followed the Swiss line of a purely external coupling of the unmodified traditional concept of neutrality with a system of solidarity essentially different from it, but were rather a real attempt to coördinate those elements of both systems, which, because of Luxemburg's exceptional position, were necessary and practicable; "... the Luxemburg Government did not in any way expect to be released from the obligations imposed upon the members of the League of Nations by the terms of Article XVI of the Covenant. It agreed to leave its territory open for the passage of such troops as the Council of the League might authorize; it also consented to participate in retaliatory measures of an economic or financial nature which might be enacted against any State in a state of rebellion against the League. Its only request was that it should not in any way be compelled to participate in military operations which the members of the League might undertake in common, nor to defend its territory by arms against foreign aggression."[308] It did not, on the other hand, request complete disarmament, but was even prepared to increase its armed forces (which at the time consisted of an army of 250 soldiers and 150 gendarmes[309]) to a force of 3,000 men. It was further intended to insert in the Belgian Constitution[310] a new provision reading as follows:

"Neutrality shall however be abandoned for obligations under the Covenant of the League of Nations so long as the Grand Duchy is a member of the League."

What gives to Luxemburg's position special interest for this study is that, at a time when its desires were still the object of consideration in the subcommittee, which was, in a way, inclined to approve them,[311] the Duchy, in a note of November 28, 1920,[312]

307 League of Nations *Records of the First Assembly (1920)*, "Report of the Fifth Committee" (*Document No. 179*) *of December 10, 1920.*

308 *Ibid.*, p. 2 f.

309 The Belgian newspaper *Le Soir* of Nov. 14, 1920.

310 This contained the following declaration: "Le Grand-Duché de Luxembourg forme un État independant, indivisible et inalienable et perpetuellement neutre."

311 League of Nations. *Document No. 179, op. cit.*: "With the general desire to meet the views of Luxemburg as far as possible."

312 The note is published as an annex to League of Nations *Document No. 179.*

to the chairman of the sub-committee, simply withdrew its original request and declared that it had no hesitation in submitting to these common obligations which, under the provisions of the Covenant, might be placed upon the members of the League, including itself, even to the guarantee obligations under Article X of the Covenant.

Luxemburg intended to imply that the obligations in the Covenant contained nothing which conflicted with her neutrality rights and obligations,[313] and the League of Nations gave actual recognition to the correctness of that view when it unanimously accepted Luxemburg as a regular member of the League.

As was explained in detail in its note of November 28, Luxemburg stated that its originally expressed desires were based on an incorrect interpretation of the provisions of the Covenant. These, it said, had been taken too literally and unconditionally. The discussions with the subcommittee and a new study of these provisions had convinced the Luxemburg government that its desire for permanent neutrality was perfectly consistent therewith.[314]

Luxemburg's view of its legal status[315] has since developed in close accord with the ideas underlying the Danish treatise of 1924, and refers to it. The military measures of Article XVI, section 2, of the League Covenant are regarded as being not an independent sanction of a military nature, but rather as an exercise of the police power for the support of the sanctions system, which in turn it understood as being of an economic and financial character. The interpretation, discussed in the treatise of 1924, regarding the right of passage under Article XVI, section 3, has also been adopted by Luxemburg.[316] Participation in sanctions is not conceived to

313 When Luxemburg at the end of this note announced that it would be forced to make certain changes in its Constitution, it later proved (in the exchange of notes, June-July 1922) that this was to be done only upon formal ratification of its admission. There have been no amendments however made to the provisions of the Luxemburg Constitution with regard to its neutrality.

314 League of Nations. *Document No. 179, op. cit., Annex 1:* "In fact, there appears to be no doubt that the idea upon which this reservation was based is perfectly in accordance with the obligations contained in the Covenant."

315 Wehrer, "Sécurité et arbitrage au Luxembourg," in *Revue de Droit International, XIII (1932)*, 331: "La compatibilité du maintien de la politique de neutralité avec les obligations de Membre de la Société des nations."

316 *Ibid.*, p. 342.

be a military action contrary to neutrality, but is the result of a pacific and peace-preserving purpose. It has been approved in advance by the League member against whom it is directed[317] and, on the contrary, cannot be exercised by any member without its own individual and prior consent. Before this consent can be regarded as having been granted, the individual League member is entitled to consider the state of its own military, geographical, and political conditions and, if the situation requires it, to refuse to participate for those reasons. This was expressly recognized by the League Council in 1925, when Germany was admitted to the League, just as it was expressed in the famous Appendix F to the Locarno treaties.[318] The principles of permanent neutrality are accordingly quite consistent with the provisions of the Covenant of the League.

6. In the sanctions against Italy in 1935-36, Luxemburg participated in the same manner as did the rest of the League members except that she placed the two belligerents upon an equal footing with respect to export prohibitions, because of her neutrality policy,[319] which agrees with the expedient suggested in the Danish treatise of 1924. It is notable that Luxemburg, in her reply, did not consider it necessary to plead her special rights and duties under the treaty of 1867, but was content to refer simply to her neutrality *policy*. This accords well with the basic position of Luxemburg (and the treatise of 1924), according to which the laws of neutrality and neutrality policy are regarded as consistent with the sanction obligations under Article XVI of the Covenant of the League, and by which any state is entitled to consider her

[317] *Ibid.*, p. 335.

[318] *Ibid.*, p. 337: "Est-il besoin de relever que si un pareil régime d'exemption peut être appliqué à un puissant État comme l'Allemagne, il va sans dire qu'un petit État comme la Luxembourg pour lequel toute participation à une guerre entre ses voisins équivaudrait a l'anéantissement, peut le revendiquer comme une mesure de justice et d'équité?

"Et d'autres petits États ne seront-ils pas dans la même situation? Le Conseil de la Société des nations pourrait-il demander, au cas ou de puissants États militaires en viendraient aux mains, qu'un petit État voisin prît partie pour l'un des belligérants ou lui ouvrît son territoire pour mieux pouvoir attaquer l'adversaire?"

[319] League of Nations, *Official Journal, Special Supplement No. 155* (1936), p. 188. The Luxemburg Government's note of October 26, 1935: "In view of the policy of neutrality of the Grand-Duchy, the Grand-Ducal Decree will not discriminate between the belligerents."

individual geographical and political limitations in carrying out these obligations. During the discussions in the Committee of Eighteen (Comité des dix-huit) regarding replies from the various governments, the Prime Minister of Luxemburg, Bech, on November 2, 1935, made the following statement:[320]

> The Judicial Sub-Committee has referred in its report to the fact that Luxemburg, in applying Proposal I [the arms embargo] has not discriminated between the belligerents. The attitude of the Luxemburg government is in accordance with the traditional policy of my country with its regime of perpetual neutrality which was established in 1867 in the interests of European peace and the principles of which are inscribed in our Constitution.... This policy which is necessitated by the unique geographical and military situation of the Grand-Duchy, thus remains within the guiding lines so often laid down in the Assembly and the Council, in accordance with which each state is bound to co-operate in the collective action in so far as its geographical situation and special position of armaments permit. On the admission of Luxemburg to the League of Nations in 1920, the Assembly recognized the special conditions existing in my country.[321]
>
> This constitutional tradition of its external policy does not prevent the Government of my country from carrying out the obligations contained in the Covenant in so far as these do not conflict with its special situation. Consequently, in spite of the bonds of friendship which unite us to Italy and in spite of the very heavy sacrifices which our co-operation places upon our national economy, we have adhered to the other proposals of the Co-ordination Committee.
>
> The Luxemburg Government thus brings to the collective measures of peace loyal co-operation dictated solely by the principles of the Covenant.

By the latter phrase ("dictated solely by the principles of the Covenant") the fact is once more emphasized that the question is not one of a mere external coördination of two essentially different systems, but of an internal combination of two necessary efforts to reach a satisfactory solution which would not be in conflict with, but, on the contrary is presupposed in the Covenant. In the Com-

320 League of Nations. *Official Journal, Special Supplement no. 146 (1936)*, p. 42.

321 Since Luxemburg withdrew these reservations and was thereupon admitted to the League as is any other member, one must here assume a tacit approval of her position, as stated above.

mittee this declaration by Luxemburg was not the occasion of further discussion.

Concepts of Neutrality following the Collapse of Sanctions In the Italo-Ethiopian Conflict

1. The sanctions against Italy, 1935-36, did not lead to the desired result, but occasioned, on the contrary, a series of official repeals of laws by individual League members,[322] which resulted in the greatest defeat that League policy has so far suffered. It was, however, in no way proved or even indicated as probable that economic sanctions would be unable to stop war. It was obvious to everyone, on the contrary, and likewise easily proved statistically,[323] that even the "mild" sanctions which were applied caused a serious decrease in Italy's international balance of trade, and if carried out over a somewhat longer period, would have brought Italy to her knees. It is therefore apparent that this economic weapon, applied to the full extent contemplated in the provisions of Article XVI, section 1, of the Covenant, would have quickly put an end to the war. It is further easily shown that it was not the unsuitability of the sanction measures, but rather some entirely alien and irrelevant factors, combined with special interests in the policies of certain Great Powers and especially the completely devastating influence which the Hoare-Laval peace proposal[324] of December 10, 1935, had upon public opinion in all countries, which eventually resulted in Italy's triumph. We shall have to learn, perhaps, to accept this defeat, and if it be possible, to do so without indignation, since indignation, according to Bismarck's well-known saying ("*Entrüstung kein politischer Begriff*"), is not always good politics. One thing is certain, however, and that is that it will of necessity create a renewed recognition of the con-

[322] See the *Danish Proclamations, Nos. 172, 173 and 174 of July 14, 1936*. Denmark, Statutes (*Lovtidende*, pp. 955 ff.).

[323] See especially League of Nations, *General Publications*, 1936, p. 4. "Statistics of Trade with Italy and Italian Colonies." III, Geneva, April-June, 1936, Co-ordination Committee No. 125, also "How sanctions failed," in *Foreign Affairs* (*New York, 1936*), *XV*, 360 ff.

[324] Issued by the Secretary-General of the League on the 13th of the same month (League of Nations, *Document C. 482. M. 258. 1935. VII*).

stant vitality, value, and need of neutrality. Of all forms of participation in the efforts to prevent war, that one is the worst which turns over the League and its institutions to the Great Powers, to serve their own policies, making them interested in sanctions just so long as they can oppose the aims of a rival state by coercive measures and then to call off these sanctions when they see the advantage of supporting that state. If sanctions are not to be used solely for the object of impartial prevention of war, it is made very difficult for the smaller states to participate. While the larger states can readily come to agreement after the end of sanctions and have all necessary conditions for the reëstablishment of trade relations with the former Covenant-breaker, it may easily happen that the smaller countries, or a few of them, are left to pay the piper, since the Covenant-breaker may throw the weight of his resentment particularly against them.

There were many indications, too, following the collapse of sanctions during the Italian-Ethiopian conflict, that the concept of neutrality had come back into fashion, even if this has led to no new plan for coördination. Those states which had remained neutral during the World War (the "ex-neutrals") were becoming better acquainted, and the expressions, "the neutrals," and "the ex-neutrals" are now heard on the floor of the Assembly without that same irritation or annoyance which had been customary. The most recent developments have led to the entire rehabilitation of the concept of neutrality.

2. The League Assembly on July 4, 1936, expressed its desire that the Council should issue invitations to the various governments to make proposals for improvement in the enforcement of the principles of the Covenant. The ex-neutrals had already conferred upon this question, and on the first of that month had issued a *communiqué* in which they made a certain reservation in Article XVI of the Covenant, which can only be regarded as aiming at coördination of sanctions with the neutrality system. These ex-neutrals, for diplomatic reasons, did not use the true description, *i.e.*, the use of the system of sanctions to further the special interests of particular world policies They merely declared, instead, that in their opinion it was useless to apply some

of the provisions of the Covenant, namely the ones concerning sanctions, and then at the same time to permit others, such as disarmament, to go unused; that "so long as the Covenant as a whole is applied only incompletely and inconsistently, we are obliged to bear that fact in mind when Article XVI is to be applied." [325] The idea advanced is that sanctions are not sufficiently effective so long as a single state, and especially the aggressor, possesses large armaments.

This viewpoint is, however, not quite pertinent, and, as we have suggested, did not touch upon the real difficulty. From a legal standpoint, it is debatable whether the obligations assumed under the Covenant are not mutually interdependent, and the necessary authority for making reservations is lacking,[326] particularly where there exists a non-enforcement of a "promise" clause like that of Article VIII, where these provisions concerning disarmament are found to be merely a dream of the future with maximum reservations. Furthermore, the argument is not pertinent to this situation. It was not armaments which caused the failure of sanctions against Italy. No use was made of military sanctions at all, and economic sanctions might have been pushed further, regardless of Italy's military strength. In the last resort, the powerful armaments of an aggressor would not hinder the application of military sanctions when the states participating in the sanctions may be assumed to have armaments as great or greater; it is a question of proportion and not of the enforcement or nonenforcement of general disarmament, which under no circumstances at any time in the near future can be counted upon to render a Great Power defenseless against the joint action of the other countries.

By the particular direction which has been given to this trend of thought, the real difficulty has been veiled, that is, that political interests and international politics, by their very nature, cannot be kept out of so important and fateful a step as that of the univer-

[325] Denmark, Finland, Netherlands, Norway, Spain, Sweden and Switzerland ("declaration of the seven Foreign Ministers"); see *League Document C.376.M. 247. 1936. VII*, p. 22, and footnote 326 *infra*.

[326] See also Article I of the Covenant according to which there have not been and cannot be any reservations made with respect to its separate provisions; further see Møller in *Nordisk Tidsskrift for International Ret* (1936), p. 232.

sal boycott of a state. It is therefore of the utmost importance that such action shall not create any obligation or danger for the states participating, especially where the smaller states are being involved in military complications; in other words, they must maintain the possibility of preserving a neutral attitude toward interests and aims which are not theirs and are not in every case objective war-prevention measures in the service of the general preservation of peace. It is for each individual participating state to decide whether it could or could not, in any particular situation, assist in war-prevention, without at the same time assuming an unwarranted share in the risk, to the detriment of its own interests, while supporting the selfish interests of other states (their colonial policy, the economic or political *status quo*, and the like); they must adopt, in other words, a policy of combination of both neutrality and solidarity.

Fresh incentives for such coördination can hardly be found in the replies which the governments made respecting suggested amendments [327] to Article XVI made in accord with the Assembly's invitation. When Esthonia and Iraq proposed [328] that a prior study be made and detailed information be given by each state as to the extent of its expected assistance in the enforcement of sanctions, it was soon recognized that this would doubtless be an almost impossible task, since much would depend upon the question of which state the sanctions were to be applied to. Norway and Sweden [329] supported the view of the *communiqué*. The Norwegian Government [330] announced that

> "we are not entitled to expect that the various members will be very willing to comply with a Council recommendation . . . [concerning participation in military sanctions] so long as they are obliged to reckon with a situation in which the aggressor State will be strong enough to defy the whole power of the League . . . it is only natural that many States should make the reservations regarding participation in sanctions which the Foreign Ministers of several States, including mine, communicated to the Press on July 1st last." [331]

[327] League of Nations, *Publications VII. Political, Document C.376.M.247.1936. VII*, p. 21. "Application of the Principles of the Covenant," Geneva, Sept. 17, 1936.

[328] *Ibid.* [329] *Ibid.*, p. 22.

[330] *Ibid.*; see also Koht, *Neutrality and Peace*, pp. 287 ff.

[331] League of Nations. *Doc.C.376.M.247.1936. VII, op. cit.*, p. 22.

Argentina believed that the sanctions provisions should be given an optional character,[332] instead of being unconditionally binding. Peru expressed a definite neutrality trend when it said that "in case of a conflict in which a country has no direct practical interest, public opinion in that country is apt to object to being obliged to take part in collective action which it does not regard as having any political utility or any moral necessity superior to its own necessity of self-preservation in all its various aspects." [333] It was of particular interest to note that Switzerland had gone over to the side of ordinary neutrality, instead of emphasizing her own exceptional position; it held that sanctions had not been applied equally in all cases. In its communication to the general secretariat Switzerland says: "They have been applied in some cases and not in others, and there are clear cases in which they never could be applied.... Although the obligations assumed by each party are theoretically identical, their effects differ greatly according to whether they apply to a Great Power or to a country with more limited resources.... For a small country the application of Article XVI may be a matter of life or death.... Switzerland cannot be held to sanctions which, in their very nature and through their effects, would seriously endanger her neutrality." [334]

Definitely neutral viewpoints, similar to those put forward by the northern countries as long ago as the League's first Assembly, were also to be noted in the following statements from Peru and Soviet Russia respectively. Sanctions, says Peru

> are recommended only to such States as can put them into effective operation. It is absurd and harmful to international relations to insist on sanctions being applied by States which, owing to the small extent of their trade or financial relations with the Covenant-breaking State, or to their geographical remoteness, cannot cause it any trouble, but whose attitude can provoke an undesirable moral tension.[335]

[332] Other countries, such as Colombia, Esthonia, and New Zealand, on the contrary, attached great importance to the *automatic* commencement of sanctions. See *ibid.*, p. 23.

[333] *Ibid.*, p. 23.

[334] League of Nations, *Application of the Principles of the Covenant of the League of Nations, Publications VII. Political. 1936. VII. 9*, p. 25. "Communications from Governments."

[335] League of Nations. *Official Journal. Special Supplement, no. 154.* "Documents Relating to the Question of the Application of the Principles of the Covenant," p. 28.

Soviet Russia proposed that the Council, where it is necessary to insure common action, or in order to limit the losses involved for certain League members, might decide that certain of the duties under Article XVI, section 1, might be entirely or in part, omitted with regard to particular states.

To a still greater degree, a number of countries took further exception to all military sanctions,[336] as well as to the idea that these should be of a compulsory character. Peru proposed simply that such provisions be "struck out of the Covenant." [337] It should at most be a question of a state, upon its own request, receiving permission to defend the obligations of the Covenant in such manner. "This would increase the sense of direct responsibility in such countries, and it would not be possible for them to desire to set collective action in motion for the benefit of their private ends," [338] an utterance which lacks neither present interest nor address.

The theory of aggression was expressly referred to by several states,[339] who regarded it as being of much importance to secure an agreement upon a definition of the concepts "aggressor," "resort to war," and the like. Argentina, on the contrary, asserted that "the previous determination of the aggressor, in each case and according to circumstances, should be laid down as a condition of all sanctions." [340]

[336] League of Nations, "Application of the Principles of the Covenant of the League of Nations, Study of Proposals Submitted," *Publication no. C.376.M.247. 1936. VII*, p. 25. [337] *Ibid.*, p. 26. [338] *Ibid.*, p. 28.

[339] *Ibid.*, Lithuania, Esthonia, Latvia, and Iraq. [340] *Ibid.*, p. 29.

III
NEUTRALITY AND THE CLASSIFICATION OF WAR

Distinctions According to Different Points of View

1. THE POLICY of participating in efforts for the prevention of war but not to the degree of participating in war itself faces its first difficulty in the question of the classification of war, that is, in a statement of the diversity of kinds of war and their consequently different evaluation. Some would distinguish [1] between wars of aggression and defensive wars, legal and illegal wars, just and unjust wars, religious wars, colonial wars, wars of reprisal, punitive expeditions, and similar classifications. The distinction between war of aggression and defensive war plays a prominent part not only in the sanctions system [2] of the Covenant of the League, but also in other more recent war-prevention agreements and "pacts," such as the Locarno Treaty,[3] the Kellogg Pact,[4] and the Saavedra Lamas Treaty,[5] the very foundation of which rests on this distinction. In other proposals and agreements, efforts have been made to determine and to define further distinctions between the different kinds of wars, especially with regard to the difference between wars of aggression and defense, as witness the Geneva Protocol of 1924 and the Convention of London of July 3, 1933. Closely connected with the question of the different classification of wars, is, of course, the question of the different causes of war.[6] Some of these

[1] Oppenheim, II, 185, which incorrectly states that "the rules of the Law of Nations are the same for the different kinds of war that may be distinguished"; Bonfils-Fauchille, II, 9 ff.; Liszt, pp. 450 ff.; Moore, *Digest of International Law*, VII, 155 ff.

[2] Cohn, *Kriegsverhütung und Schuldfrage*, pp. 104 ff.

[3] Article II: Prohibition against wars of aggression, but a right to defensive war.

[4] See further "Kellogg-Pagtens retlige Betydning," in *Juridisk Tidsskrift*, 1929, pp. 38 ff.

[5] Article I (condemning wars of aggression only).

[6] Bonfils, II, 10 ff., who has made no more effort than the above authors to present any systematic statement of the causes of war, but who says, "Les

are said to be more entitled to sympathy or "understanding" than are others. In some cases it may be a question of maintaining the prestige of a race, as of the white race; in other cases it may be as reprisal for an affront. Sometimes there may be need for expansion because of over-population; in other cases it may be the lack of raw materials which drives a nation to war. We next come to unattained "historical" rights, real or imagined, expressions of psychological inferiority complexes,[7] the need to divert internal disorder or dissatisfaction, preventive wars aimed to anticipate the outbreak of a war at a later and less favorable moment, and many others.

If we so evaluate war in its varied forms and then find considerable legal difference between, for example, wars of aggression and wars of defense, or between raw-material wars and prestige wars, we shall be led easily to the conviction that the attitude of states outside the controversy must also be similarly classified, for such states should in certain cases intervene, but in other cases are justified in regarding the dispute as none of their affair. The entire situation is then in advance rather unfavorable to the spirit of neutrality. So it was with the founders of modern international law, such as Grotius, Vattel and others. They looked upon the classification of war as a basis for distinguishing between those in which outside states should remain neutral and those in which they should not. That middle course in which states should work to end the war itself and, to the best of their ability, support a just cause without taking part in war themselves, never came under the consideration of those writers, as if they assumed that the efforts of states in the service of international justice had to express themselves exclusively in the form of war. There was next injected the notion

causes de guerre sont aussi variés, aussi multiples que sont variés et multiples les rapports entre États"; see also Strupp, *Wörterbuch,* III, 963: "Rechtlich irrelevant sind die vielfach gemachten Einteilungen in die verschiedensten Arten von Kriegen." As it appears from the text, however, the differences are in no sense without legal significance.

[7] See the statement of the Norwegian Prime Minister Kolstad in 1931 on the Greenland question, according to the Oslo "*Aftenposten*" of Sept. 7, 1931: "Much is being said about complexes these days. Repressed complexes. It is something which stores itself up in the minds of individuals. It has something to do with memories of the past. If this is true, may there not be such complexes also in the memories of a people," etc.

of morality, similar to that of the domestic circle or of small communities, applied to the domain of international law; hence it became morally wrong, and therefore wrong under international law, not to aid an innocent victim of aggression and especially to support the aggressor; only in cases where the question of guilt was doubtful should a state be permitted to remain outside the controversy.

That this point of view was abandoned under the régime of traditional neutrality was due to a number of economic, political, and military factors, and especially to the rapid development of all these forces together during the nineteenth century. The attempt to create a common front of moral and political indignation [8] against the wars of the French Revolution and the later Napoleonic wars, led to no lasting results ("the Holy Alliance"). The world was vast in those days, and interests were varied and incalculable. There was much to be done in Asia (India), Africa, and America. Young new states, just released from the burdens of absolute monarchy or of a colonial status, first sought the development of their own economic and cultural life. Distances were still great; commercial and cultural relations, measured by those of today, were slight, and peoples had little knowledge of each other.

In international relations, liberty and independence were regarded as the supreme good which led to the doctrines of nonintervention and neutrality. In international law there existed a parallel with the Manchester school of economic philosophy, and with Darwinism in the field of science. In a time which must seem a Golden Age to people of the present day, the feeling of international solidarity had as yet had no opportunity to unfold itself, at any rate not in the field of war-prevention.

[8] Schmidt-Phiseldek, *Darstellung des Dänischen Neutralitätssistemes,* I, 63 and 148 ff.; Count Bernstorff's famous note of July 28, 1793, with its attached mémoire, expressive of classical neutrality in its purest form: "Une guerre peut certainement différer de l'autre par ses motifs, par son but, par sa nécessité, par sa justice ou son injustice; cela peut être de la plus grande importance pour les parties belligérantes: cela peut et doit influer sur la paix, sur les dédommagements, sur toutes les considérations accessoires, mais cela ne regarde absolument pas les Puissances neutres. Elles s'intéresseront sans doute pour celles, qui ont la justice de leur côté, mais elles n'ont pas le droit d'écouter ce sentiment; la neutralité n'existe plus, dès qu'elle n'est pas parfaite."

This Golden Age suddenly collapsed during the World War, at the beginning of the twentieth century. But out of the horrors of the World War there was born the hope and the idea of an international solidarity with regard to the prevention of future wars. The hope and the idea were one thing; their practical or technical application was something quite different. The nations stood with no past experience to guide them. Many conflicting interests and many more misunderstandings and mistakes led to the compromise which found its ultimate expression in the war-prevention system of the League of Nations. The World War had been fought under the watchword of the awful guilt of the adversary.[9] The demand for the punishment of this adversary prevailed over everything else, and found its expression in those documents by which the war was ended.[10] Never before had a world-wide propaganda aroused passions to such a degree as in that war. It was therefore natural, indeed inevitable, that the new law of war-prevention should have its roots in those conditions—the moral and legal duty of participating in the great struggle against aggression. And so a new system with new principles was born. These ideas, in a sense, go back to the founders of the older international law, to those of Grotius and Vattel: no neutrality toward aggression.

2. If we accept the idea of the classification of war, the next question logically is: which are the wars, or reasons for war, or causes of war, which call for the intervention of outside states, and which are not? We thus arrive at the technical and practical problems involved in carrying out the classification which is to validate the principle.

Some writers would separate the various causes and reasons for war into such categories as those wars which are permissible or those which are at least excusable; all other wars would be classed as unjust and as such prohibited. This would be a distinction of a material nature. In like manner classification of a material and formal nature might be made—an intermediate position—by which it would be a matter of the distinction between just or unjust war, or of a still more formal distinction—that between wars

[9] Cohn, *Kriegsverhütung und Schuldfrage*, p. 19.
[10] *Treaty of Versailles*, Articles, 222, 227 ff., 231 ff.

of aggression and wars of defense. Finally we may associate these distinctions with purely formal criteria, where even the question of right and wrong, or of aggression and defense, becomes unessential. If these purely formal criteria—for example, the omission of a certain procedure such as waiting a certain time—are established, a duty of intervention may be created for the members of the League. Otherwise, they may remain neutral, even though ordinary moral and legal considerations argue strongly for one or the other party.

The system of the League Covenant cannot be designated as the expression of any one of these methods, but acknowledges, to some degree, its debt to all of them. It classifies wars sometimes by their causes, as just or unjust, sometimes as aggressive or defensive, and, finally, by fixed formal criteria. But it did not attribute to these various classifications the same importance. It must be remembered that the Covenant is not the expression of a single system of war-prevention. It contains a more general system of a preventive nature which is expressed in a number of rules of law, or in other cases, by a number of points of procedure for future regulation. There is also a more specific system of prevention which is to go into effect when war threatens to break out or has broken out. Thus there is ample room for many different classifications of wars and for their consideration under various groupings.

In the first place, the system of the League Covenant takes into consideration a number of different *causes of war* which it attempts to obviate more or less energetically. A cause of war toward which the system is sympathetic—one is almost tempted to say recognizes—is that which has its source in social privation and misery and wide differences in the living conditions of the working classes in the various countries. Part XIII of the Versailles Treaty lays down a comprehensive socio-political program, after asserting that the "present working conditions involve such injustice, hardship and privation to large numbers of people as to produce unrest so great that the peace and harmony of the world are imperilled."

Another type of war which the Covenant certainly regards

as justifiable is the war of execution. The circumstances presupposed in this case are that one party to an arbitral settlement refuses to comply with the award when the decision has gone against it. What is then to be done by the injured party except to assert its rights by armed force, that is, through war? And so it is stated in Article XIII, section 4, of the Covenant, that the members of the League agree not to resort to war against any other League member who complies with the award of arbitrators. Against a member who does not so comply, war is permissible.

Causes of war which receive recognition in the Covenant are those for the maintenance of international law and order and for national defense. The justice of both is assumed, as a matter of course in Article VIII, section 1, and in Article XVI. By characterizing a breach of the Covenant as an act of war against all the other members of the League, Article XVI, section 1, gave to each member the express authority to commence war against the Covenant-breaker without further formalities, even in cases where sanctions (for instance, economic) might attain the desired result without a state of war. Although the first part of that Article appears to set up purely formal criteria for the commencement of sanctions, it is certain, nonetheless, that these are intended to strike only at the "aggressor" who "resorts to war," and not at the "defender" who does likewise. That defensive war is justified, even to a certain degree regarded as necessary before the assistance of the League can be invoked, was asserted on several occasions; for example, in the discussions over the Geneva Protocol of 1924.[11] It is aggressive and not defensive war, which the Assembly resolution of September 24, 1927 stamped as an international crime.

[11] See the commentary prepared by Beneš and Politis, printed as an annex to the *Report of the Danish delegation to the Rigsdag, 1924* (p. 51), in which Article VIII of the Covenant is so interpreted that it is "recognized as being a duty to protect the national security of members of the League and to do this not only by the maintenance of the necessary minimum of armed force," and so forth; (see p. 56 f.): "without waiting for support ... it may *and should* immediately defend itself with its own resources. ... On this point there can be no doubt." The same idea was assumed as a general rule during the discussions regarding the admission of Luxemburg to the League, as that country desired to be expressly excused from the duty of self-defense ("n'être point tenu de ... défendre son territoire par les armes contre une agression extérieure"); League of Nations, *Report of the 5th Committee of Dec. 10, 1920 (179)*. (Our italics.)

The Locarno and Saavedra Lamas Treaties and the Kellogg Pact were all concerned, as we have mentioned before, with wars of aggression. Defensive war was justified as necessary and even as praiseworthy.

3. Although the League Covenant in such cases does not deny to war its high esteem, there are other situations where it recognizes, without extending actual justification, that it would be impossible to prevent its occurrence. This is true, for instance, of the more serious race conflicts, which have found expression particularly in the immigration legislation of America, Australia, and elsewhere. At the Peace Conference, Japan voiced its demand for the fundamental equality of the rights of all races. But this could not be granted, as it met with opposition from Great Britain and also from America.[12]

It may seem surprising that such a proposal, made by a country which not only had become a Great Power long before, but was already laying its plans for a Japanese empire of the world, and which had just participated in the World War on the side of the Allied Powers, could not be complied with on that occasion. But right here prejudice overcame intelligence. Article XV, section 8, of the Covenant provides that no power on earth is to meddle with questions which one of the parties claims, and which the Council recognizes, as being solely within the domestic jurisdiction of that party; the Council then dare not even make proposals for the settlement of the question, but must refrain from comment.[13] So there exists in this situation another cause of war which

[12] Miller, *The Drafting of the Covenant,* I, 293 ff. (Viscount Ishii's Speech in New York of March 14, 1919); Schücking-Wehberg (3d ed.) I, 135 ff., on Baron Makino's proposal of Feb. 13, 1919, which expressly referred to race differences as one of the most dangerous causes of war. The proposal was opposed by Robert Cecil and rejected by 17 votes to 11. In the first Assembly, 11th plenary session, the Japanese delegate Ishii once more stated Japan's desire "que l'égalité devant la loi serait accordée à tous les hommes sans considération de nationalité, de race ou de religion," and that the Japanese Government and people "ont vivement regretté que les premiers rédacteurs du Pacte se soient trouvés incapables d'accepter la proposition japonaise sur cette question."

[13] ". . . shall make no recommendations as to its settlement." This provision, moreover, is in direct conflict with those in Article XI of the Covenant in which *any* threat of war gives to the League, and in particular to the League Council which is to be summoned forthwith, the authorization to take *any* action which may be deemed wise and effectual to safeguard the peace of nations. For

eludes the methods of the Covenant and which must eventually be settled by armed force.[14]

Other causes of war are to be found in the so-called "secret diplomacy" and in the unregulated private manufacture and sale of armaments. The Covenant endeavors to cope with the former problem—to a quite insufficient degree, however—through the rule in Article XVIII requiring the prompt publication of international agreements. The latter problem of private manufacture and sale of armaments is treated rather lightly in the Covenant (Article VIII, section 5), since there was rather apparent concern for those members of the League who are unable to produce munitions and implements of war for themselves in sufficient quantities.

There are, of course, many other causes of war, and consequently, various classifications of war.[15] The Covenant has been unable to give consideration to all of them, as it would lead us too far afield. In some instances it has presumably been restrained by political and similar considerations, as, for example, the problem of the distribution of raw materials,[16] or that of the legal status of national minorities. But a clear recognition of the dynamic character of the causes of war convinces us that the Covenant never intended to abolish war in all instances, indeed not even in a majority of them. On the contrary, it starts out with the idea that war is lawful, if the formal procedure outlined in the Covenant has been observed in advance by the parties. Apart from a few exceptional cases of absolute war prohibition, the war-prevention system of the Covenant consists of its enforcement of a waiting period, a "moratorium," in which the forces for the preservation of peace in the society of states may have an opportunity to express themselves. If this does not lead to the desired result, the

further reference see Kunz, *Die intrasystematische Stellung des Art. XI des Völkerbundpaktes*, p. 62, who believes that the special provisions of Article XV, section 8, cannot serve to limit the general provisions of Article XI, section 1.

[14] For an interpretation of this provision, see Cohn, *Neutralité et Société des nations*, pp. 168 ff., and Haase, *Wandlung des Neutralitätsbegriffes*, p. 58.

[15] See Melamed, *Theorie, Ursprung und Geschichte der Friedensidee*, pp. 26 ff.; Lacombe (four causes: economic, genetic, prestige, and sympathetic); Novicow (five causes: physiologic, economic, genetic, political, and intellectual); Lagorgette (three causes: impulsive, special, and general); and others.

[16] For more upon this question, see *Raw Materials and Colonies*, publication No. 18 of The Royal Institute of International Affairs, London, 1936.

permission to make war exists, as under the former rules of international law.

4. The possibilities of neutrality within such a system of war-prevention have, in the League Covenant as in traditional international law, been stated only from the position of their relation to war. When the neutrals made trouble about this, they were told that if they did so it was because they lacked the moral and legal qualifications which the new legal system expected of its members.[17] This legalization of war occasioned further dislike of the non-participant. The very concept of the neutral position as that of the passive rôle of a spectator, without an independent value, created the demand that the neutrals, too, must bear their share of the burden and take part in the struggle. This moral demand became, within that system of law, a legal duty.

In this manner the spirit of war still asserted itself in the new international law. Neutrality and nonparticipation were to be accorded no independent status. Only from the standpoint of an armed opposition to war were they to be considered at all.[18] All neutrality's other objectives, especially its preservation of the peace, health, and existence of millions of people, saving generations from moral and economic collapse, and the like, are ignored.

[17] It is these reproaches which, in different forms, have been directed at the neutrals from the very establishment of the League up to the present moment; see among others, Ray, *Commentaire*, etc., p. 534; Gonsiorowski, *Société des nations et problème de la paix*, II, 420 ff.; Politis, *La Neutralité et la paix*, p. 121 f.; the report of the Belgian delegate Rolin in the Assembly of 1929; Cohn, *Kriegsverhütung und Schuldfrage*, p. 175.

[18] This is clearly expressed in the original Swedish proposals for amendments to the provisions for the application of economic sanctions, which they believed should be based upon the individual vital interests of the neutral state applying them ("... Members of the League which, from smallness of their resources and their geographical position, might be in serious danger if they carried out to the full their obligations under the first paragraph of Article XVI") and which were given in the Resolutions of 1921, wherein great importance is attached to the need of granting special privileges to such countries in their application of sanctions. See League of Nations, Assembly. *Records of the First Assembly, Plenary Meetings* (1920), p. 394; also *Records of the Second Assembly, Plenary Meetings* (1921), p. 436; see also various meetings of the Committee during 1921 and the Resolutions in League of Nations, *Document A. 14. 1927. V.* Reports and Resolutions on the Subject of Article XVI of the Covenant, for numerous references.

The neutrals must, at all events, be forced into the war. By cheap pseudo-moral considerations, prepared and inflated by an elaborate and cunning use of political propaganda, the public, which is without first-hand and reliable knowledge of the motives and influences actually working behind the scenes, is to be stirred up to regard one of the parties as pure and innocent and the other as the blackest of criminals, and on the strength of this mental bias to sacrifice the lives, the health, the peace, and the welfare of its people to the Moloch of war.

It is obvious that any honest system of peace preservation must approach the matter from the opposite—in other words, from the neutral's—viewpoint. The initial aim must be the preservation of peace and it is the security of trade and other relations of the neutrals, which under all circumstances, must be protected. War, on the other hand, must be seen as the irrational and worthless thing which it really is. There will naturally exist always for neutrals the clear-cut humane obligation to contribute according to their means to prevent the outbreak of war, but their first and most important duty, after all, must be to keep their own people out of war and to try to preserve peace and normal international life to its broadest possible extent.

If the belligerents were now to approach the neutrals and demand the latter's participation in the war, such action could be justified only from two viewpoints: first, they might assume the position that what they mean to abolish through international cooperation is war itself; second, they could assert that the concept of war is no longer to be recognized as a legal one and that therefore the question of neutrality no longer exists, but only one of a common front against international violence, which would henceforth be classified and regarded as are homicide, theft, robbery, and similar crimes. Under such conditions the surrender of neutrality would have some moral and internationally legal foundation. Such views had been advanced at the end of the World War as arguments to persuade the neutrals to join the new system; [19] they also underlay the American movement for the *outlawry* of war,

[19] Cohn, *Kriegsverhütung*, p. 32.

at least in its original form, namely the abolition of neutrality *as a consequence of the abolition of war.*[20]

Even if the neutral countries would not go so far, but on the other hand should insist upon the classification of the various kinds of war in such manner that some should be recognized as legal in international law while others should be prohibited, one could nevertheless consider that the idea of outlawry was inherent. Since the wars to be prohibited thereafter would thereby be deprived of their internationally legal character, including all the rights which international law had formerly conferred upon belligerents, there might, even within this restricted category of prohibited wars, be justification for demanding from the neutrals their participation, for the very reason that if the laws of war no longer applied to the situation, then the laws of neutrality were likewise inapplicable. What the neutrals had gained in that case would be that war itself had been abolished, at least within that limited sphere where their coöperation in a solidary front could be required.

As we know, the system of the Covenant of the League is the expression of neither the one nor the other of these two views. Neither the abolition of war nor its general outlawry was there in question.[21] On the contrary, war is not only tolerated by the Covenant, it is even recognized there as an important factor in international relations of the future. Even within that restricted field in which a particular war is to be regarded as unlawful and to be fought with sanctions, war as an institution is recognized in its traditional international-law sense as conferring upon the belligerents[22] all of those rights formerly connected with it. In other words, in the Covenant, the abolition of neutrality is *not a consequence of the abolition of war*, even within its limited sphere of prohibited wars. The abolition of neutrality may thus be re-

[20] Morrison, *The Outlawry of War* (p. 29), "War must be outlawed and declared a crime by international agreement"; (p. 215), "This phrase, 'outlawry of aggressive war,' has had a deceptive and confusing influence upon public understanding . . . it means just one thing and that is *nothing*"; (p. 294), "The *outlawry* of war is not the same as the bare *renunciation* of war."

[21] The same holds true of the Kellogg Pact; see the Article by Cohn, "Kellogg-Pagtens retlige Betydning," in *Juridisk Tidsskrift*, 1929, pp. 52 ff.

[22] Cohn, *Kriegsverhütung*, p. 66.

garded merely as a *means for the prevention of war*[23] within the sanctions system. It is required of neutrals that they shall offer themselves as participants in those particular wars, while they may remain neutral in others.

In this way the problem of the classification of war becomes of the utmost importance. It is not only a question of determining which war is so serious in comparison with others that sufficient reason may be advanced for neutrals to take the far-reaching steps which abolish their neutrality; it is also a question of ascertaining clear and definite criteria for classification of the different kinds of war, so that a quick decision may be made as to when the obligations commence and when they do not. Both problems present difficulties which are anything but insignificant.

Four Main Categories for Classification

1. When we turn to the four categories of classification of wars suggested above: (1) according to causes; (2) just and unjust; (3) aggression and defense; and (4) violations of formal criteria, it will be seen that the first named category is not very well adapted as a standard and therefore has not been used in the Covenant system. It would be very difficult to draw a line separating the differing causes of war, which would determine the duty of neutrals as to participation. Article XV, section 8, of the Covenant rests upon the supposition that some of the most important causes of war, such as the race problem, or the distribution of raw materials, are insoluble, so that the Council of the League itself is powerless in such cases, and it would therefore be unreasonable to require of the neutrals their intervention in the war. In other cases the Covenant has only temporarily and not definitely precluded the possibility of war, and it is then only natural for the neutrals to ask why they should abandon their neutrality to prevent war for a short period, when such action will not prevent the same war being commenced with complete legality upon the expiration of that time. The system, in other words, is too frail

[23] Carnovale, *Only by the Abolition of Neutrality Can Wars Be Quickly and Forever Prevented*, Chicago, 1922.

to support such far-reaching and dangerous measures upon the part of the neutrals.

If any distinctions are to be drawn between the various causes of war, we must decide whether such classification is to be made subsequent to the (*objective*) threats to world peace, or after the (*subjective*) determination of the war to be unjustifiable from political, legal, or moral viewpoints. This would require a very delicate weighing, for which there are practically no objective measures or lessons in past experience. Most often the real objectives of the war will be concealed and not see the light of day until it has been discovered in which direction the fortunes of war are turning. Sometimes the real causes of a war are unknown to the parties themselves. Finally, these very questions of war, either in general or in the particular situations mentioned or suggested in the Covenant of the League, may be made the object of serious doubt from various other angles, which we shall discuss later. For these different reasons there should no longer be a doubt as to whether we should or should not consider such causes when the question of abandoning neutrality arises.

2. There may appear at times to be strong arguments here to support the previous classification of wars as just or unjust. Everyone is willing, as we know, to fight for right against wrong, especially when it is a question of right or wrong with respect to one's own interests. But even where it is a question of fighting for the interests of others, or in the interests of justice, the idea of right is a powerful motive. We must, then, consider the problem as to which of the belligerents has essential right on its side—for example, which one is really sovereign over the territories in dispute—and not the question of the mere formal violation of the prohibition against war. Frequent reference is made by the opponents of neutrality [24] to the founders of modern international law, such as Grotius, Wolff, and others, saying that these writers suggest that *material interests alone* often determine a country's position of neutrality, implying that this is rather reprehensible. Thus Grotius says [25] that there are three well-founded causes of

[24] So, for example, Politis, *Neutrality and Peace*, pp. 75 ff.
[25] *De jure belli ac pacis* (1734 ed.), p. 146.

war, namely, self-defense, recovery of one's possessions, and punishment.[26] War is therefore permissible not only to defend one's life and for security and international justice, but for the defense of other important interests as well.[27]

With regard to neutrals,[28] these countries are obligated to do nothing which might strengthen the unjust party,[29] or to oppose the one waging a just war (*justum bellum*). They are to be impartial, however, only when the question of right or wrong is doubtful,[30] and they may then grant the privilege of passage over their territory to both parties impartially or supply the armed forces of both with provisions, but they may not render such assistance to besieged forces.

Vattel, too, regards the "justice of the cause" [31] as decisive. The question of right and wrong plays a large part with this writer in determining the attitude of the neutrals, and even, to some extent, as to whether a particular belligerent shall be granted all the usual benefits under the laws of war.[32] According to the international law of his day, neutrals might permit passage over their territory; Vattel, none the less, believed that the neutral state should refuse it in case of an evidently unjust attack by one of the parties against another. He gives, as an example of such unjust aggression, the occupation of another's territories "without any reason or even colorable pretext." [33]

The classification of wars as just or unjust may also be a heritage of earlier tenets of the law of war, as a final means of enforcement of their legal requirements, and with the recognition of wars of execution as legal by the Covenant of the League.[34]

26 *Defensio, recuperatio rerum et punitio*. Note that Grotius restricts defensive war in the same manner as is that of self-defense in municipal law.

27 "Pro rebus defendendis interfectionem non esse illicitam jure naturae."

28 *Ibid.*, p. 719: "De his, qui in bello medii sunt." 29 *Ibid.*, p. 722.

30 *Ibid.*, "In re vero dubia."

31 I. "The justice of the cause. If that be evident, injustice is not to be countenanced. . . . If the case be dubious, the other nations may suspend their judgment. . . ." See Vattel, *The law of nations* (J. Chitty, tr.), Philadelphia (1883), pp. 332-33.

32 *Ibid.*, p. 378: "He who is engaged in war derives all his rights from the justice of his cause." 33 *Ibid.*, p. 345.

34 Schücking (p. 616), in his understanding of the whole sanctions system, follows the same line of reasoning, regarding it as a compulsory execution ("Zwangsvollstreckung"–"internationale Exekution").

Further consideration will quickly prove, however, that it is not possible to make this classification of wars the basis for determining the question of neutrality, just as it in no way formed the basis for the system of the Covenant of the League.[35] The moral-political views of the older writers of the "justice" or "injustice" of a war would most certainly be useless as a basis for an effective system of war-prevention, and references by the opponents of the neutrality idea to such older theories are therefore ill-considered. "The justice of the cause" may, for want of positive rules of international law, be merely a moral dictum which is in no way confirmed from an examination of the internal national legislation of one country or another. A "colorable" pretext or an excuse for the occupation of a territory can always be found. If we should make the question of just or unjust a criterion in modern times, it would have to be positive international law that would decide it. But there are many reasons—apart from wars of execution involving an arbitral award—why this cannot be done.

First, it will be difficult or impossible in many cases, indeed in most, to determine for the neutrals which of the parties has right on its side. Such a decision would require exact, protracted, and detailed legal and historical investigation. If the outside states, in the opinion of Grotius and Vattel, should conduct themselves as neutrals when "the case is dubious," this in practice would mean that in most cases they would take a passive attitude,[36] which merely says, in other words, that this proposed classification of war is unfit as a basis for an effective system of war prevention.

A modern American author [37] observes that

> Of all the clichés which infect patriotic exhortations, the most subtly poisonous is that which calls the war in progress at the moment "different from all other wars," "a war for right and justice" and "high ideals" "involving no base or selfish motive."

He quotes the opinion of Benjamin Franklin that "there never was a good war or a bad peace," and adds:

[35] Cohn, *Kriegsverhütung*, p. 47.
[36] Cohn, *Neutralité et Société des nations*, p. 161.
[37] Jessup, *Neutrality IV*, "Today and Tomorrow," pp. 76 ff.: "No new thing under the sun."

It should always be remembered that the people of a country—minus certain minorities whose views cannot be freely expressed at such times—never think they are fighting for an unworthy cause, no matter what the sinister motives of government officials may be. In the current war against Ethiopia the Italian people hold the belief that they are right just as tenaciously as people in some other countries hold the belief that they are wrong. In Japan, Japanese expansion upon the Asiatic mainland is right; from the Chinese point of view it is wrong. In some cases there may be absolute standards of right and wrong against which these conflicting beliefs can be measured; few citizens of either belligerent country are competent to apply the test contemporaneously. Nor should it be forgotten that the conviction of self-righteousness is usually sincere and not hypocritical.

It furthermore happens that the question of just or unjust refers to a subject which, in the judgment or in the ordinary political activities of a state outside the dispute would not give it sufficient reason for making war even if it were in its own interests; for example, if it concerned merely a question of financial claims, a claimed insult to its honor, or territory of minor importance. No state can permit its freedom of action or of judgment on the all-important question of war and peace to be at the discretion of another state. It is quite possible that a participant state may be in the right and, at the same time, that it should not—in the opinion of a neutral—declare war for this reason, or permit the situation to become one of war. Such a decision should then be made only upon the most serious questions, and this takes us back again to the impracticability of classifying war according to its causes. Even if a very important right [justification] existed, it would be unreasonable to demand of outside states that, before the war had broken out, they should align themselves on the side of one or another of the parties to the dispute, and then support that party's legal demands through war—and this particularly within a system which aims at the prevention of war.[38] If this much ought not to be required of non-participants in advance, it is difficult to understand how something more could be required of them on that ground after war has broken out.

[38] The classification of just-unjust in traditional international law leaves out of account the classification aggression and defense. A just aggressor should be aided; an unjust defender opposed.

The fact of the matter is that the question of right or wrong has little to do with war-prevention. Grotius, Vattel, and other classical authorities on international law did not themselves intend to prevent wars by the views they set down, but only to guide neutrals as to their proper behavior during wars between foreign powers. This is an entirely different question, which the opponents of the neutrality-idea in our day mistake for or associate with a duty of war-prevention. If essentially "legalized" wars are to be permitted and only the essentially illegal ones prohibited, there will not be much room left for war-prevention, since at least one of the parties will, as a rule, have right upon its side, and so, according to this assumption, be justified in making war. In opposition to this whole train of thought, an effective system of war-prevention must uphold the principle that being right still does not give one the permission to resort to war, and that consequently the classification of war as just or unjust is unimportant to the question of war-prevention.

3. There remain, then, two other formal classifications, namely, that of aggression and defense, and that of the violation of fixed and purely formal criteria. These two classes are, by their content, quite dissimilar. It is primarily the former (aggression and defense) which has played a major part in the establishment of the current rules for war-prevention and of neutrality, both within and without the League of Nations; and this although it is in reality not decisive for the system of the Covenant of the League, which rests, rather, upon the classification of violation of fixed formal criteria, at least in so far as its expressly established rules are concerned. It is authorized, according to Article XVI of the Covenant, if the belligerent has followed the prescribed procedure of Articles XII, XIII, and XV, and waited the three months term there specified. Under these circumstances war—even a war of aggression—is legal, and there can then be no question of a nation abandoning neutrality. War is absolutely prohibited in only two situations: one where a state has accepted an arbitral award, the other where it has accepted a unanimous decision of the Council.

Under these conditions, it seems somewhat surprising that recent discussions of the rules of neutrality should have concerned themselves with the classification of war by aggression and defense and have ignored the classification by violation of fixed formal criteria. The Declaration in the Assembly, in 1927, declaring war of aggression an international crime, and the like, contains many eloquent arguments which tell us how wrong it is for neutrals not to take up arms against the aggressor. One might fairly say, however, that the system of the Covenant does not look too unfavorably upon an aggressor. War of aggression is quite just, at any rate is as much justified as is defensive war, when merely the formal rules have been observed. And even in the Covenant's two real prohibitions of war, it is quite in accord with these provisions for the state which complies with the award of an arbitral board or a unanimous decision of the Council deliberately to attack the adversary which has not done so.

Since the express terms of the Covenant do not, then, concern themselves with the classification of aggression and defense, but merely with that of the violation of fixed formal criteria, one may justly state that those modern opponents of the idea of neutrality, who constantly and reproachfully hold up to the neutrals the notion of aggressive and defensive war, have a false basis for their position. The Covenant does not prohibit aggression; it does not require neutral coöperation on such occasions unless there is a violation of the purely formal standards which it has created and which an aggressor can very easily circumvent. In the case of a violation of these fixed criteria, defensive war is as much forbidden as is war of aggression, as, for example, when an illegal occupation of foreign territory has occurred without war and the injured state wishes to defend its territory by war.

However, when we inquire why these classifications have been reversed by modern opponents of the neutrality idea, the answer is not difficult to find. As we have said, classification by violations of fixed formal standards, especially when the latter have only the character of delay, is a very slender and tenuous basis for a demand upon the neutrals to throw themselves into a destructive war. The classification of aggression and defense is more useful, because it is not an entirely formal one and, at the same time, it sounds something like right and wrong. Although the League Covenant does not support the view, one could, if the need arose, inflame public opinion by asserting that the aggression was unjustified and was, after all, the original and possibly the sole reason for the war; while the defender, even if it does not in this instance enjoy the protection of the Covenant, is assumed to be the one inclined toward peace and is for this reason, if for no other, entitled to sympathetic support.

Furthermore, it is necessary to say that the classification by violation of its formal provisions in the Covenant cannot be applied in a purely formal manner, and in this lies one of the greatest difficulties for the application of its entire system of war-prevention. The criteria of Article XVI, namely, where a League member resorts "to war in disregard of its covenants under Articles XII, XIII or XV, are in reality not purely formal ones. There is actually contained in this, besides the formal reference to the other Articles, further, and to a high degree material, assumptions. One lies in the phrase "resort to war"; the other is the inherent fact that to make war at least two parties are required, and Article XVI aims at only one of them.[39] But which one? The answer is that the thought was only of the aggressor, and not of the defender, even if the circumstances of the latter's acts are exactly the same, within the words of the text, as the others'. Defensive war is permissible, indeed is to be regarded as necessary and laudable.

The effect, even in the specific circumstances alluded to above, where resort to war has occurred, must be very dubious.[40] There exist international procedures which include the use of force and which nevertheless cannot be described as resort to war; such are retorsion,[41] reprisals, blockade, and so forth. How far such measures may go without developing into an actual state of war is a

[39] Cohn, *Kriegsverhütung und Schuldfrage*, p. 123.

[40] Liszt (p. 449) claims: "Einseitiger Angriff, der keine Abwehr findet, ist nicht Krieg." Contrasting with this is Article XVI of the Covenant which appears to assume that only *one* of the parties resorts to war ("should any Member of the League resort to war"); Schücking, p. 508 ff. on retorsion and reprisals, non-military occupation of foreign territory, etc.; Oppenheim, II, 110 f. (views of doubtful correctness); Haase, *Wandlung des Neutralitätsbegriffes*, pp. 15 ff.

[41] On the distinction between retorsion and reprisals see Matzen, *Statsforfatningsret*, III (1909), 189 ff.; Strupp (ed.) *Wörterbuch*, II, 349 ff. and 357 f.; Liszt, *op. cit.*, pp. 438 ff.; Moore, *Digest*, VII, 105 and 131.

question; or, vice versa, if one party takes far-reaching measures of such a nature and the other party opposes them by force of arms, are we then to assert that the latter has resorted to war? The system of a violation of fixed formal criteria gives no answer to these questions.

Classification by Aggression and Defense

1. There is a further difficulty, moreover, in the second question, namely, against which one of the two belligerent states, where the circumstances of both come within the text of Article XVI, and where both may be said to have resorted to war, shall sanctions be directed? The question might well arise in a specific instance requiring a decision after war has broken out. It has also a more general aspect, namely, by what criteria shall one determine whether or not a particular war comes within the provisions of Article XVI? It is this doubt which underlies the great problem of the classification of war according to aggression and defense. Outside the Covenant, for example in the Locarno Treaty, the Kellogg Pact, and the Saavedra Lamas Treaty, the classification is made upon this basis. Within the Covenant (Article XVI) it must be understood [42] in association with the classification of the violation of fixed formal criteria. If the latter classification did not exist, that of aggression and defense could have no legal significance.

How shall we determine the difference between an aggressor and a defender? There has been no dearth of replies, and many of them have confused theoretical definitions and the practical conditions of a particular case. We shall here emphasize a few main points:

It seems natural enough to identify defensive war with the right of self-defense, and this, then, is perhaps the explanation of its frequently expressed authorization.[43] This theory gives the additional advantage that its assertion makes unnecessary a proof of its validity; this is always a bit awkward to do for a system of war-

[42] Cohn, *Kriegsverhütung und Schuldfrage*, p. 123.
[43] Such as was very typical of Grotius.

prevention which is unable otherwise to justify itself. So Mr. Kellogg, in his famous address to the American Society of International Law, in 1928, resorted not a little to this method.[44] That defensive war was not included in the Kellogg Pact was asserted to be a matter of course, which need not have been mentioned at all. For a state cannot be deprived of the right of self-defense, any more than can an individual; this right, as far as we know, is presumed to be inherent and inalienable. Similar views were expressed by Mr. Saavedra Lamas [45] regarding his pact, and the same holds true for those theorists who would make the classification by aggression or defense the basis for the system of the Covenant. At the same time, they make use to some extent of the concept of unrestricted sovereignty, which has been incorporated into the system of the Covenant and which is likewise inconsistent with the acceptance of a prohibition against defensive war without further regard to the consideration that the same philosophy could be applied to wars of aggression.[46]

This theory of the right of self-defense overlooks completely the distinctions which exist, on the one hand, between the municipal law concept of self-defense and, on the other hand, defensive war as it is authorized under traditional international law, as well as in the League Covenant. Self-defense, that is, the right to use force for protection against an attack [47] (*vim vi defendere*), is subject to quite definite legal restrictions (depending upon the purposes) for which there is no exact analogy nor application with respect to defensive war. The right of self-defense presumes the preëxistence of a certain relation between the object of the attack and the means of defense which can be used. These limita-

[44] "The Legal Significance of the Kellogg Pact" in *Juridisk Tidsskrift* (1929), pp. 38 ff.

[45] *Pacte de Non-Agression et de Conciliation Argentin. Recueil de Documents.* Buenos Aires, 1936, pp. 308 ff.

[46] Cohn, *Kriegsverhütung und Schuldfrage*, p. 181.

[47] In the absence of an attack there still exists the "right in case of necessity," the situation which is subject to other legal restrictions. But this idea, which plays a certain part in the law of war as "nécessité de guerre" or "raison de guerre" (Liszt, p. 455 f., distinguishes between "right in case of necessity" and "raison de guerre": "Notstand und Kriegsnotwendigkeit sind verschiedene Begriffe") cannot be pleaded to justify defensive war as such.

tions[48] upon the right of self-defense naturally vary somewhat in different penal codes; nonetheless a common thought pervades them, which clearly indicates the distinct difference between this right and that of defensive war. Thus the Danish penal code, Law Number 126, of April 15, 1930, section 13, requires that an act of self-defense must be (1) one necessary to resist or to prevent an actual or (2) impending illegal assault, "and that (3) it shall not exceed what, as such, is justifiable." For example, to protect a quite minor privilege, one must not apply such measures of self-defense as might expose the life of the assailant to danger, and in particular one must not use the assault as an excuse to commence a new or an independent counter attack against the lawful interests of the assailant, which have no relation to the interests originally assailed. It is for the protection of the latter alone that the right of self-defense exists. What is evidently unnecessary for this specific purpose is not lawful. But defensive war recognizes no limitations of this nature. If an aggression occurs—and here again we must notice the contrast with the principles of self-defense, since no regard is here paid to the essential right or wrong of the parties[49]—war by the defender becomes a war in the ordinary sense of international law, with no limitations upon it other than those which the laws of war and neutrality permit, and so in reality a war of quite the same nature as that made by the aggressor. Defensive war, like aggressive war, permits the invasion of the opponent's territories and their occupation (rules of the Fourth Hague Convention, 1907, Articles XLII ff.) and the taking over of the administration of them. It permits the defender to annihilate its adversary's forces by land, sea, and air; indeed to subject it to cessions, restrictions, indemnities, or to permanent complete subjugation, without regard to the originally threatened objective as a guide for its defensive war or for the terms of peace.

[48] See further Torp, *Den danske Strafferets almindelige Del*, pp. 295 ff.: "Defense must not go further than is necessary to ward off the attack, a requirement common to all penal law."

[49] *Ibid.*, pp. 287 ff. (on self-defense): "The attack must have been an illegal one." A French translation of this Danish law is available: see Denmark, Statutes. *Code pénal danois du avril 1930* (Goll and Schroll, tr.) Paris (Association internationale de droit pénal), 1935.

This appears clearly from the Treaty of Versailles, which, as we know, resulted from a war which the Allied Powers avowed to be purely defensive. Attempts to parallel the legal situation therein with that of the municipal law concept of self-defense are quite impracticable. One need only read the discussions in the American Senate and Mr. Borah's explanation [50] as to what kind of "self-defense" comes within the category of "defensive war," to realize the impossibility of an analogy. It was actually asserted there that any threat to American interests, even within the territory of a foreign state and without any possible threat of war from that state, justified the United States in armed intervention on the principles of self-defense and defensive war.[51] It is then possible to understand better how the war lusts of other countries have permitted them to swallow the provision of the Kellogg Pact for the general "abolition of war," and how they subsequently have felt quite unburdened by this Pact, when exercising "military pressure" in safeguarding their political and territorial interests.

This lack of relation between the interests to be protected and the extent of the measures to be used for their defense, with the limitations deriving from this dissociation, separates defensive war from the idea of self-defense. When an aggression [52] occurs, it is immaterial under the existing pacts as to what particular interest

[50] U. S. Congress *Congressional Record. Appendix* (Jan. 5, 1929), pp. 1274 ff.; especially p. 1279: "Each nation will determine for itself, under the circumstances as they arise and the conditions which are presented, what it conceives to be self-defense."

[51] This is also true, in Mr. Borah's opinion (*ibid.*, p. 1274), in the case of the Monroe Doctrine: "The Monroe doctrine is our doctrine. We announced it ourselves. It is the principle of self-defense. *We alone interpret it.*" (Our italics.)

[52] Or the pretense of one. During the discussions in Congress (*ibid.*, p. 1274), Senator Reed referred to the Spanish-American War, replying to Mr. Borah's speech: "Does not the Senator recall that when the *Maine* was blown up the Spanish Government *immediately disclaimed the act,* and that the Spanish Government *made almost every conceivable effort to avoid the war by peaceful means?* If this treaty (namely the Kellogg Pact) had been in effect, surely we would have been bound, under the representations of the Spanish Government, to have arbitrated that matter." To which Mr. Borah replied: "We would not be bound under this treaty, in my opinion, in any different way than that in which we were found at that time . . . after the incident as it occurred, after our property had been destroyed and American lives destroyed, it was for the Government of the United States to determine *what constituted a real defense* of our rights." (Our italics.)

is threatened or by what sacrifices the aggression might be averted; instead, a broad title is granted to wage defensive war and thereby permission is extended, through a defensive attack, for the complete destruction of the aggressor. In other words, by the classification of aggression and defense, neither the question of just and unjust nor the protection of interests plays much part in determining the effects of the war. Defensive war is *war* just as much as is war of aggression, and as such has no determinable relation to the interests attacked. Viewed as self-defense, that is, protection of the country's interests, a war of aggression may be just as necessary as a defensive war. Even under municipal law concepts of self-defense, a person need not wait for an actual attack to be made, but may also prevent the attack ("intervention in self-defense") [53] by an act of self-defense ("attack for purposes of defense").[54]

Thus it would seem that while it may be possible to utilize the idea of self-defense in relations between states, we believe that this idea cannot be used for the purpose of the classification of war as aggressive or defensive nor to determine the legality of a defensive war and thereby, of the duty of a neutral to intervene in it. On the contrary, the problem must be to draw distinctions [55] as sharp as possible between *self-defense* in international law, which should be legal, and *defensive war motivated by self-defense,* which should be illegal, just as is war of aggression.[56]

[53] Torp, p. 295.

[54] *Ibid.*, p. 294; see also Descamps in *Académie de droit international, Recueil des cours,* I (1930), 472 ff.

[55] Cohn, *Kriegsverhütung und Schuldfrage*, p. 193.

[56] Giraud, *La Théorie de la légitime défense* (1934) and Scelle, *L'Agression et la légitime défense dans les rapports internationaux* (1936) have tried to develop an independent concept of self-defense in international law which would coincide with that of an unrestricted legal war of defense. It would seem, however, to be both superfluous and misleading then to refer to the "principle" of self-defense; see also Hertz, *Die Theorie der Notwehr*, p. 137, which correctly asserts that it is a peculiar notion to plead the principle of self-defense and at the same time to support the legality of defensive war under the theory of sovereignty or as a just cause (*justum bellum*); see also Keller, "Notwehrrecht und Notwehrtechnik," in *Die Friedenswarte* (1929), p. 11, who observes: "Die heute üblichen Kriegsmittel lassen zunächst überhaupt die Feststellung eines wirklichen Notwehrfalles praktisch nicht mehr zu. Denn zur heutigen Kriegführung gehört als eiserner Bestand eine derartige Verwirrung und Irreführung der öffentlichen Meinung... dass die gegnerischen Völker beiderseits sich in

2. Defensive war is then not self-defense, but is war, just as much as is that of aggression. Many other attempts have been made to analyze the distinction between these two kinds of war.[57] Such distinctions have been made on the basis of their internal ("*immanent*") or external characteristics, as subjective or objective, military-technical, legal, political, and other forms. The great number of possible classifications is certainly indicative in advance of the fact that no clear distinctions at all can be made.

The Geneva Protocol of 1924 attempted a classification by *external* characteristics, as it wished to attach importance to an element which is not, strictly speaking, expressive of the different kinds of war, but concerns rather the relations of the parties themselves, that is, whether they are willing or not to permit the controversy to be settled by arbitration or by a decision of the Council under the terms of Articles XIII and XV of the Covenant. The state which is willing to permit this thereby becomes the defender, the other becomes the aggressor,[58] irrespective of how the war started or how it is being conducted by the parties. This condition is *external to the war* itself; the readiness to accept arbitration is to be decisive for its classification as aggression or defense. This classification is not identical with that of right or wrong, but it does contain a significant consideration for a system of war-prevention, namely, the desire for peace. On the other hand, there seems to be too much importance attached to the purely formal method designed to make it simple for the other League members to decide with which belligerent party they should stand or take sides.[59] Thus the Geneva Protocol, Article X, states that "every

der Notwehrlage betrachten, und beide . . . sich gegenseitig für Angreifer halten." The distinction must then be sought partly in a territorial limitation, partly in a restriction or definition of international rights and consequences connected with measures of self-defense.

[57] La Brière, *La Définition de l'agresseur*, p. 624; Strupp, Der Kellogg-Pakt, p. 21: "wichtigste Zukunftsaufgabe der Völkerrechtstheorie und -praxis; Undén, *Quelques observations sur la notion de guerre d'agression*, p. 263: "critères de plus en plus objectifs et précis"; Giraud, *Théorie de la légitime défense*, p. 794 (as dictated by an international conscience) and others.

[58] For further reference, see Beneš' and Politis' commentary (on the Protocol), in the Report of the Danish Delegation to the Rigsdag, pp. 66 ff.

[59] This feature is further described by Beneš and Politis, as having a paramount importance.—"The system is therefore complete, and is as automatic as it can be made" (Miller, *The Geneva Protocol*, p. 190).

State which resorts to war in violation of the undertakings in the Covenant or in the present Protocol is an aggressor." Article XI, section 4, curiously enough assumes that both parties to the dispute may be aggressors in this sense. If hostilities have already broken out, the state which has refused to refer the dispute to pacific arbitration or to comply with an arbitral award, or with the unanimous decision of the Council, is presumed to be the aggressor.

This, however, is laid down only as a "presumption," which may be changed to the contrary by the unanimous decision of the Council.[60] There is thus the question of two different sets of criteria for classification by external characteristics, not to be deduced from the conduct of the war itself: (1) the desire for peace; and (2) a unanimous decision of the Council.

In their comment on Article X of the Protocol, Beneš and Politis say that[61] it would, of course, be most natural ("the first idea which came to mind"), to permit the Council to decide which of the parties is the aggressor. But there ensues at once the immediate difficulty as to whether the Council is to decide this question unanimously, or by a majority vote; both solutions are unacceptable, for, if unanimity is required, a single Council member may make the war-prevention efforts of the League illusory and a majority vote would be equally objectionable, since one could hardly expect neutrals to intervene when the Council itself was divided. The Geneva Protocol therefore suggested the automatic procedure, that is, the presumption of aggression when a juridical settlement is refused.

We shall not here discuss the numerous difficulties connected with automatic war-prevention machinery[62] but wish to consider only the idea of classifying aggression or defense according to the refusal or acceptance of arbitration or mediation. Such classification belongs to the far-too-frail systems of war-prevention mentioned above, since it would hardly be possible to get outside states to intervene in the war upon such a basis.

[60] The Protocol also contains some other presumptions regarding aggressors which there is no particular reason to discuss here.

[61] Beneš and Politis, p. 67.

[62] For further reference, see Cohn, *Kriegsverhütung und Schuldfrage,* pp. 128 ff.

It may be asserted with some justice that as a rule it is unjustifiable for a state to refuse to permit an international controversy to be settled through arbitration or through the mediation of the Council—although sometimes it *may be* of vital importance to this state that the question, in its existing form, remain unsettled. The state may wish to assert that the controversy has already been settled, or (which will frequently be the case) that the dispute between the parties really consists in determining just how their differences are to be formulated and expressed and what are the real points at issue—that is, just *what* is to be adjudicated by arbitration or by the Council.[63] These questions are not so simple as this type of war-prevention might lead us to assume. Even if we leave these out of account and assume that a State A, unquestionably willing to arbitrate, attacks a State B, which desires neither arbitration nor war, it would still be opposed to all reason and contrary as well to the purpose of war-prevention, if in such a case State B were to be regarded as the aggressor. It would therefore be unreasonable to apply sanctions against the latter state to prevent war, since this State B, on the assumption that it does not want war, is then, despite its unwillingness to bring the controversy up for international discussion, under the above circumstances the one actually attacked and not the aggressor. Sanctions in this instance would have the effect not of opposing war, but rather that of coercing states into arbitration, which is something quite different.[64]

[63] In practice very frequently a previous disagreement breaks out as to what the controversy concerns and how this shall be formulated, since the views of the two parties do not coincide and each desires the advantage coming from a formulation according to his own viewpoint. Very frequently one of the parties will deny that any dispute exists, and the finding upon this apparently so simple a point frequently occasions great or insuperable difficulties. See also the Hague Convention of 1907 on the peaceful settlement of international controversies, Article XLIII, where attempts of the parties to formulate an arbitration agreement (*Compromissum*) have proved futile. Corresponding provisions exist in many other arbitration and conciliation treaties.

[64] This theory of the criteria of aggression had been already stated some time before the Geneva Protocol; on this question see Ray, *Commentaire*, pp. 365 ff., who himself remarks: "Nous reconnaissons la grandeur et, si l'on veut, la vérité profonde de la théorie qui définit l'agression par le refus d'arbitrage.... Mais *l'agression n'est pas le refus d'arbitrage;* il faut tout de même laisser aux mots leur sens, si l'on ne veut pas que le désordre du langage facilite les sophismes et les manœuvres de la mauvaise foi."

To require of the neutrals under such circumstances that they throw themselves into a war to support the actual aggressor against the attacked state is, to say the least, impracticable.

In any event, the system of the League Covenant itself did not lay down such an unreasonable demand.[65] Under Article XVI sanctions cannot be invoked against a state whose only offense was that it would not accept arbitration or a hearing before the Council. Indeed the same holds true even if the state refuses to comply with an arbitral award or with the unanimous decision of the Council.[66] The text of Article XVI, section 1, could certainly not be interpreted in such manner—even if the technical possibility existed—that, in the event of war breaking between State A, which has complied with the decision, and State B, which has not done so, sanctions should automatically be applied for the benefit of the former state against the latter. Here the tacit assumption that sanctions are to be applied against the aggressor in the commonly accepted sense of the term must be of greater force than a purely formal textual interpretation. Although State B may have "resorted to war" in disregard of the provisions of Articles XII, XIII, and XV, it is none the less only against an aggressor that sanctions are to be applied (if at the same time the formal standards for such offense have also been violated).

Moreover, a mere declaration of willingness to arbitrate may not in itself prevent war. It is possible that one or even both of the belligerents might make such declaration and that war might nevertheless break out before an arbitral decision, which often takes years, was reached. In such a case, these definitions for the classification of aggression and defense would likewise fail in their purpose.

3. A notion frequently advanced and of widespread popularity is to the effect that classification by aggression or defense is simply

[65] The Geneva Protocol and Beneš and Politis comment have upon this point, as well as upon some others, an astonishingly hide-bound and impractical character.

[66] This case does not fall within the provisions of Article XVI, and Article XIII, section 4, and Article XV, section 6, cannot be interpreted as involving obligations of sanctions or of war for other League members under these circumstances.

a matter of finding out which country made the first move,[67] who fired the first shot. The aggressor is the one which starts or occasions the war while the defender is the party which follows, which is drawn into the war against its will, which waits until its adversary has made the first step. There would certainly seem to be something here to help us to distinguish between aggression and defense, but this new method, too, is just as surely impracticable.

Priority cannot be decisive, since the first shot may be a police matter, as, for example, when the dispute begins between frontier guards or between war vessels. The first mobilization, the first passing of the frontiers, proves nothing, since it may be due entirely to defensive considerations. Some military authorities believe that an attack is the best—sometimes the only possible—means of defense, just as a preventive war may really have as its object a defense against an otherwise inevitable attack. Likewise the "occasion" or "cause" of war is found to be an unsuitable standard. The "occasion" or "cause" may be incidental or unimportant, as compared with the concealed and real causes. With the words "who caused the war?" there arise great historical, legal, and moral questions of guilt, of objective and subjective responsibility, which are enormously complex and which it is entirely unsuitable to invoke in making an immediate decision for the application of sanctions at the commencement of war.[68]

Attempts have been made to base the classification "aggression and defense" upon military, tactical, and political considerations. Military factors are primarily concerned, however, with strategic and tactical considerations in the arrangement of attack and defense in warfare, and have little to do with a system of war-prevention—except where it is evident that the classification itself has nothing to do with the right or wrong, or the cause of the war, but is merely another device by which the main purpose, that of

[67] Saldana, *La justice pénale internationale,* p. 310: "L'agresseur est tout simplement celui qui attaque le premier": Knubben, "Völkerbund und Kriegsverhütung" (in Strupp, *Wörterbuch* III), p. 1162: "Angriff bedeutet immer und jedenfalls eine *erste Bewegung,* die Zwang enthalt."

[68] For a further discussion of this entire question, see Cohn, *Kriegsverhütung und Schuldfrage,* 1931.

the conquest of the adversary, may be attained. The Committee on the Reduction of Armaments of the League of Nations took up and examined the question of tactical and political criteria, but with a definitely negative result. We have their report of 1923,[69] which considers the problem of the determination of the aggressor and which points out the difficulties of applying the various tests.

Mobilization under modern conditions is such an extensive and protracted affair, involving such disarrangement of industry, procuring of necessary raw materials and supplies, provisioning, and other items, that it may last for years. It would be extremely difficult to put a finger upon any one point and to assert that there the aggression began.

Nor can the passing of the frontiers by armed forces be used as a test, since hostilities may begin between border police, volunteer units, or entirely unorganized mobs. If hostilities commence between war vessels on the high seas, no passing of the frontiers exists at all. It is, moreover, often very difficult to determine aerial frontiers, if war should happen to start because of a battle in the air.

Regarding the general preparation for war in one of the countries concerned, this is most often concealed or difficult to prove. Preparatory measures may have various purposes in view, and are quite impossible to classify. They are at any rate but ill-suited for use as criteria for determining the application of sanctions. Finally, the general impression by others of the policies of a state, its propaganda, the mentality of its press and people, and others similar, are measures of too ill-defined a nature to serve the purposes of classification, so much the more since the minds of people in a number of countries are being prepared at this very moment for an immediate attack. The report of 1923 really concludes that the question of a definition of aggression is an insoluble one.[70]

The report of the Dutch delegate, Rutgers, in 1928,[71] summarizes

[69] *Ibid.*, pp. 124 ff. Also see League of Nations, *Official Journal, Special Supplement* (1923), "Minutes of the Third Committee, Annex 4," pp. 183 ff.

[70] "It may, however, be accepted that no satisfactory definition of what constitutes aggression could be drawn up." *Minutes of the Third Committee*, p. 184.

[71] *Official Journal* (1928), pp. 670 ff.

those acts which, under certain circumstances, might be regarded as criteria of aggression, but admits [72] that a satisfactory definition of this term cannot be given. Moreover, it would, he believes, be dangerous to define it, since it might, in some unforeseen circumstance lead to the designation as an aggressor of a state which was actually in no way responsible for the outbreak of hostilities.

Rutgers further correctly maintained that "it was not necessarily the State to whose conduct the original crisis was due which is to be regarded as the aggressor; in certain eventualities it might possibly be the other party which ought to be regarded as the aggressor, if it has deliberately refused to conform to the Council's recommendations." [73]

Since the Locarno treaties were signed, a new classification has arisen by which writers no longer speak merely of aggression, but rather of *unprovoked* aggression, a test which has since been included in several treaties.[74] In Article II of the Final Protocol of the Locarno Conference there are two new tests of aggression in war, namely, "attack" (priority) and "invasion"; it was there agreed that the parties would in no case resort to war unless it were a question of "the exercise of the right of legitimate defense," in other words, the right to oppose an unprovoked act of aggression.[75] Such right was here associated with the right of self-defense, which can hardly serve to give it validity. Actually the signatories did not reserve the right of self-defense under these terms, but that of making war in the old-fashioned and time-honored way. It should be here noted that if a real question of self-defense in the municipal law sense of that term were involved, the right created could not be made dependent upon the attack having been an "*unprovoked*" one. Such a claim could not be logically asserted by an individual person in a situation involving self-defense, since such person has at all times the right to protect his interests against

[72] *Ibid.*, p. 686.

[73] *Ibid.*, p. 677; see also Eagleton, *Faut-il proscrire seulement les guerres d'agression ou toutes les guerres?*, pp. 507 ff.

[74] See the Treaty of Guarantee dated Jan. 15, 1931, between Poland and Rumania, Article II, Martens, *Nouv. Rec. Gén., Ser. 3,* XXX, 36: "se verrait attaquée, sans l'avoir provoqué."

[75] See also Article IV, section 3, wherein immediate assistance is promised in case of "an unprovoked act of aggression."

an illegal attack without regard to its being provoked or unprovoked.[76] If we were to make provocation the decisive test, this would alter the relation between the right of self-defense and the interests protected thereby. It should also be evident that there was in the Locarno agreement no intention to introduce new concepts of the right of self-defense into international law differing from those of its accepted sense of defensive war but that it did intend to provide an argument (untenable, incidently) for the legality of defensive war. When aggression was therein qualified as unprovoked, the qualification was a recognition of the inadequacy of the usual classification of wars as either aggression or defense.[77]

The result, however, would be the complete overthrow of the classification of aggression and defense by the introduction of the new concept of provocation. We would then be back to the classification of just or unjust, provided we made the classification in a legal sense, or to an entirely useless psychological classification if we made a mere factual application of the term. The decision, at any rate, would no longer be based upon the existence or nonexistence of a situation of aggression or defense, but upon the question as to whether there was reason for the aggression, which in turn presupposes that there sometimes is reason for aggression. The consequences of this are almost incalculable. Shall the guarantee Powers, in case of provoked aggression, hurry to the aid of the aggressor, or may they remain passive? Is defensive war, or even self-defense, against provoked aggression, unlawful, because, according to the treaty, it is legal only in case of unprovoked aggression? What is meant by provocation, and is it sufficient in itself so to classify war that aggression may become defense and defense may become aggression, that is to say, that defense against *provoked* aggression constitutes an aggression itself, and that the provoked aggression is really defense? If there are several existing

[76] With regard to the Danish law, see Torp, *Den danske Strafrettens almindelige Del* (the Danish penal-law code), p. 293: "Nor is there, according to the code, justification for making extraneous claims, such as that the attack must have been an unprovoked one. . . ."

[77] A survey of different kinds of reservations according to provocation may be found in Giraud, *Théorie de la légitime défense,* p. 756.

degrees of provocation, to what particular degree is it necessary to provoke someone to produce that effect, or shall we regard the legal situation as being such that certain lower degrees of provocation give the guarantee powers a right to passivity, while certain higher degrees of it create a new classification? It is evident that all this was not thought through, and that the further qualification of aggression as unprovoked not only contributed nothing to the simplification of the legal situation, but, on the contrary, introduced a new factor which may be so combined with the previous classification of aggression and defense as to create an interminable multiplicity of new problems. This is likewise true of the theoretical attempts made to explain the classification of aggression and defense by further qualification of other kinds.[78]

The Conventions of 1931 and 1933

1. Following the Geneva Protocol of 1924, which had little practical significance, two further attempts to define aggression were made by means of multilateral treaty agreements which merit mention here. One of them is the general convention of September 26, 1931, to improve the means of preventing war,[79] which placed the decision in the hands of the Council. If the forces of one power have invaded the territory or territorial waters of another, or have flown over these territories, the Council, under Article II, may prescribe measures to assure their evacuation. In Article III the Council is empowered to fix boundary lines which must not be passed. If such provisions are violated, and if, as a result of such action, war breaks out, the presumption [80] is created that the party guilty of these acts has resorted to war within the meaning of Article XVI of the Covenant (Article V, section 2, of the convention). Such decision of the Council must be unanimous "other than the parties to the dispute" (Article VII).

78 See especially Knubben, "Völkerbund und Kriegsverhütung," in Strupp, *Wörterbuch*, III, 1151 ff.

79 See League of Nations, *Doc. A.* 78. 1931. IX.

80 "...Such violation shall be regarded by the High Contracting Parties as *prima facie* evidence that the guilty party thereof has resorted to war within the meaning of Article 16 of the Covenant."

This convention, so far as it goes, moves in the right direction, since it places the efforts at war-prevention in the hands of the Council. It is based upon the principle of complete mutuality with respect to both belligerent Powers, and not before one of the parties has definitely violated one of the provisions applicable to both, will there be a question of special measures being taken against such party, based upon this violation of the Council's regulations, regardless of original question of aggression. The fault in this system is that the idea has not been followed [81] consistently; it ceases to operate upon the outbreak of war. Instead of speaking of a violation of the ruling of the Council, it then speaks of the presumption of aggression, in accord with Article XVI. Instead of continuing the Council's endeavors to prevent the war, these are to be suddenly discontinued and to be replaced by the system of Article XVI, an entirely different type of measure—in other words, the prevention of war through the intervention of individual League members, with their possible declarations of war.

It is, moreover, characteristic of the weakness of the entire theory of aggression that the Convention of 1931, even in such an obvious instance, speaks only of a *presumption* of aggression, not of actual aggression. It is not certain, on the other hand, that the party violating the formal regulations of the Council is, after all, an aggressor in the sense which Article XVI assumes. The formal violation may, upon consideration of the relative strength of the parties, their strategic position, preparation, and causes of the war, be determined by a comparatively unimportant offense,[82] indeed may even be a step which the state involved was compelled to take in true self-defense, not to mention the frequently difficult problem of factual proof. A mere formal violation of the provisions of the Council is to be judged according to its real importance in each individual case and not by general presumptions regarding "aggression," with the incalculable consequences connected with the

[81] On the preparatory work, see Cohn, *Kriegsverhütung und Schuldfrage*, pp. 194 ff.

[82] See also Udén, *La Guerre d'agression comme problème de droit international*, p. 19: "l'attitude de refus opposée aux invitations de la Société des Nations ne peut être toujours interprétée comme l'indice d'un geste effectif d'agression, et qu'on doit avant tout y voir une *attitude d'indifférence*."

provisions of Article XVI. It can be neither just nor right to put the machinery of war into operation for mere formal reasons. With regard to the party which, while it complies for the time being with the Council's rulings, is none the less in all other respects the real aggressor, it will doubtless prove impossible to force outside neutral states into war on the side of such state, even if its adversary were guilty of a purely formal breach of the Council's regulations.

2. The second attempt was that of the London Convention of July 3, 1933, regarding the definition of aggression.[83] This resulted from the initiative of Soviet Russia in connection with that country's ratification of the Kellogg Pact of 1927, which, as we know, was directed entirely against wars of aggression. The formulation of its details was made by the Greek delegate, Politis, in a report dated May 24, 1933,[84] to the Committee on Security Questions of the Geneva Disarmament Conference which declared its purpose to be determining acts of aggression. The Conference attempted to collect a number of criteria which had been previously mentioned as definitive for the classification of aggression, on a basis which should be, as far as possible, objective.[85] For further discussion of this report on the Disarmament Conference, reference may be made to the following chapter; we here set forth only a few observations upon the text of this Convention in its final form.

In the introductory passages the Convention stresses the prohibition in the Kellogg Pact against wars of aggression, the necessity of preventing any pretext for justifying aggression, and the need of defining this concept as specifically as possible.

Article II provides that the rôle of aggressor shall hereafter be

[83] See the Conventions between Russia and Lithuania dated July 5, 1933, and between Rumania, Russia, Czechoslovakia, Turkey, and Yugoslavia dated July 4, 1933, in League of Nations, Treaty Series (1934), p. 80 and p. 212.

[84] League of Nations, *Geneva Conference for the Reduction and Limitation of Armaments, Conference Documents* (*Conf. D./C.G. 108*), "Report of the Committee on Security Questions," pp. 679 ff., Geneva, 1935: "... determining acts of aggression in a definite, practical and direct manner."

[85] *Ibid.*: "In the opinion of its supporters, this method would constitute the foundation of any system of security envisioned by the Disarmament Conference for putting an end to doubts and controversies on the point of whether States which resort to force have committed an aggression or not."

regarded as being that of the first state to commit any one of the following acts (which are enumerated in Article I): [86]

(1) Declaration of war upon another state

(2) Invasion by its armed forces, with or without a declaration of war, of the territory of another state

(3) Attack [87] by its land, naval, or air forces, with or without a declaration of war, on the territory, vessels, or aircraft of another state

(4) Naval blockade of the coasts or ports of another state

(5) Provision of support to armed bands formed in its territory which have invaded the territory of another state, or refusal, notwithstanding the request of the invaded state, to take in its own territory all the measures in its power to deprive those bands of all assistance and protection

No political, military, economic, or other action shall, according to Article III, be sufficient to justify such attacks as are considered under Article II. This is to hold true for both the internal and the foreign situations of such state, as is further exemplified in the Annexes.

If this Convention were to serve merely as an interpretation of the Kellogg Pact or of other similar pronouncements against wars of aggression, such as the Saavedra Lamas Treaty or the Assembly Declaration of 1927, it would be innocuous. One might then at most object that, by its emphasis upon certain specific situations, it would unwarrantably narrow the concept of wars of aggression, since several equally serious offenses of a warlike nature might be found, which with equal justice might be included or considered as aggression.

If, on the other hand, we are to use the definitions of this Convention for the classification of aggression and defense and thus for the application of Article XVI of the Covenant, which according to M. Politis is its intent, as well as a basis for a demand upon neutrals for their participation in the war, the above-mentioned objections to this classification arise at once, both separately and

[86] See Geneva Conference (Annex I), 683.

[87] The Convention thus tautologically defines aggression as attack.

in their reciprocal interrelationship. We can in no way admit that "aggression" can be so "objectively" [88] defined and limited to such quite specific circumstances to the exclusion of others. A formal declaration of war, for example, might well be made under circumstances which clearly show that it is the defender which is making it and not the aggressor, and that its purpose is to prevent its suppression by the aggressor under the claim that no war situation exists. If, for instance, during the conflict now existing between Japan and China, one imagines the latter country as able to issue and carry out a declaration of war, it would hardly be possible for anyone to regard China as becoming thereby the aggressor. The mere factual passing of a frontier by armed forces had already been declared by military experts at the Disarmament Conference of 1923 an unsuitable criterion of aggression. When the 1933 Geneva Convention in Article II, section 3, defined the aggressor as being the first state to commit an act of aggression, this was pure tautology which led nowhere, because the question in each instance is just that—who *was* the first to attack?—and the question can hardly be its own answer. Next, with regard to the blockade of the coasts and harbors of another state, there is in ordinary international law agreement that this may take place under some circumstances which cannot be characterized as war and thus involving no aggression (the so-called pacific blockade); [89] indeed, Article XVI, section 1, of the Covenant, and the Resolutions of 1921 both assume this. There is, finally, the fifth act named in the Convention regarding the support of armed bands or the omission of assistance to them, a quite special situation brought up without regard to the numerous types and degrees of such acts. These are so varied that it would be impossible to put them all into the one category of aggression, especially since there exists in some cases a strong tendency to create and magnify such pretexts into acts of war and which would be greatly facilitated and encouraged if it were possible at once to classify as an aggressor a state so accused.

There exist, moreover, a great many other situations of just as

[88] Cohn, *Kriegsverhütung und Schuldfrage*, p. 140.

[89] Liszt, p. 444 f.; Oppenheim, pp. 124 ff.; on *de facto* blockades, see Moore, *Digest*, VII, 283.

dangerous a nature; for example, the failure of a state to punish or pursue persons who have assassinated high officials of another state, as in the Serajevo and Corfu affairs. Any objective definition of aggression (attack and defense) is at once both too restricted and too broad; too restricted, because many other situations offer themselves for similar classification; too broad, because any of the acts so designated can be conceived as occurring under circumstances which should make it illogical to consider them aggression.

If we were to enumerate, as Article II of the Convention of 1933 does, a list of the various acts which, taken separately, should be considered as conclusive for the determination of the aggressor, we would reach the further complication that several of these acts may take place simultaneously on opposite sides. One state may have made the prior declaration of war, while the other may be guilty of the first attack; one state may have blockaded another, which in turn has refused to abandon its support of the armed bands mentioned above. Therefore in concrete cases such lists will lead to more confusion and argument, rather than to a simple and clear determination of the classification.

Proceedings of the Disarmament Conference

1. The report of Politis mentioned above, with the draft convention attached, was presented to the Disarmament Conference through the so-called Committee on Security Questions.[90] This report was thoroughly discussed during the meeting on May 24, 1933, and on the days following, when the problems arising from the definition of aggression and the attitude of various governments toward it were discussed and illuminated in a very interesting fashion.

M. Politis asserted that the definition of aggression was the keystone of the system of security. It would warn the states against committing any of the acts so defined; it would guide public opinion in forming a judgment as to which state was the guilty party,

[90] League of Nations, *Records of the Conference for the Reduction and Limitation of Armaments.* Series B. "Minutes of the General Commission," II (1933), 499 ff.

and it would make it simpler for an international body to designate the aggressor. He felt that the greatest value of the definition was in its clarity and inflexibility. One might here object that the acts so defined might, in a complex political situation, be common to both parties; the answer was then to be that decisive word "*first*." The aggressor is he who *first* commits one of the forbidden acts, and the other party thereafter acts in lawful self-defense, he asserted.[91] Another objection, however, is that states which rush to the assistance of the party attacked must also be regarded (according to the definition) as aggressors, since they by their relationship with the original aggressor have *first* committed an act of war. M. Politis attempted to avoid this difficulty by regarding this new Convention as an extension of the Kellogg Pact, which said that any state which, in violation of its agreement, resorted to war, forfeited its rights under the Pact, and the other states under the provisions of the Pact were thereby released from their obligations to assist it. The same theory was therefore to apply, he said, to the agreement regarding the definition of aggression.

Politis then discussed the five forbidden acts of aggression, as they were called: declaration of war, violation of frontiers, attack upon territory or vessels (upon which he said "no comment was required"), naval blockade, and support of armed bands. Of special significance to him was Article II of the Convention, which stated that no considerations of any nature, whether political, economic, financial, or otherwise, could be offered as justification for committing any of the defined acts of aggression. He himself[92] regarded this act as "an advance." He felt that the defect in the Geneva Protocol of 1924[93] had been that it was tied up to the sanctions system of Article XVI of the League Covenant. That handicap had now been entirely eliminated. The new draft did define aggression, but it omitted the question of the use to be made of this definition by other international agreements and authorities.

2. It is strange that M. Politis, who after all could not have failed to note somewhat the sharp criticism to which the Geneva Proto-

[91] *Ibid.*, p. 500.

[92] *Ibid.*, p. 501.

[93] Which as we know was also prepared by Politis, in coöperation with Beneš.

col had been subjected, should appear so unaffected by it as to continue here the same train of thought in an even more extreme form.[94]

The Geneva Protocol had laid down a number of *presumptions* regarding aggression, but the Committee's report at Geneva in 1933 now made them objective and irrevocable, and this was supposed to be progress. The Protocol had after all aimed at certain practical results because of its connection with the system of the Covenant of the League; these new definitions of aggression in the report of 1933 floated on thin air. They could not be decisive for the application of the League system, according to which not aggression but a purely formal standard of violation is to be regarded as the criterion for commencement of the prescribed procedure in the application of sanctions. Nor are they of any greater value for the more recent non-aggression treaties which make *unprovoked* aggression—not mere objective aggression—their criterion, while M. Politis' definitions of aggression purposely leave out of account the question of provocation, which he holds to be of no concern to a definition of aggression. Moreover, how can such an experienced politician as M. Politis continue to believe that public opinion or an international tribunal would permit itself to be bound in a complicated and troubled international situation by a mere formal definition, and one, moreover, of such insignificant and tautological nature as to assert that aggression is constituted by a declaration of war or an attack on land or sea, and so forth? Certainly one might discover this even without M. Politis' definitions, if these quite obvious criteria are appropriate to the case under consideration. If they are not appropriate, should they still be applied, merely to satisfy the formal text of a Convention? What nation, for example, might not, if in the situation of China under continued Japanese pressure, consider the necessity and desirability of issuing a declaration of war; and, if China were to do so, who could regard her for that reason as the aggressor? And while we

[94] It is also strange that M. Politis is so strong an advocate for the theory of aggression based on subjective guilt of a state, since he elsewhere (*Les Nouvelles tendances du droit international*, pp. 43 ff.) goes far in the opposite direction in denying the possibility of collective guilt of a state. See also Donnedieu de Vabres, *Droit pénal international*, pp. 423 ff.

might fairly regard the formal first passing of a frontier as an important consideration, it is quite impossible to apply this test with regard to war upon the high seas. It will never be possible to ascertain who fired the first shot nor to attach any significance to the fact, inasmuch as the shooter may have had good reason to believe that hostilities had already begun on other parts of the front and that his particular shot was not the first act of war.

It is furthermore incorrect to assert that the question of legitimate self-defense can be answered from a purely formal standpoint by saying that the other party had struck first. It does not hold for the municipal law concepts of self-defense,[95] nor can it be maintained in the realm of international law. Whoever is exercising the right of self-defense is justified in striking first when only by such means can he ward off a threatened or impending attack. The fact that the real aggressor is thereby put upon the defensive would then not constitute legitimate self-defense for the latter.

Just as untenable is the reference by M. Politis to the Kellogg Pact, which places the intervention of third states outside the definition. First, such an exception must find its authority in the text of the 1933 Convention itself, and, second, the value of any definition of aggression must lie in its objectivity and its universal character. There can therefore be no more reference found for its interpretation in the Kellogg Pact than in the Covenant of the League, in any of the more recent non-aggression agreements or in any other similar agreement, since any such provision would deprive the definition of its universal and objective character.

3. This draft was naturally supported at the meeting of May 25 [96] by Soviet Russia—which referred to its similarity to the idea of President Roosevelt that states should obligate themselves to hold their armies within their own territories—and by Poland and Chile. It was opposed, on the other hand, by the British delegate, Mr. Eden, in a very detailed and appropriate address, who maintained first,[97] that the criteria called for in the definition are of such a nature that any state or international organization, which

[95] Torp, *Den danske Strafferettens almindelige Del*, p. 294, who describes an "attack for purpose of defense" as true self-defense.

[96] League of Nations, *Records of the Geneva Conference, etc., op. cit.*, p. 510.

[97] *Ibid.*, p. 513 f.

would attempt to estimate which of two belligerents was the aggressor, would naturally and certainly take them into consideration, without being obliged by a formal agreement to do so. He said:

> No formal instrument signed by the nations of the world was necessary to ensure that result. They were the ordinary criteria which everyone would adopt.

It was worse than useless, however, for the draft to set up "a fixed and rigid criterion." It might be of significance in a few simple cases, but in those simple cases any definition would be unnecessary. It was only in the doubtful and difficult cases that such definition would be of value, but it was precisely here that the proposed absolutely rigid and automatically effective definition was positively harmful and dangerous. Any consideration of the circumstances which preceded and had occasioned the war was out of the question, Eden said, according to this definition of aggression. The controversy might, perhaps, have had its origin in a long-continued provocation, or in pressure exercised by some great power upon a lesser one; the stronger state might have consistently refused to permit a peaceful settlement of the question, or have made preparations for war and then mobilized. All this one had to disregard, according to the proposed definition of aggression.

It might further be the situation, he said, that one of the belligerents was guilty of one act, the other belligerent of another act, both being acts of aggression within the meaning of the above definitions, and that only a short time had elapsed between these two acts. Should the whole responsibility for the outbreak of war really be determined from a purely academic, chronological finding? In this manner we arrive at a conclusion to which no one in fairness or justice can subscribe. If we attempt to apply these definitions to such actual situations as have recently arisen, we soon realize that they are useless. Nor could Mr. Eden see the use of the additional list of special assertions which, he said, could not be urged as justification for aggression, because the text of the agreement itself provided that *no* considerations of a military, political, economic, or other nature whatever could be pleaded to justify them. That list could serve only to weaken the main rule. Actually the same objections had already been expressed ten years before, with regard to the Geneva Protocol, and he merely called attention to the opinions which had been expressed by Cecil as early as 1923 in the subcommittee of the temporary mixed commission, in which, referring to the work of the commission, Cecil had said, that under the conditions of modern warfare it is impossible even in theory to determine what constitutes an act of aggression. If these new definitions of aggression were put into effect, the designation of the aggressor would no longer depend upon a consideration of the existing situation in its entirety, but rather upon the ability of one of the parties to provoke the other into one or more of the acts comprehended by the definitions.

In his reply to Mr. Eden,[98] M. Politis attempted to defend his position by pleading the commonly recognized differences between Anglo-Saxon and Continental modes of legal thought. The English, he said, tried to avoid clear concepts and definitions. The question of the chronological sequence of the acts of aggression he had previously explained as being the difference between aggression and lawful self-defense.[99] Something similar applies to provocation, which must not be considered as being associated with the question of the aggression itself. Provocation either does not justify an attack, or else the provocation constitutes the aggression itself and hence *apparent* aggression is really lawful self-defense.

These formal considerations of M. Politis did not, however, touch upon the main point, which was simply whether provoked aggression and unprovoked aggression were to be treated alike. Recent non-aggression treaties clearly show that this is not the case. Equally out of order was the reference by M. Politis to the distinction between the English and the Continental modes of thought, which had nothing to do with the present question. Mr. Eden's comments provided a *positive criticism* of the proposed definitions, and were not made merely because he desired a more vague formulation of them or no formulation at all.

4. In the addresses following this, Turkey and Persia subscribed to the proposed definitions of aggression, as did the Rumanian delegate, Titulesco, who declared that the three states of the Little

[98] *Ibid.*, p. 515.

[99] As shown above, this argument is untenable.

Entente fully accepted the Soviet's delegation's definitions of aggression and considered that M. Politis' striking speech should remove any doubts about their value.

In the meeting of May 29,[100] the Spanish delegate, Madariaga, expressed several opinions concerning the differences between Anglo-Saxon and Latin mentality and the value of a purely automatic criterion for the definition of the aggression, which he said would exempt the state from the individual responsibility of designating the aggressor. Spain, he said, would give the automatic definition its sympathetic support. The Italian representatives, however, referred to a statement of Scialoja in 1927, in which he had expressed an opinion according with the British point of view, that a state which had decided to use military force against its neighbors never needed to act openly as an aggressor—its diplomacy would always be able to maneuver in such a manner that the intended victim would be forced to attack, and no special skill was required for this. Assume, for example, the wholesale slaughter over several days of the citizens of another state; should not the injured party be able to do something about it without recourse to the slower methods of juridical procedure? In any definition of aggression it is impossible to neglect the question of provocation.

Hungary and Bulgaria also supported the British view. The Chinese, however, felt that even an imperfect definition was better than none at all, and they therefore subscribed to the proposal for the definitions.

The French representative, Paul-Boncour, naturally gave to the proposals of Politis for the definition of aggression and determination of the aggressor his full and unreserved support. For him, the act of aggression was the necessary foundation for the whole security system, and without such basis no system could be erected.[101] The French, he asserted, could not understand what objections could be raised against it—a very characteristic utterance.

M. Politis then spoke again, to refute once more the various objections. He referred to the fact that the instrument under consideration enumerated acts of aggression in a general fashion without drawing any practical conclusions from them, and restated

100 *Ibid.*, p. 547 f.

101 *Ibid.*, p. 553 f.

his opinions about the unimportance of the element of provocation to them, even asserting here their complete analogy with the penal codes of municipal law. The representative of the Netherlands, M. Rutgers,[102] then spoke in opposition to the proposed definitions of aggression, emphasizing especially the conflict between their ideas and those of Article XVI of the League Covenant.

Classification by Subjective Guilt

1. We must finally mention the attempts to classify aggression and defense according to their subjective and criminal-law elements which would identify aggression with guilt, intent, or premeditation, while defense was assumed to be an innocent and blameless kind of war. This classification is not identical with that of just or unjust, since it concerns only the formal immediate outbreak of war and not the material legal conditions which caused it.

There is no doubt but that the question of guilt and the viewpoint of penal law underlay to a large extent the classification of war in Article XVI of the Covenant of the League. Evidence of this can be found, for example, in Articles 227 ff., of the Treaty of Versailles, which demand the punishment of the German Emperor and his highest officers. The question of guilt was placed in the first rank in Article 231 of that Treaty, which characterized Germany as the aggressor ("l'agression d'Allemagne") and the Allied and Associated Powers as those attacked, upon whom the war had been forced ("la guerre qui leur a été imposée"), and from this determination of war guilt was drawn the legal responsibility for the war, with the consequent obligation of the payment of reparations for all losses and damages suffered because of it.[103]

Accordingly, the question of guilt and the viewpoints of penal law lay at the very heart of the system of war prevention of the Covenant of the League of Nations, and ever since that time this

102 *Ibid.*, p. 563.

103 These needlessly expressed reasons for the obligations of reparation must be seen as a result of the war psychosis. The same holds true for the express assertions in Article 232 regarding the impossibility of Germany's giving the required satisfaction, while insisting at the same time that it shall be given ("*impossibilium nulla est obligatio*").

particular emotional attitude has been reflected in the development of thought along this line, an attitude which creates a special difficulty for the idea of neutrality. If the classification of war as aggression and defense was not itself a sufficiently unfavorable basis for the discussion of the continuance of the law of neutrality, this naturally is true in added measure when moral and other strongly emotional considerations become involved with it. The idea of neutrality had therefore no defenders toward the close of the World War, when passions had been brought to the highest pitch and the question of guilt, in an international atmosphere of strong moral feeling, governed the discussions over the formation of a new system of law.

In the years since, this point of departure has influenced greatly the consideration and treatment of the question of neutrality. The subjective, penal-law form of the classification by aggression and defense has given to the word neutrality an odious connotation which has been continuously maintained by its opponents whenever the word has been mentioned.[104] It must be admitted that the war-prevention system here found a form which, *if capable of being carried out*, would be particularly likely to excite passions in countries outside the controversy and thus to involve them in the system, even where such system—like that of the League Covenant—bore a military character. To fight war with war would thus no longer be regarded by them as the paradox it really is.

When such a fundamental point of view is laid down and then elaborated in a comprehensive international system, it is very difficult to free one's mind entirely, not only in fact, but in imagination as well, from its influence. Therefore this system is maintained not only by nations (and their strategists) who are directly interested in the rapid development of a war psychology against the "aggressor," in as many countries as possible, but also by many others who would embrace this train of thought with complete conviction, as being correct and necessary. What is more natural than to go to war alongside those who are fighting an aggressor—and this from

[104] See *supra* for references by Ray and Politis in their writings and the declaration of the Belgian delegate Rolin during the meeting of the League Assembly in 1929, League of Nations, *Records of the Tenth Assembly. Minutes of the First Committee*, p. 32.

moral and penal considerations, as well as from considerations of international policy?

It requires a great effort to free a system of war-prevention from these powerful motives, when they are once set in motion, and to advance to the point of recognizing that a *subjective* penal-law type of classification of aggression and defense is just as impracticable, and even more so, than an *objective* one. The problem is to be understood as a purely technical one of the purposes and means of war-prevention. It is not related to a more or less extreme pacifism. A subjective penal-law construction of a system of war-prevention is regarded favorably by extreme pacifists, and especially by them, perhaps, because of their strongly accentuated emotional attitude against wars of aggression. In other circles, too, these ideas are widespread, and must still be considered as the dominant ones. As early as 1927, the Assembly unanimously characterized war of aggression as an international crime. The Kellogg Pact and the Saavedra Lamas Treaty both oppose wars of aggression from this same viewpoint.

2. The first time a fundamental doubt arose as to the validity of this attitude was in the Assembly in 1929, upon the occasion of the question of incorporating the Kellogg Pact into the Covenant of the League.[105] The Danish delegate asserted that it was purposeless and futile to attempt to distinguish between lawful and unlawful wars, between wars of aggression and defensive wars, or to take into consideration the various notions of crime, guilt, or responsibility in connection with such questions. These concepts of war, which had been taken from the penal codes of the municipal law of nations, could not without further investigation be adapted and applied as a matter of course to the mutual relationships between states under conditions of international law.

This idea was then taken up and elaborated in a Swedish article by Professor Undén.[106] While in that article wars of aggression are considered to be a crime, and to be treated from that point of view, we are not to forget, he says, that the penal codes of all countries

[105] League of Nations. *Records of the Tenth Assembly*, pp. 28-30.

[106] *La guerre d'agression comme problème de droit international.* (Publications de la Conciliation Internationale), Paris, 1930.

give them possession of means for effectively combating crime, while there is possible in the international domain only a verbal condemnation in principle without a corresponding legal means of enforcement.[107] The Kellogg Pact, he says, is a program declaration against wars of aggression rather than a real prohibition. He questions the desirability of so strongly stigmatizing as a crime something which we are unwilling or unable to combat effectively. Nor can Article XVI properly be compared with a penal statute. The League of Nations as an international organization does not have the authority of its individual component members with police at their disposal, and has made no preparations in advance for combating this "crime." The sanctions system has only a remote resemblance to its municipal law analogies. Undén believes that the duty of the League is not that of punishing the aggressor, or of compelling him to make reparation, but that the sanctions system merely affords a means of defending one's self against a possible attack.[108] If they have failed in this purpose, they may be discontinued, but nothing is provided in the Covenant concerning the legal situation or consequences which then set in.

Moreover, the aggressor state as such is here subjected to sanctions, while under modern concepts of penal law it is private persons alone and not collective units which are presumed to be subjects of penal provisions, even if the codes do recognize a few exceptional cases of collective responsibility.[109] Finally, the very action which is to be punished, namely, aggressive war, is very difficult to define in a way corresponding to the definition of personal crimes in the penal code, even if Undén does not regard the problem as wholly insoluble.[110]

There exists, furthermore, no international body authorized to make decisions similar to those of a criminal court [111] as to whether a crime has actually been committed or not. The League Council,

[107] Opponents of this opinion regard sanctions as just such means of enforcement.

[108] Undén, p. 9.

[109] A thorough exposition of the municipal law aspect of this problem can be found in Stephen Hurwitz, *Bidrag til Laeren om kollektive Enheders poenale Ansvar, Copenhagen*, 1933.

[110] Undén, p. 11.

[111] On this refer to the discussions relative to an international criminal court, in Undén, foot of p. 19.

in particular, has no such authority,[112] but the Covenant leaves it to each individual state to make the decision, according to its own sovereign judgment. The proposal to establish a criminal division of the Permanent Court of International Justice at the Hague would be extremely difficult to carry out. Should states, as such, be punished or should we blame the private persons most directly involved and responsible for the outbreak of a war of aggression? A French criminologist, Donnedieu de Vabres,[113] has called particular attention to the difficulties involved in determining the individuals who actually cause a war. Wars are usually the result of political machinations, coupled with propaganda campaigns in the press. But what lies behind these? Private passions and interests, economic and political conditions. The consideration that the interested persons, if the war is unsuccessful, might be called to account at some later date before an international tribunal, would have but slight influence upon such causes. We must, moreover, remember the maxim, *nulla poena sine lege*, and first define exactly those acts, the commission of which constitutes an international crime, and then establish appropriate penalties for them.[114]

The fundamental distinction is finally emphasized by Undén; [115] that although there is assumed to exist a situation in international law between the aggressor and the defender corresponding to that existing between a murderer and his victim in municipal law, there are really many varying degrees of responsibility in a war of aggression, which do not always have such a far-reaching purpose. There should therefore be, as in municipal law, varying degrees of guilt, with appropriate punishments for each. One would also have to take into consideration the serious question of divided responsibility between the two belligerent parties. This would be a very difficult thing to do in the field of international relations. It might be that the aggressor was the one which was in fact right in the

[112] See, however, the Treaty of September 26, 1931, for promotion of the means for the prevention of war, Article V, sec. 2 (assumption of aggression when the ruling of the Council is ignored).

[113] *Les Principes modernes du droit pénal international*, pp. 426 ff.; see also Anzilotti, *Lehrbuch des Völkerrechts*, I, 389 f.

[114] This should not appear entirely impossible beforehand—see below for a discussion of the so-called "moral disarmament."

[115] Undén, p. 25.

main question at issue. Nevertheless, sanctions for purposes of war-prevention might, it is true, be applied against such a state, while penal considerations might determine the other party to be the guilty one.[116] It might also happen that conditions would change during the course of the war; the attacked state might become the one whose terms for peace had then become an obstruction to the ending of the war, and against whom sanctions ought then to be directed.

Taken in its entirety, Professor Undén's article is a valuable expression of the Danish point of view in 1929. But it alleges mainly certain external, practical difficulties in attaining its purpose of a law of war-prevention—difficulties which no doubt might be overcome if the fundamental views of the principle were practicable and promising. Attempts have frequently been made (by Saldana and Donnedieu de Vabres, among others) to apply the analogies of municipal penal-law concepts to this international-law situation, and such efforts cannot in general be dismissed as entirely hopeless or impracticable. The only question is whether these ideas are expedient enough to be of value in the establishment of a system of rules for war-prevention.

Theoretical Criticism of the Penal-Law Concept in a System of War-Prevention

1. A basic study of the analogy between penal-law concepts and a system of war-prevention, with its resulting subjective classification of wars of aggression, is to be found in a work upon the subject of war-prevention and its associated question of guilt published in 1931.[117] This book attempts to show that the penal-law element in the war-prevention system of the League, which had its origin in the bitter feelings prevalent at the close of the World War, is really due to an application, unjustifiable both theoretically and practically, of the viewpoints and concepts of municipal penal law to a situation in international law for which they are

[116] *Ibid.*, p. 29: "l'importance d'une distinction à établir entre la guerre d'agression et la guerre defensive vaut donc bien pour l'application des sanctions, mais elle n'offre aucune base permettant de fixer des pénalités."

[117] Cohn, *Kriegsverhütung und Schuldfrage*, Leipzig, 1931.

unsuited. This question was then connected with a demand for a complete revision of the Covenant system, and the article then tries to prove that the war-prevention system of the Covenant is of a quite different nature from that which was desired for a new legal system by the nations at the end of the World War.

In the Covenant of the League, war is by no means abolished; on the contrary, it is recognized as a last resort when the "moratorium" of the Covenant has failed to effect a peaceful solution. War is expressly recognized by it in the forms of wars of execution and wars of sanctions. The position of neutrals, within such a system, is still more difficult, the author contends, than under the régime of the traditional rules of neutrality. Neutrality is not abolished as a logical consequence of the abolition of war; neutrals are merely to be deprived of those rights which they obtained through centuries of effort. The very limited system of war-prevention—or rather, the "moratorium" system—of the League Covenant cannot be regarded as a counter concession for the sacrifice of the tested rules of neutrality and of neutrality policy, in which these states have hitherto sought refuge during dangerous international conflict.[118]

The book discusses particularly, and opposes especially, the penal-law analogy for a system of war-prevention and the subjective approach to the classification of war as aggression or defense. This idea of making guilt the basis for such classification is due to special motives which, if followed logically, lead to conclusions of a nature most unsuited to a system of war-prevention. Analysis[119] of Article XVI of the Covenant shows that it was originally drawn up under the assumption that a universal war of sanctions against the Covenant-breaker would go into effect but this assumption had already been abandoned before the final adoption of the Covenant, without any effort being made at that time to think through or reconsider the legal problems thus raised, as a consequence of this revision in principle. The result has been a self-contradictory complexity of rules, creating a situation which can be understood neither as that of a state of war, a state of neutrality, or a state of peace, nor yet as a new system of law, since

[118] *Ibid.*, p. 34.

[119] *Ibid.*, pp. 45 ff.

the former laws of war and neutrality are assumed as continuing.

The possibility that there is such a thing as collective responsibility is recognized[120] by the author, but traditional international law contains no legal concept of responsibility corresponding to this, and the theory of collective responsibility cannot be useful therefore as a basis for the classification of aggression and defense. Moreover, the concept of guilt in municipal law has likewise gradually lost its significance in the penal codes. It is now indicated to what extent the concept of aggression is really an impracticable attempt to objectify the subjective concept of guilt. Aggression and defense are, in the final analysis, merely concepts in military tactics which have no relation to situations in international law and do not lend themselves for use in a system of war-prevention or as a basis for such a system.

The treatise goes a step further when it makes the statement that war—including a war of sanctions—cannot be used as a means of preventing war. The desire to fight war with war is characterized as a *paradox*, not only in pure theory, but practically as well. War is unfit to be used as a penal measure[121] because it cannot be limited in its objectives and because it does not strike at the real criminal, but does strike principally the large elements of society which had nothing to do with making it but are rather the victims of its propaganda and promotion, or which by force are compelled to take part in it. An effective system of war-prevention must disregard the question of guilt, and find and organize other means of compulsion which are really suitable for preventing or opposing war. Among such means war itself must be ruled out. Neutrality, however, is not inconsistent with such means, if it is the expression of a definite policy and of a legal situation the object of which is to keep a state under all circumstances out of war. Limitation and isolation of the condition of war is a sturdier and more virile principle than that of the system of Article XVI of the Covenant, and because of this is bound to prevail.[122]

2. In opposition to these ideas it has nonetheless been held by some that there is a need and a possibility of classifying wars according to aggression and defense, with its resultant subjective

[120] *Ibid.*, pp. 102 ff. [121] *Ibid.*, pp. 146 ff. [122] *Ibid.*, p. 191.

qualification, from the analogy in penal law. As an example of this attitude, we refer the reader to a book of M. Politis, which we have previously mentioned in another connection, entitled *Neutrality and Peace.*[123] The general ideas are stated on the title-page, together with the motto: *Qui peut et n'empêche, pèche*, in other words, who can but does not prevent war is himself an accessory to it. It would hardly be profitable to go into the details of this idea and inquire if the smaller neutral countries can really prevent war by their participation in it, or can materially contribute to that result, or to emphasize the fact that here it is not a question of the *will* to prevent war but of the nature of the *measures* or *means* through which this will can be given expression. M. Politis, who prepared the foundation upon which the Convention of London of 1933 was erected, and was co-author of the Geneva Protocol of 1924, with its definitions of aggression and its automatic war-guilt mechanism, naturally implies that it is possible to determine clearly and definitely who is the aggressor and who is the defender, and upon these conclusions to set up moral and legal criteria, not for the use of League members alone, but for states outside the League as well (e.g., the United States), so that they too will be prepared to abandon their neutral status and join in the war against the aggressor.

It is the moral aspect which the author constantly presses upon the neutrals, while disregarding those other moral obligations which a neutral government has toward its own citizens against the misuse made, in the name of morality, of the complete ignorance of the real motives for the war, which is generally prevailing with the public, especially in states outside the controversy. He asserts that it is a moral duty to abandon one's neutrality and to oppose the aggressor. But who is the aggressor? Politis here refers to President Roosevelt's statement, according to which "the simplest and most accurate definition of an aggressor is one whose armed forces are found on alien soil *in violation of treaties*." [Our italics.] [124]

This, however, is really also an impracticable definition, since the question in every case is just that—is there a violation of a treaty or not? So far as the Covenant of the League is concerned, Politis

[123] Politis, *Neutrality and Peace* (F. C. Macken, tr.), Washington, 1935.

lays down a distinction in the criteria between formal and material aggression. The formal criterion is to be found in the system of Article XVI. The material criterion of aggression he finds in Article X[125] of the Covenant. A war which may be regarded as legal, according to the formal text of the Covenant, becomes illegal, "not by its cause, but by its effect," if it proves to have been aimed at the territorial integrity or the political independence of another state.

These standards for the classification of aggression and defense are moreover useless for the basis of a system of war-prevention, since the real aims of the war, especially the question of whether territorial changes are intended, will often not appear until the conclusion of the negotiations for peace. And, if we examine the intentions and possibilities which are already evident at the beginning of the war, we will see that almost any war, regardless of its character, holds a threat against the territorial integrity and political independence of the other state, since the purpose of war is the complete subjection of the adversary to the will of the victor.

It is certainly incorrect to cite Article X in connection with the system of war-prevention in Article XVI, just as it must be asserted that the obligations of sanctions under Article XVI do not apply to such a case. Article X has an independent significance within the system of the Covenant and is applicable even if the "external aggression" cannot be characterized either as war or as a war of aggression. This Article will furthermore apply also where a war, originally begun as distinctly defensive, ends in a victory over the opponent. At any rate its relation to war-prevention is only an indirect one. Its specific purpose is that of a guarantee of territorial integrity.

From other viewpoints as well, the ideas expressed in the treatise of 1931 have been made the subject of criticism, for a further consideration of which we refer to the discussions in the Conference on Security in 1934-35 (Lauterpacht, Scelle, La Pradelle, and others).

[124] Politis, p. 69.

[125] *Ibid.*, pp. 47 ff.

Any War Classifiable as both Defensive and Aggressive

1. Opposed to the classification of aggression and defense is the fact—depending upon the starting point selected—that it is possible to classify all wars both as wars of defense and as wars of aggression. Not only do states almost [126] invariably contend that the war upon their part is a defensive one and that the adversary is the aggressor, but it is quite true as a rule that a state resorts to war only when it considers itself compelled to do so for the defense of its national interests. It is therefore with a certain justification that the assertion is made that the danger of general war is more threatening from defensive wars than from wars of aggression.[127]

In his popular work, *The Outlawry of War*,[128] C. C. Morrison speaks of "the myth of 'aggressive war.'" For him there appears to be no such thing as aggression any more; [129] the real causes of war are generally hidden ones, unknown to the public; they are, as a rule, so complicated that even the war ministries would have difficulty in discovering which of the parties is the real aggressor (what with considerations of aggression as self-defense, of provocation, and others similar). The responsibility usually lies with both parties; "aggression is reciprocal." He believes that efforts at war prevention should be directed not against aggressive war, but against the system of war itself.[130]

The opposite opinion, in which all wars are regarded as wars of aggression, is set forth with some very interesting material in Georges Demartial's book, *Le Mythe des guerres de légitime défense*.[131] Voltaire long ago asserted that "toutes les guerres sont

[126] The Italian Government itself characterized its war against Ethiopia as an attack.

[127] Flüsser, *Krieg als Krankheit*, p. 59: "*Es gibt selbstverständlich nur Verteidigungskriege* ... Deshalb sollte nicht der Angriffskrieg verboten werden, den es doch überhaupt nicht mehr gibt, den schon Kant geächtet hatte, sondern nur der Verteidigungskrieg; dann wird es keine Kriege mehr geben, denn die einzige Gefahr droht von Verteidigungskriegen." (Our italics.)

[128] Pages 215 ff.

[129] "... in modern civilization there is no such thing as aggressive war.... No nation to-day fights a war of aggression" (see however above regarding Italy).

[130] Morrison, p. 223: "to destroy the myth of a single guilty nation and to locate the guilt in the war system itself."

[131] Paris, 1931.

offensives." Demartial demonstrates that the legal, moral, and religious basis for the outbreak of the World War was that war was a necessary and a logical attribute of state sovereignty. Men who chose this calling—a profession like any other—were highly respected. The public was willing to bear the expense of it as a very essential part of their heavy tax burdens. For many people war as such appeared to have a very high moral and spiritual value. As a rule their sympathies went out to the nations which started the war, as to the Boers in South Africa, to Japan against Russia, and to the Balkan states against Turkey. Even eminent scholars and pacifists, such as Montesquieu, had declared that a preventive attack was necessary in certain cases, as when another state appeared to be growing far too powerful.[132] At the Hague in 1899 and 1907, "*peace* conferences" had been held, but the result was merely a series of regulations for *war* and neutrality.

If we attempt to find a distinction between war of aggression and defensive war, he says, it must be found in the belief that one state (the aggressor) secretly prepares and suddenly launches an attack. But such a situation does not exist under modern conditions.[133] War cannot be conceived as self-defense against aggression. It is a duel which takes place with the consent of both parties.

2. This, according to Demartial, appeared clearly at the outbreak of the World War in 1914. If Serbia had accepted Austria's ultimatum, or if Austria had tempered this ultimatum as Russia desired, or if Russia had not intervened in the controversy, or if Germany had not placed herself at Austria's side, or if France had not aligned herself with Russia, or if England had not joined with France, there would have been no war. But all these states abandoned the cause of peace and took a position that was bound to lead to war because they believed it their opportunity and regarded it as their right and in their interest to do so. None of

[132] *L'ésprit des lois,* Chap. X: "Une plus longue paix mettrait cet autre en état de le détruire, et l'attaque est alors le seul moyen d'empêcher cette destruction."

[133] Here, however, note the special situation in the Italo-Ethiopian conflict in 1935; see, further, Marshal De Bono's book on the preparations and first military operations (1937).

them was innocent, but there is no reason for stamping any one of them more than any other as the guilty party or as a criminal.

This is of course not to say that they all were equally right or equally wrong. In making a decision upon this question, it is necessary to weigh the various reasons for which they were going to war. But the point is that all these nations *desired* war under the given conditions.

Not until after war had broken out did they each don the white robe of innocence, refute with horror the very thought that war was welcome, and explain that they had no reason at all to go to war except that they had been forced to do so by a sudden and unprovoked attack on the part of their adversaries.[134] The truth is that they were all armed to the teeth, that they had long expected the war, and had prepared themselves for it,[135] and that they all undertook that mobilization which each had severally declared would make war inevitable.

Demartial then examines those trains of thought which were expressed in the various countries upon the occasion of the outbreak of the World War, and demonstrates their falsity and absurdity. They assert motives which never existed and in which no one believes, and hide their real motives. During the Moroccan crisis in 1911, Russia had said to France: "no war for the sake of Morocco." If France in 1914 had said: "no war for the sake of Serbia," there would have been no World War. But when she agreed to the war "for the sake of Serbia" this still was not the real motive. If M. Viviani had told the parliament that he had agreed to this terrible war in order to save the Serbian officials from the humiliation that Austrian officials were to coöperate with the Serbian police in investigating the Serajevo murder, a howl of indignation would have risen against him. No, Serbia was merely a pretext, and this they all knew. Just as Russia entered

[134] "Der Krieg ist uns aufgezwungen worden" is the everlastingly asserted claim of the Germans, while the Allied and Associated Powers in Article 231 of the Treaty of Versailles speak of "la guerre, qui leur a été imposée."

[135] P., "Les neutres et la crise européenne," in *Revue générale de droit international public*, 1914, p. 506: "derrière ce rideau de faits mesquins et d'intérêts limités se cachaient de vastes combinaisons politiques. Personne ne l'ignorait, et chacun savait que tout le danger de la situation résidait dans ces combinaisons inavouées."

the war to obtain Constantinople, and Great Britain because she felt herself menaced by the attack on Belgium and because she wished to rid herself of an objectionable competitor upon the world's highways, so France went to war to recover Alsace-Lorraine, which had been wrested from it in 1871, and to regain which it now saw its opportunity. These things could not, of course, be said in public, for then the opposition in the parliament would not have voted the necessary grants. To obtain the support of their people and their allies, these states had to present themselves as innocent victims of aggression, acting in self-defense. For France, it was consequently a question of making Germany appear as the aggressor;[136] in this she succeeded because of the Russian mobilization. Because of this, Germany, as Austria's ally, was drawn into the war, and at the same time it declared war against France as Russia's ally. It happened to be true that Germany for a long time had considered war against France, recognizing that the five-milliard indemnity which Bismarck had required in 1871 had let that country off far too cheaply, and that the economic exhaustion of France could now be obtained on a quite different scale.[137]

On the part of both the French and the Germans, it was considered desirable that their adversary should be the first to declare war, for then they could claim that they were acting on the defensive in the war which they both knew was bound to occur, and which both desired should take place at just that time. When the Russian ambassador called upon the French government, with a demand for fulfillment of the obligations in the existing agreement calling for France to attack Germany if the latter should attack Russia, the French replied:

> You can absolutely rely upon us, but since everything points to the fact that Germany will declare war upon France, let us wait. It is

[136] Even in the Ethiopian war, Italy tried—according to De Bono's abovementioned book—to provoke Ethiopia into attacking her, and only when this failed did Italy assume the rôle of aggressor. See the letter of Mussolini to De Bono (*La preparazione e le prime operazioni*, 1937, p. 80): "Qualora il Negus non abbia intenzione di attaccarci, dobbiamo noi stessi prendere l'iniziativa."

[137] On this see Kerr, *Walther Rathenau, Erinnerungen eines Freundes* (Amsterdam, 1935), pp. 92 ff.

highly desirable that the declaration of war should not come from France but from Germany.[138]

Germany, on its part, wishing to make the most of the slower tempo at which the Russian mobilization had to take place, was urged toward a rapid attack against the French and was impelled for that reason to declare war against France on August 3, 1914. Nevertheless, in order to assume the rôle of the party attacked, says Demartial,[139] Germany alleged some flying over her territory by French planes, which probably had not occurred,[140] and was, in any case, a minor offense, which of course would never have given cause for a declaration of war if war had not already been decided upon for other reasons. Germany acted as little in self-defense as did her adversaries.[141]

3. In their propaganda, says Demartial, both sides made equally false assertions as to the exclusive guilt of their adversaries; in this the Western powers showed much greater ability than did Germany. In consequence of the use of such propaganda, France made the question of guilt the core of its entire war policy. It was beaten into the public conscience of the world that Germany's warfare was a crime because it was aggressive, while the war of the Allies was sacred because it was defensive. The same assertion was taken over into the Treaty of Versailles: "You stand before your judges to defend the greatest crime in history," said that old sadist, Clemenceau ("ce sadique vieillard de Clemenceau") to the German delegates upon their arrival at the Peace Conference. This crime was the declaration of war. But most of the "judges," namely, Great Britain, Japan, Italy, and the United States, had become participants, through their own voluntary declaration of war. Demartial describes this as the "acme of human hypocrisy, stupidity and malice."

When the war was over and a new and permanent organization

138 Demartial p, 39. Cited by him from the official Russian documents. (Our translation.)

139 The Kaiser's speech of August 4: "In aufgedrungener Notwehr, mit reinem Gewissen und reiner Hand ergreifen wir das Schwert."

140 On the false assertion that France was the first to violate Luxemburg's neutrality, see Luxemburg, *Neutralité du Grand-Duche*, p. 7.

141 See further Graux, *Les Fausses nouvelles de la grande guerre*, I, 345 ff.; de Visscher, *La Violation de la neutralité belge et le plan Schlieffen*, pp. 911 ff.

under international law was to be created, the authors of the Covenant were not ashamed, he notes, to build the entire system upon that same hypocritical falsehood, namely, the distinction between wars of aggression and defensive war.[142] The Kellogg Pact, too, rests upon the same presumption; it is not war which is prohibited, but aggression, and no criterion for this exists. The declaration of the League Assembly of 1927 likewise stigmatized aggression alone as an international crime. The nations reserved to themselves the right to defensive war, according to the usual pretext: "tout le monde invoquera la légitime defense et personne n'y croira." [143] Demartial arrives at the conclusion that future wars should be begun only after a referendum—a conclusion which cannot be accepted and in which there is not much security, as such popular votes and plebiscites on questions of foreign policy in recent times have clearly proved.

In a supplement, he shows that governments, in their diplomatic correspondence behind the scenes, take the established position that it is impossible to give definite criteria for distinguishing between war of aggression and defensive war, although outwardly, for the benefit of the great public, they maintain that that is the only criterion. During a discussion in March, 1912, between the British and French governments concerning the procedure of each during a possible future war, the Foreign Minister, Poincaré, instructed the French ambassador at London, M. Paul Cambon, as follows: "It is of the utmost importance that England should not obligate herself to remain neutral [during a war] between France and Germany even in case it should appear that the attack came from our side." The following day M. Cambon advised him that he had communicated this to the British government and "insisté sur l'impossibilité de reconnaître le véritable agresseur." [144]

Similar discussions took place between Great Britain and Germany. What the British desired was the assurance that Germany would agree to British superiority upon the sea. On their part, the demand of the Germans was that Great Britain should bind herself

[142] Demartial, p. 72: "Mais sur quelle base veulent-ils fonder la paix? On peut a peine le croire: sur cette même distinction entre les guerres agressives et les guerres defensives, qui leur a servi à justifier cinquante-deux mois de carnage."

[143] *Ibid.*, p. 87.

[144] *Ibid.*, p. 152.

to remain neutral in any war in which Germany might be a belligerent. The British Foreign Minister then suggested the formula that the two countries should mutually bind themselves to "benevolent neutrality during a war in which one of them was a participant and in which the aggressor could not be established." The Germans, however, refused to accept this, because "one might designate as the aggressor that country which first declared war, and that this might not of necessity constitute aggression, since such a state might regard its position as one of lawful self-defense, while it had, at the same time, assumed the offensive." [145] These negotiations with Germany therefore led to no result. Furthermore, a number of pronouncements [146] of prominent statesmen in France, Germany, Great Britain, Russia and the United States at the beginning of the World War indicate that these men were carefully attending to the interests of their respective countries by participating or refraining from participating in the war, and were making efforts in the former case to provoke their opponents to make the first attack so that they themselves might appear to be the victims of aggression, while, in their public addresses, they used flowery and bombastic phrases, and avowed only the purest idealistic purposes in entering the war, giving as their main reason their aversion to aggression.

The Classification of War in the Practice of the League

1. One might wonder, perhaps, why such an outstanding and important question as that of the possibility of the existence of neutrality within the classification of aggression and defense could still be the occasion of such wide differences of opinion, since it had to be solved in some form or other in the League's war-prevention machinery. The fact is, however, that in the fifteen years from the establishment of the League to the outbreak of the Italo-Ethiopian conflict in 1935, the Council was able to dodge this issue and to avoid taking a stand upon the question. This fact in itself constitutes a strong argument in favor of a new system of neutrality law for the prevention of war. In some few special

[145] *Ibid.*, p. 154.

[146] *Ibid.*, pp. 158 ff.

instances, it may be claimed that the Council has recoiled from the consequences of designating the aggressor, in fear of the danger to the existence of the entire system connected therewith.[147] But this explanation does not hold true for all cases. Even where the question involved only the smaller states and where the problem of determining the aggressor offered slight difficulty, the system of Article XVI of the League Covenant was disregarded, and a procedure was followed which gave no consideration to concepts of guilt or aggression, its sole purpose being, through identical treatment of both belligerents, to bring the war to an end, while the questions of responsibility, compensation, and the like, were tabled for later discussion and settlement. A typical case of this kind was the Greco-Bulgar incident of 1925. There was no doubt, by ordinary standards, as to which country was the aggressor.[148] The Chairman of the Council, Briand, however, rejected any attempt to make use of the classification of aggression and defense, with its consequent application of the Covenant through the system of sanctions under Article XVI. He succeeded, however, in stopping hostilities and preventing the outbreak of war by uniformly enjoining both parties to the dispute.

In other instances, too,[149] the Council has succeeded in settling the dispute before it became necessary to resort to the application of special measures of compulsion, and consequently without raising the issue of neutrality at all. The dangerous dispute between Greece and Italy in 1923, when Italy shelled Corfu, was also settled by Italy's quitting Corfu before the question of the application of Article XVI [150] arose, and only the dispute over the applications of Articles XII-XV was referred to a committee of legal experts.

[147] So also in the Corfu incident between Italy and Greece, and in the controversy between China and Japan over Manchuria.

[148] An account of this incident and its exemplary solution through the League machinery may be found in *Redegørelse for Danmarks folkeretlige Stilling efter Folkeforbundspagten og Kellogg-Pagten* (Copenhagen, 1931), pp. 213 ff.; see also Oppenheim, II, 139.

[149] A detailed report of the war-prevention activities of the Council may be found in Conwell-Evans, *The League Council in Action*, London, 1929; see also Schücking (1924), pp. 469 ff.; Philipse, *Le Rôle du Conseil de la Société des nations dans le règlement pacifique des différends internationaux*, The Hague, 1929.

[150] Conwell-Evans, pp. 76 ff.; Oppenheim, pp. 132 ff.

On the other hand, certain economic sanctions were applied in the dispute between Bolivia and Paraguay over the Chaco territory,[151] and on this occasion, too, from the beginning in a uniform way to both belligerents, without regard to the classification of aggression and defense. In February, 1933, the British government, with the support of the French, proposed to the Council that it prohibit the sale of arms and munitions of war to both Bolivia and Paraguay, and in the following year this proposal was laid before thirty-five governments, of which the majority gave their support to it.[152] This identical treatment was carried out, despite Bolivia's claim that it handicapped Bolivia (which has no seacoast) more than it did Paraguay.

Not until after the extraordinary session of the Assembly of the League of Nations in November, 1934, had submitted a number of proposals to both of the disputants for a solution of the controversy, was one of these finally accepted by Bolivia, while Paraguay rejected it. Those countries which had issued export prohibitions against shipments of arms and munitions were requested to cancel these with respect to Bolivia, so that they thereafter were applicable only against Paraguay (with certain increases in their severity). In June, 1935, hostilities were suspended between the two countries [153] and the prohibition with regard to Paraguay was then discontinued.

It might be possible to maintain that the Council considered its own measures of war-prevention from the viewpoint of their uniform application to both parties as being safer, at least in the beginning, with the immediate aim of ending the actual state of war without taking a definite position regarding the questions of aggression and defense. This tendency in fact is officially asserted in a report [154] approved by the Council on March 15, 1927, regarding procedure in case of threatened war. The chairman was

[151] There is an account of this dispute in the *Danish Report to the Rigsdag regarding the 15th Assembly of the League of Nations,* 1935; see also Oppenheim, p. 603.

[152] Some of these countries made it a condition for their support that certain others also subscribe to it.

[153] On the settlement of this dispute see the *Danish Report to the Rigsdag of the 16th Assembly* (Copenhagen, 1936), p. 38, also Oppenheim, II, 603.

[154] League of Nations *Reports and Resolutions* (Document A.14.1927.V), p. 76.

thereafter to send telegraphic appeals to both parties to refrain from hostile acts. In order not to disturb the legal situation, he might request both parties to avoid certain troop movements or acts of mobilization. He might designate a neutral zone from which both parties should withdraw their troops, the control of which could be established on the spot, with regard to both parties. Only when it appeared that one of the parties was not complying with the ruling of the Council, was the latter to put into effect various measures, such as to pronounce official censure, to invite the members of the League to recall their diplomatic representatives from the state in question or to take still more serious steps, such as naval or aerial demonstrations of a military nature.

2. The same tendency exists in the draft [155] of an agreement regarding the strengthening of means for preventing war, which was submitted to the Assembly in 1928, and which with various amendments was later incorporated into the previously mentioned Convention of September 26, 1931. Under Article I of this model treaty the parties obligated themselves to apply the provisional recommendations of the Council relating to the object of the controversy. Article III and IV are of special interest, because they deal with a situation which, in a sense, should be covered by Article XVI of the Covenant, namely, "in the event of hostilities of whatever kind having broken out." [156] In such cases, too, the parties are pledged to comply with the unanimous decision of the Council, first to withdraw their forces from the other's territory or from any zone demilitarized by agreement. This is really a war-prevention system of an entirely different character from that in Article XVI of the Covenant, and does not necessarily presuppose a classification of aggression and defense nor any other element of criminal responsibility. It requires in no way the sacrifice of the neutrality of the non-member states, in fact it is consistent with compulsory neutrality [157] because the efforts of

155 Published in the *Danish Report to the Rigsdag regarding the Ninth Assembly* (Copenhagen, 1929), pp. 223 ff. Also League of Nations, *Official Journal. Special Supplement No. 64* (1928), p. 116, and Annex 16 to the same, p. 459.

156 See League of Nations, *Official Journal* (1928), p. 1210. (Our italics.)

157 Cohn, *Kriegsverhütung und Schuldfrage*, p. 189 f.

the Council might easily be thwarted if one of the outside states should suddenly take advantage of the opportunity to declare war, as is considered in Article XVI of the Covenant.

In the Convention of 1931 these draft proposals were weakened in various ways. Thus the obligations in Article I include only measures of a non-military character. Article II covers the case of the invasion, by the armed forces of one of the powers, of the territory of another power or of a demilitarized zone, *except* during a state of war. If, despite the measures taken by the Council, war occurs, Article V, section 2, provides that such violation shall create the presumption of an *aggression* on the part of the guilty party under Article XVI of the League Covenant, an assertion the correctness of which we have previously refuted.[158] The Convention appears to be a compromise between the systems of the draft convention of 1928 and that of Article XVI, but proves to be a step backward when compared with the former.

The Theory of Aggression and Sanctions Against Italy in 1935-36

1. One might well say that the problem of harmonizing the two systems was still unsolved when the outbreak of the Italo-Ethiopian conflict in 1935 suddenly gave it a new direction. If emphasis had already been placed upon those realistic and legal uncertainties which must always exist with regard to the more important objections to the classification of aggression and defense —that doubts will always exist in fact as well as in law with regard to this classification—here was a case at last in which not the slightest doubt could exist. If it could be asserted of almost all former wars that both parties claimed to be acting in self-defense, here was one situation in which one of the parties frankly acknowledged its rôle of aggressor, because this rôle was quite in harmony with the social philosophy and domestic policies of that state. It was that "heroic" effort, the attack, the slaughter, which was supposed to give to war its value, according to that philosophy of life. There could, then, be no cause for doubt, either practical

[158] *Supra*, pp. 230 ff.

or theoretical, concerning the classification of this conflict; the problem appeared clear-cut. Sanctions were started against the aggressor and the neutrals were forced to show their hands.

This instance [159] offered a unique opportunity to test the war-prevention system of the Covenant of the League and to form an estimate of the value of the classification of aggression and defense as a basis for that system. It is true that sanctions were to be applied, in this instance, against a Great Power, but this did not prevent almost all of the League members from loyally declaring themselves as ready to support these sanctions. Neither could the lack of universality be pleaded as an excuse, since the outside major Powers were either entirely neutral or, like the United States, in a semi-neutral position which would later come to mean their actual support and direct coöperation with the sanctions provisions of the League of Nations. All conditions required to put the system into operation were propitious—and what happened?

Italy, which had over a long period transported large numbers of troops to its colonies bordering on Ethiopia, crossed the border and commenced hostilities on October 3, 1935. Italy admitted being the aggressor and acknowledged that its purpose was to conquer Ethiopia, or the major part of it, for use as colonial territory. It was a war in direct violation not only of Article XVI, but also of Article X. The Italians offered no legal excuse or explanation; they made allegations of a purely extraneous nature, such as stating that slavery was not yet abolished in Ethiopia, or that their action involved merely a colonial war, which is just as certainly not permitted by the League Covenant and cannot be put forward as a limitation of the general obligations assumed there concerning the prohibition against war.

On October 7, 1935, the Council decided that Italy had resorted to war contrary to the obligations of member states under Article XII of the Covenant. The question of application of sanctions was referred to the Assembly, who approved it by a vote of 50 to 3, whereupon sanctions were authorized to go into effect against

[159] An account of this conflict is found in Serup, *L'Article XVI du Pacte et son interpretation dans le conflit Italo-Ethiopien*, Paris, 1938.

Italy. A Co-ordination Committee was appointed to bring about unity in the system of enforcement of the measures [160] to be taken under Article XVI.

2. The first fact of interest for the question of neutrality was that the major Powers almost immediately discovered that there was no way to apply the so-called automatic sanctions system of Article XVI, or rather the Resolutions of 1921,[161] with their successive (truly, in this case, very slowly successive) application of sanctions. There was no trace to be found of the famous Brouckère's Report,[162] which had gained such considerable support, particularly from the French, British, and Belgians, the object of which had been to prove that the Resolutions of 1921 had lost their legal significance. Not a voice was raised for the application of the ideas of that Report, or to reassert its contention that the successively severer measures of the League system must find their authority within the text of Article XI of the Covenant wherein there appeared no loophole for avoiding the immediate and automatic application of its severest penalties.[163] It was the Resolutions of 1921 which provided the only possible basis for the application of such sanctions in practice, those Resolutions whose origin lay in the proposals of the neutral countries and which were founded upon the report of the Blockade Committee of 1921.[164]

The measures thereupon taken by the League were much delayed and too restricted in their nature, and were in any case unsuited to their aim of placing obstacles in the progress of the war, let alone actually stopping it. In accord with a resolution passed by the Assembly on October 10, 1935, the Co-ordination Committee made a number of proposals to the League members regarding prohibition of the export of arms to Italy; such pro-

160 Material on the application and failure of the sanctions is found in League of Nations, *Official Journal, Special Supplements* Nos. 145-49, Geneva, 1935-36.

161 *Ibid.* (*No. 145*), p. 30 f., where the Little Entente and Great Britain arranged that the Resolutions of 1921 should not be specifically mentioned. In the debates upon the Danish bill of Nov. 5, 1935, concerning the enforcement of sanctions against Italy the wording of the Resolutions was used.

162 *Ibid.*, p. 60 f.

163 *Ibid.*, p. 70: "...to say that certain commercial relations will be gradually severed when the text demands that they shall *all* be broken off *forthwith*, is to make an almost ridiculous use of a clause...."

164 *Ibid.*, pp. 15 ff.

hibition was not to be applicable to Ethiopia.[165] Shortly thereafter a number of measures of a financial nature were proposed, designed to prohibit all direct or indirect loans to the Italian Government, including all bank and other credits, and the like. There followed, on October 19, a proposal for the prohibition of the importation of all Italian goods (with the exception of gold and silver bullion) and against the exportation to Italy of certain additional articles for use in war.

The Co-ordination Committee also assumed charge of the organization of material support among the sanctioning countries, in accord with Article XVI, section 3, of the Covenant. A number of very complicated rules were proposed to prevent those countries which participated in the sanctions and who thus lost Italian markets from suffering thereby. A sub-committee was appointed to solve in advance such legal problems as might arise in the enforcement of the sanctions, to formulate regulations for juridical procedure in case of complaints, and for similar purposes. In particular, it examined the "most favored nation" clauses in various treaties in order to clarify the position of those countries which, had been granted under its terms certain privileges by Italy, and to determine, on the other hand, how to prevent these "most favored nations" from claiming the special membership privileges conceded in the text of Article XVI, section 3, of the Covenant, and which had suffered special losses because of their participation in sanctions.[166]

There was thus an excellent spirit and much business in the air at Geneva. The Committee appealed to the states outside the League in order to discover to what extent they would be willing to support the League efforts. Telegrams were being dispatched daily to members to keep them informed of developments and in particular of the measures which other members were taking for the carrying out of sanctions.

A wonderful and gratifying event had occurred. Practically all the League members had subscribed to sanctions with the greatest

[165] A statement of the various measures taken together with enclosures, exists in the Danish Report to the Rigsdag of the 16th Assembly (1936), pp. 45 ff., entitled "The Sanctions against Italy" (Sanktionerne mod Italien).

[166] *Ibid.*, p. 50 f.

loyalty and discipline. Only Austria and Hungary had declared themselves unable to join in the Council's decision, and Albania alone had declared that she could not take part in sanctions.[167]

It was of the greatest interest to the question of neutrality to observe next the attitude of Switzerland and of Luxemburg, the general policies of which countries with regard to neutrality have been discussed above. The Swiss views were expressed in a note of October 28, 1935, and concerned the claims of Switzerland for a special position in two respects. In the first place, Switzerland had *carried out the export prohibitions equally against both belligerents*, Italy and Ethiopia. In the second place, she would not forbid importation from Italy to Italian Switzerland, since this would occasion irreparable losses which could not be compensated for by the means prescribed in Article XVI, section 3. Switzerland, however, would arrange that the normal importation should not be exceeded.

The latter exception finds a certain authority in the Resolutions of 1921 whereby economic compulsory measures may be postponed by certain countries, in order to reduce as much as possible the losses which these countries might suffer therefrom. It was presumed, however, that the Council alone was to possess the authority for granting such postponement, and that an individual League member could not so act on its own initiative.

The reservation of neutrality mentioned above is, on the other hand, of the greatest interest, because it proved that, when faced with the issue, Switzerland would not apply its own earlier theories concerning the possibility of a combination between the systems of neutrality and of sanctions—which were, that its neutrality was consistent with full participation in economic sanctions, except where no military sanctions were involved. On the contrary, Switzerland now took the position outlined in the Danish treatise of 1924, according to which a combined system of neutrality and sanctions must be carried out in the military as well as in the economic field, against both belligerents equally when necessary to maintain neutrality.

[167] In a note of Oct. 30, 1925, Panama offered certain amendments to the proposals of the Co-ordination Committee.

The position which Switzerland assumed on this occasion must therefore not be considered as the expression of any special status within the League, but simply as a position which any League member, desiring to combine a system of neutrality and sanctions, would be justified in taking.

Luxemburg took the same position in a note of October 26, 1935, although that little country had no treaty guarantee of her status within the framework of the League under neutrality law. She simply referred to her neutrality *policy*.

3. Apart from these exceptions, the neutrality question was not raised for the moment by the members of the League,[168] who agreed to apply the system of sanctions unilaterally to the detriment of Italy [169] and to the advantage of Ethiopia.[170]

Of the greatest interest, however, is the Dutch law of October 9, 1935,[171] because it makes a sincere effort to avoid the conflict between neutrality and sanctions by separating the measures of sanctions from the condition of war of Article XVI, and to tie these up with the general efforts "for promotion of international coöperation in the interest of peace or to protect certain vital interests of the Kingdom during times of strained international conditions." [172] By thus placing the efforts of the state at the general service of war-prevention, one may justly assert that war-prevention has been put upon a higher plane than merely distin-

[168] For Denmark's part, see Law No. 298 of Nov. 16, 1935, Denmark, Statutes (*Lovtidende*, p. 1177), the text of which avoids reference to any special position upon this question.

[169] See *Proclamations* Nos. 299, 300, and 301 (of Nov. 18, 1935), *ibid.*, pp. 1177 ff.

[170] An account of the Norwegian sanction measures is published in Statute nr. 10 (1936), *Aktstykke vedkomande Noreg og konflikten millom Etiopia og Italia* (a document concerning Norway and the Italian-Ethiopian Conflict), together with a series of royal resolutions, it can be found in Norway, Statutes, *Norsk Lovtidende* (1935), pp. 985 ff. For Swedish materials, see the Swedish *Proclamation* No. 560 of Nov. 14, 1935, regarding prohibition against importation into the country of articles from Italy, in Sweden, Statutes, *Svensk Lovtidende* (1935), pp. 1213 ff., the Swedish Law No. 123 of April 24, 1936, regarding the right of the Crown to prohibit credits, *Svensk Lovtidende* (1936), p. 191, etc.

[171] Netherlands. Statutes, *Staatsblad van het Koninkrijk der Nederlanden*, No. 599 (1935).

[172] ". . . ter bevordering van de internationale samenwerking in het belang van den vrede of ter bescherming van de levensbelangen van het Rijk in tijden van buitengewone internationale spanning."

guishing between participation in war and neutrality. These measures—despite the assumptions in Article XVI of the Covenant—should also be taken during strained international situations *before* war has broken out, indeed especially to *prevent* its outbreak, a situation which has no relation to the traditional concept of neutrality. Article I of the law expressly places war situations upon an equal footing with those of pre-war ones, since it reserves to the crown the right "to take measures of international coöperation for the purpose of *prevention* or *cessation of hostilities*."[173]

A similar law,[174] with the same statement of reasons, applying to the importation of goods from a number of countries including the aggressor and belligerent nations, and relating also to the extension of credits, the dispatch of merchant vessels to ports in those countries and the arrival at Dutch ports of vessels therefrom, or the transfer of ownership to the Governments or citizens of such countries was passed on October 26. The objects and the texts of these laws are undoubtedly superior to those of the Scandinavian countries. In Norway and Sweden there was no general enabling ordinance, as this is not a constitutional requirement there. The Danish Law Number 298, of November 16, 1935, gives a rather general and broad authority to the Government to comply with the membership obligations assumed under the terms of Article XVI, section 1,[175] of the Covenant, the text of which accords with the earlier and previously mentioned idea that it is permissible to distinguish between the obligations of the first and the second sections of that Article to the extent that a member may undertake one group of obligations and decline the other.

The states outside the League remained neutral. With particular

[173] ". . . als maatregel van internationale samenwerking tot het voorkomen of het beëindigen van vijandelijkheden."

[174] *Op. cit., Staatsblad No. 621* ("*Sanctiewet 1935*").

[175] The text of the law is as follows: "The Government is authorized, after consultation with the Committee on Foreign Policy and with the approval of the Finance Board of the Rigsdag, to take such measures as Denmark has assumed the duty to take by virtue of her membership in the League of Nations in order to effect the terms of Article XVI, section 1, of the Covenant, and for the co-operation which in any given case the League authorities may request."

reference to the United States, that country had originally taken a position under its new neutrality law,[176] described in detail above, which implied, in fact, its complete support of the system of sanctions. The situation, for that matter, was an ideal postulation of the theory of aggression, a united front against the aggressor, a disregard of neutrality principles with the support of the United States.

4. But now the rôles were strangely reversed; the mechanism was there and its functioning was perfect, but the sanctioning states weren't in the right mood to enjoy it. They felt sure that something was the matter. Great Britain, from the beginning, had taken over the direction of the sanctions policy and had given it emphasis by assembling a large fleet in the Mediterranean. By closing the Suez Canal to the Italian troops, that country might in an effective manner have prevented[177] the continuation of the war.[178] Another effective device would have been to stop the supply of oil[179] to the aggressor. But this they did not wish to do. France hesitated. Public opinion in the other sanction countries began to question whether the ideals which had in this case mobilized world opinion against "the aggressor" were the real and decisive motives, or whether possibly other and political motives underlay the attitude of the Great Powers. The newspapers told of British interests in northern Ethiopia and at the sources of the Blue Nile, and of

[176] *Supra*, pp. 125 ff.

[177] The Italians had counted upon the possibility of the closing of the Canal; see the letter from Mussolini to De Bono (*La preparazione e le prime operazioni*, p. 110): "Tu devi predisporre viveri e munizioni per almeno tre anni e per quanto sembri assurdo, anche perchè convenzioni formali esistono circa il passaggio del Canale di Suez in pace e in guerra, bisogna prevedere difficoltà di passaggio."

[178] According to Article I of the Treaty of Oct. 29, 1888 (Martens *Nouv. Rec. Gén.*, II, ser. 15, p. 557), the Suez Canal is to remain open at all times, including time of war. The question of the validity of this provision as conflicting with Article XVI of the League Covenant was the object of some theoretical discussion, but it did not arise in practice. The correct interpretation, of course, is that Article XVI should have precedence; see also Article XX of the League Covenant; for other opinions that the Canal should have been closed to Italian war vessels see Lauterpacht, *The Covenant as the "Higher Law,"* p. 64; Hoskins, *The Suez Canal in Time of War*, p. 101.

[179] See Jessup, *Neutrality*, IV, 132 f., on the British exports of oil to Italy and the consequent unwillingness of the United States to halt its own oil exports.

France's desire to keep Italy in the common front against Central Europe. Had Italy been promised in advance that oil sanctions would not be applied? Instead of a simple and sincere proposition of applying effective sanctions against the aggressor, it was here evidently a question again of an intricate game of world politics, in which the pieces were being moved from considerations and motives entirely unknown to the great, credulous, and ignorant public.

Then came the decisive act which converted the sanctions program into a mere stage performance, and turned the interest of the United States away from its new-neutrality policy, back to that of traditional neutrality, namely, the French-British [Hoare-Laval] peace proposal of December 10, 1935. At the very moment when all the countries of the world had been encouraged to agree to sanctions, when it was evident to everyone that an extension of these to include supplies of oil would have quickly brought the war to a stop, when the entire system, to everyone's surprise, had proved to be completely workable, Great Britain and France, the leading Great Powers of the League, made a joint proposal by which Ethiopia was to be pressed to cede half its territory to Italy and in addition, was to give to the latter country the control of the remainder of its territory, with a view to its annexation in the future.

The proposal was forwarded, together with a joint note of December 13, 1935, from the French and British governments to the Secretary-General of the League, who in his circular note of the same date (League document C. 482. M. 258. 1935. VII) made it known to all the other League members. With no authorization from the League of Nations and referring only to those desires which quite naturally arise at frequent occasions within the Council and the Assembly that disputes might be settled by peaceful means, Great Britain and France had made a proposal to Italy and Ethiopia "advising" the Ethiopian government (and only that government) to cede to Italy large parts of its territory with exact geographical boundary delimitations. Great Britain and France then would "use their influence in Addis Ababa and in

Geneva[180] to get his Majesty the Emperor to agree to, and the League of Nations to approve, the creation in southern Ethiopia of a sphere of economic expansion (*zone d'expansion*) which was to be reserved to Italy, the comprehensive boundaries of which were also stated. Within this huge territory Italy was to enjoy, through a newly created company, "de droits économiques exclusifs," ownership of the land, a monopoly of rights to exploit mines, forests, and natural resources, and so forth. The British and the French governments were to coöperate to the effect that this company, the further details of the arrangement to be prepared by the League of Nations, should "secure to their fullest extent the interests of Italy in this area." It was impossible that those making this "peace proposal" could have any doubts about its psychological and political effects. It is true that there arose such indignation and disappointment, indeed consternation, all over the world and even in influential circles of the proposing countries themselves, that it had to be withdrawn without even being discussed by the League of Nations. It is also true that its proposal caused changes in the governments of those two countries themselves and that they shortly thereafter returned to what were known as League of Nations policies. But all this cannot erase the fact from the knowledge of the world that the sanctions system had proved to be an instrument for secret interests of higher politics, which were of no concern to those numerous countries whose coöperation had been given under entirely different assumptions, so much the more in that they did not continue after that time the extension of further sanctions, which would have been an important step toward ending the war, but simply permitted matters to take their course, regardless of the original question of aggression or defense.

It is quite possible that the reasons against the application of effective sanctions were serious and compelling. To this no importance can be attached; what is important for us here is that the classification of war as aggression or defense is entirely insufficient

[180] There was no mention of any efforts having been made in Rome to influence the Italian Government to accept these proposals!

to support the system of sanctions which the theory of aggression presupposes. The Italian-Ethiopian conflict proved this, first, because there was no doubt about the classification in that instance; and, second, because such classification had proved to be without important influence upon the sanctions policies of the leading nations.

IV

NEO-NEUTRALITY AND THE "DISQUALIFICATION" OF WAR

Meaning of the Terms "Disqualification" and "Neo-neutrality"

1. THE TERM "disqualifiation" will be used here in two senses. In the first place, it will be used in its literal sense, namely the lack of qualification, in other words, denying either that any distinctions exist or, if they do, that there is any reason for taking them into account. In the second sense, the expression will be used to describe that which is not entitled to be qualified, or which is not considered in making a decision, as when a participant in sports is disqualified.

The disqualification of war means, then, first, that there is no need, in a system of war-prevention, to attach importance to the differences in classifications of war, differences in the various causes of war, or the various explanations for war. These differences may have great importance in other situations, such, for example, as deciding the question of right or wrong for the purposes of affecting the decision of an arbitral court or for the determination of obligations to pay reparations. Consideration of the various causes of war may, perhaps, be of value as an indirect means of preventing war, or in the application of such social, political, and economic measures as may abate the force of these measures. But when a system of war-prevention aims at the abolition of war itself, it is of no consequence to introduce distinctions between the various kinds of war, so that, for example, only wars of aggression would be prevented while other kinds of war would in principle be recognized as legal. The task would thus become insoluble, both theoretically and practically: theoretically, because it is impossible to determine, in a manner sufficiently clear and unambiguous, those factors upon which the distinction is to be based; practically, because any war, including defensive war, has a tendency to keep war in general, and thereby wars of aggression, as an institution. As long as we continue to recognize war itself as legal, and base our classifications upon moral, legal, strategic, or similar considerations, we preserve the institution of war, which has so strong a hold upon the minds of people that it will reassert its original influence.

2. But the disqualification of war also means the refusal to accord to the various causes or reasons for its origin, any value in a system of war-prevention. The disqualification of war is therefore merely another term for the "devaluation" of war. As we have seen, the League Covenant does not take this view, since it gives to war certain important functions in the maintenance of international law and order, among these being wars of sanctions, execution-wars, and defense. This is opposed to a system of war-prevention in various essential ways. War should in no sense be legalized under international law any more than is revolution in the constitutions of states. If war or revolution does occur, nevertheless, we have thereby broken its relation with the existing system of law. It is possible that wars are no more avoidable than are revolutions. It is possible that both have, in particular cases, a certain moral background, or that there may arise from them a new system of law, but they cannot themselves be incorporated into that system.

So far as war itself is concerned, it uses such means and has such consequences that it must under any and all circumstances be described as a catastrophe, which can never be justified by its few possible useful consequences. As we have said, it may in some particular cases be inevitable. In such cases, outside states must confine their efforts to extending assistance in the most feasible form to those states which the disaster has hit, without, however, permitting themselves to become involved in the war. On the other hand, their sympathetic endeavors for the prevention of war should be equally for the benefit of the "aggressor" state, the people of which, or at least a large proportion of them, no more desire war than do those of the "attacked" states. In this sense, war-prevention is thus more of a supranational than an international problem.

When we examine the nature of war and the possibility of its prevention, we can and therefore should consider war in its universal aspect, regardless of possible qualifications of this aspect. War is, then, what it always was during the régime of traditional neutrality, a conflict conducted with military arms between two or more states, for the purpose of subjugating one to the will of the other. It is against war in this sense that war-prevention is directed, and which it will no longer recognize as a legal situation under international law; that is, it will no longer associate with war those belligerent rights such as were granted in the Hague Conventions of 1907 and the London Maritime Declaration of 1909. On the contrary, it should refuse to concern itself with classifying war in such ways as might, after all, make war permissible or praiseworthy in special cases. Its task must, so far as possible, be to oppose war of whatever nature and under whatever classification.

3. Such an attitude toward war is clearly consistent with the idea of neutrality. Classification of war is an argument against neutrality, while disqualification argues in its favor. Nevertheless, neutrality as a part of the system of war-prevention (Neo-neutrality) is essentially different from traditional neutrality. The latter was based on an equal *evaluation*[1] of the belligerents, with consequent impartiality toward both under detailed rules for war and neutrality. Traditional neutrality took a dependent and passive attitude toward war. It was oriented by war. Neo-neutrality, on the other hand, is based on an equal *devaluation* of the war in all cases; it does not seek its own *raison d'être* in reflections as to whether it has in one situation or another a moral or legal claim to assert its nonparticipation as a right; it takes an exception in principle to participation in war in any form. It does not recognize the supremacy of the law of war; it replaces it instead with a system of combined sanctions and neutrality which centers about an effort to suppress and prevent war of every kind. The neo-neutral states are in reality those states which, without becoming a party to war, are participants in the system of sanctions designed

[1] Moore, *Digest of International Law*, VII (1906), 860: "the state of *neutrality* recognizes the cause of both parties to the contest as *just*."

to prevent war. They do not participate, and under no circumstances will participate, in war. Moreover, they do not recognize war as a legal situation, they recognize no obligation of impartiality, and they are willing to apply any means to prevent or to stop the war to the limit of their ability without themselves participating in it. How such an attitude can be made consistent with the existing rules of the Hague Conventions and of the Covenant of the League is a *technical problem* which we have discussed before. We shall here proceed to examine those new ways in which a system of war-prevention under new-neutrality law must develop unhampered by those formal ties.

The Causes of War

1. The historical study of war proves that it had an importance, especially in early times, in the preservation and development of nations, which cannot be characterized as an entirely absurd or unreasonable one. It has, in many instances, meant the elimination of conflicting tendencies which had accumulated and which required a solution. Just so, in revolutions and the detaching of colonies from the mother countries, war meant in some cases a release from certain intolerable restraints which could be shaken off in no other way. Most nations, in reviewing their history, can find wars which could hardly have been avoided under the conditions existing at the time, and which in a very real sense form an important factor in their rise and development.

One must admit, for what it is worth, that there are certain necessary, and thus rationally well-founded, causes of war. But this historic point of view must not be carried to such extremes, as frequently happens, that war may be claimed to be a logical and necessary part of historical evolution or of the future. Such thought often lies at the root of a discussion of the causes of war. One pretends to find certain definite situations which will as surely in the future as in the past lead to war, and thus will nullify any efforts at war-prevention. Such a position cannot be recognized as justified.

Properly to oppose or prevent war, it is above all necessary to study intelligently the nature of war—to see what it really is. This problem must be solved independently of all classifications of war, and apart from all evaluations of a moral or legal nature, let alone strategic considerations, so that we may be able to view war as something which needs an explanation for its existence, not for its justification, just as criminologists seek an explanation for a crime without assuming it to have been a justifiable act under the circumstances. These "causes of war," which are usually stated to be such and which the Covenant of the League itself takes into account, are of a qualifying nature, in that certain reasons are given which are considered as rendering war excusable or even permissible in certain cases, just as elsewhere the system of the Covenant justifies war as of value for the maintenance of law and order. A rational system of war-prevention looking to the future cannot apply that sort of evaluation of "causes." Several of these so-called "causes of war" are, moreover, only pretexts which cannot be taken seriously.

2. If we examine the qualifying statements in the League Covenant concerning the causes of war, we shall reach the conclusion that they are at best ill-founded.[2] In its war-prevention system the League has included this question in a broader sense, namely, as the basis of measures intended to prevent war. It assumes that by opposing certain *causes* of war, and especially those causes which are stressed in the Covenant, we are fighting war itself; that is, that we lessen the danger of wars which would be prepared for and which would occur for those reasons.

The League Covenant, however, has by no means included all the factors which in popular opinion make for war, as for example the unequal distribution of raw materials, the legal status of national minorities, and others. There is moreover a wide difference in the degree to which the Covenant has taken up the question of the positive elimination of these causes. In some instances a question of positive law of war was involved as, for example, the abolition in Article XVIII of so-called secret diplomacy. In other instances

[2] The views herein expressed were first stated in a report presented by the writer to the London Conference on Collective Security in 1935: "*Les Causes de la guerre et le désarmement moral*," of which abstracts were published in Bourquin (ed.), *Collective Security*, Paris, 1936, pp. 287 ff.

the Covenant contained only rules of procedure, or more or less specific representations, such as those in Article VIII, for example, concerning disarmament; that in Article XIX, concerning the revision of obsolescent treaties; and that in Article XXII, on the protection of colonial peoples. There are, finally, a number of causes of war for which the Covenant has for the present merely devised a program along broad lines, reserving to the future its fulfillment. This holds true particularly for Article XXIII, on humane working conditions for labor; criminal international traffic in human beings, dangerous drugs, and arms and ammunition; and on the "open-door" policy.

With special regard to social distress, Part XIII of the Treaty of Versailles gave express consideration to the question of war-prevention, for it asserted that world peace "can be established only if it is based upon social justice, and that conditions of labor exist which create for many people such injustice, hardship and privation" that there is always occasion for dangerous threats to the peace of the world. With this preamble, Part XIII creates within the framework of the League of Nations a comprehensive labor organization for the adjustment of the interests of employers, workers, and states, an organization which from its original purpose was regarded above all as a means of consolidating world peace.

Without proceeding to details, we may suppose that the direction of these ideas is obvious. It is true that the causes mentioned are not intended to explain nor to excuse wars arising from such conditions, but that the conditions are made to be jointly responsible, and there is given here one path along which an effective war-prevention plan might progress.

3. One might reasonably oppose certain objections to this entire train of thought. In the first place, no real proof exists that there is any connection between working conditions and the danger of war.[3] The desire for war and the war spirit are not to be found

[3] This question of social privation is not among those which the Institut International de Coopération Intellectuelle has investigated; see further League of Nations. International Studies Conference, *Collective Security* (Bourquin, ed.), French ed., II, 295 (hereafter cited as "Bourquin, ed."), where it is stated that for the present only the following causes of war—population problems, colonies, raw-materials, and markets would be discussed.

particularly in the lower classes of society, where social and economic discontent are assumed to be present. Nor is it at all likely that in the not-too-distant future the hopes expressed can be attained, for example, that the standard of living between the workers of the Occident and those of the Orient, can be equalized, if such equality was ever intended or desired by the parties concerned. Nor has anything occurred in practice which would indicate that the International Labour Office has contributed, or in the future would be able to contribute, in any essential degree toward lessening the danger of war.

Quite recently other ideas have been expressed, which aim at the real conditions through the League of Nations emphasizing the great importance of a supply of food, reasonable and sufficient for public health, and the efforts to secure such food for the poorer classes. During the Assembly in 1936, the English (Lord Astor) strongly emphasized the effects of malnutrition, such as apathy and hyperexcitability,[4] upon discontent and disturbances, and their dangerous social and international consequences. The economic and sociopolitical causes of war coincide in this way with the pathological concepts of the meaning of war, which we shall discuss later.

What holds true for social and economic conditions also holds to a certain degree for the other causes of war dealt with in the Covenant of the League. It is advantageous, both statistically and for general political purposes, that all treaties should be made public, as is required in Article XVIII of the League Covenant, but this has slight importance in preventing war. Those agreements or "understandings"—which, as we know, need never be put into written form—which involve a real threat to world peace, do not gain their force or validity from the legal requirement of their publication, as Article XVIII supposes, but rather from the continuing existence of certain political conditions which gave them birth. The policy of the "open door" in the colonies, which was regarded as important by many as a means of establishing peace,

[4] League of Nations, Document A. II. P. V. 5. 1936, p. 7: "la mauvaise alimentation influe également sur l'état mental et les manifestations peuvent en être de l'hyperexcitabilité ou de l'apathie."

has so far remained a vision of the future; it is a line of thought which has little practical importance, since it assumes that colonies are a sort of object of trade or means of exploitation for the mother country, who can arrange their trade policies at pleasure. In reality, the tendency has been for colonies to devise and enforce a policy based on their own interests, so that, so far as colonies are concerned, there is no more question of a more "liberal" policy, or of any policy at all, than there is for the mother countries.

A somewhat different situation exists, to a certain degree, as to the provisions in the League Covenant regarding disarmament, armament manufacture, and armament trade, because the mere existence of large armies and military supplies may of itself sooner or later lead to war. But these serve rather as a barometer of a desire for war or military action than as real causes in themselves, just as the League Covenant itself has in a most peculiar and demoralizing manner retarded progress in this direction by referring to "those Members of the League which are not able to manufacture the munitions and implements of war necessary for their safety," which is in reality a disguised defense of the trade in armaments and of armament manufacture.

The League Covenant makes no direct mention of economic advantages, such as war profits, acquisition of territory, and so forth, as causes of war, although such motives were held by many to be the most influential of all. With respect to the law of neutrality, as well, this opinion has been made the basis of a comprehensive study, in four volumes, by Jessup and others.[5] It must be admitted that most things in this life have an economic side, but it is nonetheless incorrect to identify them with it. War considered as business is, in the long run, a pretty poor investment for both belligerents and neutrals. To be able to estimate the advantages gained through war, we must compare these with its indirect and harmful consequences, such as economic depressions in the postwar period, weakened international confidence or good-will, economic blockades, and political isolation, among others, with their consequent restrictions upon trade relations.

If we examine the "causes of war" mentioned in the League

[5] New York, 1935-36.

Covenant, we may say of them in general that there exists no proof, perhaps not even a probability, that these are really the causes which lead to war; further, that they refer partly to reforms, the attainment of which lies so far in the future that for a long time to come they must be of but slight practical importance, and that, finally, the actual abolition of some of them was not sincerely desired by the authors of the Covenant. In this way such "causes" come to exist as a defense or justification for the necessity of war under the existing conditions, so long as these conditions could not be changed by other means.

4. Under such circumstances, it is natural to inquire whether the problem of the "causes of war" is really stated in its proper form, and whether we should wait for the realization of this—partly utopian—program before we may seriously claim that war can be abolished. There is a consideration which must make us somewhat skeptical in our attitude toward the entire question of "causes of war," namely, the fact that war has been known for thousands of years, in times and under circumstances where economic and social conditions had none of the importance they have today, or, in any case, where they had little to do with the origin of war. Since social and economic problems play such an all-important rôle in popular discussions in our time and form the basis of our domestic political quarrels, it is natural enough to hold them responsible for our international conflicts and to assume that they are the true causes of war.

In other times, in the Middle Ages, for example, during the Crusades, or in the Thirty Years' War, entirely different reasons for making war were asserted. When the native tribes in Central Africa or in Australia wage continuous war, it has little to do, we may say, with their social or economic problems. It is "custom," a conviction that this must be done because it always has been like that. Their youth are educated with a view to war; they seek honor there; indeed their purpose in life is war and the ability they can display as warriors. And so it is we may possibly recognize in the institution of war a social heritage from prehistoric times.[6]

[6] On hereditary social influences, see Freud, *Totem und Tabu*, Vienna, 1920, p. 211 f.

On the other hand we see powerful and conflicting social and economic interests competing and yet settling their differences, with no one considering the use of war in the solution. In a large country, such as in the United States, for example, there are, of course, important social and economic conflicts but no one would consider settling them through war. Such differences need not result in war, just as, on the contrary, we know of war and the threat of war where these conditions do not exist. It is thus rather a question of what is the custom, what one regards as the normal method of resolving the conflicting interests.

It is on the whole, a very complex problem, this one of the causes of war. It is quite possible that war-makers, when for one reason or another war does break out, seize upon such explanations as a sort of rationalization for their own otherwise illogical action. Thus, the famous philosopher Nietzsche [7] once said that he who kills another man has generally had an urge to do so, even if he subsequently purloins the murdered man's watch or purse to give to himself a certain rational explanation of the otherwise groundless and therefore doubly horrible urge which impelled him to the deed. A similar thought can be found in Dostoievski's famous novel on the murderer Raskolnikov [*Crime and Punishment*]. Other examples might be cited. Some thirty or forty years ago it was still the established custom in some countries in Europe for students to settle their disputes by duel, that is, through combat with often dangerous weapons. There had been invented a quite distinct form of insult which could always be used, namely that one of the parties had looked at, or, as it was called, "stared" at, another. It is obvious here that we could not have stopped the practice of dueling by fighting its "causes," namely offenses against honor among students. The true reasons did not lie in these so-called causes, but in exaggerated vanity, class pride, and arrogance. When duels were finally prohibited, these offenses against honor stopped automatically.

In similar fashion there is reason to suppose that some of the so-called causes of war are actually only pretexts which an impulsion

[7] Werke, VII (1910), Leipzig (*Also sprach Zarathustra*), p. 53.

to war seizes upon [8] in order to make a somewhat reasonable explanation of its baseless and senseless acts, but which in themselves might not have led to war. Likewise, upon the outbreak of war there are questions involving honor and questions of prestige which play a large part, and then occurs a process of the kind which may be called a "rationalizing" of the causes of war. It is not at all difficult to find in the history of modern and very recent times, examples of wars or international conflicts which have had their real origins in the vanity of senility, combined with a homicidal urge; the desire to support declining "prestige" or an outright desire for spoliation; of national inferiority complexes, associated with what are considered to be opportunities to take advantage of another state's weakness or its unwillingness to quarrel or to go to war, all of which are later "rationalized" in successive stages. There is first attempted a semirationalization by reference to alleged historical insults, which either never took place at all or have long since been forgotten, but which are now used to help arouse public opinion to that degree of sentimentality or rage which is regarded as useful. Then the final "rationalizing" takes place by references to overpopulation, the need of colonies, raw materials, markets, or means of production, and general economic interests, to such degree that the war-makers attempt during the course of the conflict to create certain objective settings for these asserted interests which will permit them to attain their rationalized aims and make the public forget the irrational ones. In this case there occurs within the group consciousness a control-and-displacement process, similar to that which psychoanalysis [9] has demonstrated as occurring in the mind of the individual, where emotions and instincts which cannot stand the light of day are forced down into the subconscious, while consciousness at the same time asserts a more civilized and rational explanation of these acts.

[8] So Hold-Ferneck, *Lehrbuch*, II, 250 f., takes the position that the arbitration idea cannot prevent war. It is in his opinion fallacious thinking. "Es wäre sehr oberflächlich zu glauben, dass der Streit zum Krieg geführt habe. Vielmehr ist es der beabsichtigte Krieg, der den Streit hervorruft. Der Krieg selbst entspringt aus den tieferliegenden Gründen," etc.

[9] Freud, "Eine Schwierigkeit der Psychoanalyse," *Imago*, V (1919), p. 5.

War in Its Pathological, Psychological And Sociological Aspects

1. The causes of war must therefore be sought further and in other directions than is presumed in the Covenant of the League. We must introduce scientific methods also into this field, which was formerly considered only from the standpoint of statesmen and politicians. War, then, is not merely a question of a demand for better economic and social conditions, of the freedom of trade, of distribution of raw materials, or of access to colonies. By ascribing it to such rational causes, we endow war with a logical and reasonable basis to which it cannot possibly make just claim. At any rate, these are not lines of thought which have a proper place in an effective system of war-prevention, let alone be of use in a scientific appraisal of the nature of war. Instead of such rational explanations for war, a system for its prevention must be based on the realization that war is *not* logical, that it is absurd and irrational, that none of its alleged causes or the aims pleaded in its defense can give a rational explanation or justification for the destruction and suffering to which any war, and especially modern war, exposes humanity.

We must therefore describe war as above all a social "super-individual" psychical state of pathological or hypnotic character.[10] This in no way, of course, excludes the idea that behind war there may lie extremely well-calculated plans which were originated by an individual or by a small clique. All policies rest upon the calculations and plans which such individuals or groups attempt to carry out by all available means, within which category fall those easily induced hypnotic states of mind in the social consciousness (public opinion). The question for these individuals or cliques is therefore how best to take hold of the masses without their knowledge of, or approval of, the real motives for the war; how to force people, who in their private lives are quiet, law-abiding and sensible

[10] On the susceptibility of the social consciousness to hypnosis, see especially the French school of sociology (Tarde and others); also Cohn, *Etik og Sociologi*, pp. 187 ff. (Hypnotic Concepts in Society.)

citizens, and "unable to hurt a fly," let alone kill human beings,[11] suddenly to become mad killers, to attack human beings whom they do not even know, women and children as well, and to slay, rob, and burn.

Flusser, in his book, *Krieg als Krankheit*,[12] sought to justify the opinion which the title indicates. For him, the evaluation of war is a constantly changing one, because men lack a sound basis for those moral values which belong to other times and circumstances, and which are in conflict with modern humane ideals without being fully comprehended. In his idea, there is no basis for a judgment upon war. On the other hand, the physician has a clear and fixed standard to follow: all which promotes life is healthy; all which harms, ruins, or destroys life is disease.

When the militarist answers satirically: "never again an earthquake," as a reply to the pacifist's: "never again war," it is therefore a misapprehension. If war is a disease, it can be controlled when we have come to understand its nature. Admittedly biology teaches us the fact that all life is a struggle for existence. But nowhere else in nature (except among ants) do conflicts exist among beings involving the wholesale killing of one's own species. Modern war, moreover, is no longer a conflict, but constitutes rather an agreement between two governments under which each may put to death by poison gas, long-range guns, and other mechanical aids, the healthy adolescent youth of the other. Two armies which wage war are in reality but one army committing suicide.

The causes of war are to be found in the internal (*endogenous*) and external (*exogenous*) causes of disease. To the first category belong, among others, the collective passions and greed for sensation; to the latter, military preparedness and conditions of social privation. In a miscellaneous category is greed for power among the leaders.

[11] According to psychoanalysis (Freud, in "Zeitgemasses über Krieg und Tod," *Imago*, IV [1915], pp. 9 ff.), however, this characterization of man is largely due to cant and an unwitting sublimation below the threshold of consciousness of the homicidal urge which still plays a very important rôle toward both friend ("ambivalent") and enemy, with the impossibility, at the same time, of imagining one's own destruction.

[12] *Krieg als Krankheit*, The Hague, 1932. With a foreword by Albert Einstein; see also Cohn, *Is War a Disease?* (Radio address of Oct. 10, 1934, Copenhagen.)

Collective passions do not rest upon a special love [13] for one's own countrymen, of which we have little enough in time of peace. The impelling force is hatred of the "enemy" as an abstract conception, and a sadistic satisfaction in seeing others suffer. Greed for sensation acts like an intoxicant or poison, and in order to attain the resulting state of intoxication, the individual is willing to expose himself to dangers and to venture his life for interests of which he scarcely has knowledge and in which, at any rate, he will have no share, since the "little man" will come to live again under the same general conditions, whether under the government of one state or of another. The benefits which can be obtained through war are illusory. Thus it was long believed in Germany that the progress of that state toward the end of the nineteenth century was due to its victorious war against France. The German people failed to see that this condition of prosperity was common to all countries, and was of course due to the great technical advances made generally during that period.

2. In the domain of the great military Powers, the people live continuously in an atmosphere of artificially stimulated fear. Just as in the witchcraft trials and the Inquisition of the Middle Ages, the trials for high treason in modern times keep the common people in a constant fear-psychosis. Formerly it was the "devil," now it is the "enemy," who devises cunning plans to deprive citizens of their homes and peace. It is a collective persecution mania which is being developed in this way.

Just as the priests of antiquity sacrificed the children of the believers to Moloch, or as princes in the Middle Ages sold their subjects as hirelings for war in the service of foreign states, so the youth of the present generations, in pathological imbecility, allow themselves to be put to death in the interest of high finance or of the armament industry. Moreover, this pathological imbecility and persecution mania here set in motion the disease of homicidal mania (ktinomania). This disease is also often present in aged generals and statesmen, who create war and feel a morbid satisfaction in the

[13] Opposed, see Freud, *Massenpsychologie und Ich-Analyse*, pp. 42 ff., on the unity of the army's "libido," which rests upon the notion that the generals (or the leaders) love all their soldiers equally.

mutilation and destruction of youth.[14] Many nurses who volunteer seek erotic satisfaction in seeing wounded and bleeding soldiers in the field hospitals.[15]

Physicians, he says, must learn to understand that ktinomania and war-intoxication are diseases which can be treated and prevented as such. Sigmund Freud and Alfred Adler have shown us the way. The former, through psychoanalysis, has found the cause of the nervous condition in the conflict between satisfaction of the ego and the sex emotions; Flusser believes, however, that the conflict exists rather between the nature of man and that of civilization in general. The Viennese physician, Dr. Adler, is the first to indicate the rôle of the medical profession in the service of education.

Wholesale slaughter of human beings must be taken out of politics, for war is a mental disease and has no rational significance. We can no more speak of *objectives* of war than of objectives of disease. Both have only *consequences*, consequences which are often fateful and destructive of life. Nor should we take the "science" or the "philosophy" of war seriously. War is not philosophy but is rather, lunacy and inebriation. When this drunkard awakes, a hang-over follows in the form of hunger or death. No rational or good effect can follow from his debauch.

Flusser, for that matter, is not the first to state these views, as the Dutch Association for the Advancement of Medical Science (Nederlandsche Maatschappij tot Bevordering der Geneeskunst) had earlier made the question of the physician's task in the service of war-prevention the object of detailed study and had sent an appeal concerning it to medical associations in other countries.

3. In October, 1935, at the time when the Italo-Ethiopian conflict appeared to endanger world peace, eminent neurologists from many countries addressed a manifesto against war to the governments of the world, in which, among other things, they called attention to "the striking contrast between the individual's positive aversion to war and the collective willingness to enter into it. This

[14] The Japanese writer, Sakurai, in his book *Niku-Dan* (Human Sacrifice), p. 137, tells of shooting down horror-stricken fugitive enemies as "a glorious business, a rare pleasure, a pleasure hunt," and so forth.

[15] Flusser, pp. 103 ff.

they explained by saying that the emotions, thoughts, and habits of the individual are quite different from those which he expresses as a member of a collective entity. Civilized man in the twentieth century is still in possession of strong and destructive drives, which have not been fully "sublimated" and which are given expression as soon as the society of which he is a member feels itself threatened by danger. This instinctive desire to "let the reins go," without fear of consequences but even with a prospect of reward, tends to promote a readiness for war. The manifesto said:

> It is terrible to note how averse the nations are to admit the realities of ordinary types of war. The usual dreams and imaginings, the full-dress uniform, military parades,[16] etc., no longer have anything to do with conditions in real warfare. The indifference shown toward the methods and intrigues of international armament makers must astonish everyone who realizes the dangers which this trade involves. It is criminally absurd to permit certain groups of people to receive and enjoy personal advantage from the death of millions of people. We earnestly advise you to arouse the realism and instincts of collective self-preservation of your nation, those powerful instincts which are the strongest allies for escape from war.

The appeal goes on to say that utterances by well-known statesmen have repeatedly told us that many of them have imaginings similar to that of the average man about war; assertions that war is the highest court of appeal or that war is the natural consequence of the Darwinian theory are misleading and dangerous, when one takes the actual conditions of modern warfare into consideration. Such statements are intended to conceal an exaggerated desire for power and are aimed at stirring up war passions among the speaker's countrymen. The power of suggestion, in the speeches of leading statesmen, is very great and may be very dangerous, says the Manifesto. The desire for war, which is so easily aroused when the cry is heard that the country is in danger, is not so easily controlled today as it appeared to be in 1914. Whole nations, like individuals, may be made insane (neurotic) under the influence of such suggestions. They may be driven by delusions and self-decep-

[16] Flusser, p. 72, asserts that he, as an army doctor during the World War, noticed how few of the wounded had been hit by bullets. Rifles have slight importance in modern war, but are still carried because they look well, and because a regiment of soldiers with empty hands would not have a military air.

tion, which impel them to adventures dangerous to their own safety as well as to that of other nations. The Manifesto closes with these words:

> We neurologists hereby declare that our science is sufficiently developed so that it is possible for us to distinguish between real, pretended and subconscious motives even among statesmen. The attempt to hide one's militarism by constantly talking of peace will not absolve such political leaders from the condemnation of history. These secret inciters to militarism are responsible for the endless disaster which another war will certainly involve.[17]

This declaration was signed with the name, title, and address of 350 of the most famous neurologists from all countries of the world, and was the first attempt of the medical profession to participate in their professional capacity, in the policies of states in the service of war-prevention, an attempt the justice of which is evident. As Professor Brisman[18] correctly says, this manifesto, despite the fact that its immediate effect was not great, is of epoch-making significance. It is an expression of the fact that the great progress of modern psychology not only marks a general scientific advance, but that it is equipping us to change radically our aspects of existence. One need only refer to the influence which psychoanalysis has exerted upon modern psychology; it has pointed the way to hidden springs in the consciousness of both the individual and the social group. It likewise reveals the real nature of war so clearly that there need be little attention paid in the future to statements of politicians regarding the causes and classification of war.

4. With regard to the above definitions of war as a disease, it is necessary to emphasize the fact, however, that the disqualification of war does not depend upon this pathological point of view alone. Psychoanalysis of the nature of war does not necessarily give a pathological result. The sources of war may be found also in base instincts, which resist exposure, but which by no means need be morbid. Sigmund Freud[19] recognizes, as does the modern physiological theory of Hering, that the life process is completely divisible into two elements: one ("assimilative") which builds up, the other

[17] *Ibid.*, pp. 72 ff.
[18] In *Göteborg Handels-och Sjöfarts-Tidning* for Oct. 22, 1935.
[19] *Jenseits des Lustprinzips*, Vienna (1923), p. 70.

("dissimilative") which tears down; and that desires, urges, emotions, and instincts may likewise be so classified with their antitheses, as a life urge and a death urge, and so on; to maintain, develop, and protect life, there thus runs through all functions of life and consciousness an instinct to kill and to destroy; with desires to suffer and to inflict suffering on others. This statement may properly be set against the theory of Flusser that while it is possible to identify this building up of life with what is healthy and desirable, it by no means follows that everything which tears down or destroys life is morbid. There would then, for example, be no difference between disease and old age. But there does exist a normal and natural process of "healthy" demolition, which must not be confused with disease; it is not necessary here to discuss this question in detail, as the distinction is ultimately one of terminology. What cannot be denied, however, is that bloodthirstiness and the impulse to kill are so common in nature that we cannot, without doing violence to facts, describe them in all cases as morbid or abnormal. The ferocity and killer-instinct of a tiger, hawk, or marten, are not abnormal. Throughout nature, both in the animal and the vegetable kingdoms, among birds, fish, and insects, we find a distinction between those species which obtain their nourishment from inert vegetable foods or from lower and simpler animal organisms, and those which attack and kill animals as highly developed as themselves, for food. Why should a similar distinction among nations be inconceivable? The recognition of such a possibility forces us more and more to realize that there do exist radical differences in types of societies, that the ways of states are different both in their objectives and in their means of attaining them; that there are some states which aim to develop through a process of peaceful, economic, and political growth,[20] while others have no ability for, or understanding of, these methods, but believe that such expansion must be attained by wholesale slaughter and violence.

Upon the whole, it must be said that the theory of psychoanalysis and Professor Freud himself do not completely share the

[20] See Carter's book, *Conquest*, New York, 1928, on the peaceful economic conquest by the United States of her world position.

optimism of the medical profession in its opposition to war, as expressed in Flusser's views, as well as those of the neurologists' manifesto of 1935. In a very interesting exchange of opinion between Einstein and Freud on the causes of war,[21] the former raises the question as to how it is possible that a small clique in any state, without regard for its social effects and with no restraint, can look upon war and the manufacture and sale of munitions as simply a means to advance their personal ambitions, and that this small clique can sway the great majority who must bear the weight of the suffering and destruction resulting from war. To be able to do this, it certainly must have the schools, the press, and the church under its control. And why is it so easy to excite the people to such a wild frenzy for war as to induce them to sacrifice life itself for it? Only one answer is possible. There must exist in human beings instincts of hatred and destruction, instincts which, under normal conditions, are suppressed, but which it is comparatively easy to arouse to a collective psychosis. The question then is, are there means to counteract these tendencies and to secure the human mind against these mad conditions of hatred and destruction?

In his reply, Freud attaches considerable importance to the rôle which violence plays throughout nature in resolving conflicting interests. The vanquished are killed or made the slaves of the victor. Against the force of the stronger there exists but one resource: union of the weaker ones. Thus there arises that conception of "right," which in finality is merely an attribute of force.[22] This struggle is continued in society, where "the law" is an expression of the effort of the weaker members by united action to obtain the same privileges as the stronger, since law is the same for all.

With regard to the psychological basis for war, Freud refers to his earlier study of the two instincts in human consciousness: the instinct to live, that which relates to the maintenance and propagation of life—in a broader sense, the sexual emotions and instincts—and the death instinct, which aims at death and destruction.

[21] *Why War?* Paris, 1933.

[22] *Ibid.*, p. 39: "Our logic is at fault if we ignore the fact that right is founded on brute force and even to-day needs violence to maintain it."

These two forces act simultaneously, as, for example, in the instinct of self-preservation, which is of a sexual nature but necessarily assumes at times a certain aggressive attitude toward the environment. Sometimes these sex instincts are used as a camouflage for the urge to destroy. It may also happen that a strong destructive instinct endows the aforesaid instinct to life with a special strength and intensity. As examples, both these phenomena were present in the medieval Inquisition, and underlie the enthusiasm for war in modern times.

The destructive instinct is active throughout nature, where it tries to undermine and tear down all life and to return it to inanimate forms. It expresses itself *extrovertedly* when a living being defends its own existence by the destruction of other living organisms. But it may also become *introverted*,[23] as for example in remorse or conscience, or in the morbid expression of those, masochism.

All things considered, aggressive tendencies cannot be uprooted, since they constitute a fundamental element of life itself, but they can be redirected into other channels (cultivated and refined) and they may be counteracted by the instincts to life, particularly in two ways: sympathy and identification; that is, by an understanding of the similarities among men, and by the feeling of fellowship. It is a question of submitting instincts to the control of thought, and therefore independent thinkers, not political agitators and propagandists, should be the leaders of the people.[24] Freud admits that there is a long road ahead before this can be attained.

For Freud,[25] it is a bigger problem, in one sense, that any opposition to war at all should exist. Whence this strong aversion to war, he asks, instead of accepting it as just another form of the more unpleasant necessities of existence? War is, indeed, natural enough, considered from the biological viewpoint, it is sound in logic, and unavoidable in practice. The explanation of the aversion is that man feels ashamed that he is forced to kill his fellow beings against the dictates of his conscience, and that war in modern times

[23] "Introversion of the destructive instinct." See *ibid.*, pp. 40 ff.

[24] This is an idea which Plato himself expressed many centuries ago.

[25] *Ibid.*, p. 51.

gives no such opportunity for the display of heroism as it formerly did. In fine, the pacifists are as much guided by their emotions as are the militarists. The progressive development of intelligence weakens the combative instincts and turns them inward ("introversion"). Pacificism, for Freud, is an idiosyncrasy, a form of intolerance, just as militarism is.[26] How war can be abolished is right now a mystery which we cannot solve, he says, but we can say that all developments of civilization are opposed to war.

The founder of psychoanalysis is thus in no sense of the opinion that war is a phenomenon of an especially morbid nature. He regards it, upon the contrary, as an expression of something fundamental in our very existence and believes that we shall seek in vain for ways by which it can be abolished.

Freud in this discussion seems not to have considered, however, to their full extent those impulses which he elsewhere declares exist in the human mind and consequently their ability to counteract [27] the destructive effects of mass psychoses. Of special significance in this connection seems to be Freud's study of the collective mind, from an examination of the forms of the social structure in prehistoric society, of the psychology of leadership, and the subjection of the primitive mass under the will of the leader, which is inherited from prehistoric times and is still a characteristic of the social mind [28] today. On the whole, it seems to be a reasonable assumption that human emotions first arose and de-

[26] *Ibid.*, p. 56.

[27] See also Felszeghy, "Panik und Pan-Komplex," *Imago*, VI (1920), pp. 35 ff., on "Panikabrüstung." A deterrent "panic prevention" is in the opinion of this author impracticable because "explosion preparedness" is an inherent, indeed even a necessary, appurtenance of the ego and of the satisfaction of the libido of life itself. Nonetheless, mass psychoses can be diverted and used in the service of loftier aims, especially when confronted with the "parental complex" (the calm leader, the valiant hero, the woman, the mother). Following the examples which Felszeghy gives, we might perhaps comment that their women trailed along with the ancient warriors of the North to war, probably to help them counteract the fear of panic.

[28] See especially Freud, *Massenpsychologie und Ich-Analyse*, pp. 45 ff. (panic and fright in armies), and p. 95: "Der unheimliche, zwanghafte Charakter der Massenbildung, der sich in ihren Suggestionserscheinungen zeigt, kann also wohl mit Recht auf ihre Abkunft von der Urhorde zurückgeführt werden. Der Führer der Masse ist noch immer der gefürchtete Urvater, die Masse will immer noch von unbeschränkter Gewalt beherrscht werden, sie ist im höchsten Grade autoritätssüchtig."

veloped in primitive forms of society and, therefore when stimulated to higher and unusual states, often slip back along the psychical path of their evolution into the primitive conditions of their origin. In other words, although these feelings or emotions of man, as he has inherited them, may be illogical in his present environment, and the assumption of rational war aims be therefore illogical, his emotions under sudden strong collective fears follow this old path *as if* he still lived under those primitive prehistoric conditions of society in which such strong emotions of fear had originally developed; *as if*, only by blind obedience and complete submission to the will of the leader and by slaughter of the members of the hostile horde, could he still maintain his life and obtain food for himself and his own. His emotions are released in a tension of contrast between "own" and "foreign" which is quite unrelated to the actual conditions of today, with their many means of communication and of economic and cultural relationships between the nations, so much the more since the "own," especially in large countries with colonies and dependencies, includes vast heterogeneous elements with which, under normal circumstances, he in no way feels himself to be connected in such intimate or wholehearted a manner.[29]

5. In another particular we must also take exception to Flusser's expressed opinions, namely, when he appears to believe that there already exists a morbid element in the instinct of the individual to identify himself with his social milieu (*Herdentrieb*). He speaks in this connection of a malady of the "We" ("*Wirsucht*"). The little man's vanity, his desire to play a part, his urge toward greater self-importance and happiness, all impel him to turn away at times from his own unimportant and humdrum existence and to identify himself with a collective experience, more interesting, more fateful, and in that way to share [30] in its importance.

[29] The theory of aggression itself may go back to the primitive character of the war psychosis; see Sperber, *Völkerpsychologische Ursachen des Krieges*, p. 112: "denn woher kämen sonst die endlosen Diskussionen über die Schuldfrage, mit anderen Worten über das in der Kinderstube so beliebte Thema: 'Wer hat angefangen?' "

[30] Flusser, p. 32: "Die Neigung des Menschen, ein Kollektivum, ein Wir, eine Herde zu bilden und als Kollektivum, und nur als solches, nicht als Einzelner, für Affekte sensibilisiert zu sein, die über kurz oder lang zu den ärgsten Katas-

We believe, however, that it is definitely a mistake to consider the constructive social desires and a collective mind as morbid. Such an assumption is rooted in a faulty perspective of the laws and facts of sociology and an artificial segregation of the individual, who, after all, exists only as a social being and as a member of the collective consciousness. The sociological aspect is, in general, a necessary corrective for both the pathological and psychoanalytical ones. Freud and his school are, upon the whole, inclined to belittle the importance of both the sociological viewpoint and particularly the mental life [31] of the individual. The aims of psychoanalysis and the means it employs, namely, concentration upon the conscious and the subconscious mind of the individual, are separate from the problems of sociology; in other words, much of what is incomprehensible, or leads to strained and artificial conclusions when looked at from the viewpoint of psychoanalysis, has a very simple explanation when considered from the viewpoint of sociology.

We do not get far toward understanding the nature of war by becoming absorbed in the study of the instincts of the individual human being.[32] The surprising thing is just that acts and states of consciousness which are remote from the mental life of the individual man become a reality under a war psychosis. The individual is, as a rule, peace-loving, absorbed in his own interests and those of his immediate circle, and considers his existence and welfare as

trophen führen müssen, bildet die bedeutsamste endogene Ursache der Krankheit Krieg. Bedeutet nun diese Katastrophenbereitschaft des Menschen schon einen krankhaften Zustand? Ja! Ein Kollektivaffekt ist immer auf Illusionen aufgebaut, die für Realitaten gehalten werden"; see above on Freud and Felszeghy, who believe, on the contrary, that "Katastrophenbereitschaft" is an essential element of life itself.

[31] See the introduction to Freud's book, *Totem and Tabu*, where he emphasizes the differences between his theories and those of the Zürich psychoanalytic school which explains the problems of the psychology of the individual by means of social psychology.

[32] Psychoanalysis also traces mass panic back to the basic psychoanalytic phenomenon; the first and imperishable feelings of fear aroused at the act of birth which are accompanied by the strong urge to be freed from confinement. It also comprehends the mass psychosis involved in a fear of involuntary separation from the group; see Felszeghy, "Panik und Pan-Komplex" (*Imago*, VI [1920], p. 21): "Nur hinaus! nur hinaus aus dieser Masse, aus diesem Eingeklemmtsein."

the supreme good. But when war calls, he becomes a savage slayer, who in fierce rage falls upon persons who are entire strangers to him, to slaughter or to mutilate them, and to venture his own life for purposes of which he hardly has knowledge and which, under normal conditions, he would either disapprove completely or show no interest in. This is where our problem lies, and the answer can be given only in sociological terms.

War, both according to the objective acts which it involves and the subjective state of which it is the expression, is a social phenomenon. It is social groups which wage this battle of destruction against one another, and the feelings of hatred and the lust to destroy which are developed are group emotions and group instincts. We may, indeed, say that the feelings of the group are in the last analysis those of its individual members, but we can just as logically assert the reverse of this, and the latter, from the standpoint of sociology, is more obvious and more correct. The conscious life of thought, emotion, and volition of the individual comes from his external stimulae, from his social milieu, and cannot be regarded as an expression of individual predispositions, such as might be developed should we leave the individual to himself or in an isolated state (Hauser). In a sense, we might as well, or even better, say that it is the social group which thinks, feels, and expresses itself through its individual members.[33] The truth is that we see mentality clothed in varied forms. It expresses itself in individual as well as in social forms; either of these has as good a claim to independent consideration as the other.[34]

Even if it be somewhat difficult,[35] we must therefore imagine the collective mind not as a mere phrase, or a figure of speech, but

[33] See further Cohn, *Etik og Sociologi*, pp. 144 ff.

[34] This of course is true only where there are group-mind phenomena, and cannot be used for purposes of legal construction and fictions where such is not the case. On this see Hurwitz, *Bidrag til Laeren om kollektive enheders pønale Ansvar*, p. 40 f. For a study of the law of the prevention of war only the former phenomena are relevant. See further Sighele, *La Foule criminelle*, pp. 283 ff., citing a number of cases at law which go into the question of the penal law treatment of a group mind; for consideration of the problem as a whole, see Visser, *De collectieve Psyche in Recht en Staat*, Haarlem, 1916.

[35] See Bauer, *Die öffentliche Meinung in der Weltgeschichte*, p. 7, on the average person's firm belief in the independence of his individuality; Freud, *Eine Schwierigkeit der Psychoanalyse*, p. 5.

as a reality.[36] There exists, according to this view, "actually" a group "soul," which is in some respects similar, and in others different, from that of the individual "soul." [37] This group soul resembles its counterpart in the purely formal laws of its origin and destruction of conscious mental life, the threshold of consciousness, its connection with practical interests, and so forth.[38] The distinction is that the collective soul has a far more primitive and "uncivilized" character than has the soul of the individual. It is far more inconsiderate, brutal, greedy for sensation, uncritical, easily excitable, and more difficult to calm. It is, of course, somewhat difficult to characterize the collective soul with terms drawn from our knowledge of the individual one. In terms of evolution, we might compare it with that of the higher animals. It is, for example, as easily excited as is a bull by a red rag. It is in no sense a mere generality, with a uniform description in all situations; on the contrary, there are many widely divergent special types. It may change its character. It is at times calm or apathetic, at other times alert, suspicious, or excited. It may have a morbid character, when the forms of its expression resemble the varied types of mental diseases which psychiatry diagnoses and treats in the individual. Typical and frequent group insanities are those of a persecution complex and megalomania, maniac paroxysms of rage, abnormal depression, and the like.[39]

In his well-known work, *Psychologie des foules*,[40] Le Bon gives a complete psychological picture of a collective mind, as independent of the mind of the individual.[41] He emphasizes its flexibility, irritability, and credulity. It is intolerant, submissive, and reaction-

[36] On the theoretical basis for the "reality" of a collective mind, see Lehmann, *Das Kollektivbewusstsein*, pp. 225 ff., to whose particular statement we cannot subscribe.

[37] When it has been frequently so positively asserted that the acceptance of the idea of a collective mind rests upon mysticism or a fiction, it is forgotten that the conception of an individual "soul" likewise contains a number of mystical and fictional elements.

[38] Cohn, *Etik og Sociologi*, pp. 132 ff.

[39] *Ibid.*, p. 135.

[40] Paris, 1895.

[41] Bauer, *Die öffentliche Meinung in der Weltgeschichte*, p. 8, asserts that Le Bon as a chemist takes a chemist's viewpoint of the collective mind. As contrasted with a mere mechanical composite of the independent individual minds he compares the collective mind with a chemical composition having entirely new properties distinct from those of its component parts.

ary. Its moral nature and its mental capacity are of an entirely different character from those of the individual. It is mastered by catchwords, while it is entirely impervious to reason.[42] It has an instinctive desire to be governed by a leader whose psychology and behavior, whose bold assertions with constant repetition, and the dangers of contagion therefrom, Le Bon describes in a very interesting fashion.[43]

According to this viewpoint, we cannot regard the collective mind as the mere result of the interplay of the individual minds of the separate members of the group.[44] Characteristic of the typical condition of the activity of the collective mind is a suppression of the activity of the mind of the individual. The best evidence of this condition is that the individual mind becomes submerged and entirely disappears in the collective consciousness.

Wilhelm Bauer[45] describes the condition in this way: just as in chemistry, upon the mixture of certain elements, a new substance comes into existence which has properties entirely different from those possessed by its elements, so a group of people of quite different professions, regardless of their education and maturity, unite to form a social mass which does not react as a mere mixture nor as an average of the separate psychological characteristics of the individuals which compose it, but shows entirely new and distinctive qualities, as compared with those of the individuals. For Bauer the essential thing here is simply the fact that within this unity, so long as it exists, the individuals surrender more or less completely the independence of their mental character, such as high intelligence, abilities, sympathies, on the whole everything

[42] Le Bon, pp. 100 ff.: "Dans l'énumération des facteurs capables d'impressioner l'âme des foules, on pourrait se dispenser entièrement de mentionner la raison, s'il n'était nécessaire d'indiquer la valeur négative de son influence.... Les lois de la logique n'ont aucune action sur elles." When it is asserted in mathematics that mathematical results are conclusive, this has no validity for the collective mind; see further Schindler, in *Recueil des Cours,* 1933 (IV), 303 ff.

[43] *Ibid.*, p. 111 f.

[44] See also McDougall, *The Group Mind,* p. 6: "Since, then, the social aggregate has a collective mental life, which is not merely the sum of the mental lives of its units, it may be contended that a society not only enjoys a collective mental life but also has a collective mind or, as some prefer to say, a collective soul."

[45] *Die öffentliche Meinung und ihre geschichtlichen Grundlagen,* p. 39.

which we regard as personality, in favor of this new phenomenon, which may be described as a group mind, or in some similar terms. Bauer believes that it is usually some emotional act which welds individuals, who reside in the same location or in some intellectual or spiritual relationship with one another, into a group. From that moment they lose their inhibitions, moral opinions, conscience, cowardice, and other personal restraints which ordinarily determined their behavior as individuals. Some new, strange force impels them to acts which, detached from the group, they would never have committed.[46]

It makes no difference that within the group there may be individuals of lofty mental and moral character; these cannot assert themselves, as individuals, against the collective mind; they disappear into it. The nature of this collective mind appears to be determined by its meanest members, rather than by the best in the group. This we have often the opportunity of observing in political gatherings and the like. It may be that the majority of their audience on their own account believe that the speaker is a fool, a demagogue, who seeks only his personal advantage;[47] indeed everyone may privately recognize that the statements made are false, exaggerated, and absurd. If the orator makes use of the proper mixture of sentimentality and brutality, of promises, threats, and ideas of fear, *he can come into rapport with the collective mind* without paying attention to the minds of the individual listeners. Each person may tell himself what he pleases, that the speaker is not going to persuade him against his judgment; he feels, nonetheless, that an appeal has been made to something which will certainly carry weight with the entire group and that his own mental resistance will not be strong enough to overcome the evident effects. Something akin to a hypnosis has occurred. The hypnotized subject may realize in advance that what the hypnotist will ask him to believe is foolish. Gradually, however, as his will

[46] Elsewhere (*Die öffentliche Meinung in der Weltgeschichte*, p. 11) the same author describes "die Abkehr vom eigenen Ich" as the vital element in the formation of the group.

[47] In some countries politicians are so corrupt as to be regarded with contempt, but this does not prevent them from asserting their authority in political affairs.

is broken down by the stronger will of the hypnotist, he abandons his mental resistance. The collective mind is far stronger than that of the individual, and can completely overcome its resistance.

6. In the lower stages of the evolution of the collective mind lies also the explanation for the moral distaste which the civilized man feels for some decisions made in the realm of foreign policy, especially in those regarding war and peace. He forgets that what controls here are collective groups, the minds of which operate upon a low plane of intelligence and morals when compared with that of the individual man. It is only an illusion that the policies of states appear to be conducted by idealistic individuals. The eminent qualifications of these leaders, as individuals, are insufficient to put them into a position to assert themselves against what the group regards as its interests. They would otherwise not be permitted to hold their position.

According to the arguments adduced here, the ease with which the desire for war can be aroused offers nothing peculiar. Even the normal existence of the collective mind is easily affected by promises, threats, and ideas of fear, and is credulous of absurdities, no matter how vulgar. If it feels itself sufficiently strong, it breaks out in a sadistic spree of destruction. If it believes itself weak, it can, by introducing fear, be driven almost immediately into a collective neurosis, a group insanity, in which all composure ceases. In both cases inhibitions of an intellectual or moral nature are unable to assert themselves.

Still stronger is the effect when the collective mind passes into a permanent state of insanity. This situation may result from the effect over a long period of these sadistic influences or from the creation of institutions which can have logical existence only under permanent danger of war, and leave no way by which the group mind can recover from the neurosis in which it finds itself. To this category belong first and foremost, armaments, encampments, military parades, and trials for high treason. There are suggested delusions of grandeur (megalomania) or of contempt and injustices suffered, and of others (abnormal depression). In a collective mind wrought up to this pitch of insanity, the voice of reason can be heard no longer; the frenzy must spend itself until exhaustion sets in.

The question raised by Professor Einstein as to how that small governing clique is so easily able to drum up a war, contrary to the interests of the great majority, who in general are peace-loving, may then be answered in this way, that the clique of which he speaks is working upon the collective mind and not upon the minds of the individual members of society, and that this collective mind (public opinion) is a simple, convenient, and also safe instrument for the clique to play upon if it but strike the notes attuned to the low intellectual and moral level of this collective mind. It can easily lose its self-control when someone persistently cries "Fire!" in a crowded theater while the lights are out, or when the communications of a large city are cut off, or when an emperor appears upon a balcony with a long scroll, spouting that here are the proofs that the country has been betrayed and is encircled by enemies who are even now over the frontier. It is necessary only that a large number of people be assembled and that a sudden paralyzing fear be created.

We need thus refer to no other special sociological theories on the nature of war. In particular, however, we may take exception to the theory of the conflict of races, formerly expounded by Gumplowicz.[48] This writer opposed the idea of the common origin of man and asserted, on the contrary, that there was originally an infinitude of different races, whose conflicts with one another form not only the content of the world's history but also underlie internal social and political disputes, as for example the class struggles in ancient Rome, where, he asserts, the patricians and the plebeians were originally of different races. He believed that a primitive society will never become a state by mere growth, but only through wars with other races, which it either conquers or to which it succumbs. For him international as well as domestic conflicts between those of the same race are fought out with means which are to the highest degree immoral.

[48] *Der Rassenkampf*, Innsbruck, 1883; *Grundriss der Sociologie*, Wien, 1885; see also Cohn, *Etik og Sociologi*, pp. 138 ff.

There is no reason to regard this pessimistic view as correct. Apart from the many other objections which may be raised against it,[49] it cannot be accepted by a generation which went through the experiences of the World War of 1914-18 where the white race tore itself savagely to pieces, and where practically all the different races of the world joined in the war upon the Central Powers. Race conflict belongs among those other false pseudo-scientific explanations of war, along with overpopulation, the distribution of raw materials, and general social and economic conditions, or classifications of aggression and defense. When the torch of war has been lighted, the race problem no longer plays any part. All members of the collective mind are first seized with a common attack of "nerves," and thereafter with collective insanity. Thus Italy, in her war with Ethiopia, while strongly emphasizing the point that it was a race war of white against black, made the widest possible use of black colonial troops against the enemy.[50] Under a collective psychosis this has no relevant rational explanation, but neither has it any irrational one; no explanations hold at all except that of the rage of a groundless[51] insanity.

Apart from the theory of racial conflict, modern sociology has not laid down any special theories of the nature of war. Nor is this necessary, when ordinary sociological laws and facts explain it sufficiently. Moreover, the sociology of war, as well as its pathology and psychology, is still to be written. War has hitherto mainly been permitted to remain, to the highest degree, in the hands of politicians and diplomats. But the sciences mentioned

[49] Cohn, *Etik og Sociologi*, p. 151.

[50] Compare here also the extensive use of Moorish soldiers by the "Nationalists" against the Government troops in the civil war in Spain which began in 1936.

[51] Violent and uncontrollable emotional reactions had, however, logical purposes in the primitive social conditions under which they originated; see also Felszeghy, "Panik und Pan-Komplex," *Imago*, VI (1920), p. 4: "Die zufolge unerklärbarem heftigen Entsetzen für das Individuum bedeutungsvolle, affektgeschwellte aktuelle Situation *ist nur Symbol*, von dem sich bei entsprechender Analyse herausstellt, das es *nicht die im Bewussten auftretenden Verhältnisse*, sondern die Erfüllung von weitaus wichtigeren, weitaus bedeutungsvolleren und begründeteren Gefühlsbeziehungen, *Urwünschen* darstellt . . . geht auf *längst vergessene Ursachen* zurück." (Our italics.) In modern times they are on the contrary groundless and meaningless.

above [52] have in our time reached that stage of development which entitles them at least to undertake the consideration of this social phenomenon. Only upon the basis of a scientific investigation of the nature of war will it be possible to make an effective effort to suppress or to oppose it.

Further Development of Neo-neutrality

1. As we have indicated above, the general disqualification of war, whether regarded from the pathological, psychological, or its sociological viewpoint, is well adapted for the rehabilitation of neutrality. The mere fact that a neutral state is able to keep a larger or a smaller bit of the earth free from war is in itself of such paramount importance that the moral and political considerations which call for neutral participation in the war lose their force by comparison with it. Numerous other considerations, however, plead above all for a study of the question of war-prevention itself. As has been stated elsewhere,[53] a universal privilege or obligation of states to throw themselves into war against another state, whether it be an aggressor or not, is certainly no contribution to a system of war-prevention. On the contrary, the task, as soon as war breaks out, must be to attempt to isolate and restrict it, and so far as possible to stop it. This is true not only for the smaller states, for whom it is a question of life or death to keep out of war, but also for the larger countries, whose best opportunity to contribute to the easing of the situation, through their mediation and political and economic influence, disappears, when they enter the war as participants and thus abandon their status as an impartial third party. They may, perhaps, by taking part, so affect the result that one party and not the other wins the war—this they will only do when their own interests so dictate—but they will be unable by such procedure to counteract the war itself.

The form of neutrality, "Neo-neutrality," which we shall dis-

[52] The question of the "causes," of war was taken up in an investigation in 1936 by the League's "Institut International de Coopération Intellectuelle"; Bourquin (ed.), *Collective Security* (French edition), II, 295.

[53] Cohn, *Kriegsverhütung und Schuldfrage*, pp. 189 ff.

cuss here, is in no way in conflict with such efforts as war prevention. It is, as we have pointed out previously, both practically and logically consistent with them; it is, indeed, a necessary condition for them. It is not identical with traditional neutrality as established by former international law, but does have in common with it (1) an unconditional demand for the privilege to remain outside the war, and (2) provision of the necessary means or measures for doing so, albeit in a somewhat modified form. Beyond this it recognizes no obligation of impartiality. It does not recognize the two parties to the war as having equal rights, nor one as having greater rights than the other. It disqualifies and rules out war, both morally and legally, regardless of its causes or motives, whether it is a war of aggression or a war of defense. It requires that really effective measures be applied against both belligerents. It is just as desirous of stopping the wholesale slaughter of the nation's youth in the aggressor country as in the defending one, since the people, as a rule, are equally innocent and equally helpless in both states. It is war as such with which it is concerned, and in which it will under no circumstances participate. It attaches no value to any particular kind of war, neither wars of execution nor wars of sanctions. It is therefore the expression of ideas which differ not only from those of traditional neutrality, but also from those in the system of the Covenant of the League.

The theory of aggression and that of traditional neutrality have this much in common, that nonparticipant states must either join with the injured party as allies or remain entirely passive. Neo-neutrality does not recognize this "Either-Or." It avows the possibility of preventing war, and thereby the right and duty of active participation in efforts to prevent war without participation in the war itself upon the side of either belligerent.

This new neutrality in its original form appeared in the author's treatise of 1924, which takes up for consideration the problem of *a new construction of the ideas of neutrality*. The fundamental differences between the classical conception of neutrality and the new system of the Covenant of the League are discussed,[54] with the advantages and disadvantages connected with each of them. It

[54] Cohn, *Neutralité et Société des nations*, pp. 201 ff.

is demonstrated that the conception of neutrality contains important elements which still retain their full *raison d'être*, under the new legal situation as well. It is further stated that the

> problem therefore is to separate these component parts from their earlier association with the laws of neutrality, and to combine them with the new principles which go to form the system of the Covenant of the League. One might, perhaps, be inclined in advance to doubt the possibility of combining elements of such diametrically opposite legal systems. There is, however, nothing impossible in such an attempt. It is merely a question of analyzing correctly the different component parts and then of adapting them to the new system. We may list, for example, the passive and precarious character of the law of neutrality, as being one of its older and undesirable elements. On the other hand, in its tendency toward restricting the war, there is a still vital element. It is therefore a question of finding forms for measures of international compulsion and a combination of the best in both systems which will best express the ideas underlying both the solidarity of membership and the limitation of the extent of the war. This is a theoretical and practical problem, as is any other, and cannot in advance be pronounced insoluble.[55]

The Danish treatise of 1924 was also founded upon the idea that the entire system of sanctions should be of a financial and economic nature and should in no way involve a duty to participate in actual military operations. But it had to concern itself first with the purely technical task of proving that the two systems could in practice be combined. This combination had therefore to be carried out along the lines of the traditional concepts of neutrality.

Neo-neutrality, however, abandons as a matter of principle its connection with the system of traditional neutrality, by which it no longer considers itself bound. It requires, therefore, a further and independent formulation of its own fundamental conceptions.[56]

2. Such an exposition of Neo-neutrality in complete form was proposed and discussed at the Conferences on Security in Paris

[55] *Ibid.*, p. 203.

[56] A tentative survey of a "System for Prevention of War Omitting the Question of Guilt," which points in the same direction as Neo-neutrality is expressed in Cohn, *Kriegsverhütung und Schuldfrage*, pp. 192 ff.; see also the subject "Neutralitet og Solidaritet" in "*Redegørelse for Danmarks folkeretlige Stilling efter Folkeforbundspagten og Kellogg-Pagten*" (1931), pp. 220 ff.

in 1934 and at London in 1935, where it held the center of the stage, since it clashed with the directly opposite doctrine, the theory of aggression, which is a logical necessity of the classification of war. These two conferences were held for the purpose of discussing collective security, which had for the two years immediately previous been the object of an investigation by the Committee on Intellectual Co-operation of the League of Nations.[57] The four main points around which the discussion centered, namely:

(1) The fundamental principle of the problem of collective security
(2) The prevention of war
(3) Determination of the aggressor and application of sanctions
(4) Neutrality

are of considerable interest for an examination of recent developments of the idea of neutrality.

As a basis for the labors of the Conferences, the preparatory memoranda and agenda [58] had been prepared by Professor Bourquin in March, 1934, in which the legal philosophy behind the question of the demand for security, together with the theory of aggression, played a prominent rôle.

This agenda was forwarded to a number of learned societies, among which was the Danish Institute of History and Economics, for expression of opinion; the latter replied with some "observations" upon Professor Bourquin's proposal,[59] in which was summarized the doctrines of neo-neutrality and their opposition to the theory of aggression.

The Danish Institute took exception, in their reply, to all mere philosophic discussions of the problem of security, and proposed to limit the term "collective security" to include only "prevention by international means of the outbreak or the continuation of war." All war as such was to be included, regardless of the ideology

[57] See Bourquin (ed.), *Collective Security* (French edition). See also *Coopération Intellectuelle*, Nos. 53-54, Paris, 1935.

[58] Printed in *Coopération Intellectuelle*, II, Nos. 5-6, p. 165, "Preparation of the agenda of a general study conference on Collective Security."

[59] *Coopération Intellectuelle*, Nos. 40-41, "Observations concernant le programme d'études sur la sécurité collective, pp. 222 ff.

or circumstances connected therewith,[60] that is, defensive war as well as aggressive; war as an instrument of national policy (Kellogg Pact) as well as wars with other aims.

The distinctions between war and other resorts to armed force, in the opinion of those who drew up the "observations" should be as clearly marked as those distinctions for defensive war, that is, which of such means should be prohibited and which were to be regarded as true self-defense,[61] finally which were to be permitted to a state within its own boundaries under terms analogous to those of self-defense [62] in municipal criminal law.

These "observations" further included a rejection of the system of Article XVI of the Covenant of the League, which upon essential points was branded with the customary laws of war, and which, they assert, attempts to oppose a particular war by means of a general state of war. The consequence of this is the necessity of a formula for the determination of the aggressor and the abolition of the law of neutrality. It was asserted that such a system was inconsistent with a real security arrangement. It is in theory a paradox, and in practice impossible, to prevent war by means of war. A system of security must be directed against war as such, regardless of assertions of one kind or another connected with it. Nor is there any value in this connection in deciding as to who is the aggressor or in preparing detailed rules of procedure for this purpose. The measures which should be taken must not be directed toward determining the guilty state and punishing it, but should be intended to prevent or to stop war itself. The questions of guilt and indemnification must be postponed for a later and independent discussion. Such procedure was followed, for instance, by the Council during the Greco-Bulgar incident [63] in 1925, which is a model for the formal procedure recommended as a general rule to be followed. These "observations" [64] then gave an account of the new system of neutrality.

60 "Comme un fait pur et simple."

61 The distinction between "guerre défensive" and "légitime défense."

62 As in imminent or threatened assault; only what is necessary to repel or prevent the assault without deriving right therefrom to continue the fight for purposes of subjugation, conquest, etc.

63 *Supra,* pp. 237 and 285.

64 *Coopération Intellectuelle,* Nos. 40-41, p. 227 f.; *op. cit.,* p. 52 f.

Neo-neutrality then must not be confused with traditional neutrality with its passivity and impartiality toward the belligerents; it does not coincide with the conception of "pacigérat" propounded by the Belgian writer Descamps,[65] nor with pacifism. It attempts, on the contrary, to be alert and active in the preservation of peace and the prevention of war. For this cause it is both ready and eager to fight. It demands that whatever sanctions are applied must be readily effective, but that in no case must they involve the use of military measures.

In former discussions at Geneva there has been an extensive misuse of the invocation of moral sanctions, proclamations, declaration of wars of aggression as international crimes (1927), and security pacts, one after the other. In contrast with this, the "observations"[66] designate as insufficient sanctions, such pressure as public opinion (including world opinion), the proclamation of peaceful intentions, treaty obligations, and breaking off diplomatic or consular relations. They attempt to give a general summary of the real and effective compulsory measures of legal, economic, and even military nature which neo-neutrality wishes to see applied for the prevention of war, and above all call for a revision of the former laws of war and neutrality, as these find an expression in the Hague Conventions of 1907 and the Declaration of London of 1909. Those broad rights which the laws of war formerly gave to belligerents against their adversaries and against the neutral states, must all cease to be valid. The duty of the neutral not to assist either belligerent is to be strengthened. The right of capture of vessels carrying contraband is to be conferred upon the government vessels of the neutral states. No duty of impartiality is incumbent upon these states.

It was further proposed in the "observations"[67] that there be a

[65] *Revue Générale de Droit International Public*, VII (1900), 629 ff.; "Le Pacigérat, au regime juridique de la paix en temps de guerre." See also in the same volume, "Les grandes étapes du progrès dans le droit des neutres, et la vocation de notre temps à la constitution du Pacigérat," pp. 705 ff.; and his work: "*La neutralité de la Belgique*" (1902) pp. 353 ff. For the distinction between Pacigérat and Neo-neutrality the reader is referred to the following pages of the present work.

[66] *Coopération Intellectuelle*, Nos. 40-41, p. 223.

[67] *Ibid.*, p. 226.

considerable extension of the duties of belligerents to pay indemnification, a codification of the rules for the non-recognition of territorial changes brought about through war,[68] of rules regarding the appropriation of property of the belligerent state and its citizens abroad, and so forth.

With respect to economic measures of compulsion, it was proposed that the system of Article XVI of the Covenant, as modified by the Resolutions of 1921, be taken as a basis, but that these be made more stringent in several respects, particularly by the confiscation and sale of the property and outstanding obligations of belligerents and their subjects in the other countries, the proceeds of which would be expended in the service of preventing or suppressing the war. Furthermore there was proposed the forfeiture and appropriation for similar uses of sums provided in time of peace as a guarantee [69] fund for this purpose.

Finally, Neo-neutrality takes the position that,[70] in case of necessity, military sanctions may also be applied for the purpose of preventing or opposing war, but in such manner that there is no obligation put upon the separate states to extend military assistance. The Council is to discuss any particular situation with the states regarding voluntary contingents, and there shall also be an international force, particularly an air force, at their disposal. But all hostilities, according to the "observations," were to be conducted only through international coöperation; in no case might this action take place through a declaration of war or by actual warfare on the part of individual states, such as Article XVI of the Covenant and the Resolutions of 1921 provide.

Finally the "observations" of 1934 declare that the status of neutrality of the nonparticipating states is in no way in conflict with the system of security aimed at, but, on the contrary, is an indispensable element of it. It is war itself which is to be fought,

[68] For the origin of these principles see Cohn, *Kriegsverhütung und Schuldfrage*, p. 185.

[69] *Coopération Intellectuelle*, Nos. 40-41, p. 50. This proposal has a certain resemblance to the international Convention on Financial Assistance of Oct. 2, 1930, proposed by Finland which has been signed but not yet ratified, but gives it an entirely different direction and significance.

[70] *Ibid.*, p. 51.

and not neutrality. Nonparticipating states should not be entitled, much less obliged, to resort to military measures against a belligerent state. The obligations of non-assistance to a belligerent must be strengthened considerably. The system naturally presumes, as every effective method of war-prevention does, a real and earnest desire to oppose war to the utmost.

The term "neutrality" is itself somewhat misleading, therefore, since it implies that same passivity and impartiality toward the belligerents which characterized traditional neutrality. The "neutral" states are really those upon which rest, through their common efforts, the duty of opposing the war. There should therefore be found another designation ("Neo-neutrality")[71] to better express this new status.

3. From a number of other countries also, reports[72] had been prepared for the use of the first conference in Paris, in 1934. These preliminary drafts dealt mainly with the problem of "collective security," and what the various countries understand and intend by that term. The questions of the revision of treaties (Article XIX of the Covenant) and of the causes[73] of war were also prominently placed for discussion.

Italy,[74] in accordance with the fascist philosophy, advanced fundamental objections regarding the value and practicability of the notion of security. In the draft of a systematic presentation of this problem from an American point of view,[75] Professor Philip C. Jessup also embarked upon the question of neutrality.[76] He proposed first to examine the legal status of neutrals at the present day, with regard to the changes which might have occurred during the World War or through the League Covenant and the Kellogg Pact. The next point was the question of how far an observance

[71] *Ibid.*, p. 53. The term "Neo-neutrality" was not, however, used in the "observations."

[72] These observations of 1934 are published in *Coopération Intellectuelle*, Nos. 40-41, pp. 222-229 (Paris, 1934).

[73] See the Spanish memoir by Professor Bayon y Chacon, in *ibid.*, pp. 228 ff.

[74] Coppola, "Aperçu sur l'idée de Sécurité Collective," in *ibid.*, pp. 256 ff.

[75] See the American memorandum by Jessup to the International Studies Conference (1934) in Bourquin (ed.), *Collective Security*, pp. 100 ff., and Jessup, *International Security* (New York, 1935).

[76] *Ibid.*

of the established laws of neutrality could be considered as in conflict with the general program of collective security, in situations where a united front is to be formed against a law-breaking state, and in situations where no such mutual agreement existed. Very interesting, moreover, is Professor Jessup's idea that if it should actually prove necessary to abolish neutrality in order to obtain a system of collective security, we should at least allow *neutrality, as a connecting link* with the new system of law, to remain.

He finally made concrete proposals calling for revisions in the existing rules of neutrality, whereby the duties of neutrals would be made more rigorous and their rights limited for the sake of a common front against the law-breaker, a theory which was in harmony with American neutrality policy at that time.

Under the impression that the general discussion concerned the question of the theory of aggression, which shortly before this (in May, 1933) had arisen in the Security Committee of the Disarmament Conference, and which [77] we have previously discussed, a large number of these reports deal with the question of the definition of aggression, since this definition was believed in some countries to be an important element in any system of collective security.

The theory of aggression, which is in fundamental opposition to that of Neo-neutrality, also held a prominent place in the preparatory conference which met in Paris in 1934. Professor Bourquin saw in the definition of aggression the pivot upon which the entire system of security turns. He called it "the fundamental norm" of the system,[78] that initial action which puts the entire sanctions machinery into motion.[79] In the same way, the Polish delegate,

[77] *Supra*, pp. 213 ff.

[78] *Coopération Intellectuelle*, II, Nos. 5-6, p. 160.

[79] As we have stated above, the sanctions system of the League Covenant is not tied, however, to aggression but to a formal violation of the terms of the Covenant. Moreover, M. Bourquin wished to distinguish between definitions of aggression, according to the view that *aggression* is the prohibited action but that the *aggressor* is the state against which the measures of compulsion are to be applied. These two need not be coexistent, in his opinion, since it may be the state originally attacked whose later conduct forms the essential obstacle to peace. Actually this quite correct view serves only to further demonstrate the impracticability of the aggression theory. See *ibid.*, pp. 157 ff.

Deryng,[80] argued at the beginning of the discussions in 1935 that the definition of aggression should constitute the basis of the system of security. M. Bourquin accepted this view to the extent that, when he mentioned the Danish views in his introductory report,[81] he admits that they regard war itself, not aggression, as "the crime," although they take strong exception to this penal law classification of wars of aggression, and naturally the more so with regard to defensive wars.

That the French would, both in the preparatory meetings and in the Conference itself, insist so strongly upon the theory of aggression, goes without saying. La Pradelle and Le Fur mention in their reports[82] at the London Conference of 1933 the "great advance" which was made in an objective and automatic determination of the aggressor. The situations enumerated in these Conventions, do more than create a mere presumption, as did those of the Geneva Protocol of 1924. They are irrefutable, since no views of a political, military, economic, or other character can be adduced to weaken them.

4. It was natural enough, therefore, that these views should come into a sharp collision upon the question of neutrality. Following the adjournment of the Conference, May 26, 1934, a number of the participants met again in an unofficial session,[83] where the new views set forth in the Danish memorandum were made the object of a detailed and interesting discussion. The American, Professor Jessup, desired to raise a fundamental point upon the question of neutrality. It would, in his opinion, be necessary to give the system of neutrality a place within the framework of any war-prevention system, and it should therefore have an important place in the coming conference at London in 1935. Neutrality had in the course of history assumed various forms and would probably assume new forms in the future. It held a prominent place in the Latin-American Saavedra Lamas Treaty of 1933, which had already been signed by nineteen states.

[80] Bourquin (ed.), *Collective Security*, pp. 324 ff. [81] *Ibid.*, p. 12.

[82] *Coopération Intellectuelle*, II, Nos. 5-6, "General view on the question of 'Collective Security,' " pp. 178 ff.

[83] League of Nations, *Conférence d'études préparatoire* (1934), pp. 299 ff.

The Englishman, Mitrany, pointed out [84] that there were actually two different positions of neutrality; one within the framework of the League of Nations, the other for large non-League countries such as the United States. M. de la Brière, of France, attacked neutrality from its moral and legal [85] aspects, and M. de la Pradelle, also of France, from the technical point of view.[86] There exist in the opinion of the latter two differing concepts of law: on one hand, the Continental-European, attaching importance to the objective side of the theory of aggression as a decisive criterion for putting into effect the two systems, that of the League and the Kellogg Pact, which cannot therefore recognize neutrality; and, on the other hand, the Anglo-Saxon,[87] in which these new ideas had not yet been accepted. To this the Englishman, Professor Zimmern, correctly replied that the difference had nothing to do with the opposite legal viewpoints of the English and the Continental systems. He reminded them that it was the report of a Continental state, Denmark, which first put forward the idea of preserving neutrality, as well as a plan for adapting it to the sanctions system.[88] Professor Zimmern further referred to the fact that the Danish theory had been made the basis of the Saavedra Lamas Treaty. The Conference of 1934 was not prepared, however, to accept his ideas. M. de la Pradelle insisted that [89] a state of neutrality could exist only so long as the aggressor had not been established, but in this connection raised an interesting question as to whether there might not be duties even toward an aggressor,

84 *Ibid.*, p. 300 f. 85 *Ibid.*, p. 301 f. 86 *Ibid.*, p. 302 f.

87 That England had been and still was one of the severest opponents of a neutrality program does not seem to have been considered here.

88 *Ibid.*, p. 303. "M. Zimmern fait remarquer que, malgré la distinction que vient établir M. de la Pradelle, entre la conception 'continentale' de la neutralité et la conception 'anglo-saxonne,' la Conférence a reçu un mémoire venu d'un pays continental: le Danemark, et qui soutient encore l'idée de la neutralité. Ce mémoire tâche de concilier l'idée de neutralité et celle des sanctions. L'auteur voudrait que son pays n'entre pas dans la guerre et désirerait une neutralité organisée. M. Zimmern cite un passage de ce mémoire qui lui parait caractéristique: La conception traditionelle de la neutralité, y est-il dit, n'est en aucune mesure en opposition avec un arrangement effectif de la sécurité; bien au contraire, elle en constitue un élément indispensable; ce qu'il faut supprimer c'est la guerre et non pas la neutralité. Sans s'associer à cette argumentation, M. Zimmern la trouve extrêmement intéressante," etc.

89 Except for permanently neutralized states such as Switzerland.

such, for example, as permitting him shipments of food.[90] Le Fur opposed the Danish memorandum,[91] taking the position that merely because one *wished* to abolish war one should not pretend that it had already been abolished. The Kellogg Pact assumes guilt in the one who resorts to war; it was therefore necessary to have a determination of the aggressor. This, from a purely military point of view, is perhaps difficult, but from a legal point of view is simple. Neutrality can no longer be recognized in modern war, he said.

This statement was answered by the English delegate, Manning, who pointed out that neither the Covenant of the League nor the Kellogg Pact obliges the states to abandon their neutrality. The question, in his opinion, was of a *moral* nature. Professor Jessup proposed a compromise.[92] If the machinery of the League Covenant and of the Kellogg Pact functions, there is, in his opinion, no need of neutrality; but if there were some doubt as to the determination of the aggressor, we should then have to rely upon the Danish views.

In opposition to Manning, the Frenchman, Scelle, asserted that the problem was of a legal, and not of a moral, nature. The states, it is true, were free with regard to the question of the legality of the war. But when once they had decided that it was illegal, they were then legally bound to abandon their neutrality.

In reply to this, Jessup inquired if the United States, upon its signature of the Kellogg Pact, had really renounced its rights as a neutral. These rights were still being referred to, in diplomatic documents and elsewhere.

The President (the Englishman, Toynbee) then observed that war has changed its character. In Bismarck's time one might obtain certain advantages—which could be foreseen—from war. But in our time, any war was an incalculable catastrophe which must necessarily draw all nations under its sway; a point of view which was further discussed by de la Pradelle and Bourquin.[93] M. Scelle

[90] So in the Resolutions of 1921. Article XVI of the Covenant, however, does not take this position, since it requires the immediate and complete discontinuance of all relations with the covenant-breaking state.

[91] *Conférence d'études préparatoire*, p. 304.

[92] *Ibid.*, p. 306.

[93] But which experience has since refuted (Ethiopia).

even went so far as to assert [94] that the conception of neutrality was based on a reactionary legal idea.[95] The progressive jurist should distinguish between war and an exercise of the police power. When war had been declared because of a crime, the use of compulsion upon other states was no longer war; it was police power. Therefore he could not even accept de la Pradelle's idea with regard to the permanently neutralized states. These might very well take part in all sanctions, including military ones, because again it was not a question of war but of the exercise of police power.[96] To this Manning replied that M. Scelle's distinctions between progressive and conservative jurists were less to the point than the important question as to what the legal situation itself was.[97]

Following the Paris Conference in 1934, Professor Bourquin summed up its provisional results in an agenda, with comments,[98] for the use of the final conference to be held in London in 1935. In this agenda the theory of aggression was retained as a logically necessary basis for any war-prevention system, "for if we cannot point out the guilty party, the entire fight against war will necessarily be paralyzed." [99] The neutrality question is nonetheless described as being one of the most important topics [100] for investigation, and the following points of view are stressed:

(1) Historically considered, the law of neutrality has taken many and varied forms. It is, therefore, not essential to retain those principles which characterized it at the end of the nineteenth century, especially with regard to its demand for unconditional impartiality and passivity.

(2) Rules for war-prevention necessarily require common action against the aggressor. To what extent is this fact consistent with the conception of neutrality?

94 *Ibid.*, p. 308 f.

95 This hardly flattering term he directed particularly against the author of the Danish memorandum, *ibid.*, p. 309.

96 Only in the instance dealt with in Article XV, section 7, of the Covenant of the League would M. Scelle still recognize the right of neutrality.

97 *Ibid.*, p. 310.

98 *Ibid.*, pp. 318 ff.

99 *Ibid.*, p. 335. That Bourquin's own ideas of the application of sanctions do not always coincide with the concept of "aggression" here planned, seems to have been overlooked.

100 *Ibid.*, p. 336. See also *Coopération Intellectuelle*, II, Nos. 5-6, p. 165.

(3) This must be carefully studied for each separate type of sanctions about which there may be a question (moral, legal, diplomatic, financial, economic, military). Even where a purely theoretical assertion is made (Scelle) that a neutral state may participate in all these types of sanctions, since it is a question merely of police power and not of war, this will hardly be of value in practice. It is therefore a question of determining clearly the extent to which this claim may be realized in practice. Obviously this cannot be answered for all types of sanctions in the same manner.

(4) A different question is that respecting the nature of the legal situation which arises when a state outside the League, for example the United States, while insisting upon its rights as a neutral, wishes not to act contrary to, and even so far as possible to support, the common action of the League against the aggressor.[101]

(5) Finally, inquiry should be made as to whether neutrality itself, as suggested in the Danish memorandum, should be used as a dam against the flood of war. Carried to its logical conclusion, Professor Bourquin believes that this action would lead in the contrary direction from that of the prevention of war. At the same time, it had to be admitted that these Danish views had also been expressed in Article III of the Saavedra Lamas Treaty.

At the Paris Conference in 1934, the neutrality question, which had been put aside for many years, again came to the fore, and its new expression (Neo-neutrality) was stated in sharp fundamental contrast to the theory of aggression.

The London Conference, 1935

1. During the interval between the two conferences, a number of proposals were prepared,[102] under the auspices of various national learned societies, which were to form the basis for the final discussions at the London Conference in 1935. Denmark prepared

[101] Professor Jessup afterwards made this question the subject of a thoroughly detailed examination in his book *The United States and the Stabilization of Peace*, New York, 1935.

[102] A summary of all these proposals is to be found in the appendix to Bourquin (ed.), *Collective Security*, pp. 469 ff.

two memoranda, with the assistance of the Danish Institute of History and Economics. One of these[103] reports contained a refutation in principle of the theory of aggression and that of rational causes of war, such as those which found expression in the Covenant of the League. It especially attempted to refute the theory which underlies Part XIII of the Treaty of Versailles, according to which the danger of war may be reduced by socio-political institutions, especially by the International Labour Office, established in Geneva. It contended that the real causes of war must be sought in the psychological and pathological conditions within the group mind and it tries to deduce the consequences of this as regards the efforts to prevent war.

The second Danish memorandum concerned the question of neutrality[104] and showed that the problems of neutrality and that of its combination with the sanctions system already appear in the very text of Articles XVI and XVII of the Covenant. It was next pointed out that the theory of aggression presumes that sanctions are to be applied to only one of the belligerents (the guilty party); if there is guilt upon both sides, or upon neither side, or as long as the question of guilt is undecided, this memorandum held that the members of the League have the right to remain neutral. There are further adduced a number of situations demonstrating the continued existence of the law of neutrality. Of course all this constitutes a weakening of the system, and the task will therefore be so to change it that the conditions for its establishment are made clearer and, in particular, freed from the element of guilt, which is so difficult to demonstrate.

> ...The system of sanctions should be directed against war as such, as a fact, without regard to its psychological basis. From this point of view defensive war must be included as well as offensive war, so that the states not involved in the conflict may not be obliged to make a choice which would at the same time necessitate the moral condemnation of one of the Powers, but may simply be confronted with the state of war as a fact which must be prevented and combated, in the

[103] "The Causes of War and Moral Disarmament," in Bourquin, pp. 287 ff., has abstracts of this.

[104] "The System of Sanctions of Article 16 of the Covenant and the Future Rôle of Neutrality," included in Bourquin, pp. 402 ff.

common interest of all the nations. It is of little importance to determine who, from a purely formal standpoint, is playing the part of the aggressor. War is forbidden in all cases and for all parties . . .[105]

This memorandum gives a report, similar to that of the memorandum of 1934, of the legal conditions under which Neo-neutrality can assist in the suppression of war as a fact—with its wholesale slaughter of the youth of all nations, regardless of the purposes or the name under which this takes place.

The views[106] of the 1934 memorandum thus restated were attacked in various memoranda prepared by other countries for the consideration of the Conference in 1935. The theory of aggression as the "fundamental norm" and a determination of the aggressor in accordance with the London Conventions of 1933, still dominated the discussion and were defended by the Rumanian representative, Pella, among others, who[107] finds in such definitions the best means of determining the requisite conditions[108] for the conception of a universal self-defense. The automatic definition of the London Conference is regarded by him as the best guarantee[109] of security. "La méthode pour définir l'agresseur constitue le fondement de tout système de sécurité." Consideration of provocation is rejected by him, from the same line of reasoning as that of M. Politis in the Conference of 1933. Rather naïvely, M. Pella's statement concludes by asserting that *if* all states would accept the Convention of 1933 and observe it in practice, important progress in the organization of peace would be made.

A more thoroughgoing analysis is to be found in the report of the French representative, Camille Jordan: "Definition of the Aggressor."[110] The theory of the aggression, he says, is based upon

[105] Bourquin (ed.), *Collective Security*, p. 402.

[106] At the Conference of Paris in 1934 and at that in London in 1935 Neo-neutrality still remained an entirely new theory not fully comprehended. See Bourquin (ed.), p. 12.

[107] *La Détermination de l'agresseur*, Bukarest, 1935.

[108] *Ibid.*, p. 4. The entire study has a rather superficial character. It is obvious that there is no real attempt to lay down any conditions at all for a concept of self-defense under international law, if it is to be considered sufficient for that purpose to determine the aggressor.

[109] *Ibid.*, p. 7. "Le premier effet des Conventions de Londres est d'avoir mis le territoire des États contractants à l'abri de toute guerre, violence ou acte de force."

[110] Printed in abstracts in Bourquin (ed.), *Collective Security*, pp. 296 ff.

Article 231 of the Treaty of Versailles, dealing with war guilt. Theologians of the Middle Ages (Augustine and Thomas Aquinas) had already worked out theories of "the just war," but this might be either defensive or aggressive, as for example, when a state was to be punished for not having called its subjects to account for violations of law or the like, a distinction which may also be found in some later writers, as Grotius.[111]

The Covenant of the League first introduced the new principle that that state is the aggressor which, before war starts, does not follow the procedure which it provided for the peaceful solution of the dispute. The Geneva Protocol of 1924, he says, constitutes great progress by its introduction of a purely automatic determination of the aggressor and the automatic operation of the presumption of an act of aggression. The weakness in his opinion lay in the fact that these presumptions might be invalidated (and a similar mistake is made in the Locarno agreements) by introducing the concept of provocation, which once again makes the determination of the aggressor dependent upon a subjective judgment.

The Kellogg Pact once more appeared to represent an advance, in that the guilty party is defined as the one who takes the initiative in hostilities, and in this way leads to an identification of the theories of aggression and unjust war; but the interpretations given to this Pact, especially by Americans themselves, have only weakened its significance. Jordan further holds that the first London Convention of 1933 produced a final solution of the problem, since its definitions functioned automatically and their assumptions were irrefutable.[112]

It is strange that the author could be so enthusiastic over this result, since he cites some of the objections, and in our opinion completely decisive ones, which can be raised against it. The objection that both parties might fulfill the criteria, he dismisses by asserting that the aggressor is that party who *first* fulfills them. Intervention by third states would not constitute aggression, be-

[111] Who describes the motive of punishment as a just cause for war; see *supra*, p. 188.

[112] Bourquin (ed.), *Collective Security*, p. 297: "This presumption will no longer be a simple presumption, as in the case of the Geneva Protocol, but *irrefutable, juris et de jure*. The proof of the contrary can in no case be admitted."

cause the London Convention, he says, is an outgrowth of the Kellogg Pact.[113] The distinction between a purely formal criterion of aggression and real responsibility for the entire war situation, which must be decisive in the question as to how sanctions should be applied, is also mentioned; further, the exceptions which the attached protocol makes in the automatic character of the principal rule, the inapplicability of the Convention when fixed frontiers do not exist or when the administration of the territory is divided between several states, the right of self-defense to forestall an attack when necessary, without conceding to these overwhelming objections, which are in no sense satisfactorily answered, any decisive importance. He asserts that "... the definition of the aggressor introduces into international relations a great clearness and sharpness of outline," and that this irrefutable assumption will in the future make it an easy task to establish the aggressor and make it no longer necessary to inquire into the psychological motives behind the resort to force.[114]

In a brief memorandum entitled "*Naming the Aggressor,*" the English member, Mr. Horsfall Carter, agreeing with him. The Polish member, M. Komarnicki (*Definition of the Aggressor*),[115] agrees that M. Politis was correct in his assertion before the Committee on Security that the definition of the aggressor is the basis of the entire system of security. This author attempts to give a quasi-legal and philosophical explanation of the territorial criterion of the aggression theory, using the conception of modern international law that its territory is not merely an adjunct of the state, but that it is an element of the entity of the state itself. Any attack upon its territory is therefore an attack upon the state itself and not merely an undertaking directed at the property of the state.[116]

It is not easy to see what difference this theory would have, one

[113] This explanation was previously used by M. Politis, but it is incorrect, as the text of the 1933 Convention says nothing about it.

[114] Bourquin (ed.), *Collective Security*, p. 304.

[115] *Ibid.*, pp. 313 ff.

[116] Bourquin (ed.), p. 316. "... contemporary opinion regarding territory, which does not separate the territory as object from the State as subject, but considers that the territory is an element in the personality of the State. Any violation of territory is therefore a violation of the State itself, and not merely an attempt upon the property of the State."

way or another, for the undeniable fact that an attack upon its territory is an attack upon the state, but the author seems to have forgotten that such attack may likewise occur upon the high seas or upon the territory of a third state, to which situations this theory—whatever its value might otherwise be—does not apply. His conclusion, however, was that the London Convention had solved the problem of the definition of the aggressor, and therefore represented real progress in international law.[117]

We may finally mention Professor Scelle's memorandum,[118] "Theory of International Government," in which he discusses the distinction between war and international police. For him, illegal war is a crime, and war waged to punish the criminal is not war, but exercise of the police power. The concept of neutrality must therefore disappear.[119] In the determination of the aggressor and in the application of sanctions, the Council demonstrates its rôle as a superstate government, he asserts. This applies especially to situations comprehended under Articles X and XVI of the Covenant. The author admits, however, that neutrality is still valid for situations dealt with in Article XVII, section 7. In the Locarno Treaties this police power is acknowledged by certain states. Scelle holds that the London Convention of 1933 gives us an entirely objective definition of aggression.

His pamphlet hardly justified the hopes which the author held out in the Paris Conference of 1934. Whether we *call* a war a "war" or the "exercise of the police power" makes little difference so long as the rules of international law on this situation have not been changed. The view of the Council as the government of a superstate is directly contrary to the spirit and wording of the League Covenant and to all theory and practice in this field. Just as incorrect is Scelle's assertion regarding the application of sanctions under Article X of the Covenant.

2. Aside from these memoranda, which oppose both Neo-neutrality and the continuation of the *raison d'être* of traditional

[117] Bourquin (ed.), p. 313 f.

[118] *New Commonwealth Quarterly*, I (1935-36), pp. 18 ff.; see *Collective Security* (Bourquin, ed.), p. 25; for an outline of the memorandum, see *ibid.*, p. 476 (Appendix).

[119] *Ibid.*

neutrality, more as a logical consequence of their strong support of the theory of aggression, especially in the form this conception received in the London Conventions of 1933, the new neutrality was further criticized in other preliminary drafts for the Conference of 1935. In a memorandum entitled "The Evolution of Neutrality," [120] Dr. Paul de La Pradelle asserts that certainly it is incorrect for certain writers, among them Madariaga, Politis, Brierly,[121] and Crichton,[122] to say that neutrality has been entirely abolished, or is an anachronism. It would appear from several political documents of most recent date, that the concept of neutrality still exists. Nonetheless, he believes that traditional neutrality according to the rules of the Hague Conventions has played its rôle, since it assumes an impartiality which is in conflict with the obligations of states under the Covenant of the League, and further because it is contrary to morality.[123] President Wilson's idea was that neutrality should disappear, and this stand was restated by Leon Bourgeois, and conveyed to the representatives of the neutral countries during their discussions at the Hotel Crillon in Paris.[124] This was also the view of the Council of the League in 1920, when they recognized an exception for Switzerland. In the years following there have nevertheless been attempts, by means of hair-splitting and revised interpretations, to avoid the clear meaning of the text in those provisions of the Covenant which necessarily require the abandonment of neutrality, so that the logical meaning

[120] In Bourquin (ed.), *Collective Security*, pp. 404 ff. Cited here, however, from the original mimeographed edition (March 1935) from which some of the more spiteful sallies against neutrals—the sharpest ones—were later omitted from Bourquin's book.

[121] See for example his address: "Neutrality of States under the Covenant of the League of Nations and the Kellogg Pact" (1936), published by the Danish *Akademisk Forening for Udenrigspolitik og Folkenes Forbund.*

[122] "The Pre-War Theory of Neutrality," in the *British Year Book of International Law*, IX (1928), pp. 101 ff.; with a woman's consistent logic, Miss Crichton uses throughout the article the past tense in order to emphasize her contention that neutrality is a thing of the past.

[123] "La neutralité est amenagée dans le sens de l'égöisme. Sa maxime est 'enrichissez-vous.'" La Pradelle further describes the neutrals as "neutres par profession" (p. 18 of the mimeographed text).

[124] Munch, "Les États neutres et le Pacte de la Société des nations," in *Les Origines et l'œuvre de la Société des nations*, I, 177: "la participation aux sanctions économiques, acceptée en principe par le Danemark et la Suisse, involvait à son avis l'abandon de la neutralité."

and extent of those provisions have been altered. But neutrality is no longer a question of interests, it is a question of morality and conscience. The belief that this question can be solved by making a distinction between economic and military sanctions is not tenable. Traditional neutrality is *inconsistent with all kinds of sanctions.*[125]

The Kellogg Pact, which also promised to seal the doom of neutrality, was a tremendous disappointment to its adherents because it contained no detailed rules for the punishment of the aggressor. Nevertheless, he believes all good men ("les auteurs, que la seul souci de la justice et la logique juridique anime") will not fail to recognize that neutrality was deliberately disaffirmed in the Kellogg Pact. It is certainly true that the United States itself maintains the existence of the law of neutrality, but the American view of neutrality is in process of development, and might be regarded as a "benevolent neutrality," as he tries to prove in a study of recent American neutrality legislation. The Saavedra Lamas Treaty is in his opinion also an expression of the obsolescence of traditional neutrality, because it creates a new common front of neutrality instead. This tendency, in the opinion of the author, aims in all cases to remove from the rules of neutrality their principal motive, profits. The author's temperamental language thus obviously assumes that the waging of war is a pleasant diversion from which the neutrals restrain themselves only because of the opportunity to enrich themselves by their abstention. He apparently assumes that if export prohibitions and the like prevent them from profiting through such sordid business, they will, of course, enter with pleasure into the quarrels of the belligerents.

The English representatives made a very interesting statement of the problem, in a report by Professor Lauterpacht.[126] This

125 "En réalité, il ne faut pas s'y tromper. Le régime classique de la neutralité exclut toutes les catégories de sanctions, car c'est l'idée même de sanction qui est à la source de leur incompatibilité." La Pradelle in Bourquin (ed.), p. 18 (mimeographed text). The "expurgated" edition can be found in Bourquin (ed.), *Collective Security*, pp. 404 ff.

126 "The Notion of Neutrality in a System Providing for the Repression of War," in *Some British Views on Collective Security*, Part II (Feb. 1935); abstracts and translation in Bourquin (ed.), pp. 24 and 79 ff., also 134 ff. (Memorandum No. 3 of the United Kingdom). Extracts of the views of Lauterpacht for this and

author recognizes, and accepts as a matter of course, the conclusions of the Danish memoranda upon this question, but he gives them a different slant as interpreting the legal situation in Article XVIII so that it appears to be an explicit agreement among the League members for a special form of neutrality which does not require impartiality. In his opinion, the Covenant merely returns to the conception of qualified neutrality.[127] This would be the result, he suggests, of any system of war-prevention, the members of which have obligated themselves to oppose the aggressor and to assist the party attacked, short of war.[128] On the other hand, the Swiss theory, according to which a distinction should be made in neutrality law between economic and military sanctions, he cannot approve.[129]

Viewed historically, it is evident that partiality and neutrality are not mutually exclusive.[130] This was the view of Grotius and of Vattel. It was Bynkershoek who, in 1737, first put forward the idea of complete impartiality, but even he recognized that a previously concluded agreement to render assistance in war is valid and would not be a violation of the obligation of neutrality. This view ("the admissibility of qualified neutrality in case of a preexisting treaty") was shared by eminent scholars in international law (Wheaton, Bluntschli, and others) as late as the middle of the nineteenth century,[131] and it also coincides with the practice of

succeeding references can be found (in English) in that book, pp. 412 ff.; we use the original mimeographed French text for his quotations in the present work.

[127] Bourquin (ed.), p. 413. ". . . While, therefore, the Covenant has not abolished neutrality even as between the belligerent Covenant-breaker and the members of the League applying sanctions against him, it has abolished, as among its members, the current conception of neutrality as an attitude of absolute impartiality. It signifies, as a matter of positive law, the return to the conception of qualified neutrality."

[128] Lauterpacht's theory of the League system as an agreement on qualified neutrality is unacceptable for the very reason that there exists no such agreement regarding it; the idea of neutrality is not even mentioned in the Covenant of the League and is not mentioned for the very reason that they wish to abolish it, although they did not do so. The juridical construction of a legal system cannot function as an explicit or implicit agreement under it when it is necessary to make use of such an agreement as a legal explanation.

[129] Lauterpacht, in *Some British Views on Collective Security*, p. 15 f.

[130] See also Oppenheim, II, 531 ff.

[131] *Ibid.*, p. 18 f.

states.[132] In the war between Denmark and Germany in 1848, England, as a neutral acting under its treaty obligation to Denmark, prohibited the export of arms to Germany. In the Boer War in 1900, Portugal, a neutral acting under a treaty agreement, permitted English troops to land on Portuguese territory. Even during the World War, several of the neutral Central and South American states permitted the United States to make use of their ports as bases for its naval forces. The Hague Convention conception of neutrality is therefore not an absolute one, says Lauterpacht, but is historically conditioned.[133] According to international law, there is nothing to prevent its conception being altered by treaty, as has happened, for example, in the Covenant of the League of Nations.[134]

If we should next inquire concerning the advantages and shortcomings of such qualified neutrality, within the sanctions system of the League, Lauterpacht freely admits[135] that the idea of neutrality has certain advantages. It permits a certain gradation, elasticity, and consideration of the greater of the lesser guilt of an aggressor. It averts the necessity of resorting at once to the extreme measures of a general war, in unimportant cases. It prevents a localized condition of war from spreading into a world conflagration. It corresponds to the present legal status of the reciprocal relations between the states. It proves that war is not the only means of sanctions which is at the disposal of the League, and that

[132] *Ibid.*, p. 19: "In 1848, during the war between Denmark and Germany, *Great Britain*, in fulfillment of a previous treaty obligation, prohibited the export of munitions to Germany. In 1900, during the war between Great Britain and the South African Republic, *Portugal* complied with a treaty with Great Britain allowing the landing of British troops on Portuguese territory. During the World War, after the United States declared war on Germany, a number of Central and South American States departed in a conspicuous manner from an attitude of impartiality. In April, 1917, *Costa Rica* offered her ports and waters for the use of the navy of the United States, *Guatemala* followed suit, *Brazil*, *Uruguay*, and *Peru* expressly modified their neutrality regulations. *Uruguay* issued a special decree announcing that she would refrain from treating as a belligerent any American country engaged in the defence of its rights, in a war with States in other continents."

[133] *Ibid.*, p. 20: ". . . absolute neutrality is a historically conditioned phase of international law."

[134] This construction, as we have already stated, is unacceptable.

[135] *Ibid.*, pp. 22 ff. See also Bourquin (ed.), *Collective Security*, p. 415 f.

a collective system of sanctions, and, at the same time, the neutrality of the individual members, are not mutually exclusive.[136]

On the other hand, it cannot in Lauterpacht's opinion be denied that the conception of neutrality involves a weakening of the system. There would be no positive assurance of security.[137] Moreover, neutrality is morally unjustifiable. In case of an aggression in violation of international law, the neutral state is in the same position as the private citizen who witnesses a crime against national law and does nothing, says Lauterpacht, an act which, in certain countries including England, is punishable. In a moral, if not in an internationally legal, sense we may therefore conclude that collective security and neutrality are mutually exclusive. "The more there is of the one the less there is of the other." [138] Very often the armed forces of the aggressor will be so powerful as quickly to crush and annex the attacked state. In such circumstances, collective security which recognizes the right of qualified neutrality is an empty phrase. Only a system which requires "a complete formal identification of the members with the attacked State" gives real protection. Lauterpacht has no doubt that this will be the eventual system of security. He therefore opposes the view [139] that the question of guilt has no right to be considered in a system of war-prevention merely because it is an inapplicable carrying-over, into the field of international law, of municipal penal-law concepts; or that it is a paradox to fight war with war; or that we should apply the system to war as such, against defender and aggressor alike. Such ideas in his opinion, are contrary to those which lie at the heart of the League Covenant, and to morality which, in the development of international law and order, should be analogous with that which regulates the relations of individuals within the states. They are therefore definitely rejected by Lauterpacht as being suicidal for

[136] All these good arguments have been borrowed from the Danish treatises of 1924 and 1931.

[137] As if the theory of aggression would give absolute security (see the result of the Italo-Ethiopian conflict)!

[138] This applies only to the traditional conception of neutrality and not to qualified neutrality, which in Lauterpacht's opinion underlies the system of the Covenant of the League and to a lesser degree, that of Neo-neutrality. See Lauterpacht in *Some British Views*, p. 24.

[139] *Ibid.*, p. 25.

the smaller states, as dogmatic, and as naïve. Quite different proposals had been made by the French-English fellowship, with regard to the forms under which the United States, without surrendering its traditional position, might coöperate with the League.

From the standpoint of international law, we see no reason here to criticize this English statement since it takes at once the same position as that of the Danish treatises of 1924 and 1931. Its efforts to construct a legal basis similar to the treaty provisions as that of qualified neutrality we have answered above. Its moral and political condemnation of the conception of neutrality however rests upon an error in judgment. Neo-neutrality is no less vital an element of a system of war-prevention than is the theory of aggression. In reality it is more so, since it applies not only to aggressive war, but to defensive war as well. The *measures* to be used are somewhat different, in that Neo-neutrality does not, under any circumstances, include war among them. It does insist, it is true, that non-military sanctions, too, can be very effective, indeed even more purposeful and effective than war itself, the results of which are always so uncertain and fortuitous. In the "observations" of 1934, dealt with above,[140] there was developed a system of sanctions, which, so far as efficiency is concerned, were much more thoroughgoing and more clear in purpose than the measures of the League Covenant, which are not consistent. When Lauterpacht makes the great moral requirement as to the claims of the smaller states, he assumes a system in which only legal considerations, and not political or opportunist ones, are valid. But actual conditions in this world are quite different from that, and his accusations of naïveté and dogmatism must, I fear, be directed rather against the jurist who disregards these realities. Neutrality is not self-destructive for the smaller states, but is their attempt to obtain a certain measure of security, just as the armaments of the Great Powers are their answer to the same problem. In an ideal league of nations neither armaments nor neutrality would exist, because war would have been abolished. So long as this ideal league does not exist, none of the nations can afford to abandon the foundation

140 *Supra*, pp. 285 ff.

upon which they have built, through history and experience, their foreign policy.

The Norwegian memorandum "Collective Security," by Dr. Raestad,[141] likewise is mainly concerned with a statement and a criticism of the new theory of neutrality. He asserts that the question of neutrality appears in three different forms, the American, the Swiss, and the Danish. The American is held to be difficult to understand, since it follows no consistent course and is not the expression of any clearly defined views. The Swiss form is practically identical with that of traditional neutrality. The Danish, on the other hand, is an effort to lay down a general political system, to be accepted by as many states as possible. It finds the causes of war *not* in normal economic, political, and social conditions, as the League Covenant assumes them to be, but in antisocial, irrational, or pathological conditions, to which peoples and their governments from time to time succumb. Thus it is highly desirable that as large a number of states as possible should remain apart from war, with its hatreds, passions, and bitterness, in order to help the belligerents back to peace and to the reëstablishment of normal friendly relations—in other words, to restore their mental balance. This duty the neutral should undertake at all times—during the war, at the conclusion of peace, and in the difficult postwar period. The conduct of a neutrality policy of this kind, supported by certain effective but not warlike compulsory measures, is regarded as relatively the best means of reducing the frequency of war, of preventing its spread once it has broken out, and of bringing it to a stop in every case. Dr. Raestad here repudiates the assertions made by others that neutrals intend, or that they are able, to enrich themselves through wars between other nations.

The objections which Raestad finds in the new theory are of a different nature. The principal weakness he believes to lie in the purely logical situation that neutrality can exist only when there is war and that it is thus a function of war. But war, he reminds us, is not the only form of international encroachment. Recent history has many examples of how one state may oppress another and de-

[141] In Bourquin (ed.), pp. 150 ff., in much abbreviated form; quoted here from the original mimeographed text.

prive it of large parts of its territory, without necessarily resorting to war. The question of applying sanctions to gross violations of international obligations, for example to those of disarmament, even where there has been no question of war, was taken up for study by the League of Nations in April, 1935. Collective security may require extreme measures, even in time of peace.

So far as conditions of war are concerned, a neutrality policy similar to that suggested here will lead only to half measures and will be insufficient for a real fight against war. The truth is that no policy exists which can be adapted to all situations and for all states. In some cases a neutrality policy will be necessary to a small state, to preserve its existence. In other situations that very neutrality might become extremely dangerous. For him, the problem of neutrality is one of armaments and expresses itself in varying forms according to the situation of the different states. At any rate a fixed neutrality policy of any kind has a tendency to lessen the solidary character of collective security.

With respect to the pathological nature of war, Dr. Raestad claims that this exists rather as an accompanying circumstance rather than as a motivating cause. In any case, he believes that this is not an important element of war. "As experience shows, a disposition toward crime and the homicidal instinct or brutality have so many opportunities for expression in private life that one might easily imagine a condition in the world where force dominated so completely that there would be no need of any international war." [142] History, he says, shows that pressure, applied with judgment by a sufficiently strong group of Powers, may without difficulty obtain the desired security for such nations. In the international, as well as in the national, sphere, he says, it is a question of assisting reason to win out ("la réalisation du rationnel"). The difficulty we face is that there are two opposing groups of states, one of which relies upon ententes and alliances, the second of which systematically endeavors to remain neutral.[143] One of these groups makes demands upon the other, with which it cannot com-

[142] Raestad, *op. cit.*, pp. 53 ff. (translated from the original mimeographed text).

[143] This distinction, too, appears to be somewhat questionable, because there exist states which contemplate war without relying upon alliances, and because,

ply; just as within the national society one class sweats and oppresses the other, so, in international society, one group of states exerts a pressure which the other may regard as unjust. The problem of the organization of collective security thus ends with a question mark.

Against these objections the following arguments may be brought: it is, of course, true that war is not the only form of international encroachment, and that in cases where the difference in strength is very great, wrong may triumph without actual resort to war. In such cases, which belong under a war-prevention system in a broader sense, new means of regulation should be found which the Covenant of the League has not as yet considered. But even in these cases, Neo-neutrality, the system of sanctions of which is certainly *not* dependent upon mere verbal or logical distinctions between war and neutrality (the more so, since it does not recognize war as a legal situation), seems to come much nearer to the intent and purpose of a general system of war-prevention than does the theory of aggression, which must of necessity be limited to an actual situation of war. Just because Neo-neutrality does take exception to war in all its forms, it can adjust the sanctions system very well to other extreme types of international encroachment. It attaches no importance to defining aggression nor to classifying the war; and its principles may readily be applied to situations not involving an actual condition of war,[144] particularly because it will not consider, as a matter of principle, military countermeasures against international encroachments under any circumstances.

Dr. Raestad's statement that Neo-neutrality, during a war, would lead only to half measures has previously been answered here several times. The energy with which a war-prevention system would be put into effect is hardly dependent upon the character of the system which is used. In practice it has been shown

on the other hand, the author himself looks to a strong grouping (alliance) of the Powers for the purpose of maintaining peace.

144 Examples of the possibility of a system for the practical enforcement of the prevention of war and international violence on a neo-neutral basis, without attaching importance to the question of the formal outbreak of war, are the above-mentioned Dutch *Law No. 599 of Oct. 9, 1935* and *Law No. 621* of the same month. See also the above-mentioned Danish memorandum of 1935 above, on "The Causes of War and Moral Disarmament," in Bourquin (ed.), pp. 287 ff.

that even the most flagrant instances of aggression are met with half measures by states, when for political reasons they do not wish to apply sanctions. No perfect security against war is given by any system. But in our judgment the fact that this system is aimed against war as such, and not against certain kinds of war, affords possibilities for greater consistency and efficiency than the aggression theory.

When Dr. Raestad says that it depends upon conditions in various parts of the world as to whether participation in the war by outside states, or neutrality, will be of greater advantage in a system of war-prevention, we cannot agree with him. Experience proves that the tendency of a war to spread is a universal phenomenon. Hence the war-prevention program of Neo-neutrality is of equal importance in all situations. The cause of peace everywhere has the most to gain, I do believe, by fighting war upon a neo-neutral basis, and it has most to lose when the nonparticipants have been drawn into it. There is an apparent confusion between the question as to what is best for the national policies of particular states and that of the general question of a policy of war-prevention in the supreme interest of all states. Only this latter question can be taken into consideration here.

With regard to the question of the pathological causes of war, Dr. Raestad's opinion was doubtless based somewhat too much upon a single statement of the Danish position.[145] Neo-neutrality builds upon a far broader foundation. As we have seen previously, it does not depend, either exclusively or primarily, upon the pathological nature of war, but quite as much upon the psychological, and, above all, upon the sociological, characterizations of the facts which we shall here have to consider (partly because insufficient attention has been given to the above-mentioned memorandum of 1935 concerning the causes of war). The belief that rational causes are insufficient to explain war constitutes an essential element of Neo-neutrality. Thereafter the distinction between the causes of war and its accompanying circumstances are of no importance, or—if we may express it differently—it is the accompany-

[145] Cohn, *Er Krig en Sygdom?* [Is war a disease?] Radio address of Oct. 10, 1934, from Copenhagen.

ing collective-psychical circumstances which create the effect that existing political and other practical aims are transformed into causes of war. The desire for raw materials, colonies, personal ambitions, party success, avoiding of internal political or economic difficulties, and the like, are generally present and may be extremely "reasonable" in themselves, but they are not rational, not sufficient to be *causes of war*. No one who intelligently contrasts the aims with the gains possible through war and with the sacrifices required can believe that any reasonable relation between these things exists. Nonetheless such purposes, and still others of an even more meaningless nature (such as prestige and prejudices of all kinds), are transformed into causes of war through the collective psychosis described above. It is thus the conditions conducive to the origin and the disappearance of these elements that one must study, if war is to be prevented; while the numerous rational and irrational causes of war which are generally pleaded, will always be present under changing forms. This certainly does not prevent our working for a peaceful settlement and adjustment of those conflicting interests which, as we have learned from experience, give rise to disputes and difficulties between states, a work which may be of the greatest importance in lessening the danger of war. In this sense a correct idea underlies the theory of the causes of war and its prevention.

Dr. Raestad, in closing, stated that hatreds and a homicidal instinct had many other modes of possible expression, as within the national policies of states; this is undeniable. There are many other human relations, particularly in a national society; there is for instance an element of sadism and brutality in men toward other individuals, which we are likely to overlook. The answer to this is that Neo-neutrality takes up the work on one front, namely, where these tendencies manifest themselves in the form of war. Other movements must take up the fight on other fronts. Beside the above-mentioned memorandum concerning the "causes of war and moral disarmament," efforts have been made to prove that a rational system of war-prevention must begin at a much earlier stage than that of awaiting the outbreak of the war, and must discover those forms under which those internal policies which experience has shown lead to war sooner or later may be exposed to the light of day, and oppose them with all possible energy by international means, regardless of the antiquated and obsolete concept of unlimited state sovereignty.

3. The agenda and preparatory memoranda were sent in advance to all participants in the final conference which took place in London, June, 1935, where they were made the object of renewed examination and conclusive discussion. A general survey of the different problems was given, in an introductory report by M. Bourquin, who continued to assert the necessity of the aggression theory in any war-prevention system.[146] This theory of aggression was made the object of a discussion during the meeting of June 6, and it was still the territorial criterion (Politis-Litvinoff Conventions) which was regarded as the best. M. Bourquin,[147] however, emphasized the fact which had already received attention in the discussions of the Committee on Security in 1933, that one must distinguish between the definition of aggression and the determination of the aggressor. When war has broken out, the question of the application of sanctions cannot be determined from the purely formal consideration as to which one made the first attack; but one must rely upon a judgment of the entire situation to determine which one of the states is really to blame for the outbreak or which one now constitutes the obstacle against the limitation or the repression of the war. The natural corollary of his acknowledgment, namely, that a purely formal criterion of aggression cannot therefore form the basis of a system of *war-prevention* was not mentioned, however. The Italian representative, Forges-Davanzati, asserted also that "if we cannot determine the aggressor . . . all discussion about the sanctions to be applied to the aggressor loses its value." [148]

The other objections to the Politis-Litvinoff Conventions—which had also been referred to in the discussions in 1933 as attaching too much importance to the purely formal situation exist-

[146] Bourquin (ed.), *Collective Security*, "General Report on the Preparatory Memoranda Submitted to the General Study Conference," Paris, 1935, p. 23: ". . . if we do not succeed in identifying the guilty party, repression is necessarily paralyzed."

[147] *Ibid.*, p. 329.

[148] *Ibid.*, p. 333.

ing at the moment of the outbreak of war and avoiding the whole previous history and the preliminary incidents, particularly the provocation, which play so decisive a part in a number of the more recent war-prevention agreements—were again expressed.[149] These objections were answered by Mantoux,[150] who quoted the proposal previously made by Politis—but which in reality is inacceptable—that provocation can form no part of and cannot be treated in the same manner as an actual attack. For him, provocation does not justify aggression.[151]

The question is *not*, however, whether provocation justifies aggression, but, can provocation be entirely disregarded, *when* an attack does occur, *when* war has broken out, and *when* we are faced with the question of the application of sanctions? This question alone is pertinent. The problem exists in the same form in municipal private law. Provocation does not excuse insults to honor nor assaults upon the person, but when such attacks do occur, the penal codes of many countries give consideration in a very definite way to that provocation, in determining the liability for punishment.[152] That such factors cannot be left out of consideration in international law appears from recent treaty agreements which provide that not aggression, but only *unprovoked* aggression shall form a basis for the initiation of sanctions.[153]

Professor Bourquin emphasized the question of neutrality, in his introductory report,[154] as being one of the most important problems of the Conference, an extremely satisfactory decision for the

[149] *Ibid.*, p. 319 f.

[150] *Ibid.*, p. 335.

[151] *Ibid.*, p. 336: "No provocation . . . justifies the use of force. . . . The question of responsibility is not to be confused with the fact of aggression."

[152] As for example in Denmark. Statutes, *Danish Penal Code No. 126 of April 15, 1930*, § 244, sec. 2 ("inoffensive") and § 272 ("improper behavior of the injured party").

[153] Apart from the large number of treaties which follow the model of the Locarno Treaties, and which expressly mention provocation, there are also other formulations which mean practically the same; for example, the neutrality treaty between Hungary and Turkey of Jan. 5, 1929 (Martens, *Nouv. Rec. Gén.*, XXIX (1934), 373; Art. 2: "malgré son attitude pacifique."

[154] Bourquin (ed.), *Collective Security* (French edition), pp. 29 ff.: "Il suffit de formuler le problème pour saisir l'intérêt qu'il presente. Intérêt d'ordre scientifique, car il met en cause certaines conceptions fondamentales;—intérêt d'ordre pratique non moins considérable, car la solution qu'on lui donne peut influencer considérablement l'attitude de nombreux États."

supporters of this topic, especially since some of its opponents [155] had hoped to exclude consideration of this subject from the agenda of the Conference. The three principal problems which, in Bourquin's opinion, should be studied under the heading of neutrality were: [156]

(1) Is the notion of neutrality essentially bound up with the system of absolute abstention and impartiality as embodied notably in the Hague Convention of 1907?

(2) Is there not a distinction to be established from this point of view involving participation in war and those which, by their nature, permit the state applying them to keep out of the hostilities? Can a sufficiently elastic sense be given to the notion of neutrality to make it compatible with this second category of sanctions?

(3) Would it not be proper to establish a further distinction between *active* participation in sanctions and a *passive* collaboration, the latter having as object to facilitate the application of measures without taking part in their execution? How could this passive collaboration be organized so as not to deprive of the advantages of neutrality, the states which have undertaken it?

During the discussions at the Conference, the traditional Swiss views were presented by Professor Schindler,[157] according to whom neutrality is "essentially a military concept," without significance in the economic field: "There is such a thing as economic war, but there is no economic neutrality." [158] A member of the League may therefore preserve its neutrality when it participates in economic sanctions, but not when it applies military sanctions. This is the well-known Swiss position, the validity of which has been discussed above.[159]

From the general viewpoint of legal philosophy, neutrality may, in the opinion of Professor Schindler, be held as consistent with the principle of collective security, since there is a distinction

[155] Lauterpacht, "The notion of neutrality," in Bourquin (ed.), p. 416: "A system of collective repression of unlawful war is, by its very terms, not compatible with the absolute neutrality of its members."

[156] See Bourquin, p. 27.

[157] Bourquin (ed.), *Collective Security*, pp. 422 ff.; the Swiss also prepared a brief memorandum for the use of the Conference, "on the problem of neutrality within a system providing for the repression of resort to war," by Schindler.

[158] *Ibid.*, p. 423.

[159] *Ibid.*

between national and international public safety; for the state may require from its citizens the sacrifice of their lives for the defense of their native land, while nothing comparable to this holds true for the lives of states themselves; collective security must have no greater value for one state than another; it has significance only when the security of all is guaranteed.

The obligation to participate in sanctions should therefore have certain limitations, he asserted. Special geographical or other conditions may be of such nature that the neutrality of a particular state may be of more value to the cause of peace than its participation in military sanctions. This holds true especially in two situations: [160]

(1) If participation in the war by that state exposes it to destruction; this is true for small countries with great and powerful neighbors. The right to remain neutral in such cases is not an extension of any special favor, but is merely an effort to distribute the burden fairly.

(2) If the neutrality of a state forms an essential element for the pacification of a part of the world. This has been recognized with regard to Switzerland's century-old neutrality.[161] The share of the neutral state, in a system of collective security, consists then in its promises never to lend military assistance to another state at war.[162]

This latter, however, may be considered a somewhat doubtful equivalent. Furthermore it can hold true only for permanently neutralized states, and not for those mentioned in the previous classification.

On the part of the United States, Professor Jessup [163] declared that his country had noted with great interest the change which had taken place in the views on neutrality, a topic which had for

[160] *Ibid.*, p. 424.

[161] One often hears that a neutral Switzerland keeps watch over the passes of the Alps. Just why these passes must be guarded more than any other frontier is an unanswered question. Historically the Swiss have attempted to base their claims to neutrality on many different circumstances, but have been unable to advance for their exceptional position any arguments which do not apply more or less to other countries as well.

[162] This negative promise is as important for collective security, in his opinion, as any positive guarantee.

[163] Bourquin (ed.), pp. 425 ff.

so many years been excluded from discussion in the United States as well as in Europe. During the World War (before its entry therein), the United States had been legally impartial, but in practice partial. The new system would permit it to take a position against war itself, while remaining impartial toward the belligerents.[164]

The usual view of neutrality, Professor Jessup said, is that it is possible thereby to stay out of war. It has meant, and still means, something more, however; unconsciously in the past, and consciously in the future, it may be regarded as an arrow in the quiver of collective security, contributing toward a suppression of war or limiting its duration.

If it be possible and expedient to apply a system of economic sanctions against that state which has been recognized as the aggressor, why should it not be possible, he asks, to establish a neutral front against both belligerents? The League of Nations, he says, did exactly this in the beginning of the Chaco War, where it imposed an embargo upon both the belligerents, pending a final settlement of the dispute and the determination of the guilty party. The same principle was incorporated into the Argentine Anti-War Treaty of 1933, which envisions a unified and solidary action of the neutrals, without armed intervention.[165]

He believes that the experience gained during the war years with particular regard to organizing coöperation in the economic field may form the basis for a further investigation to make common action of the neutrals practical in that field hereafter. If, during the World War, there had been a group of "allied and associated" *neutral* countries, with a common economic and financial "general staff," conditions might have been quite different today.[166]

It is true, Professor Jessup admits, that belligerents have a stronger motive for coöperation than have neutrals, but it is equally true that the neutrals have stronger motives for action dictated by

[164] *Ibid.*, p. 426: ". . . in the past it has been possible to have legal impartiality and factual partiality, as was well illustrated in the case of the United States during the war of 1914-1917. As Dr. Cohn suggests . . . it is a question of partiality against war and impartiality in one's treatment of the belligerents."

[165] *Ibid.*, pp. 426-27.

[166] *Ibid.*, p. 427.

their own interests than has a group of states applying sanctions in accord with Article XVI of the Covenant. Neutrals have an interest in avoiding involvement in the war, in shortening the war, and in protecting their own economic and financial existence; consequently coöperation offers all kinds of advantages to them. In all former wars there has been a simultaneous economic war, he says, between belligerents and neutrals,[167] and this cannot be prevented *unless there is developed an entirely new system of neutrality*.

It is certainly true that many of the neutrals desire the increased profits resulting from their neutrality, and this motive must be removed, as would be done by a *system of collective neutrality* which is directed against the belligerents.

Professor Jessup suggested finally a sort of *compromise* between the theory of aggression and this new theory of neutrality, through the application of a collective neutrality policy, as a means of war-prevention, in those situations where agreement cannot be obtained as to which state was the aggressor. So far as the United States was concerned, it would probably be willing to take a less impartial attitude in situations where the members of the League of Nations applied sanctions unanimously, if the League members would agree upon a form for the determination of the legal status of neutrals in those other situations where such unanimity could not be effected.[168]

Professor Zimmern then spoke and said that before he had heard Jessup's remarks,[169] he had regarded the neutral as "an antisocial being, leading an isolated life. . . . By the end of his speech, I got the conception of a neutral as a social being . . . ready to act vigorously on behalf of his social principles." [170] He wanted to know, however, what would happen if one or more of the members of this united neutral front were unable to enforce these export pro-

[167] In his book *Neutrality*, IV ("Today and Tomorrow"), pp. 20 ff., Jessup describes the whole concept of neutrality as being simply a euphemism for economic war.

[168] In Bourquin (ed.), p. 435. Jessup concludes by saying: "In those cases I see no alternative for the other nations of the world but to adopt what Dr. Cohn suggests is an attitude of impartiality against war, and apply *through the function of neutrality some collective system against both belligerents.*" (Our italics.)

[169] *Ibid.*, p. 428. [170] *Ibid.*, p. 428.

hibitions against their own citizens. Jessup replied that the neutral countries would each be responsible for the acts of its own citizens, and in an emergency the same economic measures might be applied against a state which broke from the united front of the neutrals, grouping such members with the belligerents for that purpose.

The English writer, Lauterpacht,[171] attacked the "resuscitation" of neutrality and the new neutrality theory along the lines laid down in his memorandum. It was true, he agreed, that the status of neutrality had recently required greater consideration, and that from a legal standpoint it was quite consistent with the system of Article XVI of the Covenant. The opposite view, assumed by the Council at the time of Switzerland's admission to the League, had been proved incorrect. But morally considered, the two systems are nonetheless in conflict with each other. The theory of aggression is an essential condition for the application of the sanctions system, and the definition of the London Conventions is, upon the whole, a correct one.[172] English authorities in international law, discussing the régime of traditional neutrality, regarded it as a legal monstrosity and a moral disgrace. It cannot then be the task of a jurist, he believes, to defend it now, under a régime of collective security.

The reply to this appears to be that it is hard to see what these moral condemnations of traditional neutrality—with its principle of impartiality—by former writers on international law have to do with the qualified neutrality of Article XVI of the Covenant, of which Lauterpacht makes himself the spokesman, let alone with Neo-neutrality, which offers complete solidarity of the states in the fight against war itself, with the sole reservation that states shall not use war as one of the means of opposing war.

The Spanish representative, de Luna,[173] conceded that logically

[171] *Ibid.*, pp. 429 ff.

[172] *Ibid.*, p. 431: "The arguments against the definition are very effective in debate for the simple reason that they are based on exceptional situations," and he goes on to show that the definition is essential to collective security. Upon this point Lauterpacht finds himself in opposition to the position of the English government itself and the pertinent observations upon it which Foreign Secretary Eden made in 1933 during the discussions in the Committee on Security.

[173] *Conférence générale d'études sur la sécurité collective* (Paris, 1935), p. 147.

there was a distinction between war-prevention and neutrality, but said that the question could not be decided by logic alone. For his part, he accepted the idea that neutrals must unite in a league having no aggressive character, but which intended exclusively to protect the rights of neutral states.

Lord Lytton and Mr. Mitrany,[174] stating British views, also took issue with Professor Jessup. The former felt that the Kellogg Pact made neutrality impossible. Mitrany regarded it as important to find a formula under which neutrality and collective security could coöperate. This might be obtained through a change in neutrality law to the effect that neutrals preserved the right to remain outside the war, in exchange for relinquishing the economic advantages which the right of neutrality had formerly involved.

In opposition to Lord Lytton's contention, Professor Jessup insisted[175] that the Kellogg Pact had not abolished the system of neutrality. He supported the fundamental logic and justice of common neutral action against the war as such in those cases where it had been found impossible to determine the aggressor.

The Polish delegate, Ehrlich,[176] was also of the opinion that neutrality, in its previously accepted sense, was no longer possible, either under Articles X and XVI of the League Covenant or under the Kellogg Pact. M. Cassin, of France, subscribed to this opinion. When the League Council had officially recognized that Article XVI had been violated, all states were *ipso facto* in a "state of hostility," which was inconsistent with neutrality. On the other hand, he would admit that the same type of obligations did not devolve upon all states. The result was that neutrality "if it is not obsolete, is visibly transformed. . . . *Allow us to give it another name*."[177]

At the close of the conference Professor Bourquin drew up a "Final Report,"[178] in which conclusions regarding the ideas of aggression and neutrality were given. M. Bourquin retained the theory of aggression as being a necessary condition for any system of war-prevention. Only the proposals advanced by the Danes

[174] Bourquin (ed.), *Collective Security*, p. 433 f.
[175] *Ibid.*, p. 434 f.
[176] *Ibid.*, p. 436 f.
[177] *Ibid.*, p. 439.
[178] *Ibid.*, pp. 443 ff.

were of a different nature, he said, and did not involve discussion of the difficult question of defining aggression.[179]

This theory was made the subject of further discussion in connection with the question of prohibition of the use of force[180] and of the ideas regarding the place of neutrality in a system of war-prevention.[181] According to these, the legal status of outside states might still be described as that of "neutrality," since they retain equality of rights as between the belligerents and in principle are obligated to a uniform and impartial treatment of both. Nevertheless, this concept of neutrality is *quite different from the one which assumed a set form during the nineteenth century*[182] and found final expression in the Hague Conventions of 1907 and the Declaration of London of 1909, because it breaks with the second principle, that of passivity.

The Relations between Neo-neutrality, Traditional Neutrality, Armed Neutrality, and Qualified and Collective (Coöperative) Neutrality, together With Pacigérat and Pacifism

1. The differences between traditional neutrality and Neo-neutrality are thoroughgoing. Traditional neutrality relied upon the two principles of unconditional state sovereignty and of non-intervention. Its natural *consequences* were passivity and impartiality. These consequences were made the *legal conditions* for its recognition and continued existence, and were at the same time the *means* by which it could be enforced. Passivity and impartiality were thus the basic elements of both the law of neutrality and of neutrality policy. They did not, however, constitute the real *substance* of neutrality, and this point has often been overlooked or misunderstood. The essential function of neutrality was to keep the neutral country out of the war, or—more broadly stated—to

[179] *Ibid.*, p. 12: ". . . in a study entitled 'Danish Memorandum No. 1,' Dr. Georg Cohn . . . declares in favor of a system directed against war as such. In his eyes, defensive war as well as offensive war ought to be considered as an antisocial act and to give rise to the application of sanctions by other states."

[180] *Ibid.*, p. 233 f. [181] *Ibid.*, pp. 256 ff. [182] Our italics.

isolate and restrict the war to the belligerents. Passivity and impartiality were the means best fitted, under the given condition of international law, for attaining these aims of neutrality. That term "neutrality," even during the régime of traditional neutrality, was thus misleading, because it emphasized the *means* instead of the *objectives.* Passivity and impartiality as well as an equal regard for the motives or justice of the cause of both belligerents, were of no value in themselves, but they constituted the only conditions under which the objectives could be attained at that time.

Neo-neutrality has to some extent the same goal as had traditional neutrality, but pursues it with greater energy, altruism, and consistency, under the new legal situation which is characterized by the political solidarity of the states and the right of collective intervention. Where the interests of general peace are threatened, it works for these in the individual interest of each separate state, as well as in the common interest of a society of international law.

The means, on the other hand, are different. Passivity and impartiality must yield to an active and common front. Equal *regard* for the rights of both belligerents and for their motives yields in Neo-neutrality to an equal *disregard* for those of war in all its forms, regardless of whether it is aggressive or defensive, and regardless of the motives or causes alleged for it. In this sense we may still urge a certain impartiality toward the belligerents. But this impartiality is only to be based upon an equal disqualification of all war and need not express itself in identical treatment of the two parties. Such treatment would depend entirely upon what procedure is most practical and appropriate, in the given case, to prevent war, or to suppress war after it has already begun, while at the same time maintaining the principles of international morality and law by attempting to bring about the best and most reasonable settlement, under the circumstances, of the dispute between the belligerents, through mediation, arbitration, or through a solidary economic, political, legal, or military pressure upon one or upon both parties.

2. We might well ask if under these conditions there is any reason whatever to preserve the name neutrality as a term for this legal situation, so much the more since neutrality in certain quar-

ters has an unpleasant sound and at least directs attention to traditional neutrality and its principles, which Neo-neutrality abandons. We might also question whether it is of any consequence what one calls this new condition in law: or if our interpretation of Article XVI of the Covenant was described as a combination of a sanctions system with the law of neutrality; since the rules of law contained in that Article will be what they are, whether we call them one thing or another. Furthermore, there had been, even during the régime of traditional neutrality, some efforts made to find a better term for what were then the essential elements of this legal situation, and one can say that this must be true in added measure under the new juridical system of international organization.

Nonetheless, when we here propose to preserve the expression "neutrality," with an added prefix, however, to describe this decisive change, it is for various good reasons. First, there is a legal as well as a political significance in preserving for a new institution in law—which seeks justice, not in the "special" interests of each individual impartial state nor in partiality for one party or another, but in their general and solidary efforts to prevent war—the ideas of impartiality and the equal treatment of the belligerents. Thus the weight and authority of these efforts are increased. Further, a certain degree of impartiality and equal treatment exists in the general disqualification of war itself with respect to both disputants. Neutrality then no longer implies—as did traditional neutrality—that the neutral merely does not wish to align itself with one belligerent or the other. It means that the neutral State takes fundamental exception to the whole conception of war, with regard to both parties. Irrespective of whether one or the other is right, or has on its side superior moral or legal justification, it will in no case agree that such right should be asserted by war.

There were also other compelling reasons for preserving the name "neutrality," such as the desire to preserve the "continuity of development of international law" and to retain those important accomplishments of neutrality in the evolution of international law, especially during the nineteenth century. If it were still held that the law of neutrality was no longer valid because of the establishment of the League of Nations or the Kellogg Pact,—and this was widely believed when these agreements were first discussed,—it would mean that we had wiped out a very long and important development of international law, and, with a stroke of the pen, renounced many rules of law which are highly useful in the service of peace preservation,[183] in fact, indispensable to those states which have historically built their foreign policies upon them. It is therefore not a matter of indifference whether we interpret the legal condition under Article XVI as a combination with the law of neutrality, or not. The combination interpretation answers immediately a great many, indeed almost all, of the questions which may arise in practice; while in the opposite case we would face a blank wall, since a reorganization of these precedents and problems would be a very difficult task, and could be possible only in a distant future.[184] It would be the same if we accepted the Kellogg Pact's proclamation of the abolition of war, and believed that this had simultaneously voided all neutrality law, in effect.[185] It would be a serious backward step—indeed the whole idea is so monstrous that we cannot reckon with it at all. Even those countries which deny, in principle, that neutrality is consistent with the existence of a system of sanctions, were forced to resort to the Hague Conventions' rules for neutrality during the application of sanctions in the Italo-Ethiopian conflict. And this would, of course, be the case in an even greater degree if sanctions were really enforced, let alone in that situation where one or more of the sanction countries themselves resort to war against the aggressor.

3. For similar reasons it would, in practice, be difficult to interpret Article XVI as an express or implicit agreement on *qualified neutrality* (Lauterpacht). Such qualified neutrality would not be recognized by the belligerents, especially if the smaller countries

[183] See also Jessup, *Neutrality*, IV ("Today and Tomorrow"), p. 147 f., who creates an imaginary picture of what conditions might be in maritime war if the law of neutrality became void ("obedience to law and respect for legal rights is much more extensive than the thoughtless appreciate.")

[184] *Supra*, p. 59 f., on the attitude of the British government toward the admission of Italian warships to colonial ports during the Italo-Ethiopian conflict.

[185] On this question, see the article: Cohn, "Kellogg-Pagtens retlige Betydning" [The legal significance of the Kellogg Pact], in *Juridisk Tidsskrift*, XV (1929), 32 ff.

did put it into practice. Moreover, the stand of Great Britain toward Italian warships in British colonial ports during the Italo-Ethiopian conflict [186] proves that even a Great Power does not expect to enforce individually a qualified neutrality under the application of sanctions. The concepts of qualified, benevolent, imperfect and similar kinds of neutrality are regarded as contrary, in modern times to the essence of neutrality.[187] Therefore one cannot introduce, without explicit authorization, such mutually and evidently contradictory concepts into the text of Article XVI of the Covenant.

It might then be asked if Neo-neutrality is not a form of qualified neutrality, and it is important to emphasize the fact that *this is not the case.* As appears from the above section relating to the technical problem, the combination principles of Article XVI of the Covenant were made upon the basis of the traditional concept of neutrality, in its full clarity and without any qualification. The concept of Neo-neutrality, which has developed from this combination interpretation, must also reject any connection with so-called "qualified" neutrality. The latter means that one takes the traditional conception of neutrality as a starting point, but, because of treaty obligations, adapts the rules to the advantage of one of the parties. Neo-neutrality does not take traditional neutrality for its starting point. By its general disqualification of war and the laws of war, it has chosen an entirely different foundation and a new starting point, and merely carries over into the new system certain of the rules of law developed in the former one, through a combination of the elements of both. It recognizes no obligation

[186] *Supra*, p. 59 f.; also on Lauterpacht's theory *supra*, pp. 303 ff.

[187] See Gareis, in Strupp (ed.), *Wörterbuch*, II, 124: "... die sog. "wohlwollende Neutralität (neutralité bienveillante) ist vom Standpunkte des konsequenten modernen Begriffs der Neutralität aus, unhaltbar.... Was endlich die Unterscheidung von vollkommener und unvollkommener Neutralität anlangt, so ist selbstverständlich von demselben modernen Standpunkte aus, auch diese zu verwerfen ..."; Oppenheim (by Lauterpacht himself!), II, 530: "that a qualified neutrality has no longer any *raison d'être*, and that neutrality must in every case be perfect"—according to the context, even where there exist treaty obligations to the contrary; see also *ibid.*, footnote 3: "... a neutral who takes up an attitude of qualified neutrality may nowadays be considered as an accessory belligerent party to the war"; Liszt, p. 535: "Der Begriff der Neutralität lässt Abstufungen nicht zu ... ein Widerspruch in sich selbst."

of impartiality and cannot be refuted with arguments borrowed from a criticism of the ideas of the older system.

It is equally important to stress the differences between Neo-neutrality and the so-called *collective*, or *coöperative*, *neutrality*. These latter also recognize in principle the rules of traditional neutrality, and attempt to carry them out in modern warfare by means of coöperation among the neutral states, this being an attempt similar to that of the Armed Leagues of Neutrality in the seventeenth and eighteenth centuries.[188] A proposal in this direction is to be found in Professor Jessup's recent work: *Neutrality, Its History, Economics and Law*, Vol. IV: "Today and Tomorrow."[189]

Jessup regards the entire concept of neutrality as a euphemism for economic war,[190] that is, an effort on the part of neutrals to expand their trade at the expense[191] of the belligerents, and an effort of one belligerent to strike at the trade and economic life of the other through the neutrals, with efforts of the belligerents at the same time to damage the trade of the neutrals.[192]

Jessup's text uses a terminology which in itself might be equally applicable to Neo-Neutrality,[193] but this writer aims in another direction. Collective neutrality, in his opinion, should not be an element of a war-prevention system, but should operate separately, in the interest of the neutrals.[194] In an unusual manner, Jessup gives a new interpretation of the concepts of the new neutrality, as expressed in the Conferences on Security, 1934-35, in combination with a war-prevention system; as if they were intended only to

[188] With the difference only that they would replace military coöperation with economic.

[189] New York, 1936.

[190] On pp. 20 ff.

[191] Jessup, p. 28, where a statement by Jefferson concerning the Russian-Turkish War of 1822 is quoted: "... let us milk the cow while the Russian holds her by the horns and the Turk by the tail."

[192] *Ibid.*, p. 40: "... the attempt of belligerents to utilize the war situation to injure the general trade position of neutral commercial rivals"; see also W. van Eysinga, *Die Niederlande und das Neutralitätsrecht während des Weltkrieges*, p. 606.

[193] *Ibid.* See, for example, the last three chapter headings: "The abandonment of traditional neutrality"; "The revision of neutrality"; "Peace through neutrality."

[194] *Ibid.*, p. 159: "... little work has been done on the strategy of neutrality. If peace can be organized, perhaps neutrality can also be organized."

keep the United States and some other neutral states out of future wars. The positive program of war-prevention plays no part, or at best a quite secondary and incidental rôle.

Collective neutrality Jessup considers as fulfilled when the neutrals refrain, as far as possible, from economic and financial relations with the belligerents; but in turn a mutual coöperation will ensure interneutral trade relations.[195] The neutrals should thus renounce their special war profits and make their choice between the alternatives, "Profits or Peace." [196] Various efforts, in earlier periods, to secure such coöperation among the neutrals are reviewed,[197] as are also the efforts which were made in that direction during the World War.[198] The United States was then very cool toward applications from European countries, while favorable toward desires for coöperation which originated with other American nations; [199] but even as regards these nations, Jessup believes that the United States forfeited a great opportunity to work for the solidarity of the Americas in this field.[200] Of special interest is the proposal [201] which was made as early as December, 1914, by Venezuela, for a "league of neutrals," designed to safeguard the interests of neutrals in their relations with the belligerents.[202]

Such self-limitation upon interneutral trade relations, combined with the breaking off of economic and financial intercourse with the belligerents, would, in Jessup's opinion, at the same time create a possibility for coöperation with the sanctions system of the League Covenant, especially in cases where the aggressor has not been

195 *Ibid.*, p. 194.

196 *Ibid.*, p. 213: " 'Profits or Peace' is not a wholly misleading description of the alternatives which must be faced in framing a national neutrality policy for the United States. If we choose Profits Today, we may well find that we will neither Profits nor Peace Tomorrow."

197 *Ibid.*, pp. 160 ff. (armed neutralities, etc.).

198 *Ibid.*, p. 166. The meeting of the three Kings, and the meetings of the ministers of the Scandinavian countries, the applications from neutrals to the United States, etc.

199 *Ibid.*, pp. 170 ff.

200 *Ibid.*, p. 173: "... the United States here lost a great opportunity for leading in an important step toward Pan-American solidarity."

201 *Ibid.*, p. 172.

202 Similar proposals relating to Europe were made, and are to be found in Lammasch, *Recueil de Rapports*, I, 303; Nippold, *Die Gestaltung des Völkerrechts nach dem Weltkrieg*, pp. 53 ff.

determined or where both belligerents come under that category.[203]

Collective neutrality, based upon this reasoning, cannot be accepted by Neo-neutrality as it is further presented in his book. When Professor Jessup gives to the views of Neo-neutrality, as they were stated in the conferences on collective security, the nationalistic American form which he does, it cannot be due to a misunderstanding, for his statements at the conference indicate that he was aware of their significance and scope. These neo-neutral views were also to be found in the Saavedra Lamas Treaty, Article III, with their real intent and their general war-prevention tendency. Jessup cites [204] this Article III, and can hardly have misunderstood the words emphasized by him in his book: "*they will adopt in their character as neutrals a common and solidary attitude*," as meaning that it is the *rights of neutrals* which are to be secured by this "common and solidary attitude." As appears from the context of these words in Article III, however, it is evident that they should have there the exactly opposite significance, namely, that the contracting states in their capacity as neutrals will work *in the service* [205] *of general war-prevention*. It cannot therefore be described as a correct interpretation, when these treaty provisions are alleged to be an expression of collective neutrality.[206]

The explanation for his interpretation may perhaps be sought in the moment [207] at which Professor Jessup's work appeared, that is, shortly after the Hoare-Laval "Peace Plan" for the Italo-Ethiopian conflict,[208] when public opinion in the United States was hastily retreating from Neo-neutrality to traditional neutrality.

Furthermore it would be difficult to subscribe to the fundamental view which pervades all four volumes of this sturdy work, according to which neutrality in all essentials is an economic question. It

[203] Jessup, p. 179.

[204] *Ibid.*, p. 175.

[205] *Ibid.*: ". . . the contracting states undertake to make every effort for the maintenance of peace. *To that end* they will adopt . . ." etc., as above. (Our italics.)

[206] See especially *ibid.*, p. 201: "Suppose, however, all the neutrals, taking a 'common and solidary' attitude, make this proposition to the belligerents: We will export to you or permit you to buy from us, a quota of provisions based on your normal requirements provided you permit similar quotas to be delivered to your enemies . . ." and p. 205: "Such a policy of coöperation . . . is envisaged in the Argentine Anti-War Treaty . . ."

[207] January, 1936.

[208] *Ibid.*, p. 84.

is not correct to say that neutrality is a mere euphemism for economic war. When conditions during a war make it possible for a limited group of exporting companies temporarily to make large profits, it is something which is neither aimed at by the neutral countries nor looked upon by them with particular favor. It is in no way characteristic nor decisive for the legal status nor yet for the economy of the neutral state. War is not "good business" for the belligerents;[209] it is still less so for the neutrals. The profits gained by subjects of neutral countries in the World War went for the most part for amusements and unproductive purchases which were of no value to the economy of their country and which afforded no support in the difficulties of the postwar period.[210] The economic viewpoint gives no explanation of the general development of the individual rules of the law of neutrality, nor any foundation for opposing war. In particular there is nothing to indicate that self-imposed restrictions upon trade among the neutrals would be likely to keep the neutrals out of war. The opposite, on the contrary, is certain, since an essential motive for a belligerent's recognition of a neutral status is that it is able in this way to retain some of its sources of supplies and continued trade relations, so that it has itself an interest in the continuation of neutral trade.

Just as questionable is the idea that collective neutrality should be equipped to coöperate in efforts at war-prevention. The two systems do not work in the same, but in opposite, directions. A strengthening of the conception of traditional neutrality through coöperation between neutrals must necessarily counteract solidary efforts for the prevention of war. Only exceptionally and incidentally can the two movements, with their differing, indeed opposing, aims, work in the same direction, namely, when a uniform treatment of the two belligerents is to all practical purposes injurious

[209] President Roosevelt truly said in the opening address at the Pan-American Conference on Dec. 1, 1936: "Let no man or woman forget that there is no profit in war."

[210] Professor Jessup himself admits this on p. 187, where he says: "The experiences of both the Napoleonic and World Wars show that these neutral profits are often confined to small sections of the population and do not reflect national prosperity. It is equally clear that they offer no bar to the losses involved in the usual post-war periods of depression."

to the one party against which it is really directed.[211] But if such uniform treatment tends to injure the party one would aid, a clear inconsistency arises. On the whole, no logical system can be built, nor any useful practical procedure be based, upon such opposite ideas. The new neutrality cannot find its expression in conjunction with or outside the war-prevention system, but only *within its framework*. It is an integral part of the new war-prevention system, indeed identical with it.

Thus it is clear wherein the great contrast between collective (coöperative) neutrality and Neo-neutrality lies. Collective neutrality is traditional neutrality in a stricter and stronger form. It has no war-prevention tendency; it does not oppose passivity with respect to efforts toward war-prevention, nor impartiality, nor the egoistic limitations of traditional neutrality. It is not possible to use such descriptions of collective neutrality as "waiving of traditional neutrality," "revision of the conception of neutrality," or "peace through neutrality," since it really aims at the maintenance of traditional neutrality, through coöperation among the neutrals. This may, under certain conditions, be a very reasonable and expedient policy for the states concerned, but it should then be designated by its correct name. It has nothing in common with Neo-neutrality in the form explained here.

4. The term Neo-neutrality must be chosen in preference to the designation pacigérat ("leading to peace"), used by the Belgian writer, Descamps,[212] to emphasize—and in a sense correctly—the positive and independent nature of the legal condition of states remaining out of war, while for him the expression "neutrality" describes rather the negative side and its dependence upon a condition of war. To this point of view one must raise the objection, however, that the status of neutrality derives its real significance from its association with the state of war. The state of peace, with its own general rules of law, has no interest in this connection.[213]

[211] Such as was the case in the Italo-Ethiopian conflict.

[212] "Le Pacigérat ou régime juridique de la paix en temps de guerre," in *Revue Générale de Droit International Public*, (1900) VII, 629 ff.; especially p. 639 on the harm the term neutrality has done by giving the entire initiative into the hands of the belligerents.

[213] This Descamps himself admits to a certain degree; see his own words, *ibid.*, p. 633: "Si ces deux sphères demeuraient isolées . . . le problème des rapports entre

It is true that neutrals wish to continue their peaceful existence undisturbed as heretofore, and the general disqualification of war, with its resultant abolition of belligerent rights, seems to a certain degree to argue for the correctness of this view for the need of characterizing the legal status of nonparticipant states.

It is nonetheless an incorrect conclusion. For Descamps, neutrality means that legal situation which makes it possible for nonparticipant states to avoid becoming involved in the war, and at the same time to oppose or to prevent the war itself. This is a *special* condition of law which cannot be identified with the legal status of a general condition of peace, and its rules of law. It is true that the term "neutrality" expresses this special condition in a *negative* form. But the term "pacigérat" is not meant to be merely a *positive* formulation of this; it is also an expression for the putting aside the peculiarity of this special legal status, which is not identical with the general condition of peace, but rather in contrast with it.

The same idea may, perhaps, be expressed in this way; that the term "pacigérat" is used as the expression of that view which regards the law of neutrality as a self-dependent and independent system of law, co-existent with the law of war. This view, as we have shown above [214] is incorrect. Traditional neutrality was as truly part of the law of war as Neo-neutrality is part of the law of war-prevention. They are not independent or free to say what the term "pacigérat" shall denote, but are bound by the condition of war, either passively or actively.

There is also reason for stating that we must not mistake Neo-neutrality for *pacifism,* as has sometimes been done,[215] which designation it cannot bear. Neo-neutrality in itself has no such special

belligérants et non-belligérants différerait peu de celui de la vie pacifique ordinaire entre États. . . . Mais il n'en va pas ainsi dans la réalité de la vie internationale," etc.

214 *Supra,* pp. 9-10.

215 Politis, *Neutrality and Peace,* pp. 77 ff., on the security conferences of 1934-35: "The memoir submitted by the Danish group attracted particular attention. It was inspired by the idea dear to the *extreme pacifists* [our italics] that if war between individual states is to be combated, it ought not to be done (as Article XVI of the Covenant of the League of Nations appears to require) by a state of general warfare."

program of toleration or indulgence, as for example, with regard to disarmament. On the contrary, it takes a very active and aggressive position. Whatever is appropriate or necessary to prevent war has its approval, even if it be a question of military or other compulsory measures, excepting only war. It takes, in this respect, a position not unlike that of traditional neutrality, which also required a certain military preparedness for its maintenance.[216] Neo-neutrality resembles pacifism as little as did the traditional neutrality of the nineteenth century or the armed neutralities of the eighteenth. One may be a pacifist without believing in Neo-neutrality, or vice versa. These two things exist in entirely different spheres. Pacifism is a philosophical, ethical, and religious view of life,[217] often containing broad requirements for abandoning the fight against injustice (Tolstoy). Neo-neutrality is a purely technical and practical form of organization for actively fighting war under any and all circumstances. It has one thing in common with pacifism to a high degree, an earnest opposition to war. It is like *armed neutrality*, in that it would organize economic and other social forces in the nonparticipant states, in order to fight against war, just as the armed leagues of neutrality attempted to do. They did this in order to maintain the rights of neutral states, and—in both cases—without, in principle, taking part in the war themselves.

Neo-neutrality and the Theory of Aggression

1. The clearest contrast, and the one which is best fitted to distinguish the essentials of Neo-neutrality, is the theory of aggression, of which we shall here make the final summary, with our comment.

Neo-neutrality means war-prevention without participation in war. The theory of aggression concentrates war-prevention efforts upon aggression as the act which puts its system into operation. We might imagine a purely economic system of sanctions based above all upon aggression as the critical test (as in Article XVI

[216] For example, the 13th Hague Convention of Oct. 18, 1907, Article XXV.

[217] See further Melamed, *Theorie, Ursprung und Geschichte der Friedensidee*, Stuttgart, 1909.

of the Covenant) and, vice versa, a military system of sanctions directed against war, without any importance attaching to the fact of an aggression. However, in its true form, Neo-neutrality disregards aggression, while the theory of aggression demands the participation of the outside states with armed force, in its fight for war-prevention; this marks the two theories as irreconcilably opposed upon this point.

The contrast between these two systems came up very clearly during the discussions in Paris, in 1934, and in London, in 1935. The theory of aggression is a clear expression of the *qualification* of war; Neo-neutrality stands for its *disqualification*. The matter of qualification, or classification, under the aggression theory, is a serious problem, full of difficulties; the problem disappears with Neo-neutrality. This is particularly true regarding the *definition of aggression*, which despite years of effort still cannot be stated in a satisfactory form. Under Neo-neutrality, logical definitions in this field are without significance. Wars of aggression as well as wars of defense both need prevention, and to an equal degree.

To Neo-neutrality, it is of interest only to state the limits of what constitutes self-defense in international law. These limits are to be determined by a study of the analogous situation of the limits of the concept of self-defense in municipal penal law and have nothing to do with the traditional rules of war or neutrality.

The great, indeed insurmountable, difficulties of the aggression theory have been explained in the passage above upon the classification of war. It was there shown that this theory has neither an objective nor a subjective basis, that the term aggression itself has only strategic or tactical foundations, applicable to military operations, and that it is neither formally nor actually fit to be the basis of a rational system of war-prevention. Neo-neutrality has no reason to concern itself further with all these difficulties.

If we accept the aggression theory, we must also take a stand not only upon the question of a formal definition of aggression, but likewise upon all those material factors which must be taken into consideration in making the final judgment as to who is the aggressor, how great is his guilt, whether there are sufficient grounds for applying sanctions against one state rather than against the other, and in this way we must consider the whole question of the causes of war, since this problem also lies at the basis of the system of the Covenant of the League. We are then compelled to go deeper into the examination and classification of the rational causes of war, some of which may explain and even justify the aggression, while others may not. That, in any concrete sense, this involves war-prevention in great difficulties, contradictory assertions, doubt, and uncertainty, goes without saying. Owing to conflicting political interests, such uncertainty will often become so serious that it is likely completely to paralyze the operation of the sanctions system. Neo-neutrality, on the other hand, is free from all such considerations and doubts. It is not concerned with questions of the reality of the rationality of the causes of war. It is content with the mere fact that a condition of war exists, which condition it is designed to isolate and end as soon as possible. Regardless of what the causes of war may really be or what they are stated to be, Neo-neutrality in advance makes unnecessary any discussion of them, for it will not permit the circle of the victims of war to be widened, no matter how important such causes may appear to the individual states involved. The situation, on the other hand, is to be met by effective and solidary measures of an economic or legal nature applied through an international organization of the states acting in the interest of the whole.

2. The theory of aggression makes the penal concepts of private law the basis of an international system of war-prevention. Aggression is counted a crime,[218] to be punished by the application of sanctions. The great difficulty, not to say impossibility, in carrying out these ideas in practice has elsewhere been made the object of a detailed study,[219] to which the reader is referred. It should be remarked, however, that no system of war-prevention can be founded upon the guilt of the individual leading statesmen in the aggressor state nor upon the collective guilt of an entire people. The conception of guilt between nations cannot be built upon

[218] See also Bourquin's "Final Report" in his *Collective Security*, p. 452: "... it is impossible to identify a criminal unless it is known beforehand in what the crime consists."

[219] Cohn, *Kriegsverhütung und Schuldfrage*, 1931.

analogies in municipal penal law. All the requisite conditions for a criminal arraignment of the aggressor as in municipal law, are lacking. Depending entirely upon the individual's point of view, especially with respect to the relative importance of the separate causes, every war may be described either as a defensive war or as a war of aggression; and even when the aggression is indisputable and, in fact admitted by the aggressor himself, the criminal-law analogies cannot be carried out. Through the idea of the designation of the guilty party, the theory of the aggression becomes to a certain degree the expression of a classification of war according to the concepts of just and unjust—a view, however, which paralyzes its efficiency and force, since legal questions, as a rule, can be decided only after long and careful investigation, while a system of war-prevention, to be of any value, must act without delay.

Neo-neutrality, on the other hand, excludes in principle the question of guilt and of penal-law concepts in the suppression of war. This naturally does not imply a denial of the fact that criminal blame or responsibility may be connected with the outbreak of war. But this question must be put aside for treatment by means outside of a war-prevention system. Neo-neutrality repudiates for this reason also the penal-law concepts, because these are likely to extend the scope of the war by arousing widespread bitterness and exciting popular feeling; it cannot deny to the people, and even to the army of the aggressor nation, that same sympathy which it has for the people and the army of the attacked state, since as a rule they will be equally guilty or equally innocent of the war in which by threats of capital punishment or other severe military penalties they have been forced by their governments to take part. For him who knows how powerless the individual is against a collective war psychosis, there can be little difference between the moral and the legal judgment of the situation by civilians or by members of the armed forces of the two belligerent countries. Soldiers would be shot from behind by their own leaders [220] if they did not march against the enemy to permit them-

220 Crozier, *The Men I Killed*, p. 168.

selves to be shot from the front, while the civilian populations of both countries are in such a condition of morbid intoxication that they are irresponsible in a penal-law sense.

If the theory of aggression were to make an actual attempt to carry out criminal law analogies for the prevention of war, this attempt would face such extensive technical difficulties that we may in advance declare it to be impracticable. The theoretic viewpoint alone led to insoluble difficulties, which came to light during the discussions of the Committee on Security in 1933, and during the discussions in Paris and London in 1934-35, particularly concerning the relationship between preparation for war and the causes of war, on one hand, and the actual outbreak of war, on the other. So the definition of aggression may well be—as Austen Chamberlain once called it—"a trap for the innocent and a protection for the guilty."

Next there is the question of provocation, which in reality completely invalidates the theory of aggression, since it no longer regards an aggression—when it is provoked—as a crime punishable by sanctions. Of what use is it to have a clean-cut definition of aggression—for example, a territorial basis, as in the London Conventions of 1933—when an assertion that there was provocation by the other side knocks the pins out from under the definition? Those efforts which Politis, and several authors after him, have made to surmount this difficulty, have been shown to be untenable, and have furthermore been refuted by the practice of those states which still make the concept of an *unprovoked* aggression the basis for their war-prevention agreements.

There is, finally, the relation between the formal outbreak of war and the application of sanctions. It has been demonstrated that these two things cannot be brought into such close relationship with each other, as the theory of aggression originally assumed. But again what value is there in a clean-cut definition of aggression, if it cannot be applied automatically and instantaneously to select the state against which sanctions shall be directed, since the answer to this question now requires new and special consideration as to guilt and expediency, independent of the formal circumstances under which the war originally broke out? It is, then, a definition for the mere sake of a definition, so much the more, because its originators definitely repudiate the idea that there is any question of presumptions, or of prima facie evidence, and claim that the value of the definition lies in the fact that it gives an objective, automatic, and irrefutable proof of the existence of an aggression.

Neo-neutrality need go no further into these numerous difficulties and the various efforts to avoid them. It regards the whole train of thought involved in their consideration as impracticable. It is impossible to construct an adequate definition of a war of aggression or of an attack (except in the realm of military tactics or strategy, which can have no significance for a system of war-prevention). Even if a formal definition of some kind or another could be laid down, it would be nonetheless without importance, since one cannot induce the leaders of nations to go to war on the strength of a violation of a technical formula, however logical and finely spun, but only upon issues involving their own political interests.

3. A further important difference exists in the two theories, in that in the theory of aggression one must draw a sharp distinction between efforts to prevent war and efforts to counteract a war which has already broken out; and, on the other hand, between such efforts with respect to war and the prevention of other dangerous or intolerable international situations, such as evident violations of international law, acts of violence, suppression of weaker states, sudden surprise attacks and the like, in all of which no actual state of war exists. It is obvious that a war-prevention machine cannot be built upon the theory of aggression when an aggression does not yet exist, but, on the contrary, is merely to be prevented. In such situations the theory would have to work by the same means as does Neo-neutrality, namely, through diplomatic negotiations, mediation, or by economic, political, and legal pressure. The same holds true for all international disorders and violations of rights of nations which fall short of actual war. But as soon as an aggression has been committed, although the situation may be otherwise unchanged, there sets in, under the theory of aggression, a sudden reversal of the methods to be applied. All at once it is no longer a question of opposing war and restoring peace,

but of punishing the guilty party. Now, in accord with Article XVI, war is to be let loose over all the world. Now each member nation is free to follow its own sovereign judgment (despite the fact that negotiations and peace proposals between the parties may have already begun), to use the situation to upset the entire war-prevention system, and to apply sanctions against whichever state it chooses to regard as the aggressor.

According to Neo-neutrality, there is, on the other hand, a continuity and a consistent purpose throughout the different stages of war-prevention and counteracting war, once it has broken out. The attitude of the nonparticipating states is the same, whether the dispute relates to war or other international encroachments. There is no point at which peaceful methods are to be discontinued so that the outside states may range themselves alongside one or the other of the belligerents. Under no circumstances can they resort to the paradoxical procedure of extending the theater of war, in order to restrict and oppose war. Neither economic nor military sanctions are considered to be punitive measures, but are merely pacific though effective steps to prevent or to oppose war and other forms of international encroachment.

Even when we examine the situation which the theory of aggression especially postulates, that is, when war had already broken out, Neo-neutrality provides much greater opportunities for war-prevention than does the theory of aggression. This latter theory has but one string upon which to play; it has put its all on one card, the existence of aggression. Where an aggression does not exist or cannot be demonstrated, its movements are paralyzed, and it must withdraw from the game. When the existing situation is not exactly in the form which the theorists had planned it to be, and does not fit neatly those "objective, automatic and irrefutable" criteria, there is nothing more to be done about war-prevention.

It is obvious that this creates an extraordinary limitation of the field of war-prevention, indeed prevents its work. When Professor Bourquin, in accord with the prevailing opinion of the Security Conferences in 1934-35, asserted that aggression is the necessary basis for any system of war-prevention, he then had to assume—if the entire attempt was to have any practical importance—that every war necessarily begins with a clear and indisputable attack by a guilty state upon an innocent one. But this is contrary to fact, since unquestioned aggression is rarely present (as it was in the Italo-Ethiopian conflict). There will probably be much doubt and uncertainty as to how the war actually began. It may have started on the high seas, where the territorial criteria of the London Conference are inapplicable; there may be guilt on both sides and a simultaneous attack, or conversely, absence of guilt or any intention to attack on both sides. A system which excludes in advance all such situations and which really aims at quite special and minutely determined conditions, which will rarely exist in their exact presupposed form,[221] has already so limited its sphere of action that it can hardly be of importance in the service of war-prevention.

Opposed to this is Neo-neutrality, with its broad and comprehensive basis and a program for the prevention of war. It places no limitations or conditions upon the kind of war which it is to oppose. It is not concerned with questions of aggression or defense, whether the intention is to pursue one's own interests—execution war or punishment—whether there is guilt upon one or upon both or upon neither of the parties, whether the outbreak was due to evil intentions or unforeseen circumstances, Neo-neutrality is always prepared to take up the work, to acknowledge its responsibility, and to do its best to oppose war and to bring it to an end. It requires the defining of a clear distinction between a defensive war, which is prohibited, and true self-defense in its strictly technical sense, in the exercise of which no belligerent rights are obtained by the defenders.

Neo-neutrality has sometimes been objected to because it is said to lead only to half measures, while the theory of aggression, which identifies the nonparticipant states with the attacked state and resolutely places them on its side, is supposed to give the only real security against war. This assumption is incorrect; good faith and energy in carrying out one's share in any war-prevention program

[221] This the French had to experience to a high degree in 1936 during the German reoccupation of the Rhineland where it was shown that the Locarno Powers as well as the League of Nations were legally powerless because the special conditions of aggression as defined in the Locarno treaties did not exist.

is not dependent upon the nature of the system to be employed. There has never been an example in practice of a state going to war against its own political interests, merely to enforce an international decision against an aggressor state; but there are a great number of instances of the opposite kind, where states, despite the fact that aggression existed in an evident and indisputable form, not only have *not* identified themselves with the attacked state and gone to war against the aggressor, but have even neglected to apply those economic sanctions which would have led to the cessation of war. The theory of aggression, so defined that certain Great Powers viewed it as imposing the duty of general participation in war when it accorded with their own political interests and as not so doing when it was contrary to their interests, is without practical value as a means of war-prevention, and is a mere caricature of an institution under international law.

We dare assume, no doubt, that the mere maintenance of general international law and order is not a sufficient objective to cause the participation of other states in war, when it meets political or economic opposition, or is contrary to their military interests. It would be much better to rely upon Neo-neutrality, which attempts to organize the political and economic interests of the nonparticipating states for the purpose of *avoiding war* or bringing it to an end by a well-prepared and efficient system, which in time will gather strength enough to prevent war. It is a viewpoint which Professor Jessup correctly emphasized during the discussions at the London Conference in 1935, and which comes naturally from Americans, who have built up their world empire not through war and conquest, but through an active and energetic display of economic and political power. The supporters of Neo-neutrality will thus be united by great and important economic and commercial interests in the preservation of peace, just as the members of the armed leagues of neutrality about the year 1800 were interested in the maintenance of neutrality, except that these interests under modern conditions prevail to a much greater degree. Neo-neutrality thus deals with realities which can gradually acquire real value for the preservation of peace in the world; while the aggression theory operates, through national and international channels, to create an agitation which is directed only to the uneducated masses so long as the true objectives have not been disclosed to them, and which, at least in the field of international relations, will be without effect when such objectives are in conflict with these economic and political interests of the state whose participation in the war is requested.

4. The theory that outside states should enter the war if an aggression exists—and this, as we know, is not only the original idea of Article XVI of the Covenant, but the theory upon which the conclusions of the Security Conferences are based,—that they should rely upon this fact alone (the aggression) to defend a step so far-reaching and dangerous to the people of their country, to world-peace, to everything that is called moral and right, is actually so monstrous, unjustified, and impracticable politically, morally, and legally that one must marvel, not because it was adopted in Article XVI of the Covenant of the League (which after all was drawn up under a war-psychosis and the intoxication of victory), but that such a large number of prominent statesmen and scholars in international law, over a number of years and after full deliberation, should have made themselves spokesmen for it. One speaks of the solidarity of the states in this connection, but what influence can this exert upon one another's policies, and what influence especially do the smaller and weaker states have upon the development of world policies? How is it possible, in this far-reaching and fateful way, that such states be made responsible for the policies of other states, with which perhaps they do not agree and at least cannot influence? How is it possible to prevent a state or a group of states from making foolish and improvident commitments of policy, from entering into ententes, or concluding agreements, which the outside states can clearly see must sooner or later lead to war, and which they themselves would under no circumstances enter upon? If all states unconditionally renounced war, there might perhaps be made a reasonable claim for the support of solidarity of so broad a nature, in order to prevent a single individual state from resorting to this means. But when states reserve the right of defensive war, wars of execution or of sanctions, indeed, all kinds of war not included within the rigid limits of the

definition of aggression or the purely formal rules of the Covenant, outside states must assume the position that in such cases they cannot become participants, because they cannot undertake any common responsibility as to whether a situation of war arises from one circumstance or another, and because they had no part in determining the previous history or in the diplomatic game which led to the aggression situation.

The real consequence of the theory of aggression is to bind the outside states to the policies of the major military Powers, to cause them to risk life and limb and the entire existence of the state in the service of foreign interests. The final decision as to whether aggression exists or does not exist—which in turn will be a decisive factor in the attitude of other states—will always lie with the Great Powers; if the Powers disagree among themselves, it will depend upon the differing political influences and the greater or lesser efficiency of their war propaganda machinery.

Conditions would be different under the rule of Neo-neutrality. There is no possibility here of war propaganda, for it is certain in advance that the outside states will not let themselves become involved in the war, since their whole policy is aimed at avoiding war, or isolating, restricting, or ending it. Since their participation cannot be required, the outside states will be much more independent in their judgment of the situation, than under traditional neutrality, freer to preserve their calm, and, through mediation and organized united action, to oppose the war. *The system of war-prevention should be a development of the neutrality policies of the countries at peace, and not of the war policies of the great military Powers.*

As we have noted elsewhere,[222] the statement that aggressive war is prohibited and defensive war permitted, is only a paraphrasing of the desire to preserve the right of making war in one's own interest, but refusing the same privilege to one's adversary. This is self-contradictory and absurd, but it is the real thought which lies behind this classification of war.[223] By a war of aggression is meant a war conducted by others; while one's own war is always a

[222] Cohn, *Kriegsverhütung und Schuldfrage*, p. 181.

[223] According to fascist philosophy, this distinction is avoided, since all war is of itself praiseworthy, wars of aggression as well. These are ideas which we see no reason to examine further here.

defensive war. Indeed, Article XVI was aimed at a very specific condition of war with the rôles of aggressor and defender segregated. From the beginning, therefore, the theory of aggression was encumbered with ambiguity.[224] Each side hoped or even expected, as a matter of course, that it would succeed in convincing the world that it was acting in self-defense, and that the adversary was the aggressor.

It is this hope which the neutrals are determined not to fulfill. Against this whole line of thought, which is entirely inconsistent with a real war-prevention system, traditional neutrality said: "It is not certain that you will convince us"; Neo-neutrality says: "It is certain that you will not convince us." For this reason the theory of neutrality is most unwelcome to the adherents of the theory of aggression. It disturbs a delicately constructed mechanism, which camouflages a propaganda for war under particular conditions in the form of an apparently general system for war-prevention.

The same line of thought is really behind the system of the Locarno Treaty, which was in form general, but in reality had quite specific war situations in mind. Those states for the benefit of whom the security arrangement was not intended, will not have much profit by it, even if their case should ever come within the formal text of the provisions, since no one, when it comes to the point, will consider applying it to them. The theory of aggression is itself, therefore, a theory which is marked at least with definite political aims, and this certainly was the reason why it was so obstinately insisted upon during the Conferences of 1934-35.

In contrast with this, the policy and the aims of Neo-neutrality are clear and unambiguous. They are always the same. The idea of the mobilization of the economic interests of the neutrals against war does not accord with any specific political grouping, but by its very nature will safeguard equally and in all cases the interests of the entire membership. This also gives its war-prevention efforts a greater authority with the belligerents than does the theory of aggression. The belligerent will be unable to assert that international intervention in this case is dictated by a misunderstanding

[224] The word "attack" has two meanings, just as have the expressions "peace" (general peace, Peace of Versailles), "security," and so forth.

of his motives or attitude, or by partiality, or because of secret agreements with the adversary, or by a diplomatic game among the countries participating in the sanctions. Neo-neutrality rejects in principle any regard for the causes of the war or for motives of whatever nature. There will be no reason for discussions between the belligerent and the outside states, since the mere fact of belligerency is the signal for the common intervention of the outside states. Naturally by these new ideas alone not all difficulties with respect to war-prevention are eliminated. It is for us to prepare and to organize in time of peace the non-military opposition, so that it will become effective enough to curb the law breaker, not only in case of war, but also in other cases of international violence. A system of this kind was proposed in a memorandum submitted to the Security Conference of 1934,[225] and the idea was further developed, both in the United States (by Jessup and others) and in South America (at the Pan-American Conference at Buenos Aires, December, 1936). Neo-neutrality is thus a great deal more definite and stronger than the theory of aggression with the latter's recognition of the right to resort to war in many cases, which thus opens the discussion upon the existing case to explore the possibilities of bringing it under the permissible categories. Neo-neutrality meets war with a clear and definite "No!" while the theory of aggression holds only a halting "Perhaps."

Finally, it is a peculiarity of the theory of aggression that it emphasizes to such a high degree the sentimental, emotional, and moral aspects, and holds only reproaches for the adherents of the opposite opinion. Almost all the defendants of the theory of aggression in the League of Nations and at the Conferences in 1934-35 have stressed, in their main arguments for the theory, that it was not a question of law, but of morality, that made neutrality a "monstrosity" (Rolin), a "disgrace" (Lauterpacht), "an attempt to enrich oneself" (de la Pradelle), "a sin" (Politis), and so forth. When emotions are appealed to in a purely scientific discussion, it is often a sure sign that arguments are lacking. But there is also another, and no doubt unconscious, reason for such emotional animosity to-

225 Published, among other places, in "*Coopération Intellectuelle*," Nos. 40-41, pp. 222 ff.; abstracts in English are available in Bourquin (ed.), *Collective Security*.

ward the aggressor, while war, in all other situations is only able to elicit a shrug of the shoulders from these eminent theorists. The real reason is that they unconsciously relieve their bad consciences for permitting war by transferring their entire indignation to an aggressor who is to be blamed for the outbreak of the war and must therefore bear the entire responsibility for it, while we others may then wash our hands of it by declaring that defensive wars, wars of execution, of sanctions, in fact all other kinds of wars, are legal. It is the aggressor, they assert, who is the "evil one"; who is to be blamed for all our troubles. There is a psychological relief-and-projection process which takes place here. Instead of the horrors of war, they speak of the horrible acts of this aggressor; instead of the wholesale slaughter of youth in the aggressor countries, as well as in the others, they speak of the aggressor's responsibility for breaking the agreements it made. The theory of aggression does not desire to look at war in its true perspective. It intrenches itself behind legal and political arguments about the various kinds of war, about the aggressor's moral and legal responsibility, about the duty of outside states to participate in the war under the dictates of morality and honor. In this web of moral and legal distinctions and argumentation, there is no room for new views or opinions upon war, or for a serious effort toward its prevention. War is accepted as a matter of course, and it is only a question of being on the right side of the barricades and the trench lines.

Neo-neutrality refuses to follow the theory of aggression in these attempts to arouse an atmosphere of war through an appeal to "morality and justice." It takes the position that in this field there is no higher moral or legal duty than to keep, so far as this is possible, the people of one's own country out of war; and, to the best of one's ability, to assist the countries directly affected by war to get out of it as soon as possible. The advocates of Neo-neutrality proclaim the disqualification of war in *all* its forms, on the basis of justice and "morality" as well. It cannot, in their opinion, accord with the dictates of ethics or of honor to participate in war. Even if the problem of war has not been fully solved in our time, some paths have been opened toward a better recognition of its nature. These paths do not lead us to the classification of war as just or unjust, as aggressive or defensive, or to any similar technical distinctions; but rather to a general disqualification of all war as a phenomenon common to the different belligerent nations, a contagious collective psychosis, a subconscious homicidal and suicidal mania, and a madness in the collective consciousness, residing far below the threshold of reason and civilization.

Neo-neutrality relies upon no single explanation of the nature of war as being the correct one, nor upon the assumption that ultimately the origin of war is to be found in economic, sociopolitical or other conditions. It considers war as a fact, regardless of the ideology associated with it. It sets itself the uncompromising task of fighting war in all its forms to the utmost, and of working for peace in the interest of the outside states and in the interest of the belligerents themselves, the aggressor as well as the defender.

The Most Recent Developments

1. As we have previously mentioned, the failure of the system of sanctions in the Ethiopian conflict quite naturally gave a new impulse to the idea of neutrality among the members of the League of Nations as well as in the states outside the League. Upon the expiration of the term of the law of 1935 (which had been extended in 1936) the United States enacted a new law by means of a joint resolution,[226] which embodies a further development of the tendencies then prevailing in the United States. This law cannot be regarded as an expression of the idea of Neo-neutrality, since it has no general war-prevention tendency, but at the same time it diverges from traditional neutrality and such neutrality's passive dependence upon the action of the belligerent states.[227] Its aim is to keep the United States out of future wars, in so far as this is possible, by an endeavor to avoid situations which, according to previous experience, are most likely to involve neutral states in war. It follows the "*cash and carry*" principle with slight modifications.

[226] United States, Congress, *75th Congress, First Session,* "Public Resolution No. 27, Chapter 146 of the Statutes at Large."

[227] The Chairman of the Committee on Foreign Affairs, Senator Pittman, who presented the bill in Congress, therefore proposed that the law should not be a neutrality law, but the "Peace Act of 1937."

The main point of this law, according to its section 2(b), is that export goods may not leave American territory "until all right, title and interest therein shall have been transferred to some foreign Government." On the other hand, the law does not unconditionally require cash payment before such departure, nor does it forbid transportation on American ships. As Mr. Hackworth, legal adviser to the State Department, put it in a speech on May 15, 1937, at the Earlham Institute of Foreign Affairs: "Certainly resentment by the American public will not be so easily aroused over the seizure of cargoes if there is no longer any American interest in them." [228]

By section 8 of this law the President's authority is extended so that he may forbid not only submarines but also armed foreign merchant vessels from entering American ports or territorial waters. Section 9 forbids [229] American citizens to sail on ships belonging to any of the belligerent parties. Section 10 prohibits American merchant vessels from trading with any of the belligerent states or carrying arms, with the exception of small arms and the ammunition therefor, as the President may deem necessary. The law does not discriminate between the aggressor and the party attacked.

On the whole, it may be said that this law is an expression of the predominant opinion upon neutrality in the current American theory of international law (Moore, Borchard, Jessup, and others) viz: that neutrality is chiefly of importance within the economic sphere, and that, consequently, it should be possible to prevent neutrals from becoming involved in war by avoiding or diminishing the economic conflicts between neutrals and belligerents. As we have previously said, this point of view is not recognized and is perhaps not even understood in the neutral European countries, which do not profit and do not wish to profit economically by their neutrality.

But also between the member states of the League of Nations, the result of the Italo-Ethiopian conflict naturally entailed a weakening of the system of sanctions under Article XVI of the Covenant, and a return to the idea of neutrality. The declaration of the

[228] From his address entitled "Neutrality and Recent Legislation."
[229] According to the former law they could do this at their own risk.

former neutral countries in 1936 has already been mentioned.[230] The Committee of Twenty-eight, appointed in the same year by the League of Nations at its annual session of January-February, 1938, dealt in particular with a report [231] on the participation of all states in the League of Nations submitted to the Committee on September 8, 1937, and was made by the British representative, Lord Cranborne. In this report Lord Cranborne raised the question as to whether it might be advisable to sacrifice some of the main principles of the Covenant, especially that of compulsory participation in sanctions, in order to induce a greater number of states to join the League. In this report three systems were considered: (1) a system essentially like the present one with its obligatory participation (a "coercive League"); (2) a system without obligation to impose sanctions of any kind (a "non-coercive League") and (3) a system which does not impose any obligation upon the members to participate in sanctions, but leaves the question to be decided in each individual case after a consultation in which the members of the League are obliged to take part (an "intermediate League").

The author gives no one of these three systems his decided preference, but later pronouncements by British statesmen show that the third system is given special consideration by Great Britain. During the meeting of the Committee, the Swedish representative, Professor Undén, pointed out that the system of sanctions had in reality been suspended, and that the present state of affairs, under which the League lacks universality, might be said to correspond to Lord Cranborne's "intermediate" type. The Swiss representative, M. Gorgé, agreed with Mr. Undén, and at the same time emphasized the notion that Article XVI had become optional. The Russian representative, Mr. Litvinoff, and the French representative, M. Paul-Boncour, however, argued for the obligatory character of Article XVI. France and Russia are of the opinion that this Article is the backbone of the League and that it cannot be nullified by the unilateral declaration of an individual member.

During the Council in May, 1938, Switzerland obtained, however, a formal recognition of its complete (traditional) neutrality.

[230] See *Supra,* p. 172 n.

[231] League of Nations, *Document C. S. P. 20,* "Report No. 1."

Squeezed in between Germany and Italy—who are no longer members of the League and disapprove of its fundamental principles—Switzerland had, during the Italo-Ethiopian conflict, realized the untenability of its former theory of neutrality based upon a distinction between economic and military sanctions. In December, 1937, Mr. Gut had carried a motion in the Swiss National Council concerning Switzerland's future position as a member of the League.[232] On April 29, 1938, the Swiss Government submitted a memorandum [233] to the Secretary General of the League of Nations, asking for "a declaration that the traditional neutrality of the Confederation is consistent with the provisions of the Covenant" and a recognition of the "unique position of Switzerland's neutrality."

In the League Council meeting on May 14, the Swedish representative, Mr. Sandler, presented a report [234] which fully approved the Swiss point of view. This report was adopted by the Council; Switzerland is hereafter under no obligation to participate in sanctions of any kind, and will not be invited by the Council to take part in such sanctions. Switzerland declares that it will remain in the League of Nations and safeguard its activities and institutions within Swiss territory. In an exchange of notes in May-June, 1938, the Swiss Government informed the Italian and the German Governments of the Council's resolution.

The Scandinavian countries had for some time considered a revision [235] of their neutrality laws of 1912 (based upon the Hague Conventions of 1907), these laws being more or less obsolete. By a joint declaration regarding neutrality, signed in Stockholm on May 27, 1938,[236] the participating states agreed not to alter their neutrality regulations without prior consultation "if possible." At-

232 An account of this debate is to be found in the *Neue Zurcher Zeitung* for Dec. 23, 1937.

233 League of Nations *Document C. 146. M. 87. 1938. V*, Geneva, April 30, 1938.

234 League of Nations *Document C. 191 (1). M. 103 (1), 1938. V.*

235 The revision was considered by a small committee, the members being: Dr. Georg Cohn (Denmark), Mr. Kivikoski (Finland), Professor Frede Castberg (Norway), Professor Undén and Dr. Th. Gihl (Sweden). Iceland also, as a member of the northern group, adopted the new neutrality rules.

236 See Sweden. Statutes, *Sveriges Overenskommelser med främmande Makter*, 1938, No. 17 (p. 103).

tached to this declaration were new and separate sets of neutrality regulations, these being on all essential points the same for each country. The rules relating to belligerent aircraft and submarines especially are an innovation; in general such devices are not to be admitted into neutral territory, with the exception of such international waterways as the Sound and the Belts. New neutrality rules in conformity with this were subsequently issued by the Baltic States as well (December, 1938).

A clear definition of the attitude of the Scandinavian countries toward the system of sanctions in the Covenant has not yet been reached.[237] On July 23 and 24, 1938, the Ministers for Foreign Affairs of Belgium, Denmark, Finland, Luxemburg, the Netherlands, Norway, and Sweden met in Copenhagen; an official communiqué following the meeting stated that these countries would continue to participate in the work of the League of Nations; at the same time, however, they declared that, under the present conditions, and in view of the policy followed in the past years, they did not consider the system of sanctions as obligatory, either for their particular group of states, its individual members, or for any other member of the League.

This point of view was also voiced by the representatives of those countries at the League Assembly in September, 1938.[238] A position constituting a compromise was taken by the British representative, Earl de la Warr, who declared that although the member states were under no obligation to join automatically in military or economic sanctions, the members were, nevertheless, in each individual case, bound to mutual consultation as to the application of sanctions; furthermore, it was necessary to uphold the principle that an attack on a member state is a question of concern to all members, and that they have no right to be indifferent in this respect. France [239] and Russia, however, maintained the unconditional

[237] According to Bloch (*Zeitschrift für ausl. öffentliches Recht*, 1938, p. 583), the new neutrality rules of May 27, 1938, must be considered as a complete return to traditional neutrality. We cannot, however, agree with this point of view.

[238] See League of Nations, *Document C. 444; M. 287; 1938; VII*, Geneva, Nov. 30, 1938: "Questions relating to Article 16 of the Covenant."

[239] The French representative, Paul-Boncour, did however admit that in enforcing Article XVI it was necessary to take into consideration not only the

and obligatory character of Article XVI, and argued that this article cannot be set aside by the unilateral declarations of member states.

The League Assembly of 1938 furthermore adopted a Protocol (September 18) relating to certain formal amendments to the preamble of the League Covenant, its Articles I, IV, V and its annex. These amendments removed from the original text all references in the Covenant connecting it with the Versailles Treaty (and other peace treaties) in order to give greater independence to the Covenant.

2. It may be said that these latest developments have fully confirmed the points of view presented in this book and in the author's previous treatises of 1924 and 1931. Time has proved that a system of warlike sanctions cannot be carried out in practice, but that the idea of neutrality, which was believed to have been abolished, has preserved its vitality. But Neo-neutrality cannot accept this latest tendency to revive the fundamental principles of traditional neutrality; it is directed equally against the system of the Covenant's Article XVI and against this traditional neutrality. When the new principles of Neo-neutrality were drawn up, the object was not only to oppose the warlike system of sanctions in Article XVI, but not less to oppose the return to traditional neutrality with its passivity in the fight against war—war which might be foreseen as a natural reaction when the system of sanctions proved impracticable.

Neo-neutrality, therefore, retains its significance under the new state of affairs as well. It does not abandon the idea of sanctions and of co-intervention in order to safeguard peace. These elements, however, are not to be based upon the international law of war, but are to be incorporated into an amplified international law of neutrality.[240] It regards the system of Article XVI as a failure, because it is *too late* to put sanctions into effect when war has once started, since the prevention of war, according to Article XVI, depends entirely upon a single and generally unascertainable factor,

geographical situation and economic conditions of each member state, but also to what extent other countries joined in the sanctions.

[240] G. Sandberg, "Om Neutralitet og Sanktioner," in the Swedish periodical *Mellanfolkligt Samarbete*, 1938, p. 248.

aggression, and, finally, because the system of Article XVI opposes one war by another war, a method which Neo-neutrality regards as at once paradoxical and impracticable. On the contrary, Neo-neutrality aims at organizing and carrying into practice *even in peacetime* its war-prevention measures; it considers this to be a condition for the enforcement of its new principles in time of peace as well as in time of war. Neo-neutrality further abandons the use of all war or warlike means in its system. It calls for a large measure of solidarity [241] on the part of the states; it demands their intervention to obviate and oppose injustice and the use of violence in international relations even under present conditions, without awaiting a general disarmament or the creation of a universal League of Nations, or other measures which for the time being are unattainable objectives.

Finally, it is recognized that the struggle against war and for peace must, in our time as well, be fought out upon an ideological basis, because the distinction between those who want peace and those who want war has become so accentuated, leaving less and less common ground for liberal reasoning, that it is to be feared that there finally will be no common basis at all for an understanding. This development has not been fully realized by the general public. There is a direct line from Machiavelli's undisguised worship of power through Schopenhauer's hatred of mankind and Nietzsche's contempt of man to our contemporary theories of "sacred egotism," the glorification of war and the consistent and intransigent annihilation of all human civilization and happiness where this is not identified with one's own. Another difficulty in upholding humane and liberal principles arises from the fact that the individual and his interests today are, as it were, swallowed up by the great mass spectacle, and because our great technical advance involves such a general mechanization and submergence of the individual that he becomes an insignificant entity in the vast machinery of society. The consequence is a gradual change of the individual's mentality, whether one regards this as a return to a

[241] See for further reference Georg Cohn, "La Néo-neutralité," in *Revue de Droit International*, 1938, p. 286.

primitive "prelogical" consciousness or a development toward a higher "super-individual" consciousness.[242]

For all these reasons the fight against war and international injustice must be waged on many different fronts with the greatest energy and by entirely new methods. The system of Article XVI has long been practically obsolete; even more so are the principles of traditional neutrality. Neo-neutrality embarks upon new methods[243] in the age-long fight for right against injustice, for peace against war, for freedom against oppression, for mutual assistance against general extermination, and for the protection of the economic, moral, and cultural progress of mankind.

[242] Heard, *The Ascent of Humanity from Group Consciousness through Individuality to Super-Consciousness*, London, 1929, p. 43: "Seen in secular perspective . . . it is evident that every community when it is about to end . . . bursts into aggressive war."

[243] Cohn, *op. cit.*, "La Néo-neutralité," p. 293.

BIBLIOGRAPHY

Académie Diplomatique International, Paris. Séances et travaux. Paris, 1927 ff.

Academy of International Law. *See* Hague, The.

Action collective et neutralité. *See* Heald, S.

Alvarez, Alejandro. Le Droit international américain. Paris, 1910.

American Institute of International Law. Codification of American International Law. Pan-American Union, Washington, 1926.

American Journal of International Law. American Society of International Law, New York, 1907 ff.

American Neutrality Policy. Hearings before the Committee on Foreign Affairs. *See* United States. Congress.

Annual Digest of Public International Law Cases. Sir John Fischer Williams and H. Lauterpacht, editors. London, 1933.

Anzilotti, Dionisio. Lehrbuch des Völkerrechts. Leipzig, 1929.

Application of the Principles of the Covenant. *See* League of Nations. Application....

Argentine Republic. Ministerio de Relaciones Exteriores y Culto. Pacte de Non-agression et de conciliation argentine (conclu le 10 octobre, 1933) Recueil de documents.... Buenos Aires, 1936.

Bajer, Fredrik. Nordens, saerlig Danmarks Neutralitet under Krimkrigen. Copenhagen, 1914.

Baker, Newton D. "Why We Went to War." In *Foreign Affairs* (New York), XV (1936), 1-86.

Bauer, Walter. Die öffentliche Meinung in der Weltgeschichte. Potsdam, 1930.

—— Die öffentliche Meinung und ihre geschichtlichen Grundlagen. Tübingen, 1914.

Bergbohm, Carl. Die bewaffnete Neutralität, 1780-83. Berlin, 1884.

Berlin, Knud K. Den danske Statsforfatningsret. 2 vol., Copenhagen, 1930-34.

Bonfils, Henry, and Paul Fauchille. Traité de droit international public. 8th ed., Paris, 1921-26.

Bonn, Moritz. "How Sanctions Failed." In *Foreign Affairs* (New York), XVI (1937), 357 ff.

Bono, Emilio de. La preparazione e le prime operazione. Rome, 1937.

Borchard, Edwin. "The Arms Embargo and Neutrality." In *American Journal of International Law*, XXVII (1933), 293 ff.

—— "The 'Enforcement' of Peace by 'Sanctions.'" In *American Journal of International Law*, XXVII (1933), 518 ff.

—— "Sanctions versus Neutrality." In *American Journal of International Law*, XXX (1936), 91 ff.

Borel, Eugene. "La Neutralité." In *Académie Diplomatique Internationale, Séances et travaux*, X (1936), 42 ff.

—— "La Neutralité de la Suisse au sein de la Société des nations." In *Revue générale de droit international public*, XXVII (1920), 153 ff.

Bourquin, Maurice. "Final Report." In League of Nations, International Studies Conference, *Collective Security*, pp. 452 ff.

—— (ed.). *See* League of Nations, International Studies Conference.

Boye, Thorvald. "Belligerent Rights of a Violator of the Kellogg Pact." In *American Journal of International Law*, XXIV (1930), 766 ff.

—— Haandbok i Folkeret. Christiania, 1918.

—— De vaebnede Neutralitetsforbund; et Avsnit av folkerretens Historie. Copenhagen, 1912.

Braun, Werner. Démarche, Ultimatum, Sommation. Berlin, 1930.

Brière. *See* La Brière.

Brierly, James L. Staternes Neutralitet under Folkeforbundspagten og Kelloggpagten. Copenhagen, 1936.

British Year Book of International Law. London, 1920 ff.

Brouckère, Louis de. "La Prévention de la guerre." In *The Hague, Academy of International Law, Recueil des cours*, IV (1934), 1-83.

—— Brouckère's Report. *See* League of Nations, *Document No. A.14.1927.V.*, pp. 60 ff.

Buell, Raymond L. "Le Canal de Suez et les sanctions de la Société des nations." In *Revue Générale de Droit International Public*, XLIII (1936), 50 ff.

Calogeropoulos-Stratis, Sypros. Le Pacte générale de renonciation à la guerre. Paris, 1931.

Carnovale, Luigi. How America Can Quickly and Easily Prevent Wars Forever, without the Necessity of a League of Nations, of a World Court.... Chicago, 1924.

—— Only by the Abolition of Neutrality Can Wars Be Quickly and Forever Prevented. Chicago, 1922.

Carter, John F. Conquest: America's Painless Imperialism. New York, 1928.

Cavare, L. "La Reconnaissance de l'état et Mandchoukouo." In *Revue Générale de Droit International Public*, XLII (1935), 5 ff.

Codification of American International Law. *See* American Institute of International Law.

Cohn, Georg. Etik og Sociologi. Copenhagen, 1913.

—— "Haevdelsen af Danmarks Neutralitet under Verdenskrigen." In *Juridisk Tidsskrift*, VI (1920), 33 ff.

—— "Kellogg-Pagtens retlige Betyding." In *Juridisk Tidsskrift*, XIV (1928), 1 ff.

—— "Kellogg-Pakt und Völkerrecht." In *Zeitschrift für Völkerrecht* (1929), 169 ff.

—— "Kollektiv Sikkerhed." In *Tilskueren* (1936), 237 ff.

—— "Kriegsverhütung und Schuldfrage; mit einer Einleitung über die Mischung völkerrechtlicher und landesrechtlicher Elemente." In *Frankfurter Abhandlungen zum Modernen Völkerrecht*, XXIII (1931), 1 ff. Also cited here as the (Danish) Treatise of 1931.

—— "La Néo-neutralité." In *Revue de droit international*, XIX (1938), 281 ff.

—— "Neutralité et Société des nations." In Munch (ed.). *Les Origines et l'œuvre de la Société des nations*, II (1924), 152 ff. Also cited here as the (Danish) Treatise of 1924.

Cohn, Georg, and N. Cohn. Folkeretskilder. Copenhagen, 1911.

Commissie van rechtsgeleerden. Algemeen verslag der Commissie van rechtsgeleerden, belast met de studie van en het uitbrengen van bericht over de herziening van het oorlogsrecht. The Hague, 1923.

Conférence de la limitation des armements. *See* Washington, D. C., Conference on the Limitation of Armament, 1921-22.

Conférences d'études préparatoires sur la "Sécurité collective," 1934-35. *See* League of Nations, etc.

"Conférence générale sur la sécurité collective." In *Coopération Intellectuelle* (No. 53-54), London, 1935.

Conférence Internationale de la Paix, The Hague, 1899. *See* Hague, The. International Peace Conference, 1899.

Conwell-Evans, Thomas P. The League Council in Action. A study of the Methods Employed by the Council of the League of Nations to Prevent War and to Settle International Disputes. Oxford, 1929.

Coopération Intellectuelle (monthly), Paris, 1931 ff.

Coppola, Francesco. "Apperçu sur l'idée de 'sécurité collective.'" In Coopération Intellectuelle (No. 40-41), 256 ff.

Coudert, Frederic R. "La Neutralité des États-Unis." In L'Esprit international (1936), 60 ff.

Cour Permanente de Justice Internationale. *See* League of Nations. Permanent Court of International Justice.

Crichton, V. M. S. "The Pre-war Theory of Neutrality." In *British Year Book of International Law*, IX (1928), 101 ff.

Crozier, Frank P. The Men I Killed. London, 1927.

Curti, Arthur. Der Handelskrieg von England, Frankreich und Italian gegen Deutschland und Oesterreich-Ungarn. Eine neutrale Darstellung. Berlin, 1917.

Cybichowski, Zygmunt. Das antike Völkerrecht. Breslau, 1907.

Danish Treatises of 1924 and 1931. *See* Cohn, Georg.

Demartial, G. Le Mythe des guerres de légitime défense. Paris, 1931.

Denmark. Rigsdag. Rigsdagstidende (1920). Copenhagen, 1920.

—— Statutes. Proclamations No. 298, 299, 300 and 301, of November 16-18, 1935. Lovtidende (1935), 1177 ff.

—— Statutes. Proclamation No. 216, danske borgerlig Straffelov av April 15, 1930, sections 244 and 272. A French translation is available under the title "Code pénal danois du Avril 1930." Paris, 1935.

—— Treaties. Danske Traktater (1751-1800) udgivet paa Udenrigsministeriets Foranstaltning. Copenhagen, 1882-85.

—— Udenrigsministeriet. Folkeforbundets første Tiaar, udgivet i Anledning af Ti-Aarsdagen for Danmarks Indtraeden i Folkeforbundet. Copenhagen, 1930.

Descamps, Edouard E. E. F. La Neutralité de la Belgique. Brussels, 1902. "Le Droit international nouveau. L'ère juridique sans violence et l'avènement du Pacigérat positif." In *Revue de Droit International* X (1929), 159 ff. and XI (1930), 62 ff.

—— "Le Pacigérat ou régime juridique de la paix au temps de guerre." In *Revue Générale de Droit International Public*, VII (1900), 629 ff.

—— "Les Grandes Étapes du progrès dans le droit des neutres et la vocation de notre temps à la constitution du pacigérat." In *Revue Générale de Droit International Public*, VII (1900), 105 ff.

Despagnet, Frantz. Cours de droit international public. Paris, 1899.

Donnedieu de Vabres, Henry F. A. Les Principes modernes du droit pénal international. Paris, 1928.

Dulles, Allen W., and Hamilton F. Armstrong. Can We Be Neutral? New York, 1936.

Dupuis, Charles. Le Droit des gens et les rapports des grandes puissances avec les autres états avant le pacte de la Société des nations. Paris, 1921.

Eagleton, Clyde. "Faut-il proscrire seulement les guerres d'agression ou toutes les guerres?" In *Revue Générale de Droit International Public*, XXXIX (1932), 498 ff.

—— "La Législation sur la neutralité aux États-Unis." In *Revue de Droit International*, XVII (1936), 926 ff.

Einicke, Paul. Rechte und Pflichten der neutrale Mächte im Seekrieg, nach dem Haager Abkommen vom 18 Oktober, 1907. Tübingen, 1912.

Einstein, Albert, and Sigmund Freud. Why War? English translation by Stuart Gilbert. Institute of Intellectual Co-operation, Paris, 1933.

Esprit, L'; revue internationale. Institut International de Coopération Intellectuelle, IV (1934). Articles by Johan Bojer, Aldous Huxley, and others.

Esprit international, L' (The International Mind). Published by the Carnegie Endowment for International Peace. Division of Intercourse and Education. Paris, 1927 ff.

Eysinga, Willem Jan Marie van. "Die Niederlande und das Neutralitätsrecht während des Weltkrieges." In Zeitschrift für Völkerrecht (1932), 603 ff.

Fairman, C. "La Loi américaine de neutralité du 31 août 1935 appliquée au conflit italo-éthiopien." In *Revue Générale de Droit International Public*, XLII (1936), 678 ff.

Felszeghy, B. "Panik und Pan-Komplex." In *Imago*, VI (1920), 1 ff.

Fenwick, Charles G. International Law. New York and London, 1924.

—— "Neutrality and International Organization." In *American Journal of International Law*, XXVIII (1934), 334 ff.

—— "The Implication of 'Consultation' in the Pact of Paris." In *American Journal of International Law*, XXVI (1932), 787 ff.

Fernandez, R. "L'Amérique du sud et la Société des nations." In Munch (ed.) *Les Origines et l'oeuvre de la Société des nations*, II (1924), 137 ff.

Flusser, E. Krieg als Krankheit. The Hague, 1932.

Foreign Affairs (New York); an American quarterly review. Edited by William L. Langer and Hamilton F. Armstrong. New York, 1922 ff.

Freud, Sigmund. "Eine Schwerigkeit der Psychoanalyse." In *Imago*, V (1919), 1 ff.

—— Jenseits des Lustprinzips. Vienna, 1923.

—— Massenpsychologie und Ich-Analyse. Vienna, 1923.

—— Totem und Tabu; einige überstimmung im Seelenleben der Wilden und der Neurotiker. Vienna, 1922.

Friedenswarte, Die; Blaetter für internationale Verständigung und zwischenstaatliche Organization. Monthly, Zurich, 1899 ff.

Galiani, Fernando. De' doveri de principi neutrali. German translation by K. A. Caesar. 2 vols. Leipzig, 1790.

Gallus. "Des Amendements au pacte de la Société des nations en vue de la mettre en harmonie avec le pacte de Paris." In *Revue Générale de Droit International Public*, XXXVII (1930), 19 ff.

Gareis, Karl von. "Neutralität bewaffnete, wohlwollende." In Strupp, *Wörterbuch*, II, 124 ff.

Garner, James W. "Non-recognition of Illegal Territorial Annexations and Claims to Sovereignty." In *American Journal of International Law*, XXX (1936), 679 ff.

—— "Recent Neutrality Legislation of the United States." In *British Year Book of International Law*, XVII (1936), 45 ff.

Geneva Conference. *See* League of Nations.

Geouffre de Lapradelle. *See* La Pradelle, Albert.

Giraud, Émile. "La Théorie de la légitime défense." In *Hague, The. Academy of International Law. Recueil des cours*, XLIX (1934), 687 and 863.

Gilbert, Clinton W. The Mirrors of Washington. New York, 1921.

Gonsiorowski, Miroslas. Société des nations et problème de la paix. 2 vols., Paris, 1927.

Göteborg (Sweden). Göteborg Handels-och Sjöfarts-Tidning, 22 Oktober, 1935.

Graux, Lucien. Les Fausses Nouvelles de la grande guerre. 2 vols., Paris, 1918.

Great Britain. British White Book. Memorandum on the Signature by His Majesty's Government of the Optional Clause of the Statute of the Permanent Court. (Cmd. 3452) Mssc. No. 12 (1929), London, 1929.

—— British White Book. Papers Relating to the Proposed Amendment of the Covenant of the League of Nations. Mssc. No. 18 (1930) London, 1930.

Grotius, Hugo. De jure bellis ac pacis. Marburg, 1734.

Gumplowicz, Ludwig. Der Rassenkampf. Innsbruck, 1883.

—— Grundriss der Sociologie. Vienna, 1885.

Haase, Joachim. Wandlung des Neutralitätsbegriffes. Leipzig, 1932.

Hackworth, G. H. "Neutrality and Recent Legislation." In Earlham Institute of Foreign Affairs, 1938.

Hague, The. Academy of International Law. Recueil des cours. Paris, 1923 ff.

—— First International Peace Conference, 1899. Parts I-IV, in one volume. The Hague, 1899.

—— Second International Peace Conference, 1907 (June 15 to October 18) Actes et documents. Ministère des affaires étrangères. The Hague, 1907.

Hall, William E. A Treatise on International Law. Alexander P. Higgins, editor. Oxford, 1924.

Handbuch des Völkerrechts. Irregular. Stuttgart.

Hassman, H. Der Kellogg-Pakt und seine Vorbehalte. Brückenau, 1930.

Hautefeuille, Laurent B. Des droits et des devoirs des nations neutres en temps de guerre maritime. 2d ed., 3 vols., Paris, 1858.

—— Histoire des origines, des progrès et des variations du droit maritime international. Paris, 1858.

Heald, Stephen A., and Raymond L. Buell. Action collective et neutralité; deux études. Conciliation internationale, centre Européen de la dotation Carnegie, Division des relations internationales et de l'éducation. Bulletins No. 3-4. Paris, 1936.

Heard, G. The Ascent of Humanity from Group Consciousness through Individuality to Super-Consciousness. London, 1929.

Hedin, A. La Neutralité des états scandinaves. Stockholm, 1899.

Heffter, August Wilhelm. Das europäische Völkerrecht der Gegenwart auf den bisherigen Grundlagen. Edited by F. H. Geffcken. Berlin, 1888.

Heilborn, Paul. Rechte und Pflichten der neutralen Staaten. Berlin, 1888.

Hertz, Wilhelm G. "Die Theorie der Notwehr." In *Die Friedenswarte*, XXX (1935), 137 ff.

Hold-Ferneck, Alexander. Lehrbuch des Völkerrechts. 2 vols., Leipzig, 1930-32.

Hoskins, Halford L. "The Suez Canal in Time of War." In *Foreign Affairs* (New York), XV (1935), 93 ff.

Huber, Max. "Die schweizerische Neutralität und der Völkerbund." In Munch (ed.), *Les Origines et l'œuvre de la Société des nations*, II (1924), 68 ff.

Hubner, Martin. De la saisie des bâtiments neutres. The Hague, 1759.

Hudson, Manley O. The Permanent Court of International Justice. New York, 1934.

Hull, Cordell. "Neutrality." In *Hague, The. Académie Diplomatique Internationale, Séances et travaux*, X (1936), 41 ff.

Hurwitz, Stephan. Bidrag til Laeren om kollektive Enheders pønale Ansvar. Copenhagen, 1933.

Institute of International Law. Annuaire de l'Institut de Droit Internationale. Ghent-Brussels, 1874 ff.

Inter-American Conference for the Maintenance of Peace, Buenos Aires, 1936. Special Handbook for the Use of Delegates. Washington, 1936.

International Academy of Diplomacy. *See* Académie Diplomatique Internationale.

International Law Association. Report of the Thirty-seventh Conference, Oxford, 1932. London, 1933.

Jessup, Philip C. "The Birth, Death and Reincarnation of Neutrality." In *American Journal of International Law*, XXVI (1932), 789 ff.

—— Neutrality: Its History, Economics and Law. Vol. IV, "Today and Tomorrow." New York, 1936.

—— The United States and the Stabilization of Peace. New York, 1935. (Later edition entitled "International Security.")

Jessup, Philip C., and Francis Deák. Neutrality: Its History, Economics and Law. Vol. I, "The Origins." New York, 1935.

Juridisk Tidsskrift, med østre landrets Tidende. Copenhagen, 1915 ff.

Keller, F. "Notwehrrecht und Notwehrtechnik." In *Die Friedenswarte*, XXIX (1929), 10 ff.

Kerr, Alfred. Walther Rathenau; Erinnerungen eines Freundes. Amsterdam, 1935.

Kleen, Rikard. Kodificerad Handbok i Krigets Lagar till Lands och till Sjös, enligt Aftal och vedertagen Sedvänja bland hyfsade Folkslag. Stockholm, 1909.

—— Lois et usage de la neutralité d'après le droit international conventionel coûtumier des états civilisés. 2 vols., Paris, 1898-1900.

Knubben, R. "Völkerbund und Kriegsverhütung." In Strupp (ed.), *Wörterbuch*, III (1929), 1151 ff.

Koht, Halvdan. "Neutrality and Peace: the View of a Small Power." In *Foreign Affairs* (New York), XVI (1937), 280 ff.

"Kortskitse over Abessiniens Deling efter den Laval-Hoare'ske Plan." In *Berlingske Tidende* (aften), December 14, 1934. Copenhagen, 1934.

Krauel, W. Neutralität, Neutralisation und Befriedung im Völkerrecht. Greifswald, 1915.

Kulsrud, Carl J. "Armed Neutralities to 1780." In *American Journal of International Law*, XXIX (1935), 423 ff.

Kunz, Josef L. "Die intrasystematische Stellung des Artikels XI des Völkerbundpaktes." In *Frankfurter Abhandlungen zum modernen Völkerrecht*, XXI (1931), 1 ff. Leipzig, 1931.

La Brière, Yves de. "La définition de l'agresseur." In *L'Esprit International*, VII (1933), 616 ff.

Lacombe, P. De l'histoire considérée comme science. Paris, 1894.

Lagorgette, J. Le Rôle de la guerre. Paris, 1906.

La Pradelle, Albert Geouffre de. "L'Évolution de la neutralité." In *Revue de Droit International*, XV (1920), 197 ff.

Laursen, Laurs R. Danmark-Norges Traktater (1523-1750). In Danish and French. 9 vols., Copenhagen, 1907-33.

Lauterpacht, Hersh. "The Notion of Neutrality in a System Providing for the Repression of Recourse to War." In *Some British Views on Collective Security*, II (1935), mimeographed, p. 1 ff.

—— "The Covenant as the 'Highest Law.'" In *British Year Book of International Law*, XVII (1936), 54 ff.

Le Bon, Gustave. Psychologie des foules. Paris, 1895.

League of Nations. Application of the Principles of the Covenant. Documents Nos. A.31.1936.VII. and C.376.M.247.1936.VII., Geneva, 1936.

—— Assembly. Records of the First Assembly. Geneva, 1921.

—— Assembly. Report of the Fifth Committee. Document No. A.II.-P.V.5.1936. Geneva, 1936.

—— Council. Procès-verbal of the Seventy-eighth Session of the Council.

—— Council. Report of the Committee. Document No. C.191 (1) M.101.(1)1938.V.

—— Council. Reports and Resolutions on the Subject of Article XVI of the Covenant. Document A.14.1927.V.

—— Disarmament Conference. Records of the Conference for the Reduction and Limitation of Armaments. Series B, Minutes of the General Commission. Document No. B.II.1933.IX.10., Geneva, 1934.

—— Geneva Conference for the Reduction and Limitation of Armaments. Report of the Committee on Security Questions. Conference Document No. C.G.108. Geneva, 1935.

—— International Studies Conferences. "Collective Security." Edited by M. Bourquin. A Record of the Seventh and Eighth International Studies Conferences, Paris, 1936. Also published in French under the title "La Sécurité collective."

—— Eighth International Studies Conference. Minutes of a General Studies Conference on "Collective Security." Document No. K.24. 1935. Paris, 1936.

—— Ninth International Studies Conference, Madrid, 1936. Preparation and Short Record of the Meetings on the Peaceful Solution of Certain International Problems (Peaceful Change) Edited by the International Institute of Intellectual Co-operation. Parts I and II, Paris, 1936.

—— Official Journal. Geneva, 1920 ff.

—— Official Journal. Special Supplement, Nos. 145-149. Geneva, 1935-36.

—— "Questions Relating to Article XVI of the Covenant." Document No. C.444.M.287.1938.VII. Geneva, 1938.

—— Treaty Series. Geneva, 1920 ff.

Lechartier, Georges. "Neutralité et politique exterieur aux États-Unis." In *Esprit International*, X (1936), 236 ff.

Lehmann, Gerhard. Das Kollektivbewusstsein; systematische und historischkritische Vorstudien zur Soziologie. Berlin, 1928.

Lenz, Paul. "Krieg und Massenpsychologie." In *Die Friedenswarte*, XXXV (1935), 86 ff.

Liszt, Franz von. Das Völkerrecht. Edited by Max Fleischmann. 17th edition. Berlin, 1925.

London. International Naval Conference, 1908-9. Proceedings of the International Naval Conference. Held in London, December 1908-February 1909. London, 1909.

Luxemburg. Grand Duchy. Ministry of State, Director General of Foreign Affairs. Neutralité du grand-duché pendant la guerre de 1914-1918; attitude des pouvoirs publics. Luxemburg, 1919.

McNair, Arnold D. "The Stimson Doctrine of Non-Recognition." In *British Year Book of International Law*, XIV (1933), 65 ff.

McDougall, William. The Group Mind; a Sketch of the Principles of Collective Psychology with Some Attempt to Apply Them to the Interpretation of National Life and Character. 3d rev. ed., Cambridge, 1921.

Martens, Georg Friedrich von (ed.). Nouveau recueil général de traités et autres actes relatifs au rapports de droit international.... Ser. I-III, 1808 ff. Göttingen, 1817 ff.

——— Recueil des principaux traités ... de l'Europe ... depuis 1761 jusqu'à present. 7 vol., Göttingen, 1791-1801.

——— Supplément au recueil des principaux traités ..., 1801-18, 6 vols., Göttingen, 1802-18.

Matos, Jose. "L'Amérique et la Société des nations." In *The Hague. Academy of International Law. Recueil des cours*, III (1929), 5 ff.

Matzen, H. Den danske Staatsforfatningsret. I-III, Copenhagen, 1910.

——— Forlaesninger over den positive Folkeret. Copenhagen, 1900.

Melamed, Samuel M. Theorie, Ursprung und Geschichte der Friedensidee. Kultur-philosophische Wanderungen. Stuttgart, 1909.

Meurer, Christian. Die Haager Friedenskonferenz. 2 vols., Munich, 1905-7.

Michaïlidès, Ph. La Neutralité et la Société des nations. Paris, 1933.

Miller, David Hunter. The Drafting of the Covenant. 2 vols., New York, 1928.

——— The Geneva Protocol. New York, 1925.

——— The Peace Pact of Paris. New York, 1928.

Mirrors of Washington. *See* Gilbert, C. W.

Møller, Axel. Folkeretten in Fredstid og Krigstid. 2 vols., Copenhagen, 1925-34. An English translation under the title *International Law in Peace and War* by H. M. Pratt, London, 1931-35, is available.

——— "Bør Folkeforbungspagten reformeres?" In *Nordisk Tidsskrift for International Ret*, VII (1936), 224 ff.

Montesquieu, (Baron) Charles de. L'Esprit des lois. (Chapter X.) Geneva, 1748.

Moore, James Bassett. "An Appeal to Reason." In *Foreign Affairs* (New York), XI (1933), 547 ff.

——— Digest of International Law. 8 vols., Washington, 1906.

Morrison, Charles C. The Outlawry of War: a Constructive Policy for World Peace. Chicago, 1927.

Moscato, A. Le sorti della neutralizzazione belga dopo la guerra. Reprint from *Rivista di Diritto Internazionale* (irregular), Rome, 1930-31.

Munch, Peter. "Les États neutres et le pacte de la Société des nations." In Munch, ed., *Les Origines et l'œuvre de la Société des nations*, I (1923), 159 ff.

——— "Die Völkerbundspolitik der drei nordischen Staaten." In *Institut für internationales Recht, Kiel University*, 1 Reihe (Vortrage und Einzelschriften), Heft 11. Berlin, 1929.

—— (ed.) Les Origines et l'œuvre de la Société des nations. Rask-Ørsted Fonden; Copenhagen. Texts in French, English and German. 2 vols., Copenhagen, 1923-24.
Netherlands. Statutes. Law of October 9, 1935, "Co-operation with League Sanctions." In *Stattsblad van het Koninkrijk der Nederlanden*, No. 599 (1935). The Hague, 1935.
—— Statutes. Law of October 26, 1935, "Sanctions law." In *Staatsblad van het Koninkrijk der Nederlanden*, No. 621 (1935). The Hague, 1935.
"Neutrality Today." In *The Round Table* (London), XVI (1936), 762 ff.
Niemeyer, Theodor, and K. Strupp, editors. Die völkerrechtlichen Urkunden des Weltkrieges. Vols. 1-4, Munich, 1916-20.
Nietzsche, Friedrich. Also sprach Zarathustra. Vol. VII of "Werke," Leipzig, 1910.
Nippold, Otfried. Die Gestaltung des Völkerrechts nach dem Weltkrieg. Zurich, 1917.
Nordisk Tidsskrift for International Ret. E. Bruel and others, eds. Copenhagen, 1934 ff.
Norway. Statutes. Laws with respect to Norwegian participation in sanctions in the conflict between Italy and Ethiopia, *Norsk Lovtidende* (1935), 985 ff.
Nys, Ernest. Le Droit international. 2d ed., 3 vols., Brussels, 1912.
Oppenheim, Lassa F. L. International Law: a Treatise. 5th ed., ed. by H. Lauterpacht. 2 vols., London, 1935.
Organisation Centrale pour une Paix Durable. Recueil de rapports sur les différents points du programme-minimum. 4 vols., The Hague, 1916-18.
"P." "Les Neutres et la crise européenne." In *Revue Générale de Droit International Public*, XXI (1914), 497 ff.
Pacte de non-agression et de conciliation Argentin. *See* Argentine Republic.
Pella, Vespasien V. La Détermination de l'agresseur. Bukarest, 1935.
Perrinjaquet, J. "La Guerre européenne et les relations commerciales des belligérants et des neutres." In *Revue Générale de Droit International Public*, XXXVIII (1931), 127 ff.
Philipse, Adriaan H. Le Rôle du Conseil de la Société des nations dans le règlement pacifique des différends internationaux. The Hague, 1929.
Phillips, W. Alison, and Arthur H. Reede. Neutrality: Its History,

Economics and Law. Vol. III, "The Napoleonic Period." New York, 1936.

Politis, Nicholas S. La Neutralité et la paix. Paris, 1935. English translation by Francis C. Macken, entitled *Neutrality and Peace*, Carnegie Endowment for International Peace, Washington, 1935.

—— "Les Accords de Locarno." In *Revue de Droit International*, VI (1925), 713 ff.

—— Les Nouvelles Tendances de droit international. Paris, 1927.

Rambert, Georges. Le Droit de la guerre et le pacte Briand-Kellogg. Lausanne, 1931.

Rappard, William E. "l'Entrée de la Suisse dans la Société des nations; avant propos de M. le Conseiller fédéral Motta ... edité par les soins de l'association suisse pour la Société des nations." In Munch (ed.). *Les Origines et l'œuvre de la Société des nations*, II (1924), 361 ff.

Rapports et resolutions concernant l'article 16 du pacte. *See* League of Nations, Reports and Resolutions....

Raw Materials and Colonies. Royal Institute of International Affairs, London, 1936.

Ray, Jean. Commentaire du pacte de la Société des nations selon la politique et la jurisprudence des organes de la Société. Paris, 1930.

Recueil de rapports.... *See* Organisation Centrale pour une Paix Durable.

Recueil des cours.... *See* Hague, The. Academy of International Law.

Resolutions of 1921. *See* League of Nations, Reports and Resolutions. ... Document No. A.14.1927.V.

Revue de Droit International. Paris, 1920 ff.

Revue de Droit International et de Legislation Comparée. Quarterly, Paris, 1869 ff.

Revue générale de Droit International Public. P. Fauchille, ed., Paris, 1894 ff.

Richter, Siegfried. Die Neutralisation von Staaten, insbesondere die der Schweiz, Belgiens, Luxemburgs und des fruheren Kongostaates. (Rechtseinheit, Heft 11), Berlin, 1913.

Rivier, Alphonse P. Principes de droit des gens. 2 vols., Paris, 1896.

Rivista di Diritto Internazionale. Rome, 1905 ff.

Rougier, Antoine. "Le Traité de Versailles et la neutralité de la Savoie." In *Revue Générale de Droit international Public*, XXVII (1920), 40 ff.

Roosevelt, Franklin D. "La Neutralité." In *Académie Diplomatique Internationale, Séances et travaux*, X (1936), 47 ff.

Round Table, The. A quarterly review of the politics of the British Empire. London, 1911 ff.

Royal Institute of International Affairs. Information Department. Raw Materials and Colonies: Paper No. 18. London, 1936.

—— Journal. London, 1922 ff.

Rutgers, Victor H. "La Mise en harmonie du pacte de la Société des nations avec le pacte de Paris. In *Hague, The, Academy of International Law, Recueil des cours*, IV (1931), 5 ff.

Sakurai, Tadayoshi. Niku Dan (Menschenopfer) Tagebuch eines japanischen Offiziers während der Belagerung und Ersturmung von Port Arthur. German tr. by A. Schinzinger. Freiburg, 1911; English tr. by A. M. Bacon ("Human Bullets"), Boston, 1908.

Saldana, O. "La Justice pénale internationale." In *Hague, The, Academy of International Law, Recueil des cours*, V (1927), 227 ff.

Sandberg, G. "On Neutralitet og Sanktioner." In *Mellanfolkligt Samarbete* (1938), 248 ff.

Sandiford, Roberto. "La Neutralité aérienne." In *Revue Générale de Droit International Public*, XXXIX (1932), 739-75.

Savage, C. Policy of the United States toward Maritime Commerce in War, 1914-1918. Washington, 1936.

Scelle, Georges A. J. J. "L'Agression et la légitime défense dans les rapports internationaux." In *L'Esprit international*, X (1936), 372 ff.

—— Théorie du gouvernement international. The New Commonwealth Institute, Memorandum No. 2. London, 1935.

Schindler, Dietrich. "Contributions à l'étude des facteurs sociologiques et psychologiques du droit international." In *Hague, The, Academy of International Law, Recueil des cours*, IV (1933), 233 ff.

Schmidt-Phiseldek, C. F. Versuch einer Darstellung des dänischen Neutralitätssistemes während des letzteren Seekriges. 2 vols., Copenhagen, 1802-3.

Schou, P. "The United States Refusal to Join the League of Nations." In Munch, ed., *Les Origines et l'œuvre de la Société des nations*, I (1923), 297 ff.

Schücking, Walter M. A. and H. Wehberg. Die Satzung des Völkerbundes. Berlin, 1921; also 3d ed., Vol. I, Berlin, 1931.

Schweizer, Paul. Geschichte der schweizerischen Neutralität. Frauenfeld, 1895.

Scott, James B. "Neutrality of the United States." In *American Journal of International Law*, XXIX (1935), 644 ff.

—— The Armed Neutralities of 1780 and 1800; a Collection of Official

Documents, Preceded by Views of Representative Publicists. Carnegie Endowment for International Peace, Division of International Law. New York, 1918.

——— The Controversy over Neutral Rights between the United States and France, 1797-1800. A Collection of American State Papers and Judicial Decisions. Carnegie Endowment for International Peace, Division of International Law. New York, 1917.

——— The International Conferences of American States, 1889-1928. Carnegie Endowment for International Peace, Division of International Law, New York, 1931.

Séfériadès, Stelio. "La Conception de la neutralité dans l'ancienne Grèce." In *Revue de Droit International*, XVI (1935), 641 ff.

Serup, A. L'Article XVI du pacte et son interpretation dans le conflit Italo-Éthiopien. Paris, 1938.

Seymour, Charles. "American Neutrality; the Experience of 1914-1917." In *Foreign Affairs* (New York), XIV (1935), 26 ff.

Sforza, C. "La Belgique et sa politique etrangère." In *L'Esprit International*, XI (1937), 19 ff.

Shotwell, James T. "The Pact of Paris, with Historical Commentary." In *International Conciliation*, No. 243, October 1928. Carnegie Endowment for International Peace, Division of International Law. New York, 1928.

——— "Renonciation à la guerre et non mise hors la loi de la guerre." In *L'Esprit International*, II (1928), 483 ff.

——— War as an Instrument of National Policy and Its Renunciation in the Pact of Paris. New York, 1929.

Sighele, Scipio. La Foule criminelle; essai de psychologie collective. French translation by P. Vigny. Bibliothèque de philosophie contemporaine, 2d ed., Paris, 1901.

Sperber, A. "Völkerpsychologische Ursachen des Krieges." In *Die Friedenswarte*, XXXV (1933), 108 ff.

Stratis. *See* Calogeropoulos-Stratis.

Strupp, Karl. Éléments du droit international public. 3 vols., Paris, 1930.

——— Der Kellogg-Pakt in Rahmen des Kriegsvorbeugungsrechts. Leipzig, 1928.

——— "Neutralisation, Befriedung, Entmilitarisierung." In *Handbuch des Völkerrechts*, Band 2, Abteil 2, pp. 1-441. Stuttgart, 1933.

——— (ed.) Wörterbuch des Völkerrechts und der Diplomatie, I-III. Berlin, 1924-29.

Sweden. Statutes. Law and Proclamation No. 560 of November 14,

1935. "Forbud mod Indforsel til Riget af Varer fra Italien." In *Svensk Lovtidende* (1935), 1213 ff.

—— Law and Proclamation No. 123 of April 24, 1936. "Aangaaende Kongens Ret til i visse Tilfaelde at foreskrive Kreditspaerring." In Svensk Lovtidende (1936), 131 ff.

—— Sveriges Overenskommelser med främmande Makter. No. 17 (1938), Stockholm, 1939.

Switzerland. Conseil fédéral. Message du Conseil fédéral à l'Assemblée fédérale concernant la question de l'accession de la Suisse à la Société des nations. Bern, 1919.

Times, The. London.

Torp, Carl. Den danske Straffrets almindelige Del. Copenhagen, 1905.

Treatise of 1924. *See* Cohn, Georg. Neutralité et Société des nations.

Treatise of 1931. *See* Cohn, Georg. Kriegsverhütung und Schuldfrage.

Turlington, Edgar W. Neutrality: Its History, Economics and Law. Vol. III, "The World War Period." New York, 1936.

Ullman, E. Völkerrecht. Tübingen, 1908.

Undén, Østen. La Guerre d'agression comme problème de droit international. Conciliation internationale, Paris, 1930.

—— "Quelques observations sur la notion de guerre d'agression." In *Revue de Droit International*, XII (1931), 262 ff.

Union juridique internationale. Séances et travaux. Paris, 1920 ff.

United States. Congress. Congressional Record, and Appendix, January 5, 1929, pp. 274 ff.

—— Congress. House. Committee on Foreign Affairs. American Neutrality Policy. Hearings before the Committee, 74th Congress, Washington, 1936.

—— Congress. Senate. Committee on Foreign Relations. Hearings before the Committee, 66th Congress, Washington, 1919.

—— State Department. Research and Publications Division. Policy of the United States toward Maritime Commerce in War; prepared by Carlton Savage. Vol. I (1776-1914), Vol. II (1914-1918). Washington, 1934-1936.

Vandenbosch, Amry. The Neutrality of the Netherlands during the World War. Grand Rapids, 1927.

Vattel, Emerich de. Le Droit des gens. 3 vols., Lyon, 1802. Available also in English, as *The Law of Nations*, J. Chitty, tr., Philadelphia, 1883.

Visscher, Charles de. "La Violation de la neutralité belge, et le plan Schlieffen." In *Revue de Droit International*, IX (1928), 906 ff.

Visser, Herman L. A. De collectieve psyche in recht en staat. Haarlem, 1916.

Waldkirch, Eduard Otto von, and Ernst Vanselow. "Neutralitätsrecht." In *Handbuch des Völkerrechts*, Band 6, Abt. 5. Stuttgart, 1936.

Warren, Charles. "Safeguards to Neutrality." In *Foreign Affairs* (New York), XV (1936), 199 ff.

Washington, D. C. Conference on the Limitation of Armament, 1921-22. Washington, 1922.

Waultrin, A. "La Neutralité scandinave." In *Revue Générale de Droit International Public*, XI (1904), 5 ff.

Wehberg, Hans. Die Aechtung des Krieges. Deutsche Liga fur Völkerbund Schriften, Berlin, 1930.

—— "Der Pakt von Locarno." In Strupp, ed., *Wörterbuch des Völkerrechts*, III, 977 ff.

Wehrer, Albert. "La Politique de securité et d'arbitrage du grand-duché de Luxembourg; sa politique de neutralité." In *Revue de Droit International*, XIII (1932), 326-66 and 641-63.

—— "Le Statut international du Luxembourg et la Société des nations." In *Revue Générale de Droit International Public*, XXXI (1924), 169 ff.

Westlake, John. International Law. 2 vols., Cambridge, 1904-7.

Whitton, John B. "La Doctrine Monroë et la Société des nations." In *Revue de Droit International*, VIII (1927), 561 ff.

—— "La Neutralité et la Société des nations." In *Hague, The. Academy of International Law, Recueil des cours*, II (1927), 453 ff.

Williams, Sir John Fischer and H. Lauterpacht, eds., Annual Digest of Public International Law Cases. (Irregular), London.

Woolsey, L. "The Fallacies of Neutrality." In *American Journal of International Law*, XXX (1936), 256 ff.

Wright, Philip Quincy. "The Concept of Aggression in International Law." In *American Journal of International Law*, XXIX (1935), 373 ff.

Zeitschrift für Völkerrecht. Breslau, 1929 and 1932.

INDEX